T0373870

WHEN GIANTS RULED THE SKY

WHEN GIANTS RULED THE SKY

THE BRIEF REIGN AND TRAGIC DEMISE
OF THE AMERICAN RIGID AIRSHIP

JOHN J. GEOGHEGAN

The
History
Press

This book is dedicated to my parents, who gave me every advantage;
would that they were alive to see the result.

Jacket illustrations:
Author Photo: Emil Petrinic
Front Cover: US Naval History and Heritage Command, Catalog #NH43901
Back Cover: Official US Navy Photograph

First published 2021

The History Press
97 St George's Place, Cheltenham,
Gloucestershire, GL50 3QB
www.thehistorypress.co.uk

British Library Cataloguing in Publication Data.
A catalogue record for this book is available from the British Library.

ISBN 978 0 7509 8783 7

Typesetting and origination by The History Press
Printed and bound in Great Britain by TJ Books Limited, Padstow, Cornwall.

CONTENTS

Principal Players   7

Preface   13

PART I: A Giant in Flight. USS *Akron* (ZRS–4), 1933

1   Admiral William A. Moffett: A Giant in Winter   23

2   Departures   29

3   A Night to Remember   38

4   Fight for Survival   47

5   Spotlight   54

6   Wiley on Trial   61

PART II: A Giant is Born

7   Paul W. Litchfield: A Giant in Spring   73

8   Blimps Lead the Way   80

9   Dawn of the Commercial Airship   84

10   Competition   96

11   Cutting a Deal   102

12   Pitching Commercial Airships   106

13   The Design Competition   110

14   Success within Reach   117

15   For Want of a Nail   123

16   Airship Fever   129

17   Consequences   137

PART III: A Giant in Trouble. USS *Macon* (ZRS-5), 1933–34

18 Building the *Macon*   145
19 Christening   154
20 Trial Flights   165
21 Lakehurst   172
22 Dr Karl Arnstein: A Giant Displaced   177
23 Doubts   184
24 Fulton   192
25 Sunnyvale   197
26 Up to the Task?   204
27 Flying Aircraft Carriers   229
28 Peril in the Sky   236
29 Fleet Problem XV   243
30 A Giant in Waiting   251

PART IV: A Giant Redeemed. USS *Macon* (ZRS-5), 1934–35

31 The *Houston* Incident   257
32 Lt Cdr Wiley: A Giant Revealed   264
33 A Giant Excels   273
34 A Giant in Danger   283
35 A Giant is Lost   297
36 A Giant is Rescued   310
37 A Giant on Trial   319
38 Assigning Blame   332
39 Aftermath   344
40 A Giant is Found   350

Epilogue   358
Acknowledgements   371
Sources   375
Notes   385
Index   426
About the Author   437

PRINCIPAL PLAYERS

SECRETARY OF THE NAVY

Curtis D. Wilbur (1924–29)
Charles F. Adams, III (1929–33)
Claude A. Swanson (1933–39)

US Navy

Chief of Naval Operations (CNO)
Admiral William V. Pratt (1930–33)
Admiral William H. Standley (1933–37)
Admiral William D. Leahy (1937–39)

Commander in Chief, US Fleet (CINC, FLEET)
Admiral David F. Sellers (1933–34)
Vice Admiral Joseph M. Reeves (1934–36)

Commander Aircraft, Battle Forces (COMBATFOR)
Admiral Joseph M. Reeves (June 1933)
Rear Admiral John Halligan (1933–34)
Vice Admiral Henry V. Butler (1934–36)

US Navy Bureau of Aeronautics (BUAER)
Admiral William A. Moffett, Chief (1921–33)
Rear Admiral Ernest J. King, Chief (1933–36)
Rear Admiral Arthur B. Cook, Chief (1936–39)

Commander Garland Fulton, Head of LTA Design Section
Lt Thomas G.W. 'Tex' Settle, Inspector of Naval Aircraft (embedded at
Goodyear-Zeppelin)

US Navy Rigid Airships
USS Shenandoah (ZR-1) (1923–25)
R38 (ZR-2) (1921)*
USS Los Angeles (ZR-3) (1924–32)
Commander Charles E. Rosendahl, Commanding Officer (1926–29)
Lt Cdr Herbert V. Wiley, Executive Officer (1926–29)
Lt Cdr Herbert V. Wiley, Commanding Officer (October 1928, May 1929–
April 1930)

USS Akron (ZRS-4) (1931–33)
Commander Charles E. Rosendahl, Commanding Officer (1931–32)
Commander Alger H. Dresel, Commanding Officer (1932–33)
Commander Frank C. McCord, Commanding Officer (1933)
Lt Cdr Herbert V. Wiley, Executive Officer (XO) (1931–33)
Boatswain's Mate, Second Class, Richard E. Deal
Metalsmith, Second Class, Moody E. Erwin

Curtiss F9C-2 Sparrowhawk pilots:
Lt D. Ward Harrigan, Squadron Leader
Lt Howard L. Young
Lt Frederick M. Trapnell
Lt (jg) Harold B. Miller
Lt (jg) Robert W. Larson
Lt (jg) Frederick N. Kivette

USS Macon (ZRS-5) (1933–35)
Rear Admiral George C. Day, Board of Inspection & Survey responsible for
ensuring USS *Macon* was fit to be commissioned a US Navy vessel

---

*   The US Navy agreed to purchase the *R38* from the UK with the intention of desig-
     nating it the ZR-2. However, the *R38* crashed before it could be commissioned by
     the Navy.

Commander Alger H. Dresel, Commanding Officer (1933–34)
Lt Cdr Herbert V. Wiley, Commanding Officer (1934–35)
Lt Cdr Jesse L. Kenworthy, Jr, Executive Officer
Lt Cdr Edwin F. Cochrane
Lt Cdr Scott E. Peck, Navigator
Lt Cdr Donald M. Mackey, Flight Control Officer
Lt Calvin M. Bolster, Ship's Repair Officer
Lt Anthony L. Danis, Aerologist
Lt (jg) George W. Campbell
Lt (jg) John D. Reppy
Robert J. Davis, Chief Boatswain's Mate
Ernest E. Dailey, Radioman, First Class
Helmsman, William H. Clarke, Coxswain
Elevatorman, Wilmer M. Conover, Aviation Machinist's Mate, First Class
Maximo Cariaso, Mess Attendant, First Class
Florentino Edquiba, Mess Attendant, First Class

Curtiss F9C-2 Sparrowhawk pilots:
Lt Harold B. Miller, Squadron Leader
Lt Howard L. Young
Lt (jg) Frederick N. Kivette
Lt (jg) Gerald L. Huff
Lt (jg) Leroy C. Simpler
Lt (jg) Harry W. Richardson

GOODYEAR TIRE & RUBBER COMPANY (1900–58)

Paul W. Litchfield:
Plant Superintendent (1900–11)
Factory Manager (1911–16)
Vice President (1915–26)
President (1926–30)[*]
CEO, Chairman (1930–58)
Chairman *Emeritus* (1958)

---

[*]   Litchfield also served as President of the International Zeppelin Company commencing in 1929.

GOODYEAR-ZEPPELIN CORPORATION (1924–40)

Paul W. Litchfield, President
Jerome C. Hunsaker, Vice President*
Dr Karl Arnstein, Chief Designer
Kurt Bauch, Engineer
Hugh Allen, Public Relations Director

LUFTSCHIFFBAU ZEPPELIN (1908–45)

Count Ferdinand von Zeppelin, Founder (1908–17)
Dr Hugo Eckener, Manager (1917–45)**
Dr Karl Arnstein, Structural Analyst (1915–24)

---

*   Hunsaker also served as President of the Pacific Zeppelin Company commencing
      in 1929.
**   Dr Eckener also commanded the *Graf Zeppelin* (LZ-127) as well as numerous
      other Zeppelins.

In this plodding commercial age, this day of humdrum money grubbing and of the routine though admirable round of quiet duty doing, it is a good thing, I think, for the few of us who can to leave the beaten track, fare forth into strange fields, and strive mightily to do things which are exceedingly difficult and dangerous and the more fascinating because they are difficult and dangerous.

Walter Wellman, airship pilot,
The Aerial Age, 1911

PREFACE

It is easy to dismiss the rigid airship as ... predestined to failure. But this explains nothing.

Richard K. Smith, Airship Historian[1]

Why read a book about airships?

The answer is simple: because most of what we know about them is wrong.

In retrospect, airships might seem like fragile dodo birds destined for extinction, but for the first thirty years of the twentieth century they were viewed as a more robust means of transportation than the aeroplane consistently surpassing them in range, flight duration, and load-carrying capacity. By comparison, early aeroplanes were noisy, oil-splattering affairs that could only carry a handful of passengers, flew mostly in daylight, were often grounded by poor weather, and crashed with alarming frequency. And yet, the history of aviation remains focused on Heavier-Than-Air (HTA) flight. It's not difficult to understand why, but it's a bias that overshadows some truly amazing airship accomplishments. Consider the following:

- In 1901, Alberto Santos-Dumont, a Brazilian millionaire with soulful eyes and a penchant for depression, needed only thirty minutes to complete an eight-mile, circular course around the Eiffel Tower in his No. 6 dirigible. What's more, the diminutive Brazilian did it two years *before* the Wright brothers flew at Kitty Hawk – an impressive display of powered, navigable flight.*

---

* To give the Wright brothers their due, their engineering acumen made them first to crack the code of HTA flight. Nevertheless, they were far from being the first men to

- In 1910, German airships began carrying paying passengers on a regularly scheduled route four years *before* the first scheduled commercial airline service began in the United States.
- In 1919, a British airship, the *R34*, was the first aircraft of any type to make a round-trip voyage across the Atlantic – something no aeroplane of the day could accomplish.* If that's not impressive, the *R34* completed her record-making flight eight years *before* Lindbergh crossed the Atlantic on his solo, one-way flight to Paris and did so carrying passengers.
- In 1926, an Italian airship, the *Norge*, flew over the North Pole, marking the first time any land, air, or sea expedition incontrovertibly reached that destination.**
- In 1929, another German airship, the *Graf Zeppelin* (LZ-127), circled the globe six times faster than the first aeroplane to do so. Two years later, the *Graf* commenced a regularly scheduled passenger service between Germany and South America with occasional stops in New Jersey – a performance no other aircraft of the day could match.

Lighter-Than-Air (LTA) flight may be a withered branch on aviation's tree, but its history is important because it's where human flight first began. *When Giants Ruled the Sky* will not only correct many of the popular misconceptions associated with airships but explain why so many people expected they would surpass ocean liners and transcontinental trains as the preferred means of long-distance transportation especially for the wealthy.

One popular misconception is that the *Hindenburg* (LZ-129) crash brought an end to the airship era. *Giants* will show this isn't the case. Additionally, the *Hindenburg's* fiery demise killed far fewer people than many of us assume. Of the ninety-seven passengers and crew aboard that fateful day, two thirds – sixty-two people – survived the disaster. This casualty rate of 35 per cent was far lower than the major aeroplane, train and ocean liner disasters of the day.

---

fly, which may come as a surprise to many. Additionally, they weren't quite the heroes they're painted to be as we'll soon see.

*   Although Alcock and Brown succeeded in being the first to fly across the Atlantic, a few weeks before the *R34*, they took a considerably shorter route, flew only one way, and made a very hard landing in Ireland. By comparison, the *R34's* flight was smooth sailing.

**   Despite Frederick Cook and Robert Peary each claiming to have reached the North Pole first, in 1908 and 1909, respectively, neither claim was ever verified and both remain controversial. In the case of Richard Byrd's 1926 overflight of the North Pole, he later admitted his navigation was faulty.

Given 1,503 souls were lost on the *Titanic*, the *Hindenburg*'s death toll of 35[*] is small by comparison. In fact, Germany remained so confident in the future of airship travel that she began flying a replacement, the *Graf Zeppelin II* (LZ-130), only four months after the *Hindenburg* crash and continued to operate her for another two years. The Germans even had a sister airship under construction, the LZ-131, when the Second World War intervened.

What most people don't realise is that before the *Hindenburg* disaster, German airships transported tens of thousands of paying passengers millions of miles *without a single passenger fatality* – a safety record unmatched by any other form of transportation.[2] Although it's true that the number of deaths attributable to airship crashes was astounding when compared to the small number of craft that were built, airships were promoted by their adherents as the safest form of long-distance transportation.

One reason so many people expected airships to become the dominant form of long-distance transport was that the US Navy, in partnership with the Goodyear Tire & Rubber Company and German airship manufacturer Luftschiffbau Zeppelin[**] were determined to sell the public on the speed, comfort and safety of airship travel. Twice as fast as the speediest ocean liner (to which they were frequently compared), airships seemed ubiquitous during the 1920s and early '30s, appearing over Tokyo, Washington, D.C., Rio de Janiero, the Egyptian pyramids and New York's Empire State Building. The Empire State Building (the tallest skyscraper in the world when completed) was even built with an airship mooring station at its top. As a result, airships didn't just capture the public's imagination in the way the American space programme would many years later: they held it firmly in their grasp for three decades until aeroplane technology matured enough to eventually overtake them.

What may surprise the reader is just how close America came to having her own fleet of gigantic, globe-spanning airships. Designed to carry passengers, mail, and cargo, these behemoths were not only intended to fly from New York to California, but across the Pacific, the Atlantic and down the length of South America. And yet, passenger ships ply the ocean today while commercial airlines flourish. Meanwhile, the big rigid airship is extinct. An explanation why is long overdue.

One reason airships seemed destined to succeed was that between 1917 and 1935 the United States Navy poured tens of millions of dollars into an experimental programme that built a series of increasingly sophisticated

---

[*]   One of the 35 killed was not a passenger or crewman but a line handler on the ground.
[**]   Translated from the German, *Luftschiffbau* means 'airship construction'.

dirigibles, larger and more expensive than anything that had ever flown. The biggest of the lot, the USS *Akron* (ZRS-4)* and her sister ship, the USS *Macon* (ZRS-5), were so large they equalled the RMS *Lusitania* in length. Fourteen storeys tall, and two-and-a-half football fields long, these self-contained cities in the sky could venture aloft with an eighty-man crew for days at a time when an aeroplane's range was limited, ocean liners slow and no railroad truly transcontinental. There was only one problem. The Navy's airships kept crashing. Even when the Navy was warned that its airships had a potentially fatal design flaw, it refused to listen. When it became clear the design flaw had caused at least one of its airships to crash, the Navy covered up the truth rather than risk further embarrassment.

The purpose of this book is to delve into the two most critical years in the Navy's big rigid programme, April 1933 to February 1935, and ask the question: what the heck happened? Why, after spending millions of dollars and years of effort, did the fate of the American airship come down to a brief twenty-three-month window? Central to the answer are the heroic contributions of four men instrumental in building the Navy's Zeppelins, each a giant who ruled the sky:

- Rear Admiral William A. Moffett, the first Chief of the US Navy's Bureau of Aeronautics, who envisioned a fleet of gargantuan military airships patrolling the Pacific to prevent a surprise attack by Japan.
- Paul W. Litchfield, CEO of the Goodyear Tire & Rubber Company, who not only wanted to build Zeppelins for the Navy, but also a fleet of passenger-carrying airships that spanned the globe.
- Goodyear-Zeppelin's chief airship designer, Dr Karl Arnstein, who, having built Zeppelins for Germany to bomb London, was determined to design the world's safest airships for his former enemy no matter the obstacles put in his path.
- And the *Macon*'s enterprising captain, Lt Cdr Herbert V. Wiley, upon whose shoulders the fate of the American rigid airship would ultimately fall.

Each one of these four men shared the same hope for the future – a fleet of US-flagged dirigibles that would extend American military and commercial hegemony from sea to sky. This dream not only ended up killing one of them,

---

* The Z in the US Navy's ZRS-4 designation stands for Airship (not Zeppelin as some people think), the R for Rigid and the S for Scout. The number meant she was the Navy's fourth big rigid.

but would irrevocably change the lives of the other three while leaving a lasting mark on aviation. Sadly, the contribution of these four giants is little remembered today despite their having once been famous. That these four men fought to overcome seemingly insurmountable odds to achieve their goal suggests just how extraordinary, if little known, the story of the American rigid airship really is.

But first a word about definitions.

There are three types of airship: non-rigid, semi-rigid and big rigid. Most people are familiar with non-rigid types. The Goodyear blimp, which flies over sporting events, was a good example for many years.* Blimps are designated non-rigid because their envelope contains no skeletal framework. Instead, their shape is determined by the pressure of the lifting gas inside. Non-rigids also have a gondola slung underneath, which houses the pilot and passengers along with one or two engines mounted on their outsides.

Next come semi-rigids. Semi-rigids incorporate a keel in their envelope giving them added structural strength. As a result, semi-rigids can be built larger in size than non-rigids, allowing them to lift more, and fly farther, than blimps. But even then, semi-rigids don't approach the truly gargantuan size of the rigid airship.

Whereas the envelope of a non-rigid or semi-rigid is shaped by the lifting gas it contains, the envelope of big rigids, like the *Akron*, *Macon* and *Hindenburg*, are given shape by an enormous, skeletal airframe. This enables the crew to live and work inside a big rigid's hull; unlike a blimp or semi-rigid where passengers and crew are confined to the gondola underneath. A big rigid's airframe is critical to its design because it supports a series of gas cells inflated with helium or hydrogen to float the airship. The reason why big rigids had to be so huge was to contain the enormous amount of LTA gas necessary to lift their sizeable weight. Although a big rigid's heaviness may seem counterintuitive, it's required if the airship is to be sturdy enough to transport a large amount of people and cargo considerable distances for days at a time without landing.

To give an idea of a big rigid's mind-boggling size, the *Hindenburg* was approximately 140 times larger than the Goodyear blimps of her day. She had to be, not only to transport 100 passengers and crew thousands of miles while serving gourmet meals in luxurious accommodations, but to transport a substantial amount of cargo which not only included cars, but a piano for shipboard entertainment. In contrast, blimps can only carry a few people

---

*   Goodyear retired its non-rigid blimp fleet in 2014, replacing it with semi-rigid airships.

two or three hundred miles. Only big rigids, like Germany's *Hindenburg* or America's *Akron* and *Macon*, were robust enough to cross an entire ocean or continent.

As for the difference between a 'dirigible' and an 'airship', there are none. The terms are interchangeable. The word dirigible is derived from the French verb *dirigeable*, meaning to steer or direct, so any LTA craft that has an engine which propels it forward, and a steering mechanism like a rudder, can be termed a dirigible. As for the word 'Zeppelin', it's a brand name used to describe airships built by Count Ferdinand von Zeppelin's company, Luftschiffbau Zeppelin. Considered the father of the big rigid, Count Zeppelin and his firm built nearly 200 airships for commercial or military use during the first forty years of the twentieth century. Since then, the word has evolved to represent an entire category just like Kleenex, Xerox or Hoover. For our purposes, though, Zeppelin refers only to airships conceived and built by the German count and his eponymous company.

Despite being largely overlooked, the early days of LTA flight produced a diverse number of craft, many of them awe inspiring both in size and design. Even today, airships permeate modern life in unexpected ways. Take for instance the rigid airship in Pixar's animated movie *Up*. It's based upon the USS *Akron* and her sister ship, the *Macon* – two Navy dirigibles that could launch and retrieve their own aircraft in mid-flight.

Finally, as much as *When Giants Ruled the Sky* is a factual history, there is a fair amount of personal observation sprinkled throughout. For example, as a child I never understood why the Goodyear Tire & Rubber Company had blimps. Those giant gas bags with their winged-foot logos didn't seem to have anything to do with tyre manufacturing. Hopefully, *Giants* will not only explain why a blimp fleet makes perfect sense for the company, but why it continues to operate them today.

If it's hard not to be moved by the sheer size, grace and beauty of big rigids, it's equally difficult not to be impressed by the courage and determination of the men who designed, built and operated them. Nevertheless, airship history rarely receives the respect it deserves. The USS *Akron* and *Macon* may be sterling examples of white elephant technology, but that only makes the story of the men who struggled to build and fly them all the more inspiring.

In summary, *Giants* intends to place rigid airships in their rightful heroic context. It's not only a reappraisal of the reason for their demise, but a celebration of the passion and daring of four larger-than-life figures whose efforts made the American big rigid possible.

In other words, explaining why the airship went the way of the dinosaurs is at the heart of this story. And the interesting thing is it had nothing to do with the *Hindenburg*.

PART I

A GIANT IN FLIGHT. USS *AKRON* (ZRS-4), 1933

1

ADMIRAL WILLIAM A. MOFFETT: A GIANT IN WINTER

Rear Admiral William Adger Moffett may have been a giant who ruled the skies, but the 63-year-old Chief of the Bureau of Aeronautics (BUAER) felt more like a lion in winter this dismal Monday morning. It was 2 April 1933 and the sky outside his window in Washington, DC's Navy Department was claustrophobically low: its clouds a leaden shade of grey. Like it or not, the weather fitted the admiral's mood.

Responsible for overseeing every aspect of naval aviation, Moffett was not only BUAER's first chief; he'd headed it for a dozen years. A champion of flight at a time when the field was still young, Moffett was considered the father of naval aviation. His crowning achievement was to persuade Congress to fund a thousand aeroplanes and two big rigids for the Navy – the largest purchase of aircraft ever made at the time. The congressional appropriation not only put naval aviation on the map but saved a number of American aircraft manufacturers from bankruptcy, transforming Moffett into a national figure.

Even in his waning years, Moffett made a striking impression. Although he rarely smiled for the camera, favouring a stern, granite-faced expression, he was a handsome man. His high forehead, well-proportioned nose and cleft chin lent him a patrician air that was reinforced by the pipe never far from his mouth. Not especially tall, Moffett's military bearing added inches to his height while his snow-white hair encircled his head like a laurel wreath, adding to his imperious effect.

As intimidating as Moffett appeared, there was little doubt his rigid airship programme was in trouble. Some people wondered why the admiral placed so much importance on the Navy's big rigids when aeroplanes were the coming thing. Nevertheless, Moffett was proud of his newest airship, the USS *Akron*. Nearly three football fields long and fourteen storeys tall, the

Akron was meant to patrol the ocean to forestall a surprise attack by Japan. In the meantime, her younger sister, the USS *Macon*, was set to make her first test flight in just a few weeks.

Moffett had heard the complaints about his big rigids: they were too expensive, accident prone and vulnerable to being shot down; they only flew when the sun shined; and more recently, aircraft carriers had made them obsolete. The last was ironic given Moffett was instrumental in developing carriers for the Navy. Moffett argued that airships were complementary to, not competitive with, aeroplanes, but fewer people were buying his story.

It didn't help that the Navy's first big rigid, the USS *Shenandoah* (ZR-1), was ripped in half by a violent thunderstorm over Ohio, killing fourteen of her forty-three-man crew. The Navy's second big rigid, ZR-2, also suffered a horrible demise when she collapsed in mid-air during a trial flight over Hull, UK.* Forty-four of her forty-nine-man crew were killed, including sixteen of the seventeen Americans on board. In contrast, the USS *Los Angeles* (ZR-3) flew for nearly eight years, making her the most successful big rigid the Navy had ever operated.

The *Los Angeles* had gone a long way towards putting concerns about Moffett's rigid airships to rest. But the *Akron*, the Navy's newest big rigid, had suffered a series of embarrassing mishaps calling Moffett's programme into question. An astute politician, Moffett had hoped to dispel the concerns by inviting members of the House Naval Affairs Committee, which funded his airships, to take a ride on the *Akron*. But as the congressmen waited to board, the dirigible's tail broke loose. With her bow still attached to the mooring mast, the *Akron* spun like a weather vane, her tail dragging across the ground with a sickening crunch. The damage was so severe the flight had to be cancelled. Worse, the *Akron* was laid up two months for repairs. As one congressman witnessing the accident remarked, 'When I see girders snap off like pretzels, I know something is wrong.'[1]

Then there was the Camp Kearny incident.

When the *Akron* should have been celebrating her first transcontinental voyage across the United States, three sailors holding her mooring line were inadvertently pulled into the sky over San Diego. A newsreel cameraman caught the exact moment two of the men fell to their death, making for mem-

---

*   ZR-2, which the US purchased in the UK, crashed before she had a chance to be commissioned in the US Navy. As a result, she's usually referred to by her British designation, *R38*. To add to the confusion, ZR-2 crashed in 1921 while ZR-1 wasn't commissioned until 1923.

orable if damning footage.* It was yet another black mark on the *Akron's* record that, along with rumours of substandard construction, continued to dog her.

Powerful members of Congress felt the *Akron* was a white elephant, but Moffett was confident she'd live up to expectations if given a fair chance. His reasoning was sound enough. The *Akron* had been designed to scout thousands of square miles of ocean faster, more thoroughly, and at far less expense than the sea-going cruisers the Navy relied upon. Importantly, Moffett saw rigid airships as the best means to prevent a surprise attack by the Imperial Japanese Navy against the United States.

America had been preparing for war with Japan ever since the island nation had stunned the world by defeating the Russian Navy at the Battle of Tsushima in 1905. That Japan could thrash a major Western power threatened the big four's hegemony** fuelling racist beliefs about the coming 'yellow peril'.

Not one to think small, Moffett envisioned at least ten ocean-going airships, the largest ever built, to serve as the 'eyes of the fleet'. He already had two big rigids, the *Akron*, commissioned in 1931, and the USS *Macon* (ZRS-5), christened just that March. Whether he got the rest depended on two things: his ability to demonstrate the *Akron* and *Macon* were effective ocean-going scouts and establishing a US-based commercial airship industry to help build his aerial fleet. Until then Moffett worried America was vulnerable to a Japanese attack.

Moffett hadn't always believed in airships. 'I confess to being a skeptic originally as to whether these … "gas bags" could be of any value,' he'd written. 'But after I investigated the matter, I became convinced as to the ultimate … desirability of … their development.' As far as their price tag went, he said his critics were 'apt to think too much about the money involved and too little about the benefits to mankind'.[2]

Moffett had his work cut out for him. During the darkening days of the Depression, the Navy's 'battleship admirals' considered naval aviation a threat since it competed with their precious surface fleet for scarce funding. This meant Moffett's airship programme attracted a lot of sniping inside the Navy, which is why he felt 'Putting over Lighter-Than-Air has been the toughest job I ever undertook.'[3]

Moffett may have faced increasing criticism, but he was well positioned to succeed. Two gold stripes, one thick, one thin, plus a star on his sleeve gave

---

*　　After dangling from the airship for more than an hour, the third man was pulled aboard.

**　　In 1933, the big four were defined as the United States, the United Kingdom, France and Italy.

him the clout he needed to get the job done. Spartan in taste and reserved in manner, he kept his emotions in check unless someone required a bawling out. But Moffett's southern charm helped contribute to his success. He was genuinely well-liked in the corridors of power, where he didn't just know who to put the arm on, but how hard to squeeze. A consummate insider, Moffett had an intuitive grasp of Washington politics. But his polite manner hid a steely determination; he'd even bypass his chain of command if it got him what he wanted.[4]

Moffett may have made it look easy, but it wasn't. Competing naval factions, inter-service rivalries and the sclerotic nature of decision making in Washington meant he endured many years of bureaucratic infighting. And yet he nearly always won.

If Moffett had done more than anyone else to shape the future of naval aviation, he'd paid a steep price for it. Yes, he wielded tremendous power, but Chief of BUAER was not a popular position in a Navy that was trying to figure out how to incorporate aeroplanes with its fighting ships. Yet Moffett had served three terms as head of the department, foregoing any chance of promotion. He'd also sacrificed his personal life. The father of six children, he'd been missing in action for most of his marriage. Remote and often gruff, he travelled so frequently he was rarely at home. His wife, Jeannette, fifteen years younger, was used to his being away. Prominent in Washington society, she enjoyed the power and prestige her husband's position gave her if not always his presence. If Moffett's reputation as a ladies man, earned at the Naval Academy,[5] had carried over into adulthood, he'd been discreet. As it was, his marriage was more respectful than affectionate.[6] His children suffered as well. As Moffett's eldest daughter recalled about the admiral, he made for 'a great navy officer but not a very good father'.[7]

Serving his country had certainly taken its toll. As proof, Moffett had finally begun looking his age. In fact, he'd recently lost so much weight his features had thinned to the point of sharpness. One explanation is that he suffered from congestive heart failure. If so, few if any people were aware of his condition. Still, photographs show him looking drawn and frail. That's not to say he'd lost his command presence, on the contrary, he remained tough as nails. But after forty-two years in the Navy he'd earned the right to be tired.

Moffett was proud of his accomplishments, but he'd ruffled some feathers along the way. Roosevelt wanted to reappoint him as Chief of BUAER for an unprecedented fourth term, but Secretary of the Navy, Claude A. Swanson, had been cool to the idea.[8] And so, after more than four decades serving his country, Moffett was slated to retire on his 64th birthday. In the meantime, he had almost finished building Happy Landings, his 40-acre retreat overlooking the Potomac River in Virginia. One thing was certain, he'd probably have difficulty adjusting to the quiet life after wielding power for so long.

Moffett's impending retirement meant he only had six months to get his rigid airship programme on a sound footing. This wasn't a lot of time, especially since the sharks were circling. The last thing he needed that grey Monday morning was bad weather to interfere with his plans.

The reason the weather so concerned Moffat was that he was scheduled to fly on the *Akron* later that evening. The largest, most sophisticated, most expensive aircraft built in her day, the *Akron* was Moffett's pride and joy. He'd even invited a VIP to join him on the flight. But the increasing gloom outside Moffett's window had him worried the flight might be cancelled. Picking up the phone, the admiral placed a call to Lakehurst, New Jersey, where the *Akron* was based, to make sure the flight wasn't scrubbed.

Normally, the Chief of BUAER wouldn't bother calling a base commander about a routine training flight, but Moffett wanted to make a point. It was no secret he felt his airship captains were fair-weather flyers. '[I have a] feeling,' he'd written, 'and have had it for a long time, that the ships have not been operated as much as they should.' Moffett had gone so far as to say, 'It may be advisable to take one … out … looking for bad weather … so we can … find out what these ships can really do.'[9]

Never shy about making his opinion known, Moffett had recently overseen the replacement of the *Akron*'s commanding officer with a more aggressive airship skipper, Commander Frank C. McCord. McCord agreed that airships should fly in every kind of weather.[10] After all, nobody wanted a big rigid that flew only when it was sunny, least of all Moffett.

When the phone rang in Commander Fred T. Berry's office, Berry wasn't surprised to learn it was Moffett. The commanding officer of NAS Lakehurst was used to hearing from the admiral. But when Moffett learned that the *Akron*'s skipper was in Berry's office, he asked to speak with him. Handing the phone to McCord, Berry let him know it was the admiral calling.[11]

McCord had been the *Akron*'s CO for only three months. Recruited from the fleet to command Moffett's next generation of dirigibles,[12] he knew how much the surface Navy looked down on airships. This is why McCord had embarked on an ambitious training schedule hoping to show sceptics what the *Akron* was capable of. So far they remained unconvinced.

While Moffett enquired about the upcoming flight, McCord motioned to his executive officer, Lt Cdr Herbert V. Wiley, to get the latest forecast. After calling the base's aerological office, Wiley told McCord there was a possibility of scattered thundershowers later that night. The weather over their intended destination, Newport, Rhode Island, also looked poor, which might prevent them from accomplishing the tasks they'd scheduled for the next morning.[13]

Though Moffett's exact words are lost to history, his intent was clear. He wanted the *Akron*'s fifty-ninth flight, scheduled for sunset, to proceed as planned. When McCord assured him it would, Moffett said to expect him before 1900 hours and hung up.[14]

With one seemingly innocuous phone call, Rear Admiral William A. Moffett not only changed the future of his rigid airship programme, but the fate of the American airship as well.

2

DEPARTURES

Moffett departed Washington accompanied by his naval aide at 1300 hours.[1] Normally, he preferred flying to Lakehurst Naval Air Station. After all, he was head of naval aviation. But the weather was sketchy. Not wanting to risk being grounded, he made the long drive in his staff car instead.[2]

When the admiral arrived at NAS Lakehurst nearly six hours later the huge slab-like doors of Hangar No. 1 were already open. Inside, a gigantic dirigible, her airframe poking through her canvas-covered hull like the ribs of a steer, hovered off the concrete floor. That something larger than a battleship could float in the air seemed counterintuitive – as if the *Akron* thumbed her nose at gravity. And yet there she was illuminated by overhead lights with a shadow beneath her proving she was no magic trick.

Moffett's car pulled into the *Akron's* hangar followed by a shrill whistle alerting the crew to fall in place. While the men came to attention, their breath visible in the chilly night air, McCord greeted Moffett with a smart salute.

NAS Lakehurst was the heart of Moffett's rigid airship programme, but Moffett wasn't satisfied with having a dirigible base on the east coast. He was building a second one on the west coast as well. In the meantime, the culmination of everything America knew about big rigids operated just a few miles south of New York City.

There was nothing small about Moffett's rigid airship programme. From the size of its budget to the number of sky sailors it employed to the thousands of miles the *Akron* could fly without landing, no string of superlatives quite did it justice.

There's no denying the *Akron* was a window into the future. A miracle of modern engineering, she was state of the art for the US Navy when commissioned in 1931. Some 785ft long and 140ft tall, she dwarfed everything around her including her crew, which looked Lilliputian by comparison. Even King Kong, the giant ape in a new movie released the previous month, was a chimp by comparison.

Size didn't mean she was slow, however. The *Akron* was the fastest dirigible the Navy had ever flown, with her eight Maybach engines generating a top speed of more than 80mph. That wasn't as fast as aeroplanes of the day, but she didn't need to be. The *Akron*'s job was to scout thousands of square miles for days at a time, which required range not speed. Able to travel more than 10,000 miles without refuelling,[3] the *Akron* was a marathoner not a sprinter.

Incredibly, she was a self-contained city in the sky with everything she needed to keep her eighty-man crew aloft for days on end. This included mess halls and a galley; three separate sleeping quarters for her officers, chief petty officers, and enlisted men; toilets and sinks (if not showers); a ward and navigation room; radio room, sick bay, smoking room, captain's cabin and darkroom for developing photographs all residing inside her enormous hull connected by a labyrinth of catwalks, stairs and ladders. The *Akron* not only had running water, but her own power plant to generate electricity. Eighteen telephones spread throughout the ship assisted communication, while eight machine-gun emplacements helped repel attack.* There was even a sub-cloud observation car that could be lowered on a cable to spy on the enemy below.

If that wasn't impressive enough, the *Akron* was also a flying aircraft carrier. She not only carried two aeroplanes inside her belly, which could be deployed and retrieved in mid-flight to defend against attack, but a third hung from a trapeze outside the airship. The world had seen nothing like it.

Unfortunately, the *Akron* also suffered from the same high hopes with which so many first born are saddled. Although she'd been flying for eighteen months, she had a long way to go before proving herself an effective ocean-going scout. One flight wasn't going to change that, but Moffett wanted to be on board that night if for no other reason than to show his VIP guest that rigid airships were a viable means of commercial transport.

As if being a *wunderkind* weren't enough, the future of America's airship industry depended on how the *Akron* performed. If she demonstrated she could fly on a regular basis despite inclement weather, then the financial community would feel comfortable investing in passenger-carrying airships. But

---

*   Although the emplacements were ready, her .30-calibre machines gun had yet to be installed.

if the *Akron* failed to live up to expectations, then the financial markets would steer clear of what they saw as a risky investment. Moffett had little choice. He had to show the *Akron* could fly in poor weather if he wanted an airship manufacturing industry to take root in America. Without it there was no one to build his fleet of airships. That's why he didn't want the *Akron* grounded because of a few clouds.

Nothing in Moffett's early career suggested he'd one day become a giant of aviation. In fact, he'd once told a colleague, 'Any man who sticks to [flying] is either crazy or … a … damned fool.'[4]

Never a gifted student, Moffett had graduated from Annapolis in 1890 at the bottom of his class. During the next thirty years he'd served on nearly every type of surface ship from a wooden sailing sloop to a steam-powered dreadnought.[5] In every respect he seemed a traditional line officer wedded to the surface fleet. He'd even been awarded the Medal of Honor for his actions during the Navy's Battle of Veracruz in 1914.

It wasn't until Moffett commanded the Great Lakes Naval Station that he realised the importance of aviation to the Navy. After observing pilot training up close, he became an evangelist with all the fervour of a recent convert. When he was named Director of Naval Aviation in 1921 he immediately began lobbying for a separate department within the Navy dedicated to flight.

The key to Moffett's success as Chief of BUAER was recognising that aircraft carriers were key to integrating aeroplanes with the fleet. Able to transport planes places they couldn't reach on their own, carriers were becoming central to a Navy that had long favoured battleships.

Moffett knew aeroplanes made excellent fighters and bombers, but he also believed rigid airships could play a role. They not only had an advantage over planes in terms of endurance and load-carrying capacity; they cost far less than a heavy cruiser, the Navy's traditional ocean-going scout.* Furthermore, airships could be repaired in flight; aeroplanes couldn't. Additionally, an airship remained floating in the sky even if all of its engines failed. In contrast, engine failure for an aeroplane often led to a crash.

---

*   It's important to note that some Navy cruisers also carried aeroplanes, but the cruisers' range was limited compared to the Navy's big rigids, putting them at a disadvantage when it came to scouting.

The steps leading to the *Akron*'s commissioning had been anything but smooth, however. Things got off to a rocky start when the design competition the Navy held for its next generation dirigible had to be repeated. Goodyear-Zeppelin, a division of the Goodyear Tire & Rubber Company, had won the first competition,[6] but the company couldn't build its winning design at the Navy's stipulated price, so the competition was held again.

Moffett preferred granting the contract to Goodyear outright, but Congress mandated competitive bids. Goodyear's President, Paul W. Litchfield, was not accustomed to losing, so it was no surprise when his company won the second competition as well. But if the process had been messy, the Navy contract was straightforward. It called for the Goodyear-Zeppelin Corporation, a joint-venture between the Goodyear Tire & Rubber Company of Akron, Ohio, and Luftschiffbau Zeppelin, GmbH of Friedrichshafen, Germany, to build two rigid airships for the fixed price of $8 million.

Luftschiffbau Zeppelin had built more than 120 Zeppelins by 1928, making them an expert in big rigid design. It was natural for Goodyear to partner with the leading company in the field to build rigid airships for the Navy, but Litchfield never intended to build only two big rigids. He envisioned the *Akron* and her sister ship, the *Macon*, as loss leaders – the first step in Goodyear becoming the world's leading manufacturer of passenger-carrying airships. But the *Akron* had to prove herself before the commercial market materialised, meaning Litchfield was rolling the dice.

When the *Akron* was finally christened on 9 August 1931, newspapers hailed her as 'Queen of the Fleet', 'Battleship of the Air', and 'Leviathan of the Skies'. The ceremony, held on a Saturday inside the Goodyear-Zeppelin Air Dock in Akron, Ohio, was deemed so important, President Hoover's wife was named the airship's sponsor. The city of Akron even declared it a legal holiday so residents could attend.

Some reports claim that between 250,000[7] and 500,000[8] people witnessed the event, although the *New York Times* pegged the number between 80,000 and 100,000.[9] Either way, traffic was backed up for miles.

The heat inside the hangar was so stifling, straw-hatted men and overdressed ladies fanned themselves in search of relief. Meanwhile, Goodyear sold blimp rides outside for a dollar[10] while a 500-piece brass band played 'Anchors Aweigh'. As attendees gaped at the silver whale floating overhead they noticed part of her canvas covering had been peeled back to reveal her inner workings, as if labelling her refuse tank and ventilation system could explain the miracle of flight.

Litchfield enjoyed the honour of escorting the First Lady to the dais. Mrs Hoover, looking every bit her fifty-seven years, sat in the front row partially shielded by microphones. Heavy set and frumpy, she wore a cloche hat and matronly dress as limp from the heat as the oversized bouquet she clutched to her chest.

The viewing stand, adorned in red, white and blue bunting, was tucked under the *Akron*'s bow, which jutted 75ft over the crowd like the prow of a ship. Packed with local politicians, Goodyear executives and senior Navy officials, attendees included Amelia Earhart, who'd flown in for the occasion.

Dr Karl Arnstein, the *Akron*'s chief designer, was also present for the ceremony. Arnstein was a modest man. Not one to make exaggerated claims, he shied away from the superlatives newspapers used to describe his creation, claiming it was, 'boasting before the baby actually walks'.[11]

Litchfield sat in the front row next to the President's wife. Considered one of America's most powerful industrialists, he'd taken Goodyear, which had once been a small, family-owned shop, from the brink of bankruptcy to an industrial colossus. Practically everyone in the country either bought Goodyear tyres, recognised its winged-foot logo or had seen its blimps.

If it seems odd that a tyre manufacturer sponsored a blimp fleet, it was because Goodyear was in the blimp-building business. In addition to manufacturing all six of its company blimps, Goodyear had sold another nine to the Navy. Now, Litchfield was celebrating the completion of Goodyear's first big rigid for Moffett's LTA programme. This made the day as much Litchfield's triumph as Moffett's. After all, it was Litchfield's face on the cover of *Time* magazine that week.* As the accompanying article made clear, 'Proud as he was about this week's milestone … Litchfield was frank in saying that … the new Navy ship was but a means to an end: the building of commercial air liners … to ply regular routes across the Atlantic and Pacific.'[12] The airship business never looked more promising.

The *Akron*'s christening was such a big deal that NBC Radio and the Columbia Broadcast System carried the ceremony live to tens of thousands of listeners. Litchfield was first to speak. Wearing a summer-weight jacket, and crisp, white trousers, he looked big-boned and gawky in front of the microphones. After briefly outlining the history of lighter-than-air flight, he introduced the Assistant Secretary for Naval Aviation, who was smart enough to keep his remarks short. Then it was Moffett's turn.

---

*   The illustration was so flattering as to be almost unrecognisable.

Resplendent in his dress whites, Moffett's job was to sell the Navy's airship programme to a country hard hit by the Depression. Emphasising the many new jobs the airship industry would bring, he ended his remarks by quoting Henry Wadsworth Longfellow's 'O Ship of State' – a wise choice given the shaky times:

Thou, too, sail on, O Ship of State!
Sail on, O Union, strong and great!
Humanity with all its fears,
With all the hopes of future years,
Is hanging breathless on thy fate!
We know what Master laid thy keel,
What Workmen wrought thy ribs of steel,
Who made each mast, and sail, and rope,
What anvils rang, what hammers beat,
In what a forge and what a heat
Were shaped the anchors of thy hope!
Fear not each sudden sound and shock,
'Tis of the wave and not the rock;
'Tis but the flapping of the sail,
And not a rent made by the gale!
In spite of rock and tempest's roar,
In spite of false lights on the shore,
Sail on, nor fear to breast the sea!
Our hearts, our hopes, are all with thee.
Our hearts, our hopes, our prayers, our tears,
Our faith triumphant o'er our fears,
Are all with thee, – are all with thee!

The Air Dock's acoustics were so poor few people grasped what Moffett was saying. As one wag noted, the only person who understood Moffett's speech was the admiral and the man who wrote it.[13]

After Moffett finished, the band struck up 'The Star-Spangled Banner' and everyone stood to face the flag. When the final notes echoed through the Air Dock, Mrs Hoover stepped to the cluster of microphones and, with Moffett and Litchfield looking solemn behind her, proclaimed, 'I christen thee, *Akron*.'

Though tradition dictates christening new ships with champagne, the country was in the midst of prohibition – and anyway, smashing a bottle against the bow of an airship seemed too violent an act for such a fragile-looking creature. And so Mrs Hoover, reaching with her white-gloved hand, grasped a long, beribboned cord hanging in front of her. Then, yanking it down, two hatches dropped open in the *Akron*'s bow, releasing forty-eight white pigeons, one for each state.

As the pigeons emerged, some more reluctantly than others, the crowd cheered, the band played, and newsreels' cameras recorded the moment for posterity. To acknowledge the christening, the *Akron* was allowed to rise 6ft into the air before being cranked back into place. It was the lighter-than-air version of a new ship sliding down the building ways into the sea, but the *Akron* was so massive hardly anyone noticed she budged.

Everything went downhill after that. It wasn't unusual for a prototype to fail to meet all its specifications, but newspapers made much of the *Akron* being over budget and 20,000lb overweight – a liability when getting airborne. Worse, it coloured the perception that she might not be everything that was promised.

Moffett was nothing if not accomplished at public relations. The day after the *Akron* was commissioned he took 207 VIPs up for a flight – the most people that had ever flown aboard a dirigible at one time. It was a tangible demonstration of a rigid airship's passenger-carrying capacity, which must have pleased Litchfield.

Soon, the *Akron* was generating bold-faced headlines, coast-to-coast radio broadcasts and breathless newsreel coverage every time she flew. Moffett made it a point to have the *Akron* appear over large cities hosting a parade so tens of thousands of Americans could crane their necks skyward to watch the future of aviation pass overhead. So popular was the Navy's newest dirigible there was even a line of *Akron* souvenirs including pennants, ashtrays, bookmarks and a children's cap to go along with the constant stream of newspaper, newsreel, and magazine coverage.

We take air travel for granted today, but twentieth-century America was hungry for any form of transport that could span its vast continent and two great oceans. Germany already had one airship, the *Graf Zeppelin*, which was flying a regular scheduled service from Friedrichshafen near the Swiss border to Rio de Janeiro, Brazil – an astounding round trip of 12,000 miles. Why then wasn't the United States building its own airships to compete? The stakes could not have been higher for Moffett, Litchfield, Goodyear and the Navy.

Moffett's primary goal was to ensure the *Akron* was an effective naval scout, but he was not above promoting civilian airships as well. For this reason, he'd invited 50-year-old Alfred F. Masury, Vice President and Chief Engineer of Mack Trucks, Inc., to accompany him aboard the *Akron* that evening. A lieutenant colonel in the Army Reserves, Masury had carved Mack Truck's distinctive bulldog logo out of a bar of soap before patenting the design. Looking like a bulldog himself, Masury was an officer of the International Zeppelin Transport Company,[14] a Goodyear-sponsored firm mapping dirigible routes across the Atlantic. An avid believer in passenger-carrying airships, Masury didn't need convincing of their worth. Yet Moffett was determined to demonstrate the *Akron* could fly in all sorts of weather, knowing it would strengthen Masury's case to investors.

Moffett and Masury boarded the *Akron* an hour before take-off.[15] As the sun dipped below the horizon, a heavy brown fog descended on the airfield. Lakehurst Naval Air Station may have been the Navy's premier airship base, but it had a reputation for poor weather. Carved out of coastal New Jersey's sand and scrub pines, the sparsely populated area was flat enough to make it ideal for flight operations. But Lakehurst was also smack dab in the middle of every storm blowing up the Eastern Seaboard. Moffett could not have chosen a better location for poor-weather flying. As proof, the *Akron*'s captain had visited the base's aerology office twice that day seeking the latest forecast.[16] What Commander McCord found wasn't unusual. A cold front was pushing in from the west creating a low pressure system near Ohio. Since it was outside the *Akron*'s area of operations, he wasn't particularly worried. Still, one of the *Akron*'s pilots who'd flown up from Washington that afternoon said the ceiling was so low he'd had to keep his plane close to the tree tops the entire way.[17]

None of this would have been alarming if weather forecasting hadn't been more art than science. In fact, conditions were poor enough that McCord decided at the last minute not to fly the *Akron*'s Curtiss F9C-2 fighters aboard. Instead, the N2Y-1 trainer – a two-seater bi-plane nicknamed the 'running boat' – would take their place. That way, if Moffett or his guest wanted to leave early they could be flown back to Lakehurst.

Serving on a big rigid was far more prestigious for the Navy's sky sailors than a lowly blimp. Importantly, a 50 per cent increase in salary called flight pay was earned for flying four or more hours per month. This meant a lot during the Depression, when a Navy salary didn't go very far. With Moffett on board, the crew were confident they'd fly that night. In other words, they were sure to get their bonus.

This would be Moffett's twelfth flight aboard the *Akron*.[18] He'd flown her more times than her commanding officer, McCord. As the mobile mooring mast began towing the airship out of her hangar, the admiral found an unobtrusive spot in the control car and settled down to watch preparations for take off.

As the *Akron*'s crew scrambled to get things ready, the temperature outside was a chilly 41°F, the cloud ceiling an oppressive 300ft.[19] There were plenty of buildings taller than 300ft in New York City just across the Hudson. Skyscrapers were easily spotted during the day, but flying in the clouds at night could lead to a collision in the days before radar. No wonder McCord had grounded his aeroplanes; only Moffett's airships would be out in this soup.

The *Akron* was finally ready for take-off at 1928 hours.[20] That's when McCord leaned out the control car window and, lifting a cardboard megaphone to his mouth, issued the most counter-intuitive command in the US Navy: 'Up ship!'

As the ground handlers released the land lines tethering the *Akron* to earth, the mighty airship with Admiral Moffett and seventy-five souls aboard rose slowly into the sky.* Within a minute, she'd vanished in the clouds as if erased by nature. It was the first of many indications that that night's training flight would be anything but routine.

---

*   Of the seventy-six men on board the *Akron* that night, twelve were officers, fifty-seven enlisted men and seven were guests, including Rear Admiral Moffett; Moffett's naval aide, Commander Henry B. Cecil; Moffett's VIP guest, Arthur F. Masury; and Lakehurst's commanding officer, Commander Fred T. Berry.

3

A NIGHT TO REMEMBER

If the *Akron* appeared fragile, she was at least twice as strong as the *Los Angeles*, the Navy's previous big rigid.[1] As Moffett boasted, the *Akron* was not only, 'the best airship that has ever been built; she is the safest'.[2]

The *Akron* punched through the fog at 1,500ft, the lights of Lakehurst making the clouds glow beneath her.[3] Her mission was simple: arrive at Newport, Rhode Island by 0700 hours to begin calibrating the radio direction finder stations along the New England coast. The task was mundane but important. Aircraft needed radio beacons to navigate in the days before radar and without them they got lost. But the route to Newport was fogged in, so McCord ordered the *Akron* to head inland where visibility was better. Once the skies cleared, they could make the three-hour dash across Long Island Sound. Until then, it was imprudent to bring the running boat aboard, so McCord radioed the pilot, Lt Trapnell, to wait until morning when the weather cleared.

As McCord set course for Philadelphia, Moffett observed how the officers interacted in the control car – a telling sign of how well a ship was run. The admiral had a rule when flying: don't interfere with operations, but he'd already violated it that morning when he phoned Lakehurst to make sure the weather didn't prevent their departure.[4]

A big rigid's control car is surprisingly small compared to the vast size of her hull. Attached to the airship's underbelly like a barnacle on a whale, it was positioned 200ft from her bow and 600ft from her stern. Offering a commanding view of the world below, it was not a comfortable place for those afraid of heights. Additionally, the airship's hull was so huge that its curvature prevented those on the bridge from seeing any part of her stern other than her bottom tail fin. Cut off from the rest of the crew overhead save for the telephone and a single ladder leading into the airship above them, those in the control car were in a world of their own.

As long as a city bus,[5] the oval-shaped structure was divided into three compartments: the forward-most compartment, or bridge; the navigator's compartment in the middle; and the gun room aft, which was more often used for smoking. The bridge was the *Akron*'s nerve centre. This is where her engine telegraphs were located. They not only signalled speed to her eight engine compartments spread through the ship, but forward, reverse and the angle of her propellers. The airship's flight controls (her helm and elevator wheels) were also located here. The *Akron* needed both if she was to operate in three dimensions.

The elevator wheel, located on the port side of the bridge, was responsible for altitude control. The actual elevators were on the *Akron*'s horizontal tail fins. Operating like the flaps on an aeroplane, they enabled the airship to rise or descend depending on how much and in which direction (clockwise or anticlockwise) the wheel was turned. An altimeter, inclinometer, vertimeter and superheat meter were located near the station.[6] There was also a series of small chalkboards above the windows on the port and starboard side. These boards were used to record the weight of the airship's fuel and ballast water as well as its remaining helium – important information if the ship was to maintain her equilibrium. Piloting an airship was as much about maths as anything else. As one officer put it, they 'flew it with a slide rule'.[7]

Beneath the chalkboards hung a row of toggles, which were used to drop ballast. There was also a set of toggles that could be pulled in an emergency when ballast or fuel needed to be dumped immediately to lighten the ship.[8]

The helm enabled the airship to turn either port or starboard. Located at waist level and surprisingly small for a ship's wheel, it was made of metal. The helm was connected to the rudders on the *Akron*'s vertical tail fins by cables hundreds of feet long. These cables were kept taut by a series of pulleys, sheaves and slack adjusters. One complete turn of the *Akron*'s helm moved her rudder 5 degrees,[9] but being an airship she was slow to respond.

People tend to equate dirigibles with aeroplanes because both fly, but they're more like submarines than anything else. The sky is as fluid a medium as water, with similar changes in temperature, pressure and flow. This is why airships, like submarines, had to make constant adjustments to maintain their equilibrium. It also explains why they employ a ballast system, something no aeroplane would ever require. Just as submarines face a limit on how deep they can dive, airships are limited by how high they can fly. Fly too high and the thinning air caused their helium to expand so much it risked bursting their gas cells.

The helmsman held the most commanding position on the bridge. Standing in the forward-most part of the compartment with nothing in front of him but floor-to-ceiling windows, he had an unobstructed view of the world.

The *Akron*'s executive officer (XO), Wiley, was stationed near the helm, while McCord stood near the elevator wheel in the aft section of the bridge.[10] As many as eleven men could crowd on to the bridge at one time,[11] including the captain, his XO, the officer of the deck, the helmsman, the elevatorman and their reliefs. This was a lot of men for such a small space, but everyone knew his role, so things functioned smoothly.

That evening, as the *Akron* headed towards Philadelphia, the bridge was blacked out to preserve the crew's night vision. Suspended above the darkness with only a few dim instrument lights illuminating their faces, it must have felt lonely. Less than an inch of alloyed metal separated the men from the black abyss below but it wasn't something they thought about. Still, the control car's swaying motion combined with the wind blowing in through the open windows reminded the bridge crew that the *Akron* flew at the mercy of the elements.

As the night wore on, Moffett's VIP, Masury, sat in the navigator's compartment looking increasingly worried.[12] Separated from the bridge by a sliding door, the compartment was where the navigator plotted the airship's course while sitting at a large, flat table fastened to the floor to keep it from sliding.

The control car's third, or aft compartment, had a ladder leading into the airship overhead as well as exit stairs embedded in the floor that could be lowered to the ground once the *Akron* landed

Moffett remained in the control car for the first two hours of the flight.[13] He knew his way around an airship, given the many times he'd flown aboard the Navy's big rigids. Although too old to be a Navy pilot, Moffett had qualified as a naval observer, meaning he could fly as navigator, co-pilot or support personnel on Navy planes. As a result, he was more than comfortable in the air.

As the fog slowly dissipated, the ground below became visible. In another month they would be able to stop worrying about winter storms, but for now clearing skies was an encouraging sign. By the time the *Akron* reached Philadelphia, the weather had improved enough that the city's lights could be seen twinkling below.

Next, McCord ordered a south-westerly course to Wilmington using the Delaware River as a guide. Airships were low-flying aircraft rarely venturing above 5,000ft. If they did, the valve on their gas cells would automatically vent helium to prevent them from bursting. But airships needed helium to stay aloft, so they avoided exceeding 'pressure height' whenever possible. Usually, the *Akron* maintained an altitude between 1,500 and 2,500ft. Slightly higher than the Empire State Building, it was close enough to the ground that geographical features such as rivers and railroad tracks could be used for navigation.

It's possible retirement was on Moffett's mind that night. It was almost certain that he'd be tapped to join the board of the International Zeppelin Transport Company given that his VIP that night was a director. If not, there was another Goodyear-sponsored company focused on Pacific airship travel that would be interested in retaining the admiral. Such positions were prestigious and well compensated. Importantly, they'd allow Moffett to continue the lighter-than-air work he'd begun at the BUAER.

Whatever problems his rigid airship programme was experiencing, Moffett was confident they could be ironed out before he retired. Every experimental programme suffered setbacks, and rigid airships were no exception but Moffett was convinced of their utility. He felt certain, given enough time and money, the *Akron* would prove naysayers wrong.

Once they passed Philadelphia, Wiley felt things were under control enough that the XO decided to take a smoking break in the aft compartment.[14] At 2000 hours the *Akron* reported, 'All well'[15] to Lakehurst. Fifteen minutes later, Moffett passed Wiley as he climbed the ladder into the giant erector set overhead. Stepping on to the port catwalk, which ran the length of the ship, Moffett headed towards the officer's wardroom.[16]

Along the way, Moffett encountered Richard E. Deal standing watch.[17] The boatswain's mate, second class, had flown with Moffett on all three of the Navy's big rigids. He was famous for having missed the *Shenandoah's* final flight when he switched places at the last minute with another elevatorman wanting to visit relatives in St Louis. When the *Shenandoah's* control car plunged to the ground, killing everyone inside, Deal's shipmates nicknamed him 'Lucky', as in Lucky Deal. He got even luckier when he later married the widow of the man who'd replaced him aboard the *Shenandoah*.[18]

'You on watch, sailor?' Moffett asked.

'Yes, sir. I have the telephone at this station.' After a pause, Deal added, 'You must like flying on this ship, Admiral.'

'I'm very fond of it,' Moffett replied, 'Much more so than the others. It is much better than the *Shenandoah*.'[19]

As the two men conversed, they balanced upon the impossibly narrow catwalk only 13in wide. The catwalk, also called a gangway, was covered in cork

to provide a secure grip but there was only a thin wire cable running its length
to use as a handhold. Not only did the *Akron's* engines cause the catwalk to
vibrate, they swayed every time the ship was raked by a gust. One misstep
could send a man plunging through the airship's canvas covering to their death
more than 1,000ft below. When the two men finished speaking, Moffett slid
past Deal in an effortless *pas de deux*, not giving the danger a second thought.

It wasn't until the *Akron* reached Wilmington at 2030 hours that lightning
was spotted. Wiley, still smoking in the aft compartment, felt all eight of her
engines come online. Taking this as a signal to return to the bridge, he noticed
McCord had also changed course and was now heading in an easterly direction.[20]

As lightning continued flashing in the south, McCord instructed Wiley to
get the latest weather forecast. Exiting the control car, Wiley climbed into the
airship overhead making for the aerology office. When he arrived, he discovered that static from the storm had interfered with radio reception, so they'd
only received two-thirds of the eight o'clock weather map.[21] Wiley didn't need
the entire map, however, to see a severe low-pressure system over Washington
was heading their way.

'What do you think?' McCord asked Wiley after he returned with
the news.[22]

'We certainly have a storm down there,' Wiley replied before suggesting they
take a westerly course to escape it.[23]

Airships had two options to avoid a storm: they could try to outrun it or
fly around it. One thing they couldn't do was fly above it since most storms
exceeded pressure height. The safest choice was not to fly at all, but that wasn't
an option Moffett encouraged.

Flying west to avoid a storm was standard practice for the Navy's rigid airships. Most storms followed a north-easterly direction before heading out to
sea. But McCord claimed to see lightning to the west as well as the south, so
he ignored Wiley's suggestion and chose an easterly course instead.

It wasn't the first time the *Akron's* CO had ignored his XO's advice. Though
both men acted professionally, there was tension between them, especially
since Wiley was more experienced. At first glance you'd have thought the two
men had a lot in common. Both were Midwesterners who'd attended the
US Naval Academy within four years of each other. But Wiley was a second-
generation airship officer, making him a member of the 'old guard'. In contrast,

McCord was third generation, recruited to the programme several years later. This meant Wiley had served nearly twice as many hours aboard airships as McCord, yet Wiley reported to McCord because he was junior in rank.[*,24]

Moffett had created this awkward situation by recruiting high-ranking officers to his LTA programme, believing they would 'draw more water'[25] in a Navy dominated by the surface fleet. But Moffett's policy caused resentment among long-term LTAers. Not only did it lead to crowding in the programme's upper ranks, it slowed promotion for more experienced men.[26]

It was bad enough that the *Akron* had three commanding officers in eighteen months,[27] two of them demonstrably less experienced than Wiley, but Wiley had once commanded the *Los Angeles*. Serving as McCord's first officer was a step down for him. To make matters worse, McCord treated Wiley with disdain. This rubbed Wiley the wrong way, but he had to submit if he hoped to replace his commanding officer one day. In the meantime, the situation was less than satisfactory.

Lucky Deal arrived in the control car to relieve the elevatorman a few minutes before 2100 hours.[28] As the lightning outside increased, McCord ordered another course change – this time heading north-east towards Asbury Park in New Jersey. But the fog returned as the *Akron* neared the coast. At the same time, powerful gusts began raking the airship as rain drummed on her canvas hull. Counting the seconds between lightning flash and thunder clap, Wiley realised the storm was catching up to them.

As McCord and Wiley searched for an escape route, the fog outside the control car windows was so thick they couldn't see far. Deal white-knuckled the elevator wheel as he struggled to maintain the airship's altitude. The elevator was the trickiest station on the bridge, requiring equal doses of nerve, strength and endurance.[29] After years of experience, Deal had a finely tuned instinct for flying, but controlling a big rigid in the middle of a storm was exhausting.

As Deal fought to keep the airship level, he could feel every one of her 200 tons in the screaming muscles of his forearms. At 2200 hours, he took a break, handing over the elevator wheel to his relief. Heading for the navigator's compartment, he found Moffett's VIP looking nervous.[30]

'It's pretty bad, isn't it?' Masury asked.[31]

---

* Wiley had 4,000 hours on airships compared with McCord's 2,250.

'There's nothing to worry about, Colonel,' Deal replied. 'We've been in worse storms than this. You should have been with us in the *Shenandoah* … coming from Buffalo back in 1924 … The lightning was so bad … the control car seemed … a ball of fire.'[32]

It was a point of pride among airship veterans to brag about how much worse a previous storm had been. After reassuring Masury he had nothing to fear, Deal headed to the aft compartment for a smoke.

By the time they'd reached the New Jersey coast, visibility was zero. McCord had tried flying above the fog, only to find they were hemmed in by low-hanging clouds.[33] Since lightning continued to plague them, he decided their safest bet was to head out to sea. Flying east over the Atlantic, he'd planned on eventually turning south to circumvent the storm. But this made little sense to Wiley, who was sure a westerly course was best.[34] He had no choice, however. He had to comply with his captain's order.

As the *Akron* headed over the Atlantic, she quickly encountered the full force of the storm. Lightning could be seen playing around her airspeed indicator, which trailed beneath the control car,[35] while her radio antenna had to be reeled in and out so many times to avoid a lightning strike that a fire control unit was detailed to stand by.[36] As proof of its virulence, the storm's interference was so great the *Akron*'s radio was of little use. Unable to broadcast her position, she was effectively cut off from the world.

By 2300 hours it was clear to everyone in the control car they'd flown into the heart of the storm. McCord, still looking for an escape, ordered the airship back to shore.

It was impossible to know where they were, as the storm had rendered the ship's radio direction finder useless.[37] And though they'd tried dropping flares to check their position, they were just swallowed up by the fog.[38] McCord thought they might be over Asbury Park, but visibility was so poor he couldn't be sure. Complicating matters, the weather made a landing impossible even if they succeeded in finding Lakehurst.

What neither McCord nor Wiley realised was the storm they'd encountered was one of the most violent to hit the east coast in a decade.[39] If they'd headed west as Wiley had suggested they might have escaped the worst of it, but now it was too late. There was no safe place to run.

Worried they might collide with a skyscraper over New York City,[40] McCord ordered the *Akron* back out to sea. But once over the Atlantic the storm grew fiercer. Every time a powerful gust broadsided the ship, the *Akron* shuddered, causing her Meccano-set-like skeleton to creak, vibrate or sway. Wiley guessed they were near the heart of the storm,[41] but it was hard to know for sure.

It had been five hours since they'd left Lakehurst when, shortly after midnight, Moffett returned to the control car. The admiral seemed only slightly impressed by the storm, remarking to Wiley, 'Almost as bad as the one we struck in Alabama.'[42]

Spreading his feet to counteract the ship's roll,[43] the admiral seemed to be enjoying himself. After watching for a few minutes he retired to the aft compartment to smoke his pipe.[44] Then, at fifteen minutes after midnight, the *Akron* hit a severe downdraught.

'We're falling!' the elevatorman shouted.[45]

As the elevator wheel spun out of his hands, a relief stepped in to grab it. Since the *Akron*'s fate depended on her altitude, Wiley jumped in to lend a hand.[46]

While the men on the bridge fought to keep their airship from plummeting, the *Akron* fell to 1,100ft. McCord ordered ballast dropped to slow her descent, but the ship was slow to respond.[47] As thunder crackled like cannon fire, McCord rang up the engines for more speed. Meanwhile, Wiley yanked the toggles emptying the mid-ship ballast bags. When the *Akron* reached 950ft, Wiley pulled the bow's emergency ballast toggles, dumping 1,600lb of water into the sea.[48] Hopefully, it would slow their descent.

Lighter-than-air physics are such that nothing happens quickly on an airship. Whether dropping ballast, venting helium or turning to port, every command has a delayed effect. After what seemed like an eternity, the *Akron* finally levelled off at 700ft, then began to climb.* When she reached an altitude of 1,300ft, the crew's relief was palatable.

For the next few minutes everything seemed fine. Then the *Akron* flew into a second downdraught, this one more severe than the first. Once again the airship plunged at a stomach-churning rate. McCord called for more elevator to counteract her nose-up incline, but when the airship dropped to 800ft the end seemed near.

---

*   Reports vary as to whether the *Akron* levelled out at 700 or 800ft as well as her degree of inclination, which may have ranged as high as 45 degrees. Either way, it was a dire situation.

Sounding five shrill blasts over the telephone howlers, Wiley sent the crew inside the ship running to their landing stations.[49] Moments later, a sickening lurch wracked the Queen of the Skies. For a moment, Wiley thought they'd been hit by a gust, but when the helmsman reported the rudder unresponsive he was convinced the airship had broken in two.[50]

When a 200-ton object flying at 70mph meets an unyielding surface, disaster is inevitable. What Wiley didn't realise is that the *Akron* hadn't broken in half, she'd flown into the Atlantic stern first, ripping off her bottom tail fin.[51] As the airship's eight engines laboured mightily to lift her out of the water, they probably did as much damage as the hungry waves determined to swallow her. When the control car finally emerged from the clouds at 300ft, Wiley could see the water below rising up to meet them.

'Stand by for crash!' he called out.[52]

Like a bird house nailed to a slowly falling tree, the *Akron*'s control car timbered towards the ocean. Wiley braced himself to keep upright. In the meantime, all conversation on the bridge ceased as the men contemplated their fate. Soon, the pride of the Navy's LTA programme was going to sink into the Atlantic, and there was nothing Moffett, McCord or Wiley could do to stop it.

4

FIGHT FOR SURVIVAL

It was fifteen minutes after midnight when Metalsmith, Second Class Moody E. Erwin felt the *Akron* plummet. The ship dropped so precipitously, Erwin, who was catching some shut-eye, had to grab hold of his bunk to keep from tumbling out.[1] Hearing the call for off-duty crew to assemble in the bow, the 28-year-old Tennessee native exited the compartment, pumped full of adrenalin. Seconds later, the *Akron* hit the water.

When the *Akron*'s stern collided with the sea, her forward momentum made quick work of her bottom tail fin, allowing water to flood the vessel. But the rest of the airship remained high in the sky, slanting at a crazy angle. As Erwin joined the growing knot of men on the steeply tilting catwalk, he could see the airship coming apart around them. First, one of the girders overhead gave way, blocking his path.[2] Next, a petrol tank tore loose, ploughing through the men gathered on the catwalk. The tank left three gashes on Erwin's hip before slamming into another man knocking him aft, never to be seen again.[3] But that didn't stop Erwin and the rest of the crew from fighting their way towards the bow. Forced to climg up the catwalk on his toes, Erwin grabbed anything he could to keep from falling.[4]

As the ocean poured into the *Akron*'s stern, the shriek of twisting metal could be heard throughout the ship. When freezing water reached her two aft engines, a tremendous hiss followed by a cloud of steam. Moments later, the lights went out.[5]

It was every man for himself after that. Trapped near the bow, Erwin made a split-second decision. Diving through the *Akron*'s outer cover, he plunged 30ft into the sea below.[6]

Erwin was a strong swimmer, but the frigid water was so shocking it squeezed the breath out of him. Then the ship rolled on top of him. Fearful of becoming tangled in its wreckage, Erwin dove deep as the *Akron* chased after him.[7] When he resurfaced, he'd cleared the wreck but was so chilled he couldn't stop his teeth from chattering.

At first, Erwin thought he could swim to shore, but there was no shore in sight to swim towards. Given that he was afraid of sharks, he kicked the water furiously, hoping to scare them away. As huge waves regularly dunked him, a heavy rain continued to fall. Finally, a lightning flash illuminated a fuel tank bobbing 20yd away.[8]

Erwin fought the roiling sea with every stroke. When he finally reached the tank, two men were already clinging to it. One was the *Akron*'s chief radio operator, Lt Robert W. Copeland, the other, Mechanic Lucius Rutan.[9]

A couple of hundred yards away, the *Akron*'s bow stuck out of the ocean. As she continued to sink, Erwin heard the cries of at least a dozen men in the darkness around him. With each passing minute they grew fainter.

Richard 'Lucky' Deal was resting in his bunk in the enlisted men's quarters when Chief Boatswain's Mate Carl Dean rushed in.

'All hands forward!' Dean shouted.[10]

Since the compartment had no ceiling, Deal was watching helium gas cell No. 7 billowing overhead. But when the *Akron* suddenly lurched, he was shocked to see two longitudinal girders connecting two of her main rings snap in half.[11]

Deal grabbed a pair of wire cutters before heading towards the bow, thinking they might be needed if he had to snip a slip tank. The gangway's inclination was so steep it felt like scaling a mountain. Deal grabbed what he could for support, but the lights inside the ship went out. Shortly thereafter, he felt his feet get wet.[12]

Trapped inside the sinking airship, Deal soon found himself in chest-deep water. When a fuel tank struck his head it momentarily stunned him. Struggling to free his feet from the wreckage, Deal swallowed copious amount of seawater.[13] When he finally escaped the sinking ship, the ocean was so rough he couldn't survive without something to stay afloat.

As the storm raged around him, Deal saw his fellow crewmen struggling in the water. He wanted to help, but it took every ounce of his energy to keep afloat. When a lightning flash illuminated a 120-gallon fuel tank bobbing nearby, Deal tried reaching it but was too weak to swim all the way.

Moody Erwin, hanging on to the tank, saw his shipmate go under. Reaching out, he pulled Deal to the surface.

'Who's here?' Deal asked, catching his breath.

'Rutan and Copeland,' Erwin responded.[14]

The four men clung to the cylindrical fuel tank, but it kept rolling in the waves, shrugging them off. Meanwhile, two phosphorous flares, ignited by the water, lit up the sea and revealed a hell-scape straight out of a Hieronymus Bosch painting.[15]

Erwin, Deal, Copeland and Rutan floated in the frigid Atlantic for at least half an hour. Suffering from hypothermia, they shivered uncontrollably as their speech began to slur and their pulse weakened. Of the four, Rutan and Copeland were in the worst shape. Copeland's face was a twisted grimace and neither man had energy to speak. When a wave swept Deal into the sea, he spotted a hole in the tank that was letting water in. Deal tried plugging it but it was hard to stop the flow. Locking hands with Erwin, Deal hoped to stop the tank from rolling but it was an impossible task.[16]

When a wave knocked Rutan off the tank, he was too exhausted to save himself. The last Deal saw of him was an outstretched hand slipping beneath the waves. By this time, a comforting warmth had begun to spread through Erwin's chest – the final stage of hypothermia before death set in.[17]

When the control car finally smacked down on the ocean, it was with such force it crushed the aft compartment. Seconds later the car filled with icy water, then, rolling on to its side, disappeared beneath the sea. But, before the car vanished, a wave washed Wiley out the portside window.[18] He swam underwater for as long as he could, hoping to escape the wreckage. When he finally surfaced, it was in a thick cloud of fog.

Wiley heard the cries of his drowning crew, but the towering whitecaps quickly separated the *Akron*'s first officer from his men. He thought about swimming back to the airship 400yd away but needed to rest first. As luck would have it, a board drifted by, which he grabbed.[19] Spotting a man struggling in the water, Wiley tried to help him, but a wave forced him under. When Wiley resurfaced, the man was gone.[20]

As the mortally wounded *Akron* receded in the night, waves tossed Wiley like a bathtub toy. At one point, he heard the cries of Erwin and Deal, but wasn't sure where they were.[21] In the meantime, McCord, Masury and Moffett were nowhere to be seen. Wiley was an excellent swimmer, but if he wasn't rescued soon, he'd die of hypothermia. Floating on his board to conserve energy, he was left to endure the pummelling of the storm.

The world's biggest, most expensive aircraft sank off Barnegat Light shortly after midnight on Tuesday, 4 April 1933. Although Copeland, her radio operator, managed to get an SOS out before losing electricity, static from the storm rendered most radio receivers inoperable.

Trapped inside the sinking ship, the crew cut through her outer envelope using the knives they'd been issued. Those that escaped swam away as fast as possible to avoid being pulled down by the wreck. But where could they go in a raging storm 25 miles off the coast of New Jersey?

The average water temperature in April was 46°F, although some reports suggest it was colder. The longest a person can survive in water that chilly is twenty minutes, and that's not taking into account towering waves, gale-force winds and a driving rain. On top of that, many of the *Akron*'s crew didn't know how to swim.

Given that the *Akron*'s life belts were still in the hangar at Lakehurst, the crew was at immediate risk of drowning.[22] To make matters worse, the Navy not only didn't know where the *Akron* had crashed, no one even knew she was missing.

The *Phoebus*, a German-flagged oil tanker, was bound for Tampico, Mexico, when the *Akron* went down. Having left New York City earlier that day, she'd been blown off course by the storm. Since the weather was terrible, her 34-year-old captain, Karl Dalldorf, was on the bridge when he spotted lights off the starboard bow at 0023 hours. Dalldorf realised the lights couldn't be a ship because they hung in the sky. Vanishing briefly, they reappeared three minutes later on the ocean's surface before winking out altogether.[23]

Dalldorf soon deduced that an aeroplane had crashed.[24] Ringing up the engines for full speed, he ordered his 9,000-ton tanker to head for where the lights had last been seen. Twenty-five minutes later, the crew smelled petrol as the *Phoebus* ploughed through surface wreckage. When Wiley was spotted in the water, a lifeboat was put over the side. After tossing Wiley a buoy, they pulled him into the boat, making him the first of the *Akron*'s crew to be rescued.[25]

When Deal spotted the *Phoebus*, he shouted, 'There's a ship!'[26]

Fearing they might be missed, Deal and Erwin yelled for help. But Deal worried his friend wasn't going to make it. When a wave knocked Erwin off the tank, he seemed ready to give up.

'I can't hold out!' Erwin cried.[27]

Semi-delirious, Erwin wanted to go to sleep, but Deal encouraged him to hang on a bit longer.[28] It wasn't until they heard the *Phoebus* sound a deafening blast on its ship's whistle that Deal truly believed they might be saved.

A lifeboat from the *Phoebus* soon spotted them. Erwin was rescued first followed by Copeland, who was unconscious. As Deal awaited his turn he saw the *Akron*'s only life raft drift by empty.[29] When he was finally lifted out of the water, he too slipped into unconsciousness.

It was a stroke of luck that the *Phoebus* came along when she did. Erwin and Deal, suffering from exposure, could not have lasted much longer. As it was, Copeland never regained consciousness and died later that night. The *Phoebus* launched a second boat to continue the search, but no one else was found. This left Wiley, Erwin and Deal as the sole survivors of the worst disaster in aviation history.

It wasn't until Captain Dalldorf spoke to Wiley that he realised an airship, not an aeroplane, had crashed.[30] Dashing off a message early on Tuesday morning to anyone who could receive it, Dalldorf wrote: 'Airship *Akron* with 77 men [*sic*] aboard went down near Barnegat Lightship … Chief Officer [*sic*] and three men saved.'[31]

Wiley checked on Erwin and Deal before sending a radiogram to the Navy Department.[32] When the Chief of Naval Operations replied, he ordered all three survivors to keep quiet about what had happened.

The reaction is understandable. Facts about the crash were few, so the Navy wanted to keep a lid on things until more was known. The news blackout didn't last long, however. Once newspapers got hold of Dalldorf's message, they rushed out early morning extras, the *San Francisco Chronicle*'s headline being typical of the coverage:

DIRIGIBLE *AKRON* WRECKED AT SEA[33]

The light atop Hangar No. 1 at NAS Lakehurst blinked through the night. Since the naval air station's commanding officer had been aboard the *Akron*, Lt Cdr Jess Kenworthy Jr took over responsibility for the base. Details of the disaster were few, so Kenworthy, not wanting his men to speculate, ordered them to keep away from reporters.[34]

Families of the *Akron* crew began arriving at the base's welfare building early Tuesday morning. Some had learned about the crash from boys selling newspapers, but most heard about it from one another since news spread quickly in the tight-knit community. Many of the wives lived on base or in the nearby town. They not only knew each other well, their husbands socialised and their children played together.

Several of the wives arrived carrying infants, while others were accompanied by the family dog. Four of the wives were pregnant. Seven had to be hospitalised for emotional distress.[35] Meanwhile, their husbands' cars sat in the car park near the hangar awaiting their return.

There was little information at first. One report suggested the *Akron* had been struck by lightning.[36] Another mentioned four men had been saved, but nobody knew who they were. One survivor, whose name was only partially listed, could have been Deal or Dean. Lucky Deal's wife knew her husband was a good swimmer, but Carl Dean's wife knew her husband couldn't swim a lick.[37] A Coast Guard cutter spotted floating mattresses and other debris, offering hope more of the crew would be found.[38] One report falsely claimed that forty men had been spotted on wreckage off Barnegat Light, but prospects dimmed as the day progressed.

Among the missing was Admiral William A. Moffett. The phone at Moffett's Washington home began ringing sometime after midnight. The admiral's 14-year-old daughter, Beverly, was first to answer. The caller informed her the *Akron* had gone down and asked to speak with the admiral. Confused, Beverly passed the phone to her mother, who explained that her husband was not at home. He was aboard the *Akron*.[39]

Jeannette Moffett waited patiently on Tuesday for news of her husband. When reporters sought her reaction, she held an impromptu press conference on the steps of her house. 'I have every belief that Admiral Moffett is all right and I shall hear from him,' she told reporters. 'The Admiral has a way of coming out of things safely.'[40]

Despite First Lady Eleanor Roosevelt stopping by to offer her support, Jeanette's optimism was not justified. The next day the *Washington Post* ran her husband's obituary even though his body had yet to be found. McCord and Masury, also missing, were presumed dead.

The weather remained loathsome throughout Tuesday. Seas were rough and winds high with a second storm following on the heels of the first. A massive search was launched despite the weather. At least two Coast Guard ships as well as planes from the New York Police, Marines and Philadelphia Navy Yard participated.[41] Considerable debris was spotted where the *Akron* had sunk, including pieces from the airship's envelope, but no more survivors were found.

Navy pilots based at NAS Lakehurst begged Kenworthy to let them participate in the search. Not wanting to lose more men to the storm, he forbade it.[42] When survivors were reported clinging to wreckage, Kenworthy finally relented, granting permission for a twin-engine blimp, the J-3, to take to the skies.[43]

It seemed fitting that a Navy blimp should search for the *Akron*'s crew, given Moffett's belief airships made excellent scouts. The J-3 flew along the coast off Long Beach Island until a strut on one of her engine mounts broke. Needing to make an emergency landing, she fought against headwinds to get to shore. When she finally reached the resort community of Beach Haven, she dropped ground lines for bystanders to grab. But before the J-3 could land she was blown out to sea, where her gondola crashed in the waves, drowning two of her seven-man crew. The next day, headlines trumpeted the second airship disaster in twenty-four hours.

A Coast Guard cutter had rendezvoused with the *Phoebus* by then. Wiley, Deal and Erwin were transferred to the USCGC *Tucker* (CG-23), which transported them to the Brooklyn Navy Yard. Wiley and Erwin were well enough to walk off the ship under their own power, but Deal had to be carried off. A cameraman snapped their picture as they disembarked, but none of the men would speak to the press. For the time being, details of the *Akron* crash would remain a secret.

5

SPOTLIGHT

It was a sunny day in Akron, Ohio, when Goodyear's chief airship designer, Dr Karl Arnstein, first learned of the *Akron* crash. Arnstein was in his office at Goodyear-Zeppelin when reporters caught up with him. Described as 'in shock', the bespectacled engineer revealed little. 'I can say nothing,' he told reporters in a quavering voice. 'I must know more.'[1]

One reason Arnstein didn't answer questions is that he may have been concerned that a fault in his design was responsible for loss of the *Akron*. This could explain why newspaper accounts describe him looking dazed, tight-lipped and grim.[2] Nobody knew why the airship had crashed, but Arnstein regained enough of his composure to release a statement that afternoon:

> News of the disaster comes as a profound shock to me and the entire organization at Goodyear-Zeppelin. From the viewpoint of personnel it is a staggering loss to the nation.[3]

When asked by reporters whether the *Akron* crashed because of a structural failure, Arnstein denied it, but the truth is he didn't know.

President Franklin D. Roosevelt had only been in office a month when the dirigible crashed. 'The loss of the *Akron* with its crew of gallant officers and men is a national disaster,' he told the country. 'Ships can be replaced but the nation can ill afford to lose such men as Rear Admiral William A. Moffett.'[4]

But Lt Commander Wiley was the one person everyone really wanted to hear from.

When Wiley arrived at the Brooklyn Navy Yard, his uniform was so wrinkled you could almost smell the sea. A few hours earlier he'd been fighting for his life in the stormy waters of the Atlantic. Now, he set foot on dry land for the first time since his ordeal began.

Lucky Deal was first to disembark the Coast Guard cutter, carried off on a stretcher. Moody Erwin, draped in a blanket and leaning on a sailor for support, followed next. Wiley, the senior ranking officer, came last. Wearing borrowed trousers and a khaki shirt that had shrunk after being dried on the ship's boiler, he shuffled off in a borrowed pair of shoes he wore unlaced because they didn't fit. Asked by a reporter how he was, all Wiley would say was, 'Fine.'[5]

Many people were affected by the *Akron* disaster, especially those who'd lost family members. But no one's life changed more that day than Lt Cdr Wiley. As the *Akron*'s sole surviving officer, he became the nation's most famous sky sailor overnight. Suddenly, everyone wanted to hear what he had to say.

If it was natural for Wiley to be the face of the *Akron*, it wasn't a role the 42-year-old naval officer relished. A plain-spoken Midwesterner born and raised in Missouri, he was a man of few words. Reporters described him as 'steady and quiet',[6] but what they really meant was distant and reserved.

Wiley learned to keep his emotions in check growing up. A Navy career had only reinforced this tendency. Though he made allowances for his wife and children, he was not one to express his feelings, which is why he came across as formal and flat. Having said this, Wiley's peers respected him. Commander Rosendahl, who rarely had a kind word to say about anyone, considered him first rate. But Wiley's subordinates found he could be chilly. Using his command prerogative, Wiley kept them at a distance. Given his preference for silence, he'd soon feel discomfort with all the questions he'd be asked. Until then, he kept his thoughts to himself.

That same day, doctors at the Brooklyn Navy Yard pronounced Wiley fit if exhausted. Nevertheless, it's curious that he agreed to a radio interview so shortly after the disaster. Of course, the public was hungry to know every detail about the *Akron*'s final hours. Still, no official reason had been given for the crash. A radio address seemed especially imprudent given a Navy Court of Inquiry with the power to recommend court martial would soon be convened. In the meantime, both the Senate and the House announced their own investigations, including a far-ranging inquiry into airship safety.

But the public wanted to hear from the man who'd been swimming in the icy Atlantic less than twelve hours before, so that evening NBC and the

Columbia Broadcasting System set up microphones in the hospital to capture the first eyewitness account of what happened.

Photographs show Wiley looking remarkably calm for what he'd just been through. Sitting on a hospital bed wearing a striped robe over hospital-issued pyjamas, his hair parted neatly in the middle, he doesn't look like a man who'd just survived a disaster. Instead, he calmly holds his typewritten statement, a water pitcher on a tray behind him in case he got thirsty.

'Very reluctantly I consent to speak so soon after the loss of so many ship-mates,' he said in a steady voice, 'but because of the widespread interest in this disaster ... I wish to give you a general report.'[7]

Pausing for a moment, Wiley glanced down at the papers in his hand before rubbing a pencil against his cheek.[8]

'I am not going to answer any questions as to opinion or technical observations,'[9] he said. Then he told the world what it had been waiting for.

We left Lakehurst last night at 7:30 on a regularly scheduled flight ... the ground was obscured by fog but we knew our position quite accurately ... We continued to the eastward for about an hour and then reversed course. When we reached the land again we saw a group of lights ... This was ... midnight and the course was changed to the south-east. About thirty minutes later the ship began to descend rapidly from 1,600ft and I dropped emergency ballast ... The fall was stopped ... [and] we rose rapidly ... About three minutes later the air became exceedingly turbulent and the ship was tossed about violently. I knew we were near the centre of the storm because the air is most disturbed near the centre ... [While calling] all hands for landing stations ... the ship took a sharp lurch. By this time the bow of the ship was inclined ... about 20 degrees but ... falling quite rapidly. In the fog nothing could be seen. I asked the altitude and the answer was 300ft. I gave the order 'Stand by to Crash', and that signal was rung up to the engine cars.[10]

Wiley estimated no more than thirty seconds transpired between his sounding the alarm and when the *Akron* hit the ocean. When asked if the water was cold, his affirmative response was so emphatic, it made reporters laugh. [11]

Someone asked, 'Did you see Captain McCord after the crash?'

'The water just swept me out of his window,' Wiley responded. 'I don't know what happened to him.'[12]

Wiley said he didn't believe the ship was struck by lightning, but declined to speculate on the cause of the disaster. He concluded his remarks by offering a ringing endorsement of Moffett's big rigid programme, while indirectly plugging Goodyear:

> In spite of this accident I have every confidence in airships and hope that our people will still continue to see the value of them both commercially and for naval uses.[13]

As quickly as it began, the press conference was over.

If Wiley seemed stiff in recounting his ordeal, he wasn't used to the spotlight. 'Doc,' as he was known to friends, had never been the centre of a media storm. But the *Akron*'s first officer was circumspect not just because he didn't want to say anything that might damage the LTA programme, but because he wasn't exactly sure what had happened.

The airship had certainly been caught in a downdraught, but why did she end up in the water? Had a gas cell ruptured? Was she flying too low? Or had the downdraught broken her in two? Wiley didn't admit it to the press, but he wasn't anymore sure of the answer than Dr Karl Arnstein.

Despite his measured delivery, newspapers called Wiley's account 'one of the most thrilling … broadcasts ever put on the air.'[14] What they didn't mention is that the radio interview was a sign of how fast the world was changing. That a nationwide radio audience could hear a first-hand report the same day the *Akron* was lost rather than wait for tomorrow's newspaper indicated how much technology was changing daily life. Airships were but one example, which included the rapid spread of electricity, telephones and talking motion pictures. All this new technology experienced an occasional setback as the *Akron* disaster made clear, but it was the price the nation was willing to pay for progress.

Wiley's narrative of how the world's safest airship fell out of the sky played well on the radio, but the story was custom-made for newspapers. Some dailies, including the *Akron Beacon Journal*, managed to print a Tuesday morning extra despite being an evening paper.

Every word of Wiley's account made it into Wednesday's broadsheets. Flying was so novel that many newspapers had a regular aviation column. But there had never been an aerial disaster on the scale of the *Akron*, so the press went into a frenzy.

Some papers romanticised the crash. The *Akron Beacon Journal* ran an editorial calling the bridge crew's behaviour a story that 'glorifies the traditions of the American navy'.[15] Others used it to question the sanity of building more airships. So long as the *Akron* was flying, the anti-airship contingent remained in the background but once she crashed, misgivings about Moffett's rigid airship programme erupted into view. As Goodyear's hometown paper reported, 'With the mounting determination to end the naval airship program spreading through … Congress … the fate of the boldest American bid for commercial supremacy in the air hung in the balance.'[16] Put another way, Litchfield's plan for passenger-carrying airships had hit a major roadblock.

The *Los Angeles* had flown without mishap for eight years, the *Akron* for only twenty months. Nevertheless, eight years is a long time for an emerging technology to operate without a failure. Certainly, no aeroplane, train or ocean liner could lay claim to a similar safety record, at least not in their early days. But the *Akron* crash erased any progress the *Los Angeles* had made. Now, all anybody wanted to know was what caused the disaster.

Less than twenty-four hours after being rescued, Wiley, Erwin and Deal received orders to travel to Washington. Doctors thought Wiley might require further treatment but discharged him anyway. The travel order came so quickly, Deal had to borrow a naval uniform, only to discover it had the wrong insignia, while Erwin wore an ill-fitting suit for the journey. As for Wiley, he wore the same wrinkled uniform he'd been rescued in.

The day after being fished out of the Atlantic, the three men found themselves standing in the cold at Long Island's Floyd Bennett Airport awaiting their flight. Once again, Wiley spoke to the media, this time for newsreel cameras. As a chilly wind rearranged his hair, Wiley told the gathering, 'We are now ready for duty in airships wherever we are assigned.'[17] It was a bold statement given what they'd been through.

The three men travelled by plane to Washington, DC, where they were greeted by Secretary Swanson on the steps of the Navy Department. Deal was so unwell Erwin had to help him up the stairs. Moffett may have been dead, but the Navy's PR instincts remained strong. Swanson indulged in some positive spin, bestowing a commendation on each man for the benefit of the newsreels. 'I congratulate you, Lt Commander Wiley, on being one of the survivors of as gallant a crew as ever constituted the personnel of the navy,'[18] Swanson said for the cameras.

Wiley replied, 'Thank you, Mr Secretary. I would like to say that the discipline on the ship was perfect. Even our beloved Admiral Moffett went to his station. The orders were all given in a low tone of voice and carried out quickly.'[19]

It's surprising how two-faced Swanson could be. Squirrely looking with a bushy moustache and starved physique, he had told the press the day before, 'I have never been enthusiastic over these large airships.'[20] Now he was bestowing commendations on three of the *Akron*'s only survivors for the benefit of newsreel cameras.

After the ceremony, Wiley, Erwin and Deal met Admiral William V. Pratt, Chief of Naval Operations, with whom they spent the afternoon. The next morning, they were driven to a meeting with the President.

The White House can be intimidating to those visiting for the first time. Since Wiley was the ranking officer, Erwin and Deal stayed in the background while Roosevelt did his best to put everyone at ease.

'I'm thankful you're here,' the President said greeting them. 'Sit down and tell me all about it.'[21]

After Wiley praised the *Phoebus* for their rescue, the thirty-second President promised to write a personal letter thanking the captain. Then he told a funny story about a congressman investigating the *Titanic* who didn't know where the starboard side of a ship was.[22]

The President may have appeared sympathetic, but Roosevelt had had a mixed experience with dirigibles. He'd invested in the American Investigation Corporation in 1921, which was in talks with Schütte-Lanz, a German airship manufacturer, about an airship passenger service between New York and Chicago. Franklin D. Roosevelt served on the corporate board as well as being a company vice president. But the firm ran into financial difficulties. When the *Shenandoah* crashed, it put an end to its plans.

Being warmly greeted by the President was one thing, but losing the support of the House Committee's Chairman of Naval Affairs was quite another. congressman Carl Vinson had funded Moffett's LTA programme. A curmudgeonly Georgia Democrat nicknamed 'the swamp fox', Vinson went on record the day of the *Akron* crash saying, 'We've built three and lost two; you can take it from me, there won't be any more.'[23] Additionally, Senator William H. King, Democrat of Utah, introduced a resolution calling for an investigation into the usefulness of Navy dirigibles. That same day, Representative Vinson was authorised by the House Naval Affairs Committee to conduct an investigation into the *Akron* crash. These two investigations would eventually be combined into a joint congressional committee determined to get to the bottom of the disaster. Meanwhile, the Navy's Court of Inquiry was set to convene at Lakehurst on Monday.

The loss of the *Akron*, along with seventy-three of her seventy-six officers and crew, was a grievous blow to the Navy's rigid airship programme. Not only was it the worst disaster in aviation history, but half of the Navy's experienced LTA personnel were wiped out overnight.[24] Given the *Akron*'s sister ship, the USS *Macon*, was scheduled to begin trial flights later that month, there was an urgency to the congressional proceedings. With America's flagship at the bottom of the Atlantic and her chief supporter, Admiral Moffett, dead, the Navy's big rigid programme was in danger of being cancelled.

It's not difficult to understand why the anti-airship coalition thought the programme should be buried along with Moffett. After all, the *Akron*'s fatality rate was an astonishing 96 per cent. But her seventy-three deaths didn't hold a candle to passenger-ship disasters like the *General Slocum* in 1904 (893 souls lost), the *Titanic* in 1912 (1,517 souls lost) or the *Empress of Ireland* in 1914 (1,012 souls lost). Even train accidents, which happened more frequently than airship crashes, killed at least as many people as died aboard the *Akron* and occasionally more.

However, the *Akron* crash was all anyone could talk about. Though an undeniable tragedy, nobody seemed to notice the body count was a drop in the bucket compared with trains and passenger ships. One thing was clear, however. The same rules didn't apply.

6

WILEY ON TRIAL

If Wiley felt uncomfortable his first few days as a public figure, they were nothing compared to what lay in store. He not only suffered the indignity of being chased by reporters; he had to undergo the rigours of not one but two crash investigations. By the time the hearings were over, he'd be a household name.

The first investigation, the Navy Court of Inquiry, convened inside Lakehurst's Hangar No. 1 on Monday, 10 April. The hangar was one of the largest buildings in the world, but its emptiness served as a reminder that its primary tenant was missing. The hangar, too large to be heated, was cold, damp and draughty, so the court met in the narrow, brick-lined room off to one side where the *Akron*'s gas cells were repaired.[1] The striking thing about the room wasn't its long table around which the inquiry met, or the chalk-board for diagrams, it was the huge swaths of gas cell fabric that hung like drapes around the room. Meanwhile, another powerful north-easter lashed the building's windows, demonstrating to those inside what the *Akron* had gone through.

That same day, Moffett's body was found floating 35 miles off the coast of Atlantic City. The side of his head had been crushed, presumably when the control car hit the ocean. Moffett had been in the water for a week, so his engraved cufflinks and khaki raincoat were used to positively identify him.[2]

Moffett's remains were only the fifth to be recovered. McCord had been found the previous day, along with part of an instrument panel from the control car. But sixty-seven of the *Akron*'s crew were still missing a week after she'd sunk. When informed during the court hearing that Moffett's body had been recovered, Wiley eyes were said to shine with tears.[3]

If being the only officer to survive the crash catapulted Wiley to national attention, the naval Court of Inquiry pinned him there for a month. Since only Wiley could say what took place inside the control car leading up to the crash, it was possible he might incriminate either himself or one of his superior officers. As a result, the public breathlessly awaited his testimony.

It's no exaggeration to say the future of Moffett's rigid airship programme depended on what Wiley revealed. This may explain why, over the course of three days, he spoke in such a slow, deliberate and, at times, halting manner. As the *New York Times* noted in its front-page account of the inquiry's first day, 'It was evident that Wiley testified with some reluctance … on controversial points.'[4]

It is possible Wiley suffered some form of post-traumatic stress disorder, but it's more likely he knew his testimony could tip things either way and so, being in favour of airships, he measured his words carefully.

Wiley's written account of the crash was entered into the record on the first day of the proceedings. It was the same just-the-facts explanation he'd given Secretary Swanson. Stripped of blame, drama or innuendo, about the only thing you could tell for sure was that the *Akron* had crashed. The reason why remained unclear.

If Wiley's report was absent meaningful content, it suggested (intentionally or not) he wasn't telling the whole story. The first few days after the crash Wiley thought the *Akron* had broken in two. But as the court of inquiry advanced, he backed away from this contention. Additionally, at least one of the judges suspected Moffett of countermanding McCord's orders on the bridge that night,[5] which might explain the *Akron*'s erratic course. But Wiley refused to blame either man, even though he'd objected at least once to McCord's easterly heading. Wiley's reluctance to criticise a superior officer wasn't unusual. Importantly, how could Wiley turn against a programme he'd chosen as his career path, faithfully served as one of its early recruits and succeeded in for more than ten years?

Even when the court questioned him, Wiley said little of consequence. He allowed that reports indicated severe weather over Michigan, but since it was outside their area of operations, 'We did not consider it a threat.'[6] More surprising, Wiley testified that the barometric pressure at the storm's centre might have caused the *Akron*'s altimeter to be '250ft in error'.[7] If true, it meant the airship was flying far closer to the ocean than her officers realised. But Wiley didn't think the *Akron* was lost during the latter part of the night, downplayed his suggestion to head west, didn't realise they'd flown into the water at first and wasn't even sure why they'd crashed. In other words, he knew surprisingly little for an officer on the bridge.

After the court finished questioning Wiley, he was told he could make a statement. The *Akron*'s first officer paused for a moment, then began speaking slowly.

'I do want to say that I think before and during the flight the captain … and all of the officers and men did their duty to the best of their ability. If any errors were made they were beyond the skill and experience existing today.'[8]

If it sounds anodyne that's because it was. But the biggest surprise is how close to the truth it was.

Lucky Deal was called to testify on the second day of the inquiry. In contrast to Wiley's stiff and reserved manner, he provided some colour to the proceedings. Reporters scribbled furiously in their notebooks as Deal described the *Akron*'s bow inclination as the greatest he'd ever experienced.[9] But it was Erwin who took the court into unchartered waters when he testified on the third day that it was shortly after midnight when, 'I heard something snap and looking up saw a 12in break in a girder.'

'Was it your impression that the stern was in the water when the girder snapped?' one of the judges asked him.

'No, sir. The tail was not in the water.'

'How do you know?'

'Because the ship was still flying and it couldn't very well fly if it was in the water.'[10]

Erwin's testimony was a potential bombshell since it suggested that the *Akron* had experienced a structural failure *before* she crashed, something Wiley had initially agreed with. Alarm bells should have rung, especially since a previous witness had already testified the *Akron* was due for an overhaul. This included reinforcing the airship's airframe where one of the two longitudinal girders had broken.[11] The twelve-day repair job had been recommended by Dr Arnstein and approved by the Navy following damage the *Akron* had previously suffered.

It's revealing that Wiley chose this moment to exercise his right to examine Lt Cdr Edwin F. Cochrane, Lakehurst's assembly and repairs officer responsible for maintaining the *Akron*. Cochrane had earlier told the court about the airship's impending overhaul.

'As far as you know was the ship considered perfectly safe to fly without this alteration?' Wiley asked.

'Yes, sir,' Cochrane replied.[12]

No one questioned Cochrane's judgment, in part because he was an experienced repairs officer. Nor did anyone think it odd that Wiley wanted to set the record straight about the safety of the *Akron* before her last flight. Clearly, Wiley had a dog in the fight.

In contrast, Erwin and Deal were enlisted men whose testimony was confined to events inside the ship. Whether the court deemed their account less important or less reliable than an officer's is uncertain, but the two men's testimonies never received the attention they deserved. Instead, the inquiry took a turn towards the absurd when 'Captain' Anton F. Heinen was called to testify late on the afternoon of 13 April.

Anton Heinen was a colourful if unpredictable character. As much loose cannon as airship captain, he'd piloted commercial Zeppelins for a subsidiary of Luftschiffbau Zeppelin. After that, he'd trained airship crews to fight in the First World War.

Heinen had come to America in the early 1920s to train the *Shenandoah* crew. Commissioned a lieutenant commander in the US Naval Reserve, it was an unusual position for a German national in the years following the war.

Heinen's claim to fame was saving the *Shenandoah* after she tore away from her mooring mast in the middle of a storm, leaving most of her bow behind. The damage was so extensive that the airship could only fly stern-first. After an eight-hour struggle with only a skeleton crew on board, Heinen succeeded in flying the *Shenandoah* back to Lakehurst.

Built like a jockey, small and slim, Heinen sported a red Van Dyke, which drew attention from his balding head. Famously difficult, his personality was best described as irascible. His frank, sometimes contradictory, opinions often got him into trouble with the very people he hoped to impress.

With an ego as big as the dirigibles he flew, and a penchant for self-promotion, Heinen had tried recapturing the limelight ever since leaving the Navy. He'd even promoted a small blimp for family use called the air yacht. It goes without saying that most of the officers in Moffett's programme thought him a jackass.

Heinen was the last witness heard that day. His pro-airship testimony started out reasonably enough, but it wasn't long before he got himself in trouble. Telling the court the accident could have been avoided if the *Akron* had steered around the storm, his next comment was even more indiscreet: 'There should be no whitewash of the *Akron* disaster as there was of the *Shenandoah* tragedy.'[13]

Heinen was referring to the Navy's Court of Inquiry into the loss of the *Shenandoah*, at which he'd testified that her captain had caused the crash by removing the helium safety valves from the airship's gas cells. Heinen may have hoped to make himself a home in America's fast-growing airship industry, but no one would touch him, given his tendency to shoot from the hip. Still, he had a point. The Navy did have a history of whitewashing its airship disasters, but because Anton Heinen said it, nobody was listening.

That same day, the father of naval aviation was buried at Arlington National Cemetery. Hundreds of people attended the ceremony including Mrs Moffett and her children, as well as Swanson, the Secretary of the Navy. The elaborate procession led by an honour guard included a horse-drawn caisson bearing Moffett's coffin. The admiral was honoured with a 21-gun salute, followed by a bugler playing taps, after which he was lowered into the ground. And so, a lion who'd weathered many tempests including war, politics and impending retirement, had succumbed not to winter but to a fast-moving storm no one had predicted. His wife, Jeanette, was said to accept the news of his death with 'fortitude', suggesting she was something of a lioness herself.[14]

McCord was also laid to rest that day at Annapolis' Naval Cemetery, while Masury's ashes were spread from the Ambrose lightship, 5 miles off the coast of New Jersey.[15] Sadly, the majority of the *Akron*'s crew remained missing.

Jerome C. Hunsaker, a former Navy commander who'd been involved in the design and construction of the *Shenandoah*, testified at the inquiry on 19 April. Citing a study conducted by Goodyear engineers, he said the only way girders 7 and 8 could have broken was when the *Akron*'s tail hit the water.[16] Hunsaker's testimony contradicted that of Erwin, who'd been aboard the airship at the time of the crash. Hunsaker, who hadn't, also hinted responsibility for the crash lay with the *Akron*'s operators since it was foolish to fly in the middle of a thunderstorm.

But Hunsaker had a conflict of interest. After twenty-one years with the Navy, he'd joined the Goodyear-Zeppelin Corporation as Vice President of its airship division. Put bluntly, it was in his best interest to defend the *Akron*'s design. Suggesting otherwise might have been the death knell for Goodyear's business.

Commander Alger H. Dresel, an experienced if conservative airship captain, appeared before the inquiry on 26 April. Dresel testified that he avoided flying in thunderstorms but surprised the court when he said that he thought the weather forecasts for 2 and 4 April 'doubtful'.[17] When Dresel revealed he would not have flown the *Akron* on either of those days 'unless it was an emergency',[18] it reinforced the feeling the *Akron* should never have been out that night.

Dresel's testimony is instructive because he'd not only captained the *Akron* prior to McCord, he was commanding officer of her sister ship, the *Macon*, whose maiden flight he'd overseen the previous week. The *Akron Beacon Journal*'s columnist had praised Dresel for his, 'determination to avoid unfavourable weather' when scheduling the *Macon*'s maiden flight.[19] Such behaviour may have reassured Navy officials that the *Macon* was in safe hands, but it was the opposite of what Moffett had desired.

That same day, Admiral Pratt, Chief of Naval Operations, announced that given the loss of the *Akron*, and a lack of funding due to the Depression, the Navy would decommission Lakehurst Naval Air Station as an airship base.[20] It was another sign the Navy's battleship admirals were determined to kill Moffett's programme.*

When Dr Arnstein was called in front of the Court of Inquiry on 26 April, he defended his creation. The Czech-born engineer reassured the court he'd incorporated everything he'd learned building rigid airships for Germany into the *Akron*'s design. As for her strength, Arnstein testified the *Akron* was built to a safety factor more than twice that required.

'The *Akron* was intended to excel all previous airships,' Arnstein told the court.[21] She was, in his opinion, the strongest, safest dirigible ever built. But the designer of the *Akron* was a lot less confident in private than he was in court. In a letter he sent to Wiley less than a month after testifying, Arnstein wrote, 'It would help ... if you would ... write to me your personal opinion ... as to whether the ship broke in the air or failed after striking the water.'[22] This hardly sounds like a man secure in the knowledge his design was safe.

---

*   Ultimately, the base closing never happened.

One matter that drew surprisingly little attention from the court was the *Akron*'s lack of lifesaving equipment. At least the *Titanic* carried enough life preservers (if not lifeboats) to accommodate its passengers. By comparison, the *Akron* carried no life preservers and only one small life raft.

'What are the regulations relative to carrying life preservers on airships?' Admiral Butler asked.

'I know of none,' Wiley replied, adding that the airship's pillows and sleeping bags were suitable for flotation.[23]

Various search parties had found some of the *Akron*'s bedding floating on the ocean, but there is no record of an *Akron* survivor using a sleeping bag to stay afloat, suggesting they either didn't pass muster as a safety device or the majority of her crew never escaped the inside of the airship.

Given the *Akron* was an ocean-going scout, one would think she'd have more life-saving equipment, especially since it could have reduced the death toll. Had the *Phoebus* not been passing that night, there might not have been any survivors at all. As it turned out, the court never held anyone accountable for the dearth of life-saving equipment

Two weeks after the *Akron* was lost, a naval tug snagged her wreckage with a grappling hook. Divers had discovered the *Akron* 33 miles off the New Jersey coast in 100ft of water – Duralumin skeleton mostly intact.* Only two sections had separated from her hull: her bottom tail fin, discovered 510ft aft, and the bridge section of her control car found 100ft from the main debris field. There was no indication she'd broken in half. Her fin's distance from the main wreck lent credence to the theory the *Akron* had struck the ocean stern-first, sheering off her tail.

Four days later, a submarine rescue vessel arrived on the scene.[24] Using its crane, it lifted the *Akron*'s bottom tail fin off the ocean floor. Its twisted girders, dripping canvas and spaghetti knot of cable looked nothing like an airship. It had been hoped more bodies would be found inside the wreck, but that wasn't the case. The crew were still missing.

---

*   Duralumin was the trademark for a relatively new alloy made from copper and aluminium used to make the girders for the *Akron*'s airframe.

The *Akron* crash was a murder mystery with at least five suspects. Weather was the prime suspect. A faulty altimeter could also have played a role because it misled the bridge officers into thinking they were flying at a higher altitude than they really were. Additionally, either Moffett or McCord could be viewed as culpable: Moffett for insisting big rigids fly in poor weather and McCord for his erratic course, leading to the heart of the storm. Finally, there was Arnstein's concern that the *Akron* might have experienced a structural failure while still in the air. Any of these could have been the guilty party. It was up to the naval Court of Inquiry to identify which one.

The court's findings, issued on 1 May 1933, absolved Goodyear, Litchfield, Arnstein and the Navy of any blame, finding the *Akron*'s design and construction were 'adequate to the point of excellence' and her crew 'competent and efficient in their capacity to handle the airship'.[25] Instead, the court identified two causes for the crash: weather and Commander McCord.

Certainly, the lack of accurate weather information played a role, but McCord's zig-zagging didn't help. Perhaps he was seeking a way out of the storm, or perhaps, as some suggested, Moffett was back-seat driving. No evidence has surfaced to support this claim, and at least two parties (Wiley and Deal) testified Moffett was absent from the bridge when McCord made his most questionable course changes.

What's confusing is that McCord had a reputation as an astute navigator, which makes what he did hard to explain.[26] Nevertheless, the court cited McCord as having 'committed an error of judgment in not … setting such courses as would have kept him … safe'.[27]

In retrospect, it's easy to see where the court went wrong. Moffett's insistence that big rigids should operate in unsettled weather, whether explicit or implied, influenced McCord's decision to fly that evening, meaning fault should have been attributed to Moffett as well. But nobody was going to blame the father of naval aviation for the loss of the *Akron*. McCord, on the other hand, was easier to sacrifice. He was not only lower on the totem pole, he was unable to defend himself. It was more important for the Navy to uphold Moffett's reputation, one of its most distinguished officers, than come clean about what happened.

Congressman John J. Delaney, a Democrat from New York, was first to question the court's findings. Delaney told the *Akron Beacon Journal*, 'The naval inquiry has whitewashed the whole thing.'[28] But no one should have been surprised at the verdict. All the judges were career naval officers. One in particular, Commander Garland Fulton (who we'll hear more about later), was the BUAER's chief of airship design. Fulton was hardly going to cast aspersions on an airship whose design he'd personally approved.

In other words, Heinen's prediction of a whitewash proved prophetic. Even blaming McCord proved too much for the Navy, which later expunged his culpability from the record.[29] That left only weather to blame.

As it turns out, Erwin's testimony was a lot more helpful than Wiley's. Everything about Wiley's behaviour points to him being a loyal naval officer, but his cautious choice of words, halting delivery and tortured syntax left a lot unsaid. Obviously, the *Akron*'s first officer was in an uncomfortable position. He didn't want to impugn the LTA service at a time when the sharks were circling. Nor did he want to attribute blame – that was for the judges to determine. Still, Wiley's understanding of the night's events was surprisingly lame for an officer on the bridge. Did the *Akron* crash solely because of a downdraught, a faulty altimeter or structural failure? Neither the court nor Wiley would say.

In short, the naval Court of Inquiry shirked its duty. Instead of pursuing Erwin's testimony suggesting the *Akron* was structurally unsound, the court focused on the role poor weather forecasting played in the tragedy. Though a legitimate course of inquiry, it conveniently deflected attention from the men ultimately responsible – Admiral Moffett, the BUAER and the contractors who built the airship. The court may have blamed McCord, but you couldn't court martial a dead man.

It's impossible to exaggerate the effect the *Akron* crash had on Moffett's rigid airship programme. In one fell swoop, a third of its officers were wiped out.[30] It was a devastating blow not just in terms of manpower, but negative publicity. With Moffett a casualty of the crash, the programme lost its most ardent supporter. This only encouraged anti-airship factions in Congress and the Navy to unsheathe their long knives.

But what about Wiley? One can't help but wonder what effect all this had on one of the few men to survive the tragedy.

Wiley was a celebrity now. The National Chicle Company even issued a gum card with his likeness – not the kind of attention the reserved boy from Missouri was comfortable receiving.* What saved Wiley was that his request

---

*   He was No. 509 in the forty-eight-card *Sky Bird* series. Moffett came just before him at No. 508.

for sea duty was finally approved. Shortly thereafter, he received orders to serve aboard the USS *Cincinnati* (CL-6), the very type of scout ship the *Akron* was intended to replace.

And so, for the first time in eleven years, Lt Cdr Wiley, one of the most experienced airship officers in the United States Navy, would not be serving aboard a dirigible. When the USS *Macon* was commissioned in June, the last, best hope for the American airship would be flying without him.

PART II

A GIANT IS BORN

7

PAUL W. LITCHFIELD: A GIANT IN SPRING

If Admiral Moffett dreamt of a fleet of ocean-going airships patrolling the Pacific, Paul W. Litchfield was the man to build them. Although little remembered today, Litchfield was famous enough in his time to be mentioned in the same breath as Henry Ford, John D. Rockefeller and Andrew Carnegie.

The tale of how Litchfield turned the nearly bankrupt Goodyear Tire & Rubber Company into an industrial colossus is a classic American success story. In addition to making Goodyear the world's largest rubber manufacturer, he did more than anyone else in the nation to promote airships for commercial transportation. By the time the *Akron* crashed, Goodyear had made airships both famous and commonplace.

Paul W. Litchfield (the W stood for Weeks – his grandmother's family name) worked at Goodyear for nearly sixty years. Starting in 1900 as plant superintendent, Litchfield rose to CEO and Chairman until his retirement in 1958. During this time, he grew Goodyear's tyre business to market leadership while spearheading the company's diversification into aviation.

Born a Boston Brahmin in 1875, Litchfield could trace his descendants to the *Mayflower*. A serious-minded youngster, he describes sailing on Maine's Kennebec River where he summered as a boy, growing up in 'a typical New England environment of thrift ... hard work [and] simple pleasures'.[1]

The family wasn't wealthy, but Litchfield's mother was determined that her son became an engineer. Enrolling him in MIT in 1892, Litchfield's parents struggled to pay the tuition. When he graduated with a degree in chemical engineering he couldn't even afford a copy of his yearbook.[2]

Litchfield wasn't interested in the rubber business at first. A backwards industry populated by small, foul-smelling shops steeped in soot, 'It was the last thing I ... expected to go into.'[3] But the country was in a recession in 1896, so

Litchfield took a job with a firm that made bicycle tyres – a booming business at the time. He left not long after to oversee another company's automotive tyre division. But it wasn't until 1900, when a struggling firm in Akron, Ohio, made him an offer, that Litchfield's life changed forever.

Two brothers, Frank and Charles Seiberling, had established the Goodyear Tire & Rubber Company in 1898. The fledgling concern was named after Charles Goodyear, who'd invented the vulcanisation process that allowed rubber to be shaped into a variety of forms. The Seiberling brothers didn't want to limit themselves to tyres, so they produced horseshoe pads and poker chips also made of rubber. But their best-selling product was bicycle tyres.

It should come as no surprise that the humble bicycle played an important role in Goodyear's product line. The safety bicycle, with its pedal-driven chain, was a new technology when it swept the nation in the 1890s. Safer and easier to operate than the giant-wheeled penny farthing, bicycle sales in America exceeded a million units when the Seiberlings started Goodyear. In fact, there was so much money to be made selling bicycles that two brothers from Dayton, Ohio, named Wilbur and Orville Wright, went in to the business.

The bicycle was the ideal solution for people who didn't own a horse and couldn't afford an automobile. A practical means of getting around, it not only democratised transportation but freed young couples to meet without a chaperone. Before long, single women pedalling bicycles overtook the popular culture, giving birth to the hit song 'A Bicycle Built for Two'.* Improved mobility didn't just lead to more romantic encounters, however; it led to powered flight. Both the motorcycle and aircraft industries emerged from the lowly bicycle, as Glenn Curtiss and the Wright Brothers would demonstrate.

Goodyear's job offer seemed to come out of the blue, but the Seiberlings were interested in Litchfield's experience designing automobile tyres. Fewer than 4,200 cars had been manufactured in America when Litchfield joined Goodyear, but the automobile promised to be a growth market. And since a car needed four tyres compared with only two for a bicycle, the business looked promising.

The Seiberlings' venture was only eighteen months old when Litchfield accepted their offer. Moving to Akron just two weeks shy of his 25th birthday, he wasn't sure what he was getting into. Akron, located on the Ohio and Erie Canal, was a centre for waterborne commerce; one reason Benjamin Franklin Goodrich opened the town's first rubber factory in 1871. Soon, the

---

*   The original song title was 'Daisy Bell'.

B.F. Goodrich factory was joined by Goodyear and Firestone, transforming Akron into the tyre manufacturing capital of the world.

Initially, Litchfield focused on producing tyres for horse-drawn carriages and bicycles, but his design for the first tubeless automobile tyre remade the company. By 1905, Goodyear was selling original equipment tyres to Buick, Cadillac and Oldsmobile. Ten years later, the company was the largest tyre manufacturer in the world.

Litchfield transformed the rubber business from a mishmash of back-alley shops to a billion dollar industry, but that doesn't explain why a tyre manufacturer wanted to be in the lighter-than-air business.

Litchfield had a knack for spotting undeveloped markets. The aviation business was tiny, but fast growing. Goodyear began selling the first pneumatic tyre for aeroplanes, replacing the sled runners and bicycle tyres they'd been using in 1909. Still, blimps were another story. That began changing in 1910 when Goodyear established its Aeronautics Department selling rubber-coated fabric for hydrogen-filled balloons.[4] The technology proved ideal for LTA envelopes since they required an impermeable membrane to prevent their lifting gas from escaping.

Litchfield immersed himself in the lighter-than-air market, sponsoring racing balloons much like automobile manufacturers sponsor motorsports today. Goodyear's first company-owned balloon won the Gordon Bennett Cup in 1913, a long-distance race commencing in Paris. Three years later, the company bought 720 acres near Akron for its growing LTA business, naming it the Wingfoot Lake Airship Base.[5]

The First World War turbocharged Goodyear's LTA business. In 1917, the company sold nine B-type blimps to the Navy, followed by ten C-types a year later.[6] After the military requisitioned Goodyear's airship base to train more than 600 personnel in LTA flight, Goodyear became the Navy's largest supplier of blimps.[*] In turn, the Navy became Goodyear's largest LTA customer.

But Litchfield wasn't satisfied with just building blimps for the Navy; he wanted to build passenger-carrying airships as well. This led Goodyear to construct its first company-owned blimp with the intention of selling it on the commercial market.

---

[*]   Goodyear's competitors included B.F. Goodrich in Akron, Ohio, and the Connecticut Aircraft Company in Bridgeport, Connecticut, which also sold blimps to the Navy.

Goodyear's *Wingfoot Air Express* was a 150ft-long, non-rigid filled with 95,000 cu ft of hydrogen.[7] The gondola, suspended from the envelope by cables, sported two massive overhead engines, each with their own propeller.

The weather over Chicago was sunny and clear as Goodyear's flight crew assembled the *Wingfoot Air Express*. It was Monday, 21 July 1919 and the crowd gathering at the White City Amusement Park was there to watch the strange-looking craft take shape. Located on Chicago's South Side, the amusement park boasted its own aerodrome, roller coaster, ballroom and beer garden. Left over from the 1893 World's Fair, it was a popular destination

Jack Boettner was an experienced blimp pilot when he boarded the *Wingfoot Air Express*, but he wasn't well versed in her operation since it was her inaugural flight. Technical problems had delayed the blimp's debut that morning, so it wasn't until noon that Boettner eased her into the sky. Next, he headed to Grant Park, where he planned on staging two exhibition flights.

Since the *Wingfoot Air Express* was undergoing testing, Goodyear didn't want her carrying passengers.[8] However, the company needed publicity for its creation, so the 1430 hours flight included two reporters from the *Chicago Evening Post* as well as Colonel Joseph C. Morrow, who was evaluating the blimp for the US government.[9]

Roger J. Adams, President of the Adams Aerial Transportation Company, had also expressed interest in buying the blimp. Adams was trying to attract investors for a transatlantic airship service between London and Chicago with a stop in New York. As Adams told a reporter, 'Chicago will be the blimpopolis of the western world!'[10] Unfortunately, Adams missed the White City flight. Forced to chase the blimp by car, he was still waiting to board her at Grant Park.

As the clock approached 1700 hours, Boettner prepared the blimp for her final flight of the day. But so much hydrogen had been valved during her previous flight that there was only enough left to carry five passengers. Three of the spaces were already spoken for: one for the pilot, Boettner; and two for Goodyear's mechanics, Harry Wacker and Carl Weaver. Boettner had also allowed Milton Norton, a photographer for Chicago's *Herald and Examiner*, to board along with his box camera. Finally, Earl H. Davenport, whose job was to promote the White City Amusement Park, was also invited to fly. Plump, bald and upbeat, Davenport had missed the White City take-off, just like Adams. Now he climbed into the gondola while Adams fumed about having to wait until tomorrow. As things turned out, he was happy to miss the flight.

The blimp's five passengers sat in single file. Each was issued a safety harness connected to a rope fastened to a parachute. If a person abandoned ship, the rope would unspool to a fixed length before pulling the parachute from its pack, which was attached to the outside of the gondola. 'All you have to do is jump,' Boettner told his passengers. 'The parachute takes care of itself.'[11]

Boettner sounded a siren signalling their departure. Next, the sausage-shaped blimp lifted off the ground as two American flags, one at her bow and the other at the stern, rippled in the breeze. Later, there would be talk of the blimp's engines shooting sparks as she climbed into the sky. This was always a danger when flying a blimp containing hydrogen, but the flight proceeded as planned.

Boettner sat at the controls in the bow. Behind him was Davenport, followed by the photographer and Goodyear's two mechanics. Boettner flew over Lake Michigan at first but eventually turned west towards Chicago. Flying at low altitude, the open gondola provided the five men with a commanding view of the city below. They could easily follow the rail lines bisecting Chicago as well as the smell of its many stockyards.

It's not clear why Boettner chose to fly over Chicago that day; some people think Norton wanted to take pictures for his newspaper. If so, he couldn't have timed the flight better.

It was slightly after 1700 hours when the *Wingfoot Air Express* appeared over the Loop, the heart of Chicago's business district that included some of the nation's first skyscrapers. Since people were just getting off work, the *Wingfoot Air Express* brought traffic to a halt. As the thrum of her engines beat a beckoning call, thousands of people flooded the pavements to watch the novelty pass overhead.

Everything seemed to be going smoothly until Boettner felt the control car shake. They were crossing over State Street when Boettner saw flames licking at the blimp's envelope. Realising there was no time to waste, he shouted, 'Over the top, everybody![12] Jump or you'll burn alive!'[13]

It's estimated 20,000 people watched as the hydrogen-fuelled fire engulfed Goodyear's first blimp. Gawkers included the crowd at Comiskey Park, which had gathered to see the soon-to-be disgraced White Sox play the New York Yankees. As the airship began buckling in the middle, smoke and debris filled the sky. Soon, five tiny figures were seen to jump from the gondola. Unfortunately, only four parachutes opened – three of them on fire.

Goodyear's mechanic, Harry Wacker, appeared doomed from the start. He initially had control of his descent, but his silk parachute quickly dissolved in flames.[14] Wacker's luck seemed to change for the better when his chute snagged on the cornice of the Insurance Exchange Building. But he soon lost his footing, coming to rest on a fire escape below.

Carl Weaver's parachute also caught fire. Unable to control his descent, the mechanic plummted to earth. Meanwhile, Norton, the photographer, spun wildly in the air until he smashed against the Western Union building. His body came to rest in the street below, attached to his still-smoking parachute.

The most grisly death was reserved for the White City's PR man. After Davenport jumped, the rope connecting him to his parachute became tangled in the blimp's rigging, preventing it from deploying. Dangling upside down while swinging like a pendulum, Davenport kicked and screamed as the airship overhead was engulfed in flames.

Goodyear's pilot was the last to jump. Boettner would have died, had he not landed on the roof of Chicago's Board of Trade building. There, he shed his burning parachute, and descended a fire escape to search for his passengers in the street below. When two Chicago detectives realised he was the pilot, Boettner was taken in for questioning.

The Illinois Trust & Savings Bank was in the southern part of the Loop. Looking like a Greek temple with Corinthian columns, its main feature was a two-storey rotunda capped by a massive skylight. The bank was winding up its day when a shadow momentarily crossed its floor.[15] Seconds later, Carl Weaver smashed through the skylight.

One eyewitness described Weaver's body as 'so badly burned he could not … be identified as a man'.[16] Weaver was followed by Davenport, still roped to the *Wingfoot Air Express*. Smashing into the bank's marble floor, Goodyear's blimp spewed burning petrol in a 50ft radius.[17]

While bank tellers found themselves trapped inside their cages, everyone else rushed to one of only two exits. Meanwhile, the intense fire, heat, and smoke stoked panic among employees, whose screams one newspaper called 'indescribable'.[18] 'I thought the end of the world had come,' one survivor recalled. 'Everything around me seemed on fire.'[19]

The *Wingfoot Air Express* was the first major civilian air disaster in American history. Thirteen people were killed and more than two dozen injured, including 16-year-old James Carpenter and 14-year-old Joseph Scanlon, who worked for the bank as messengers.[20] Two of the blimp's five passengers: Boettner, the pilot; and Wacker, the mechanic, survived the crash. Goodyear's other mechanic, Weaver, and Davenport, the PR man, died on the spot. Norton, the photographer, succumbed to his injuries a few days later.

Illinois' Attorney General ordered seventeen Goodyear employees arrested after the crash, including Boettner, the pilot.[21] Initially reluctant to co-operate with the investigation, Goodyear soon changed its mind, promising to pay the expenses of those injured in the disaster.[22] Ultimately, no one was charged with a crime because it turned out no law had been broken. The only practical result was that Chicago's City Council began regulating air traffic over Chicago.

The horrific crash of the *Wingfoot Air Express* is not mentioned in Goodyear's official company history, nor any of its promotional literature. Certainly, Litchfield wasn't pleased by the debacle, yet he continued manufacturing blimps undeterred. This is surprising given Goodyear had achieved the kind of aviation record no one wanted. But Litchfield's enthusiasm for passenger-carrying airships remained undiminished even after the *Akron* crash fourteen years later.

Some critics feel Litchfield's desire to build passenger-carrying airships was misguided but Goodyear was exceedingly well positioned to take advantage of the transportation revolution. That people died in the process was regrettable, but safety would improve over time. Meanwhile, the company stood to make buckets of money.

That same year, Goodyear built three Pony blimps, each containing 37,000 cu ft of hydrogen.[23] One of these blimps began offering passenger services between Los Angeles and Catalina Island in 1921. The one-hour trip covering 39 miles took place six times a day, Wednesday to Sunday, making it one of the earliest regularly scheduled airline services in America.* [24] Nothing, not even the worst aviation disaster in Goodyear's history, would prevent Litchfield from building commercial airships. He was determined to forge ahead no matter what.

---

*   Germany's DELAG began offering a passenger airship service in 1910, while A. Roy Knabenshue carried paying passengers in a blimp over Los Angeles in 1912. Both services were focused more on sightseeing than transporting passengers to a specific destination and were terminated well before Goodyear's Catalina Service in 1921.

8

BLIMPS LEAD THE WAY

Litchfield's blimp fleet was an excellent method of promoting Goodyear tyres. Although not the first dirigibles to be used as aerial billboards, the Goodyear blimp became a cherished icon for many Americans. One four-colour advertisement in 1930 shows a farmer behind his plough as the 'Goodyear Zeppelin' passes overhead. 'They make my tires!' the farmer exclaims, waving his hat in the air. It was exactly the kind of leadership position that Litchfield aspired to.

Goodyear's CEO not only hoped to use the company's blimp fleet to advertise its tyres but showcase its LTA technology as well. The strategy worked well enough that in addition to selling balloons and blimps to the Navy, Goodyear won a contract from the Army to build the first semi-rigid in America.*

Competition between the Army and Navy helped fuel Goodyear's LTA business. The inter-service rivalry was fierce, despite an agreement assigning big rigid development to the Navy. The Army had bought its first semi-rigid, the *Roma*, from the Italian government in 1921. However, when the *Roma* struck high-voltage wires killing thirty-four of her forty-five-man crew, it supplanted the *Wingfoot Air Express* as the worst aviation disaster in America. It also led to the Army Air Service hiring Goodyear to build a replacement.

Admiral Moffett fought hard to maintain Navy dominance in LTA flight despite the Army nipping at his heels. In 1922, the Navy built its first big rigid, the USS *Shenandoah* (ZR-1), on its own. Goodyear, not wanting to be shut out of the market, supplied the *Shenandoah*'s gas cells, strengthening its ties to

---

* Purchased by the Army in 1926, the RS-1 is not to be confused with the Army's first non-rigid (or blimp), the SC-1, purchased from Thomas Baldwin in 1908.

the Navy. But Goodyear didn't begin construction of its own blimp fleet until 1925. Beginning with the *Pilgrim*, a 106ft-long non-rigid, it was the company's first blimp to use helium rather than hydrogen as its lifting gas.* A few years later, the *Pilgrim* landed atop O'Neil's department store in downtown Akron, where it discharged passengers, marking one of the few times an airship ever landed on the rooftop of an American building.**

As the number of Goodyear blimps multiplied, they also increased in size. The *Defender* was the largest at 179,000 cu ft, more than three times the size of the *Pilgrim*. Christened in 1929 by Amelia Earhart, the *Defender* was followed by the *Columbia*, *Reliance* and *Resolute*, bringing Goodyear's blimp fleet to six.

Litchfield may not have been the first to use airships as flying billboards,*** but he was first to popularise the practice in the United States. Today, many companies use blimps to sell products, but the practice was new when Goodyear began flying them in the 1920s.

Litchfield's blimps captured the public's imagination in a way few advertising mediums could. With its fleet of flying billboards making low-altitude jaunts over American cities, their giant, winged-foot logo visible from the ground, Goodyear's message was hard to miss. Its trademarked logo based on Mercury, the fleet-footed messenger god, is said to have been inspired by a statue atop a newel post in Frank Seiberling's house. Thanks to Litchfield's blimps, Goodyear became one of America's most recognised brands.

It's important to remember that Litchfield saw blimps as a means to an end — building big rigids. As he conceded in his autobiography, the Goodyear blimp was a stepping stone to passenger-carrying airships. 'Any vehicle which could cut the time of steamship crossings in half was of special interest,' he wrote, describing the big rigids' main selling point.[1] As Litchfield well knew, it was more profitable to build and sell airships to the commercial market than just build for blimps for the Navy or flog tyres for aeroplanes.

Unfortunately, history doesn't tell us where the word 'blimp' comes from. One theory says it derived from an onomatopoeic description of the sound a blimp's envelope makes when finger-flicked. Whatever the root, the Goodyear blimp became widely recognised. Hundreds of petrol stations had a blue and yellow Goodyear calendar with pictures of its blimps hanging on their walls. These omnipresent date keepers were supplemented by print ads featuring

---

*   The *Pilgrim* was small, containing only 50,000 cu ft of helium.
**   O'Neil's had a lot of heart for Goodyear's big rigids. A few years later, a ground-floor window display featured a scale model of the Goodyear-Zeppelin Air Dock, including a version of the *Akron* with its original (i.e. longer) tail fins.
***   The UK, France and Germany were the first to use blimps for aerial advertisements.

Goodyear airships in the fast-growing medium of popular magazines. These colour advertisements are a good example of how Goodyear used its tyre manufacturing business to benefit its LTA business and vice versa. Goodyear even held an annual Zeppelin race for tyre dealers starting in 1929.[*]

Litchfield believed in the future of aviation; as he noted in his memoir, 'It will be more important for a boy to learn to fly than to learn to swim.'[2] But he never lost his love for the sea; that's why Goodyear's first blimps were named after America's Cup defenders. Litchfield also named his Akron estate Anchorage, filling it with nautical artefacts and incorporating anchors into its entrance gates. This makes sense for someone whose grandfather once built clipper ships. Nevertheless, the weather vane atop the flagpole in front of his house was shaped like a blimp, while the fire screen in his living room had an airship design.[3] Sailing may have been an important part of his life growing up, but LTA was his future.

Litchfield also enjoyed riding in the Goodyear blimp, which regularly touched down on the lawn of his estate.[4] One publication went so far as to call the *Pilgrim* Litchfield's 'private airship'.[5] Though probably an exaggeration, he did take some unusual trips aboard Goodyear blimps, including having the *Mayflower* pluck him off the deck of an ocean liner and being picked up off a train siding in California.[6,7]

LTA flight was so important to Goodyear that the P.W. Litchfield Trophy was created in 1925. Awarded annually for the American balloon that travelled the greatest distance, the competition promoted use of Goodyear's rubber-infused fabric for lighter-than-air flight. But Litchfield was interested in bigger game. As he made clear, blimps and balloons were a means to an end. What he *really* wanted was to supply the world with a fleet of gigantic, passenger-carrying airships that could cross the ocean.[8]

---

[*]   The contest was designed to incentivise Goodyear dealers to sell more tyres. The grand prize for the Third Annual Zeppelin Race held in 1931 was a visit to the Goodyear-Zeppelin Air Dock and a close-up look at the *Akron* under construction. There were never any actual Zeppelin races.

Litchfield was not a handsome man. Tall and ungainly with oversized facial features, deep-set eyes and a diminishing head of white hair, he bore a striking resemblance to press baron William Randolph Hearst. Litchfield didn't drink, rarely smoked and, like many tycoons, was a man of few words. Self-described as 'frugal of speech', he disliked public speaking even though he was frequently called upon to do it.[9]

Litchfield could also be intimidating. A commanding if distant figure for Goodyear's tens of thousands of employees, he was proud of his 'competitive spirit', which occasionally led to labour strife.[10] Those who reported directly to him called him P.W. to his face, and Litch or the 'old man' behind his back, and not always affectionately.

Litchfield may have been tough, but he was a forward-thinking executive. He made sure Goodyear one of the first American companies to establish an eight-hour work day. He also introduced paid holidays as well as a pension plan, and health and accident insurance. When the Great Depression took a bite out of sales, Litchfield shortened the workday to six hours rather than institute lay-offs. He even offered 'Americanisation' classes for Goodyear's many immigrant workers.

Of course, there was a Mrs Litchfield as well as two daughters but, like Mrs Moffett, she didn't see much of her husband. By the time Litchfield was named CEO and Chairman of Goodyear in 1930, the company was selling rubber-based products for cars, trucks, buses, trains, aeroplanes, balloons, blimps, big rigids and ocean liners. As one ad put it, 'The world … moves on Goodyear rubber', exactly as Litchfield intended.

When 1933 dawned, there was little doubt the 58-year-old Litchfield was at the top of his game, but he hadn't yet realised his dream of building passenger-carrying airships. When the *Akron* crashed, the question remained: could he still do it? What's surprising isn't the answer (which everyone knows), it's how close he came to pulling it off.

9

DAWN OF THE
COMMERCIAL AIRSHIP

Henri Giffard's flight over Paris in a self-propelled blimp was the first to achieve the holy grail of 'dirigibility' in 1852. Even then, the Frenchman's airship could only go in the direction he desired if a strong wind wasn't blowing. Nevertheless, the ability to steer transformed lighter-than-air flight. Until then, balloons were left at the mercy of the wind. Now, for the first time, they could be steered in a set direction. Even then, passenger airship service was slow to get off the ground. Still, Americans had been anticipating it as early as 1849. That's when Rufus Porter began selling stock in his Aerial Navigation Company. Porter envisioned an airship catering to gold miners willing to pay $200 a piece to travel from New York to California in three days. His idea wasn't crazy, just ahead of its time. Any transportation that sped passengers across the continental United States had commercial potential, especially since roads were lamentable, steamship travel slow and the railroads stopped at the Mississippi. Porter's problem was a dirigible that could be steered had not yet been invented.

Selling stock in $5 increments, Porter promised an astonishing return of nearly $21,000.[1] If it sounds too good to be true, it was. But Porter wasn't a charlatan, just an optimist. The founder of *Scientific American*, he built at least one scale model of his steam-powered 'aerial locomotive' to demonstrate its feasibility.[2] A full-sized version intended to carry 100 passengers never got off the ground, but Porter, like a lot of entrepreneurs, was convinced his business would succeed.

If Porter dreamed of airships ferrying passengers across the country, he was not alone. A San Francisco-based engineer named Charles Stanley dreamed right along with him. The 1899 prospectus for the Stanley Aerial Navigation

Company describes a cylinder-shaped airship built of aluminium with enough room for forty passengers and their luggage.[3] Although Stanley raised money, he never got further than his prospectus. His idea was too far advanced to be realised by the day's technology.

It could be hard to differentiate between money-grabbing schemes and honest attempts to invent a passenger-carrying airship. There were plenty of both, but not as many scams as one might think. One article appearing in the *Chicago Daily Tribune* in 1910 predicted an airship-aeroplane hybrid that would one day transport passengers to New York City in only nine hours, with the article asking the question, 'Would you ... Zeppelin from here to New York?'[4] Needless to say, the prediction was speculative.

Not surprisingly, a healthy scepticism prevailed during the early days of American flight. People were cautioned against airship schemes as early as 1908. In an article titled 'A Warning to Air-Ship Investors', the writer advised:

Companies to build, sell, and operate new types of flying machines will ... be seeking stock subscriptions in every city in the country. How shall we distinguish the false from the true? The advice ... is to keep clear of the whole business.[5]

The first practical dirigible after Giffard's was piloted by a short Brazilian with a droopy moustache named Alberto Santos-Dumont. When Santos-Dumont's No. 6 dirigible circled the Eiffel Tower, returning to its starting point in less than thirty minutes, he became the first person in the world to demonstrate truly navigable flight.

Until Santos-Dumont, balloons were beholden to the wind. But *le petit Santos** showed it was possible to control one's direction in the air thanks to a 12hp engine and a rudder for steering. Equally impressive, Santos-Dumont did it in 1901, two years before the Wright Brothers flew at Kitty Hawk.

Although Santos-Dumont's No. 6 dirigible had a distinguished pedigree (e.g. its wealthy owner travelled in only the finest social circles), there's no disguising the fact the American airship was born at a carnival funfair.

The first working dirigible in the United States was built by a self-styled 'captain' named Thomas S. Baldwin. Baldwin had run away to join the circus

---

*   Some reports indicate he was only 5ft tall and weighed 90lb – an ideal size for lighter-than-air flight.

at age 15. Later becoming an itinerant balloonist, he performed a series of increasingly daredevil stunts, including tightrope walking and parachuting, before deciding to follow in Santos-Dumont's footsteps. As a result, America's first practical dirigible was designed, built and piloted by Captain Baldwin in 1904. With an envelope 52ft long and 17ft in diameter, it contained only 9,000 cu ft of hydrogen.[6] What's most striking about Baldwin's dirigible is not that it weighed only 220lb, or that the airship's envelope was crafted from Japanese silk wrapped in an Irish linen netting, but that, when inflated, it looked like a giant sweet potato.[7,8] The dirigible's gondola was also odd looking. Its wooden, scaffold-like construction was little more than an open-air catwalk for the operator to cling to. With both legs planted on the two bottom runners, there was nothing to prevent a pilot from falling through the gap except a firm grip. Altitude control was equally primitive. When the pilot wanted the airship to climb, he moved backwards along the catwalk, tilting the bow towards the sky. When he wanted to descend, he moved forward, tipping the nose earthward. This meant the pilot had to be constantly moving from one end of the dirigible to the other, making for a perilous journey.

After a year of experimentation, Baldwin achieved success when, early on the morning of 2 August 1904, he rose 500ft above Oakland's Idora amusement park.[9] Spending the next forty-five minutes in the air, Baldwin traced a mile-wide circle before returning to his starting point.

'The airship has exceeded my fondest hopes,' he told the *Oakland Tribune*. 'I believe I have successfully solved the problem of aerial navigation.'[10]

The Wright brothers had flown at Kitty Hawk eight months earlier, but since they'd kept their flight a secret, there were questions about what they'd accomplished. Although the Wright Flyer was notable for using wing-warping for lateral balance, elevators for pitch control and a moveable rudder, aeroplane technology was in its infancy compared to airships. As a result, Baldwin was initially thought to be the first person to fly in America.

For perspective, the Wright brothers' trials at Kitty Hawk didn't come close to matching either Santos-Dumont or Baldwin in terms of distance, altitude control and ability to steer. Aeroplanes would eventually exceed airships in performance but it would take another twenty years for them to do so. In the meantime, the Wright brothers would sue Baldwin, alleging patent infringement.[11] When the Wright brothers later offered to manufacture propellers for Baldwin's aircraft, it solidified their reputation as 'frenemies'.

As Baldwin well knew, the engines used by early airships were heavy, underpowered and prone to break down. But as the internal combustion engine shrank in weight, it increased in output. This was a critical advance if airships were to become a practical means of passenger transportation. Otherwise, they'd have been as directionless as a balloon.

Baldwin's dirigible received an official stamp of approval when the US Army Signal Corps bought one for $10,000 in 1908 — the same year Henry Ford introduced his Model T. The Army's first powered aircraft, Baldwin's airship, was designated the SC-1 for Signal Corps Number 1. In other words, Baldwin beat the Wright brothers in selling his invention to the military by a year.

Baldwin became famous for his contributions to LTA flight, including a much-ballyhooed performance of his *California Arrow* at the St Louis Fair, but he never became rich. The LTA business rewarded him in other ways. Going to work for the Connecticut Aircraft Company, he helped win a contract to build the US Navy's first dirigible in 1917.* When the United States entered the First World War, Baldwin oversaw balloon procurement for the Army's Signal Corps, becoming a bona fide captain in the process.[12] He did well enough in the position that Goodyear hired him after the war to manage its balloon manufacturing and inspection programme, which is where he was working when he died in 1923.[13]

Giffard, Santos-Dumont and Baldwin showed that a lighter-than-air craft could be navigated, but when it came to establishing the world's first passenger airship service, Germany, not France or the United States, led the way. Founded by Count Ferdinand von Zeppelin, whose airships would soon be dropping bombs on London, DELAG (its German acronym) was the first regularly scheduled airship service in the world.** Between 1910 and 1913 DELAG built six passenger airships: the *Deutschland I* and *II* (LZ-7 and LZ-8), *Schwaben* (LZ-10), *Viktoria Luise* (LZ-11), *Hansa* (LZ-13) and *Sachsen* (LZ-17)[14] carrying 10,000 passengers a total of 90,000 miles.***,[15]

Focused more on sightseeing than inter-city travel, DELAG's airship service was a remarkable achievement for its day. The passenger cabin was not only

---

*   It was named the DN-1.

**   There were two, brief airline passenger services using seaplanes: one between San Francisco and Oakland, California, in 1913 and the other between St Petersburg and Tampa, Florida, in 1914. Both services folded after a short while.

***   Although total number of passengers carried, miles covered and flights made vary depending upon the source, the above statistics reasonably approximate what DELAG accomplished between 1911 and 1914.

enclosed for the first time, but panelled in mahogany with mother of pearl inlay and expensive carpeting. As liveried waiters served champagne and cana-pés, well-dressed passengers sat in high-backed chairs enjoying the spectacular view while sailing over the German countryside. No wonder Litchfield was inspired to build airships.

DELAG had its share of problems, though. The *Deutschland I*, which flew between Friedrichshafen and Düsseldorf, did so for only a short time before a storm landed her in the treetops. There were no fatalities, but all thirty-three of her passengers were forced to climb down a rope ladder to safety, resulting in plenty of grumbling. Another DELAG airship, the *Schwaben*, was destroyed by fire only a year after being launched. Again, there were no passenger deaths, but it's fair to say German commercial airships had a mixed operating record. However, it's important to note that they didn't kill a single paying passenger until the *Hindenburg* twenty-three years later.

German ground crews were not so lucky. A handful of DELAG employees were killed during airship operations, but their fatalities were rarely included in safety statistics. Still, early Zeppelins surpassed aeroplanes not only in passenger safety, but range, flight duration, passenger amenities and how much cargo they could carry. If it seems like dirigibles crashed more frequently than aeroplanes it's only because they had a higher profile, therefore each crash attracted more notoriety. In absolute numbers airplane crashes far exceeded those of airships. Since Zeppelins carried more passengers than areoplanes, their fatalities ran higher, which also put them in the spotlight. Nevertheless, for the first third of the twentieth century, Zeps appeared to have aeroplanes beat.

DELAG wasn't alone for long. The first airship service in the United States to carry paying passengers was founded in 1914 by one of Baldwin's pilots.

A. Roy Knabenshue (the A. stood for Augustus but everyone called him Roy) made his first balloon ascent at the tender age of 5 when a family friend invited him along. Knabenshue never forgot the experience and vowed to become a 'professional aeronaut', much to his father's dismay.[16]

Knabenshue Sr was an Ohio newspaper editor who held ballooning in low esteem. When Roy reiterated his intention to become an 'aeronaut' at age 14, his father was adamant. 'Nonsense,' he responded. 'I refuse to listen to such talk, you are going to become a newspaper man.'[17]

Undeterred, Knabenshue purchased his first balloon at age 23. When his father heard the news, he was infuriated. 'I will not have it,' he told his son.

'You will be traveling around the country … with show people of low variety … Think of your mother.'[18]

LTA flight was a disreputable business back in the day. To spare his family embarrassment, Knabenshue assumed the alias Professor Don Carlos and began touring Ohio amusement parks, where he sold balloon rides earning as much as $500 per engagement.[19] Knabenshue's expenses often exceeded his income, but he loved the aeronaut's life. Within three years, he'd progressed to more dangerous stunts including jumping from a balloon with a parachute just like his future mentor, Captain Baldwin.

Knabenshue was nothing if not ambitious. Travelling to the 1904 St. Louis Fair to sell balloon rides, he bumped into Baldwin who, realizing he'd grown too fat to get airborne, hired Knabenshue to pilot his newest dirigible, the *California Arrow*. After newspapers reported on the two men's St. Louis flights, Baldwin and Knabenshue became nationally famous overnight.

Knab's personality easily won people over. With a lopsided nose and friendly smile, his colourful manner and exaggerated repartee helped to drum up ticket sales. Waving his oversized cap at the paying crowd below, he knew how to keep them entertained by constantly upping the ante.

Knabenshue's career was a a series of crowd-pleasing firsts. These included being the first to fly an airship over New York City (1905) and the first airships to bomb a city (Los Angeles in 1908).

Constantly looking to stir up publicity, Knabenshue staged LTA competitions with other daredevil pilots. These money-making events were guaranteed to draw huge crowds. A brief film of the 1910 Los Angeles Air Meet shows just how adept a pilot Knabenshue was. The clip opens with Roy in his one-man dirigible doing a high-speed take-off from a standing start. Though the frame rate exaggerates how fast he's running, it can't hide the alarmingly rakish angle at which he takes flight.[20] Given his fearlessness, it's surprising he lived as long as he did.

But it wasn't until 1913 that Knabenshue struck upon the idea of carrying twelve paying passengers on a regularly scheduled route over Los Angeles. His dirigible, the *Pasadena*, was one of the largest non-rigids of her day. Half a football field long, the *Pasadena*'s envelope was 30ft in diameter and contained 75,000 cu ft of hydrogen. If that sounds like a lot, she was only a quarter as large as Goodyear's blimps today, but people marvelled at her size.

Knab wasn't an engineer by training. Although he had input into the *Pasadena*'s specifications, he hired Charles F. Willard to design her. His passenger service was also like DELAG's in that it was more about aerial tourism than getting some place specific. Few people had flown in 1913, but the American public was fascinated by flight. Since the *Pasadena* flew at a low altitude, she guaranteed passengers an impressive view of the city – exactly what Knab was banking on for ticket sales.

The *Pasadena*'s gondola was longer than a city bus but only half the width, making for a cramped flight. Passengers sat single file. Women wore lacy shirt-waists and long, narrow skirts, while men favoured suits with a vest, tie and the occasional derby. Meanwhile, the *Pasadena*'s open-air gondola subjected her passengers to wind, sun, rain and an occasional spray of hot engine oil. Undoubtedly, they found it thrilling.

Two weeks after Knabenshue began his first passenger flights, a delegation of women appeared at the *Pasadena*'s hangar demanding a personal audience.

'We want you to take your airship and peacefully leave our locality,' one of the women told him.

'What have I done?' Knabenshue asked.

'You have risked the lives of our husbands.'

Suspecting a mistake, the grease-stained pilot checked his manifest, only to confirm that none of the aforementioned men had ever flown on the *Pasadena*.

'Your husbands were joking,' Knabenshue explained. 'Probably they were trying to appear as great heroes. Now the thing to do is for you to take a ride with me and then you'll have it on them.'[21]

If this apocryphal-sounding story is true – and it's Knabenshue who tells it in his unpublished memoir, *Chauffeur of the Skies*, it was a shrewd move. It was just like Knab to recognise that five women flying in the *Pasadena* was not only great publicity but a tacit endorsement of his airship's safety. Given his persuasiveness, all five went for a 'short hop'.[22]

Part carnival barker, part daredevil, Knabenshue personified the hucksterism of early American flight. A showman at heart, he did everything possible to promote his airship passenger business. He even convinced a motion picture studio to feature the *Pasadena* in a movie.

The film industry, like Knabenshue, constantly sought novelty to attract paying customers. When the Universal Film Company hired him to co-star in its three-reel feature *Won in the Clouds*,* Knabenshue hoped the public-ity would boost his ridership.[23] The movie opens with Knab piloting the *Pasadena* over a Los Angeles back lot dressed to look like deepest, darkest Africa. There he startles villagers who, upon seeing a dirigible for the first time, unleash a torrent of spears. Knabenshue's character uses the *Pasadena* to

---

*   Originally titled *Flight of Life*.

locate the villagers' diamond supply, which he plans on stealing. Knab bombs the village and wipes out the natives, thereby anticipating Germany's use of Zeppelins over London the following year. Regrettably, the film is lost to posterity, but a synopsis reveals the story ends with Knab getting both the diamonds and the heroine's hand in marriage – a happy ending for everyone but the natives.[24]

Advertised as 'A Masterpiece of Sensationalism', *Won in the Clouds* didn't save Knabenshue's airship service. As it turned out, more people were interested in gawking at the *Pasadena* than taking a ride. The exorbitant ticket price of $25 didn't help, but even after Knab lowered it to $10 he was unable to keep the business afloat. Still, it is remarkable that Knabenshue flew paying passengers on a prescribed route between Pasadena, Santa Monica and Long Beach before fixed-wing aircraft, even if the service lasted only a few months.

Given the economic reality, Knabenshue eventually closed up shop, taking the *Pasadena* to Chicago. Following a few improvements, he renamed her *White City* after the amusement park where Goodyear's *Wingfoot Air Express* would embark on her first and final flight five years later.

Knab had more success selling twenty-five-minute rides over Chicago than he did in California. A brief film he produced to promote his service shows him ferrying passengers over Lake Michigan. The sky is dulled by coal smoke, the *White City*'s front-mounted propeller a fast-turning blur. Nevertheless, the female passengers seem to be enjoying themselves as they smile, laugh and wave white handkerchiefs at a passing steamer on the lake below. Knabenshue even persuaded his airship-adverse father to take a ride. In a photograph presumably taken by the aeronaut, the *White City* sails over Chicago with both Knab's parents on board. The surprising thing is how happy his father looks given his previous antipathy towards LTA flight.

The early days of a new technology often show diversity in form. Early ships, trains, automobiles and aircraft all experimented with a variety of designs. LTA flight was no exception. Marked more by failure than success, LTA's early days included such fantastical inventions as the aerial rowboat (a dirigible you rowed), the sky-cycle (a dirigible you pedalled) and a man-carrying kite. Most of these fanciful creations ended up as dead branches on aviation's tree, but as more was learned about the science of flight, dirigibles consolidated behind an accepted design.

Naturally, all this experimentation required money. Since early LTA flight received virtually no government support, market forces shaped the industry. This meant most American aeronauts were starved for funding. LTA entrepreneurs sought investors, leased their inventions or rented them as flying billboards – anything to make it a paying proposition. Aeronauts such as Baldwin were famous enough that they could earn a percentage of ticket sales in addition to what they charged the public for rides. This income was supplemented by the occasional sale of their invention, but far more LTA entrepreneurs failed as a going concern than succeeded.

If the airship industry was unregulated, so was the way the word 'airship' was spelled. At various times it was written as 'Air Ship', 'air ship', or 'Air-Ship' depending on who was doing the spelling. Nor was there agreement on what it meant. Airship was a fungible enough term that it included both dirigibles and aeroplanes during the early years of aviation. The same holds true for its practitioners, who were sometimes called 'aerialists', 'aeronauts' and, on occasion, 'argonauts'. Lighter-than-air flight was so novel it took years before a standardised description of its participants (let alone its vehicles) was agreed upon.

Thanks to the exploits of Knabenshue and other aeronauts, expectations were high that passenger airships were right around the corner. The January 1923 cover of *Popular Science* featured a dirigible named the *San Francisco Express*, promising 'Monster New Airship Will Carry Passengers across the Continent'.[25] Okay, but what people weren't quite ready for was the *City of Glendale*.

When Thomas B. Slate began working on his dirigible in 1925 he planned on offering the first airship service from California to New York. Slate had made his fortune in the early days of the refrigeration business selling dry ice to the public.[26] Using his personal wealth to fund the Slate Aircraft Corporation, he envisioned a fleet of airships carrying up to forty passengers and a five-man crew across the United States in thirty-six hours – roughly a third of the time it took by train.[27]

Slate based his company in Glendale, California, promising to name his airship after the city if the authorities leased him land at the municipal airport.[28] When they agreed, Slate built a prototype naming it, true to his word, *City of Glendale*.

Nearly a football field in length* and 58ft wide, the teardrop-shaped airship contained 330,000 cu ft of hydrogen.[29] With a mouth in its bow to accommodate its propeller, horizontal striping and a fluke-like tail, Slate's airship resembled nothing more than a giant, shiny whale.

One surprising feature of the *Glendale* was its all-metal hull. Building a lighter-than-air craft out of metal may seem counterintuitive, like a knight in armour trying to fly, but it's not as crazy as it sounds. The US Navy would purchase its own metal-clad, the ZMC-2, in 1929 and operate her for nearly thirteen years.

The *Glendale*'s metal hull was made from long, thin strips of lightweight Duralumin riveted together. Assembled in an interlocking monocoque structure, the hull looked like it was made of corrugated metal. The airship's propulsion system was also unusual. A five-bladed fan called an 'impeller' was mounted in her nose.** Part of a centrifugal blower system, it was designed to create a vacuum in front of the craft, sucking air into the bow before expelling it out her sides. If all went according to plan, Slate claimed the *Glendale* would achieve a top speed of 100mph.[30] Of course, nothing went as planned.

It didn't help that Slate claimed his steam-powered engine would be so efficient it required only 6 gallons of water to cross the continent.[31] That alone should have raised a few eyebrows. Regardless, the *Glendale* was an impressive sight. Her 80ft-long passenger cabin, attached like a keel to the bottom of the ship, contained sixteen portholes and forty windows, guaranteeing future passengers a spectacular view.

In one notable photograph, Slate poses in front of his hangar holding a scale model of his airship. Another self-styled 'captain' who favoured custom-made uniforms (his ground crew wore white jumpsuits), Slate wears a blazer better suited to yachting than flight. A white cap with gold braid, patent leather brim and a shield bearing an outline of his airship with the letter 'S' completes the nautical theme.

Slate was as much promoter as inventor. One of his airship's intended features was an 'elevator' that could be lowered to the ground on a cable, eliminating the need to land. Slate even built a platform atop the Glendale Hotel, the first in a series of rooftop landing sites he promised would span the country.[32, 33] Slate informed the press the *City of Glendale* would also include sleeping accommodation and a dining salon – all for the ticket price

---

* The *City of Glendale* was 212ft long.
** A later version appears to have eight blades.

of a Pullman sleeper.[34] Five years after he'd begun work, Slate was finally ready to debut his airship.

The maiden voyage of any craft is a momentous occasion, which is why 5,000 people gathered at Glendale's Grand Central Air Terminal on 21 December 1929 to watch the airship take flight.[35] The shortest day of the year began chilly but warmed quickly as the sun rose into the sky. Slate's ground crew walked the *Glendale* out of her hangar. One photo shows a man wearing bib overalls staring dumbstruck at the lighter-than-air craft while another reveals a dog slinking towards the airship, its tail lowered in caution.

As the *Glendale*'s gleaming hull was warmed by the sun's rays, the hydrogen inside began to expand. Sadly, her unyielding hull, rigid to the extreme, couldn't contain all that rapidly expanding gas. When the first rivet popped, sounding like a gunshot, the crowd scattered.[36] More rivets followed, after which the *Glendale*, no longer lighter-than-air, settled on the ground before rolling on to her side with an audible sigh.

Slate cancelled the flight, ordering his airship back into the hangar. Upon inspection, it was discovered at least one pressure release valve had stuck, preventing hydrogen from escaping. With no place to go, the *Glendale*'s lifting gas had forced her hull's Duralumin panels to separate. This allowed her gas to escape, causing Slate's dream to come crashing back to earth.

The inventor shook off his disappointment, telling the *Los Angeles Times* it would take only thirty days to effect repairs.[37] Then, he went to the Hollywood premier of *The Lost Zeppelin*, an unusual choice given what had transpired.

Slate soon learned he'd have to rebuild his airship from scratch. Unable to raise money during the Depression, he declared bankruptcy in 1931. Shortly after, the *Glendale* was sold for scrap – its hangar shipped to Arizona to be made into hay barns.[38, 39]

Technology rarely travels in a straight line. There are always wrong turns, double backs and false starts. Yet men like Baldwin, Knabenshue and Slate succeeded in pushing lighter-than-air flight in new directions.

But by 1933, the leaders in the field including Santos-Dumont, Von Zeppelin, Baldwin and Admiral Moffett were dead. This left only Paul W. Litchfield to carry their torch. Litchfield had already remade Goodyear into one of the largest industrial concerns in the country. Now, he set his sights on making it the world's dominant manufacturer of big rigid airships. As

Knabenshue once remarked, 'The airship business is the real thing. It beats captive balloons all hollow and there's money in the game.'[40] Litchfield might not have put it quite that way, but he had every intention of proving Knabenshue right, especially the part about making money.

10

COMPETITION

Paul Litchfield may have been inspired by the LTA pioneers that came before him, but he faced a threat from international competitors vying to establish passenger-carrying airship services before he did.

Airship travel seemed poised to explode after the First World War. Once nations settled their differences, the desire to link Europe through various forms of transportation grew. Germany had begun the trend with DELAG's inter-city service, which the war interrupted. Now Goodyear was well positioned to compete, but Litchfield had some catching up to do.

One formidable competitor was Vickers, the British aircraft manufacturer. Vickers released detailed plans for a rigid airship designed to carry 140 paying passengers between London and New York in 1919. The Vickers dirigible was the biggest ever proposed, exceeding anything built by Germany. But size wasn't her most notable feature – that would have been her rooftop passenger accommodation. Previous practice concentrated the passenger cabin in an extended gondola beneath the dirigible. Vickers' airship turned this idea on its head with passenger cabins, a restaurant and an open-air deck planned for the dirigible's rooftop.

Vickers spent considerable effort developing its proposal. It not only published technical specifications but made a compelling economic case. The company did so hoping the British government would fund its effort to connect the UK to its colonies via LTA flight, something that Litchfield would have liked to do.

Clearly, Vickers was trying to position its dirigible as a sky-going ocean liner, but its design was fanciful. An airship's centre of gravity is located in its bottom half to prevent it from becoming top heavy. Vickers' design made airship travel look appealing, but it was never built. Still, it increased the pressure on Goodyear. If Litchfield didn't jump into the rigid airship market, the UK might steal it from him.

While Vickers promoted commercial airship travel, there were plenty of other airship schemes, making it difficult to separate the signal from the noise.

In 1923, Dr Johann Schütte, designer of Germany's Schütte-Lanz dirigibles, proposed an airship service between Chicago and New York. Forecast to cut travel time in half, Schütte told the *New York Times*, 'the only thing necessary for the development of rigid aircraft in this country is capital and I might add courage'.[*1]

Schütte's background was more than credible. His Schütte-Lanz airships with their remarkable plywood airframes competed with Zeppelins just like Ford competed with GM. But if American airship entrepreneurs lacked funding (as Schütte suggested), they had plenty of courage. Schütte-Lanz entered into discussion with at least one American company regarding an airship service. The firm even developed plans for three commercial airships: the *Atlantik* (S.L. 101), the *Panamerica* (S.L. 102) and the *Pacific* (S.L. 103). Later, the company would bid unsuccessfully to build the USS *Akron* and *Macon*. Schütte-Lanz never closed these deals, but as far as Litchfield was concerned the heat was on.

Despite Litchfield's desire to enter the passenger-carrying airship business, America continued to lag behind the rest of the world in commercial airship services. A cartoon on the front page of the *New York Evening Graphic* in 1926 shows airships from the UK, France, Belgium, Germany, Russia and Japan flying over Uncle Sam, who is tied by red tape to a map of the United States. 'How Long Will The American People Stand For This?' the headline asks, while the red tape reads: 'Congressional Apathy. No Appropriations. Indifference. Politics. Delay'.[2] Litchfield could not have penned a more sympathetic message.

But the UK and Germany weren't the only countries interested in passenger airships. By 1924, Italy had her own commercial airship – a luxuriously outfitted semi-rigid designed by General Umberto Nobile. Named the N.1,

---

*   Schütte believed airships could reduce travel time between Chicago and New York from twenty hours by train to only ten for airships.

she included the first bedroom ever installed on an airship.[3] France, Spain, Russia and Japan also toyed with dirigibles. Meanwhile, America continued to lag behind.

The interest in commercial airship service was simple: anything that reduced travel time was not only desirable but thought to be profitable. Whether an express train or a Blue Riband ocean liner, speed commanded a premium. The challenge was building an airship that made economic sense. It is one thing to announce plans for a passenger airship service and quite another to execute them profitably. Dr Schütte could give all the interviews he wanted, but it wasn't the same as the meticulous studies that Vickers, DELAG and Goodyear undertook. Even then, getting an airship service off the ground would not be easy in the United States.

At this point, it's fair to ask why aeroplanes didn't overtake airships sooner.* One reason is that airships came first, giving them a competitive advantage. But nothing contributed more to airship supremacy than the Wright brothers' insistence that they were entitled to patent key aspects of flight. The early days of flight had an 'open source' feeling to them. Many of the early pioneers, such as Octave Chanute and Otto Lilienthal, freely shared the learning they gained from their success and failures. The Ohio-based brothers took full advantage of this information sharing, but were slow to reciprocate. In fact, the Wright brothers were not only secretive about their aviation efforts – they also had a proprietary feeling towards flight. After their success at Kitty Hawk, they sued virtually anyone who tried building an aeroplane, whether American or European, claiming it infringed on their patents. This impeded HTA development to the point that few manufacturers risked building aeroplanes for fear the brothers would take them to court.** In fact, HTA manufacturing was so stifled that the US still didn't have an air force when the First World War broke out in 1914 – eleven years after the Wright Flyer first flew. It wasn't until Congress intervened to pool aviation patents in 1917 that aeroplane manufacturing began to take off. Planes would surpass airships by the 1930s,

---

*   For a comprehensive look at the competition between aeroplanes and airships see
        Alexander Rose's excellent book, *Empires of the Sky*.
**   When the courts upheld the Wrights' patent claim, manufactures were forced to
        pay the brothers a 5 per cent royalty for every aeroplane they sold. This drove up the
        price of planes, making them prohibitively expensive, which hindered both private
        aeroplane ownership and industry growth.

but Zeppelins continued to beat aeroplanes in terms of range, flight duration and load-carrying capacity for years to come.

This explains why rigid airships were initially more attractive than aeroplanes for long-distance travel, but it doesn't explain why the German airship industry was so far ahead of everyone else. One reason is that Count Ferdinand von Zeppelin's big rigids were so robust they revolutionised airship travel. But another important reason was that the German government supported the industry with money. Not only did the German military buy locally produced airships, the government permitted von Zeppelin to raise funds using a state-sanctioned lottery to expand his manufacturing capacity. In contrast, the US government left its airship industry to the vagaries of the market. The US Army and Navy purchased a few non-rigids, but they did so irregularly and only on an experimental basis. In the meantime, the British and German governments were happy to subsidise their airship industries through military procurement or direct government support. This was a significant competitive advantage, ensuring America was a follower not an innovator. While DELAG provided a first-class passenger service aboard its increasingly sophisticated airships, Roy Knabenshue was doing his carnival act over Chicago.

That all changed once German Zeppelins began bombing London. These attacks fuelled a post-war arms race, first by the UK, then the United States, as both countries funded big rigid construction in a race to catch up with Germany.

Ironically, German Zeppelins were not the formidable weapon many presume. The number of bombs a Zep could carry was limited by weight. Additionally, their aiming was imprecise, with many bombs missing their target. That's not to underestimate the psychological toll Zeppelin attacks took on the British public during the First World War,* but the truth is, dirigibles made poor bombers.** Not only was weather a deadlier enemy, causing them to crash more frequently than they were shot down; they were far more effective as naval scouts. In fact, it's estimated German Zeppelins flew only fifty-one bombing raids over the UK. The vast bulk of their time was spent searching for the British fleet. When they found it, they alerted the German Navy, helping them to avoid its clutches. Buaer's admiral Moffett knew this, which is why he wanted the *Akron* employed as an ocean-going scout not as a bomber.

---

*   The British public called Zeppelins 'baby killers'.

**   Although many people think Germany's Zeppelin raids were the first time airships were used to bomb an enemy, Italy used dirigibles to bomb Turkish troops in Libya in 1912.

Once hostilities ceased, Germany was forced to relinquish her dirigibles to her former enemies. The UK, France, Italy, Belgium and Japan all received at least one German airship. However, the US Navy didn't get theirs until October 1924.*

The Treaty of Versailles prevented Germany from building any more dirigibles for the military after the First World War, but the US Navy got around this restriction by agreeing (somewhat disingenuously) not to use the *Los Angeles* for military purposes. Instead, she was classified an experimental vessel intended to train LTA crews. This explains why the *Los Angeles* was outfitted with passenger accommodations more suitable for commercial travel than warfare. Specifically, five, Pullman-style cabins with wood panelling, high-backed sofas and privacy curtains could accommodate up to twenty overnight passengers. Each one of the three-cushioned sofas were protected by slip-covers, while the carpeting was covered by a runner made by riggers who normally repaired the airship's canvas envelope. More appropriate to Nemo's *Nautilus*, these accoutrements were not usually found aboard a military vessel. Numerous VIPs, including the King of Siam, availed themselves of the *Los Angeles'* luxe accommodations, but few were fooled into thinking she was anything but a military airship.

By 1921, Germany's airship industry was on the brink of extinction, and neither the UK nor the United States were interested in preserving it. Instead, they wanted their own airship industry. No longer able to build Zeppelins for the military, Luftschiffbau Zeppelin had no choice but to restart a passenger airship service in 1919. The result was the *Bodensee* (LZ-120), which carried 2,400 paying passengers on 103 flights between Friedrichshafen and Berlin in a span of only ninety-eight days.[4] This marked the first time a dirigible was used exclusively for transporting passengers from one destination to another. It would not be the last. But it was virtually the only thing keeping the lights on at Luftschiffbau Zeppelin."

Then Germany was forced to turn the *Bodensee* over to Italy as war reparations. Meanwhile, the Allies pushed to dismantle the Zeppelin manufacturing works in Friedrichshafen. By the end of 1921, Germany not only didn't possess a single big rigid, her airship industry was bordering on extinction.

---

*   German airship crews destroyed many of their Zeppelins when the war ended rather than see their enemies capture them. As a result, LZ-126, later commissioned as the *Los Angeles* (ZR-3), was built by Luftschiffbau Zeppelin and handed over to the United States as war reparations.

With Germany on the ropes, the UK moved to fill the airship gap. She'd already built three big rigids during the First World War: the *R33*, *R34* and *R36*. Intended to launch reprisal raids against Germany, none of the vessels were completed before the war ended. As mentioned, the *R34* made history when she travelled from Scotland to New York in 1919. She was not only the first dirigible to cross the Atlantic, but the first aircraft of any type to make a round trip.

The *R34*'s achievement bode well for the future of transatlantic airship travel, but when the *R38* broke apart in 1921 killing most of her crew, it cast a temporary chill over the UK's airship business. That didn't stop Litchfield. Instead, he saw an opening in the market.

Litchfield could be as cold and calculating as the next industrial titan. With his dream of an American commercial airship service still in its infancy, he decided to press his advantage. What he would accomplish between 1923 and the crash of the *Akron* eleven years later would be nothing short of miraculous.

But first he had to cut a deal.

11

CUTTING A DEAL

When Litchfield faced a knotty business problem, he liked playing the piano while unravelling it. As his youngest daughter, Edith, noted, 'If he plays something gay and cheerful, everything is all right, we can go in and talk and laugh and sing with him ... But if he looks real mad and plays very slow, then look out. Don't go in ... even on tiptoe.'[1]

Litchfield was playing the piano a lot during the 1920s. Like most companies, Goodyear had been hard hit by the recession at the beginning of the decade. In a few short months, car manufacturers had cancelled so many orders, tyre production fell by 86 per cent.[2] By the end of 1920, Goodyear was in receivership.

The Seiberling brothers had no choice but to restructure the company's finances. When they did, they lost control and were pushed out. This paved the way for Litchfield's ascendancy. By the time sales rebounded he was Vice President of the tyre division. Now overseeing the company's largest revenue stream, he was hungry to get into the rigid airship business.

The Navy had purchased the *R38* from the UK and built the *Shenandoah* on its own. Then, it outsourced its third big rigid to Germany for construction. This meant Goodyear had missed out on building all three of the Navy's rigid airships. But neither the British-built *R38* nor the Navy-built *Shenandoah* had served Moffett's programme well since both had crashed. The admiral hoped his next big rigid, built by the masters of airship construction in Germany, would fare better.

As he tickled the ivories, Litchfield pondered how to persuade the Navy to buy its next generation of big rigids from Goodyear. The company had been supplying the Navy with a steady stream of blimps since 1917 but big rigids promised to be a more profitable market.*

One thing helping Litchfield was that Moffett didn't want to keep outsourcing construction of a strategic weapon to a foreign country. He wanted the United States to have its own airship industry and Goodyear was the natural choice. Few American companies had its LTA experience, but Goodyear would have to make a massive investment in infrastructure if it wanted the Navy's big rigid business.

Luftschiffbau Zeppelin tried interesting the US government buying its Zeppelins, but both the US Army and Navy had mixed experiences working with a former enemy. Then an interesting thing happened. Secretary of the Navy, Edwin Denby, and Secretary of War, John W. Weeks called Litchfield to Washington. They wanted to feel out whether Goodyear would be interested in procuring the rights to build Zeppelins in America. As Litchfield wrote in his autobiography, 'It occurred to someone that it might be easier for a private company … to make such arrangements.'[3]

The meeting between Litchfield and the US government was a coup for Hugo Eckener. Dr Eckener, a giant in his own right, had succeeded Count Zeppelin as head of Luftschiffbau Zeppelin after the latter's death. But the company had no more orders to build Zeppelins after delivering the *Los Angeles*. Meanwhile, the once-proud manufacturer had been reduced to making kitchenware. Now, Eckener had not only piqued the interest of an American industrial giant, he'd got the US government to do his bidding.

Litchfield was a shrewd businessman. He knew an undervalued asset when he saw one. Sending his representative to feel out Eckener in Germany, Litchfield had no intention of paying money for the North American rights to build Zeppelins. He wanted to make a trade.

Eckener was not in a strong bargaining position. Despite doing everything he could to keep Luftschiffbau Zeppelin afloat, the industrial concern seemed destined for bankruptcy. A deal with Goodyear to license its Zeppelin technology was a lifeline for the company, leaving Eckener with little negotiating leverage. But Luftschiffbau Zeppelin had the technology the Navy wanted, which meant Litchfield had little choice but to cut a deal. And so, he travelled to Germany to personally negotiate the right to build Zeppelins.

---

* Goodyear was not the Navy's sole supplier of blimps. When the Navy's first blimp, the DN-1, performed poorly, the Navy sought replacements from other manufacturers, including Goodyear and Goodrich.

Talks were held at the Kurgarten Hotel – an elegant, old world hostelry in the picturesque lake town of Friedrichshafen. 'Most of the discussion was in German,' Litchfield recalled thirty years later. 'The negotiations started … in the morning and lasted until nearly four o'clock the next morning.'[4]

As Litchfield drank coffee to stay awake, his lawyers hammered out a deal in the wee hours. Luftschiffbau Zeppelin would grant the right to build rigid airships in North America to a new entity, the Goodyear–Zeppelin Corporation. Additionally, Dr Eckener agreed to transfer all relevant patents and expert personnel to the new company. In exchange, Luftschiffbau Zeppelin would receive a one-third interest in the undertaking. Goodyear also agreed to transfer its American LTA business, related personnel and patents to Goodyear–Zeppelin in exchange for a two-thirds interest, allowing Litchfield to retain control. Remarkably, not a single dollar changed hands.[5]

Who came out ahead is hard to say. Litchfield got something for nothing. Still, he had to make a huge capital investment to make his gamble pay off. Dr Eckener, on the other hand, kept Luftschiffbau Zeppelin alive, persuading a deep-pocketed partner to invest in Zeppelin technology in the hope of future profits.

It's important to remember that the deal was made in 1923, six years before Luftschiffbau Zeppelin launched its most successful passenger airship, the *Graf Zeppelin*. This means Litchfield made a bet on Zeppelin technology when it was still unproven – at least on the scale that Goodyear and the Navy planned. It was a risk he was willing to take.

The best deals leave all participants happy. The Goodyear–Zeppelin agreement was a textbook case. Eckener had his lifeline; Moffett had an American supplier to advance his LTA programme; and Litchfield had taken an important step in turning Goodyear into a manufacturer of rigid airships first for the military, then the commercial market.* For better, or worse, Goodyear, Luftschiffbau Zeppelin and the US Navy would be bound together in a partnership lasting a decade.

Forging the deal turned out to be the easy part – the challenge lay in making it work. This was no simple task given that Litchfield and Moffett still had to convince the United States Congress to fund the construction of big rigids.

---

*   It's interesting to note that Luftschiffbau Zeppelin almost went bankrupt twice in ten years. The first time it was rescued by a dramatic increase in German military spending during the First World War. The second time, the company was rescued by Goodyear. In other words, even the leading manufacturer found airship economics difficult to make work.

Litchfield wasn't crazy for wanting to build Zeppelins. 'At the end of the war people were just as much interested in airships as they were in aeroplanes,' he recalled.[6] 'There was nothing in the record which indicated that rigid airships could not be flown safely.'[7] Additionally, airship technology was improving rapidly, as the UK's rigid airship programme showed. If Goodyear didn't enter the market soon it might get left behind.

Litchfield's plan was a bold roll of the dice. Whether it succeeded came down to the cunning and determination of a handful of men. Even then it wasn't clear whether Litchfield could pull it off, but he was determined to succeed.

12

PITCHING COMMERCIAL AIRSHIPS

When the BUAER formalised the specifications for its next-generation big rigids in April 1924, Litchfield must have felt he was finally getting somewhere. Called Design No. 60, it was the BUAER's stake in the ground – a tangible indication of what the next-gen big rigids should look like. The design described an airship two and a half football fields long containing 6 million cu ft of non-flammable helium. Intended for long-range scouting missions, what made Design No. 60 so remarkable wasn't just its size but the fact it would carry aeroplanes to defend against attack. These aeroplanes would be launched and retrieved by the airship while it was in mid-flight, making her the world's first flying aircraft carrier.

The decision to include aircraft on a big rigid had profound consequences for its design. The airships would not only have to be bigger to accommodate the extra weight; they'd have to be faster so planes wouldn't stall when flying aboard.

Goodyear-Zeppelin engineers provided input to Design No. 60, but that wasn't the same as a contract to build it for the Navy. In the meantime, the division was bleeding red ink. Litchfield must have been frustrated with how slow the Navy was moving, but that didn't stop him. He was busy promoting commercial airship travel in America, hoping it would lead to more business. In a speech he gave to the Ohio Association of Real Estate Boards in October 1925, Litchfield promoted the new age of aerial travel. Drawing a comparison between airships and automobiles, he noted neither had been recognised as superior modes of transportation when first introduced. Despite the oversight, Litchfield believed airships would surpass all forms of long-distance transportation, covering in days what now took months.[1]

Litchfield also called upon Congress to enact legislation requiring 50 per cent of airships operating between foreign countries and the United States be American built and owned. As an Associated Press reporter wrote, 'Mr. Litchfield is confident that the development of trans-Oceanic air ship service on a commercial basis is imminent.'[2]

But six months passed and no contracts materialised. While Litchfield chummed the waters for airship travel, an article appeared in the May 1926 issue of *Popular Science Monthly* shedding light on his plans.

'I went to Akron and … found a little group of German experts at work under the direction of P.W. Litchfield,' the author recounted. 'I found Dr Hugo Eckener … head of the famous German Zeppelin plant at Friedrichshafen … There, too, is Dr Karl Arnstein … builder of … nearly 100 … Zeppelins.'[3]

Aside from showing once sworn enemies working together to build a former German weapon less than ten years after the war had ended, the article gives a gushing account of the GZ-1 – a commercial dirigible Goodyear-Zeppelin hoped to build for the private sector. Described as a 'super airship', the GZ-1 was to be nearly three football fields long, carry 100 passengers and have a non-stop cruising range of 6,000 miles.[4]

For perspective, the GZ-1 was not only longer than a battleship, but surpassed in length the largest ocean liner then afloat.* If that wasn't impressive, its helium capacity of 7 million cu ft was nearly three times that of the Navy's *Los Angeles* and 1 million cu ft larger than Design No. 60, making her the biggest airship yet proposed.

The article quotes Dr Arnstein as saying the GZ-1 'will be fitted out like the finest ocean liners, with passenger cabins, staterooms, bathrooms including showers and dining rooms. It will [also] have [twin] promenades running the length of the ship … with windows from which passengers may view the world below.'[5]

Nobody thought small when it came to airship construction, largely because the economics combined with lighter-than-air physics necessitated scale to succeed. The more lifting gas a big rigid contained the more passengers and cargo it could lift, translating into greater profits. Blimps and semi-rigids couldn't fly very far, or carry enough passengers, to compete with trains or ocean liners. Gigantic-ism, along with a heavy dose of luxury and glamour, was the order of the day.

★   An article in the *New York Times* that same year describes the GZ-1 as being 1,000ft long, which is longer than three football fields.

In addition to carrying passengers, freight and mail, the GZ-1 was said to have enough horsepower to 'buck the fiercest storms' while transporting passengers from New York to London in only two days.[6] Crossing the Atlantic in forty-eight hours was more than twice as fast as the sleekest steamship, a serious competitive advantage if the GZ-1 was built.

Litchfield was so confident in Goodyear-Zeppelin's airship he was quoted as saying, 'our engineering staff … have worked out the details so thoroughly as to exclude every possibility of a serious accident that might destroy it … In fact, we are so convinced of this that we would give a gold bond as assurance of its safety.'[7]

Perhaps, but the article's tone is so admiring it reads like a plant. Hugh Allen, Goodyear-Zeppelin's head of public relations, was responsible for drumming up positive media coverage. Goodyear's PR maven had begun his career as a reporter for the *Cleveland Plain Dealer* before editing papers in Seattle, Washington and South Bend, Indiana. After working as managing editor for the *Akron Beacon Journal*, Goodyear tapped him to head up the company's public relations department where he thrived.

Allen understood how the media worked. He not only commanded a sizeable advertising budget, he had a thick Rolodex of contacts. His ability to place favourable stories is not in question. Although there is no evidence Goodyear promised advertising in exchange for positive coverage, the article's awestruck tone was unusual for a scientific publication, even one catering to the general public.

The most interesting thing the article reveals is that Litchfield was seeking private investors to finance the GZ-1. This shows he was not relying on the government or the Navy to get his commercial airship business up and running, at least not initially. What the article neglects to mention is that the GZ-1 was vapourware designed to attract buyers. It existed only on paper. The truth was that Goodyear-Zeppelin had big plans, but Litchfield would need all the help he could get to make them fly.

Support for Litchfield's commercial airships came from an unusual source: the US Navy. The Navy's General Board, an advisory group, recommended the Navy's rigid airship programme be used 'to determine their … commercial value'.[8] Moffett was also an enthusiastic supporter. In a series of speeches and newspaper articles he freely admitted, 'Our naval efforts have a direct influence on the commercial future of airships … We should grasp our great opportunity and occupy this new merchant marine of the air before our rivals.'[9]

Promoting passenger airships was always on Moffett's agenda. It was the only way to ensure a manufacturing industry capable of building big rigids took root in America. The more rigid airships built in the United States, the lower the cost to the Navy. Additionally, commercial airship infrastructure meant more places for the Navy's big rigids to land in an emergency as well as more airship crews to draw upon. This explains why Moffett promoted commercial airship travel almost as much as Litchfield. But sometimes his efforts could tip into the extreme.

In testimony before the House Naval Appropriations Subcommittee shortly after Goodyear-Zeppelin was formed, Moffett made the remarkable announcement that the Navy had designed a dirigible capable of carrying eighty paying passengers on regularly scheduled trips between London and New York. Moffett presented figures showing how the *Los Angeles*, in conjunction with two other airships, could support a year-round passenger service to London, New York and Panama. He even submitted projections forecasting an annual profit of $5 million.[10]

The Navy was not usually in the business of commercial transportation, which makes Moffett's announcement all the more extraordinary. But the admiral was doing everything he could to signal to Wall Street that commercial airships were worth investing in. How else was he going to get the manufacturing capacity he needed to build his fleet of sky ships?

After Litchfield was promoted to President of the Goodyear Tire & Rubber Company in 1926, he was able to pursue his rigid airship plans even more aggressively. Litchfield had certainly earned the promotion. Among his recent accomplishments, he'd signed a milestone contract with Sears-Roebuck & Company, marking the first time automobile tyres were sold through a mass-market retailer. Additionally, Goodyear-branded service stations and tyre centres were sprouting up around the country. These new sales channels, which prominently featured Goodyear's winged-foot logo and distinctive blue and yellow colours, both revolutionised the marketing of tyres to the American public and fattened the company coffers.

Litchfield's initiatives drove Goodyear to a commanding lead in its core tyre business. But this was necessary if the company was going to fund its expansion into rigid airship manufacturing. However, Goodyear still wasn't building big rigids for the Navy.[11] If something didn't happen soon, Litchfield's gamble might not pay off.

13

THE DESIGN COMPETITION

Finally, in June 1926, Congress authorised the construction of two giant rigid airships to be built as part of the Navy's five-year aeronautical programme. Authorisation is not the same as appropriation, however. Congress approved manufacturing two big rigids but didn't earmark funds for their construction. It wasn't until March 1927, more than three years after Goodyear-Zeppelin had been founded, that Congress authorised money to build Moffett's big rigids. Even then, it was only the paltry sum of $200,000 – not nearly enough to begin driving rivets. Instead, Congress mandated the Navy hold a design competition. Once again Litchfield's dream faced a delay.

Litchfield would have preferred the Navy to grant its big rigid business to Goodyear without having to compete for it, but Congress would not permit a no-bid contract for such an important project.[1] Now, Goodyear had the privilege of vying against thirty-seven companies for the chance to build big rigids for the Navy.

It's surprising how many bids were submitted given the rigid airship industry didn't exist in America. Submissions ranged from the practical to the improbable. It wasn't unusual for amateur inventors to send crackpot ideas in the hopes of winning, as Moffett's response to one such entrant makes clear:

> Mr. Trent's attempts to design an airship have been known to the Bureau of Aeronautics for several years. His ideas have been passed upon by various organizations and no merit found in any of the proposals he has presented … His proposed method of executing his ideas is too crude to warrant serious consideration.[2]

An overheated market can lead to inflated expectations. Big rigids were no exception. There were plenty of outrageous airship schemes during the 1920s and '30s, most no more than sketches on paper. Given the anything-goes environment, charlatans, dreamers and crackpots abounded.

Among the kookiest were proposals for hospital Zeps, solar Zeps and Zeps that floated on water. There were Zeps with wings, rooftop landing strips, hydraulic landing gears and pontoons.* One proposed airship boasted a passenger cabin that slid along an overhead rail to aid in the craft's ascents and descents, much like Knabenshue had shifted his weight on the *California Arrow*'s catwalk. There were even plans for a Soviet Zep that carried its own hangar, and a cargo Zep that enabled freight trains to unload inside it.

One of the more unusual designs was a Zep-plane hybrid named the Zepperplane. Another incarnation was a blimp with wings, while a third idea was for a blimp with an aeroplane underneath. The latter was designed by a Los Angeles vocational teacher John Hodgdon, who built a scale model. Named the *City of Long Beach*, a full-size version was never constructed. French aviator M. Cesar actually built and flew a dirigible-biplane hybrid in France circa 1910, but the design was unwieldy and never caught on.

Some of the weirder dirigibles were no more than fanciful illustrations featured in magazines of the day such as *Popular Science* and *Modern Mechanix*. Most of these seemed intent on doing nothing more than fueling a young boy's dream of flight. At one point, there were so many designs competing for attention it was hard to know which to take seriously. Success or lack thereof was dependent on funding and expertise, which were in short supply. In the meantime, the world continued thirsting for a transoceanic airship service.

The Navy's design competition lasted five months. When the winner was declared in July 1927 it was Goodyear-Zeppelin. But the Navy wanted its big rigids built on a fixed-cost basis. Litchfield knew cost overruns were inevitable since no one had built airships this big before. That's why he insisted Goodyear would only build on a cost-plus basis, meaning the Navy would have to absorb

---

*   The control car on early German Zeppelins was designed to land on Lake Bodensee (aka Lake Constance) near Friedrichshafen. This is why it was called a gondola. Nevertheless, it was generally not a good idea for a rigid airship to set down on water.

any cost overruns.[3] This was shrewd of him because it shifted the risk of building a prototype from Goodyear to the Navy.

Moffett bent over backwards to support Goodyear's bid but neither naval higher-ups nor Congress would allow a cost-plus contract. Additionally, the American arm of the Brown–Boveri Electric Corporation muddied the waters by contending its shipbuilding subsidiary could build big rigids cheaper if the Navy allowed it to use its Lakehurst hangar for construction.

Their contention was doubtful, but Brown–Boveri had clout. A special hearing was held before the House Subcommittee on Appropriations to consider their bid. In the interest of fairness, it was decided to repeat the design competition the following year. Undoubtedly, Litchfield wasn't playing many happy tunes after he heard the news.

Companies seemed to be announcing new commercial airship ventures targeting the American market almost every month. Among the most aggressive was Ralph Upson's Aircraft Development Corporation.

Upson, a former Goodyear engineer specialising in airship design, wanted to build an airship with an all-metal hull. More robust than Slate's *City of Glendale*, Upson's metal-clad was backed by automotive tycoon Henry Ford and his son, Edsel.[4]

Moffett preferred Goodyear to be the sole supplier of Navy airships, but he couldn't risk alienating Ford, whose deep pockets and political pull were not easily ignored. In 1926, Congress authorised construction of a 149ft-long, 200,000-cu ft metal-clad built by Upson. The experimental airship, designated ZMC-2 but nicknamed the 'Tin Bubble', would not be delivered until 1929.*

The Navy's second design competition attracted only nine competitors. When the winner was announced in August 1928, Goodyear-Zeppelin ruled the day. Its three designs were not only the best; they were the only bid to include construction costs – a necessity for declaring the winner.

---

*   The 'MC' in ZMC-2 stood for metal clad. After twelve years of flying with mixed results, the Navy scrapped her in 1941.

Litchfield was elated at the news. His years of hard work were finally paying off. Better yet, Congress had appropriated $8 million for construction of two rigid airships, each 785ft long with a helium capacity of 6.5 million cu ft. The first would cost $5,375,000, the second $2,450,000.[5] The reason the first cost more than the second is it would be built from scratch – always an expensive proposition. The second airship could be built more cheaply because it would benefit from economies of scale, or that was the presumption. But everything had to go just right if Goodyear was to make a profit. Otherwise, the company would take a bath.

Litchfield wasn't too worried about losing money since he expected the commercial airship market would make up the difference. But Goodyear-Zeppelin had to invest $3 million in airship infrastructure, including $2.25 million to build an air dock.[6,7] It was a considerable sum, but Litchfield was so bullish he told Dr Arnstein, 'We have to look ahead … Let's build a dock big enough for a 10 million foot ship.'[8]

The Navy declared Goodyear–Zeppelin the official winner of its design competition on 1 October 1928. Winning was not supposed to be a foregone conclusion, but Goodyear had the inside track since Litchfield had worked with Moffett for almost a decade. Litchfield could also count on his many friends in Congress to support Goodyear's bid. If that wasn't enough, the company had been building blimps for a dozen years. When it came to airship construction, Goodyear had more experience, money, manpower and clout than any company in America.

Nine men were present for the contract signing, which was held in the Secretary of the Navy's office in Washington, DC. In a photograph taken to mark the occasion Moffett, looking tight-lipped in a dark business suit, is seated at a desk next to Secretary of the Navy, Curtis D. Wilbur. None of the men in the tableau are smiling, which is surprising given there was finally a home team to root for. There would be another official photograph commemorating the actual signing of the contract with Moffett, Litchfield and Secretary Wilbur posing in front of the winning design. Dr Arnstein stands behind Litchfield staring off into the distance. Nobody looks happy in this picture either. They were probably feeling the hot breath of expectation on their necks.

If the 1920s promised big things for rigid airships, then the 1930s would deliver on that promise. Not only would Goodyear make a buck, the Navy contract would subsidise the cost of building rigid airships for the commercial market. It was a brilliant strategy, but it depended on demand for commercial airships materialising as Litchfield expected. So far, things seemed to be going his way.

The Navy's first big rigid was to be delivered in thirty months, followed by the second fifteen months later. It was an aggressive timetable for building the world's largest aircraft, especially one that had never been built before. The contract signing came five years after Litchfield's trip to Friedrichshafen – six since the federal government had encouraged him to obtain the rights to build Zeppelins in America. If Litchfield was impatient to get started, it was understandable. The UK was about to launch its Imperial Airship scheme linking its far-flung colonies, while Japan and the Soviet Union were developing their own military and commercial airships.

Litchfield realised how easy it would be for the UK to siphon off North American passenger traffic once their airship service to Canada began the following year. This was a direct threat to his commercial airship aspirations. Furthermore, the UK's latest passenger airship, the *R101*, had been paid for by the British government, while Litchfield was still seeking private investors for his venture. If that wasn't pressure enough, Goodyear's big rigid contract signing was upstaged by the arrival of Germany's *Graf Zeppelin* at Lakehurst on 15 October 1928.

The *Graf's* first transatlantic voyage was a milestone for commercial aviation. The Zeppelin offered unprecedented luxury in air travel while promising safety, comfort and convenience at a price few people could afford. Still, the *Graf's* American arrival marked the first time so many people had been transported by an aircraft of any kind across the Atlantic Ocean.* This wasn't just a handful of people as on Roy Knabenshue's sightseeing flights. It wasn't even DELAG's champagne-sipping tourist excursions between two German cities. It was the world's first transatlantic air service, and it was up and running before Goodyear could launch the same.

It took the *Graf* only four and a half days to cross 6,100 miles between Germany and America – faster than the five or six days normally required by

---

*   The *Graf* carried sixty people from Germany to the United States: twenty passengers and forty crew. This lopsided ratio was not unusual for the early days of commercial LTA flight. Once Dr Eckener and Litchfield established their transoceanic services, they intended to skew the ratio more towards passengers.

steamship. If the *Graf*'s wallpapered accommodations were somewhat cramped compared with an ocean liner, they were positively spacious alongside the aircraft of her day. Passenger cabins were similar in configuration to those of a Pullman sleeper (the standard for luxury), if somewhat larger. Not only that, the *Graf*'s dining room featured white starched table cloths, etched crystal and elegant china with fresh flowers in silver bud vases adorning every table. Fine wines and a fully stocked bar were also available, as were a variety of savoury items on her menu. Meanwhile, the *Graf*'s numerous windows not only provided stunning vistas but could be opened to permit fresh air to enter. The *Graf*'s successor, the *Hindenburg*, would even include a piano forte made of Duralumin in its passenger lounge. It weighed all of 356lbs and must have sounded terrible.

After disembarking at Lakehurst, Dr Eckener wasted no time heading to New York City. A ticker-tape parade celebrating the *Graf*'s arrival was held, followed by a series of glittering receptions, luncheons and dinners. This gave Eckener ample opportunity to talk up Luftschiffbau Zeppelin's plans for a regularly scheduled airship service between Germany, Brazil and the United States. Admiral Moffett and Lt Cdr Wiley attended some of these events, while Henry Ford also sent a representative. Ford had already built a mooring mast at his own expense to accommodate airships at Ford Field in Detroit. Now, he hoped airships such as the *Graf* would make Detroit a regular stop on their itinerary.

Lady Grace Marguerite Hay Drummond-Hay, a British journalist and society figure who made more headlines than she wrote, tacitly endorsed airships when she told a luncheon group she was more frightened speaking in front of them than travelling across the Atlantic by airship.[9] As her audience gave their rapt attention, Drummond-Hay's plummy voice was broadcast over national radio. 'The *Graf Zeppelin* is more than just machinery, canvas and aluminium,' she told her audience. 'It has a soul.'[10] The day of international airship travel had finally arrived.

Drummond-Hay cut a stylish figure. With her tailored suits, fashionable hats and occasional leather flying gear, she was the only female passenger aboard the *Graf*, making her the first woman to fly across the Atlantic east to west. Another soon to-be-famous aviatrix, Amelia Earhart, had crossed the Atlantic west to east four months earlier but she too had been a passenger not a pilot.

Drummond-Hay was so well known that her trip aboard the *Graf* helped promote airship safety. She even appeared in a print advertisement plugging the *Graf* and Lucky Strike cigarettes. Running alongside her soft-focused portrait, her testimonial read, 'The fact that we were not permitted to smoke (aboard) the *Graf Zeppelin* … only increased my appetite for a Lucky Strike. Oh, how good that first one tasted!'[11]

The *Graf*'s passengers were not permitted to smoke for good reason – one stray spark and the airship's 2.6 million cu ft of highly flammable hydrogen might catch fire. This deficit would be corrected aboard the *Hindenburg*, where passengers were allowed to light up in a specially pressurised smoking room.

Litchfield hosted a series of private meetings with Eckener to discuss a joint global airship service. But Eckener's meeting with Goodyear executives had to be cut short because he was whisked away by special train to meet President Coolidge in Washington – further validation of just how important the *Graf*'s achievement was.

The world would change drastically when the stock market crashed one year later, but the Great Depression would only dent the *Graf Zeppelin*'s business. Airship passengers were so wealthy as to be virtually recession-proof.

Litchfield had a problem, though. Goodyear still didn't have a single contract to build a passenger-carrying airship. The commercial pot, long simmering, had finally come to a boil, but it was doing so without him.

14

SUCCESS WITHIN REACH

There were three commercial airships in the world in 1929: Germany's *Graf Zeppelin* and the UK's *R100* and *R101*, which were scheduled to begin operations in the autumn. Importantly, the *Graf* had not only completed her first transatlantic trip to the United States, but circumnavigated the globe thrilling the public.

In comparison, when Transcontinental Air Transport, the predecessor to TWA, began offering the first coast-to-coast airline passenger service in 1929, it required nine separate legs all flown in daylight plus bookings on a sleeper train to span the continent – hardly a seamless affair. Henry Ford had introduced his tri-motor passenger aeroplane, nicknamed 'the Tin Goose', two years before, but it could only carry nine passengers plus a three-man crew. The year 1929 was also a record year for fatal civilian aeroplane crashes in the US, which helps explain why rigid airships looked like a more reasonable alternative for coast-to-coast travel.[1]

The Navy's big rigid programme had made enough progress by then that the American business community was ready to invest in commercial airships. With Goodyear-Zeppelin's Air Dock complete, and construction of the *Akron* under way, proof of concept was just around the corner. As a result, Litchfield had little trouble attracting partners.

Goodyear established two companies to facilitate commercial airship operations in the United States: one to map routes across the Atlantic, the other across the Pacific. The first company was the International Zeppelin Transport Corporation, with Goodyear its main sponsor. Its board included executives from the Aluminum Company of America (which made Duralumin – the main component in airship frames); the United Aircraft and Transport Corporation; the General Motors Research Corporation; Carbon and Carbide Chemicals

Corporation; and three banking groups: Lehman Brothers, the National City Company and the Greyson M.P. Murphy Company. Dr Eckener also sat on the board representing both Luftschiffbau Zeppelin and the Hamburg-America Line, which specialised in steamship travel.[2]

That same year, Goodyear formed the Pacific Zeppelin Transport Corporation. Pacific Zeppelin not only included board members from San Francisco and Hawaiian banks but also west coast steamship companies including Dollar Lines, America-Hawaiian Lines, Matson Navigational Company and the Los Angeles Steamship Company. Additionally, United Dry Docks, Inc. had a board seat, as did the Standard Oil Company of California and three fledgling airlines: Western Air Express, United Aircraft and Transport Corporation and Pan-American Airways.[3]

It's fair to ask why competitors such as the shipping and airline industries would partner with a commercial airship service. The answer was money. The ocean liner, trucking and nascent airline industries saw dirigibles as a threat. Not only could airships steal their high-margin passengers, but their mail and cargo that paid for everything. Rather than let airships siphon off revenues, airlines and transoceanic shipping companies joined forces with Litchfield in the hope of sharing profits. This is why Alfred F. Masury, a representative of the trucking industry, was on board the *Akron* the night she crashed. The only reason railroads didn't join as well is that they were engaged in a fierce pricing war with one another, leaving them starved for cash.

If all went according to plan, Goodyear's Atlantic and Pacific corporations would link with Germany's Hamburg-America Line to form one giant transport trust offering seamless airship travel between the United States, South America, Europe and the Pacific. At a time when the average person didn't stray more than 50 miles from home, Goodyear's vision was grandiose, forward thinking and unprecedented.

Litchfield presided over International Zeppelin as President, while J.C. Hunsaker headed up Pacific Zeppelin. Hunsaker not only supervised the development of operating and traffic studies but liaised with the financial community. He had little difficulty attracting interest; raising capital was another story.

To boost the business, Litchfield met with President Hoover in May 1929 to ask his support for an airmail contract that would help cover the cost of airship travel between Los Angeles and Hawaii.[4] Meeting the President in the White House accompanied by several senators, Litchfield told Hoover that Congress favoured an oceanic air service to keep the country competitive. According to the *New York Times*, Hoover was receptive.[5]

Litchfield worked tirelessly to make all the pieces of his planned airship empire come together. With his Atlantic and Pacific consortiums managing airship operations, Goodyear-Zeppelin could concentrate on what it knew best: building a fleet of globe-spanning giants.

In support of these efforts, Goodyear-Zeppelin released a steady stream of positive news throughout 1929. Shortly after meeting with Hoover, Litchfield announced the design of 'two great commercial airships ... for service on a line ... [from] California over the Pacific'.[6] A Goodyear promotional piece about the airships promised 'spacious compartments' and a 'lack of noise ... odors and sea sickness'. Luxury accommodations would include, 'a lounge, shower baths, smoking room, and a ... main saloon', features normally associated with a luxury ocean liner.[7]

The dirigibles described were essentially civilian versions of the two rigid airships Goodyear was building for the Navy. Each would transport eighty passengers (fifty-six more than the *Graf*) plus a plane to facilitate mail delivery. A follow-up article in the *New York Times* said the two airships would be ready by autumn 1933, noting that in Litchfield's opinion, 'The future holds great commercial possibilities for LTA transportation.'[8]

To drum up further support, Goodyear-Zeppelin released artist's sketches of the airships' observation deck and dining room. The company even built a full-size mock-up of part of the airship to sell future tickets as well as a scale model showing the arrangement of promenade decks and passenger cabins.[9]

Goodyear's 1933 delivery date may have been optimistic, but the time was right for an American passenger airship. With the *Akron* a year away from completion, and the *Macon* poised to follow, the day of the American commercial airship seemed finally to have arrived. All Litchfield needed was to persuade Congress to pass the Merchant Airship Act and Goodyear would become the world's largest manufacturer of passenger-carrying airships.

The Crosser bill, introduced in the House in 1930, was the last piece in Litchfield's grand puzzle. Sponsored by Representative Robert Crosser (D) of Akron, Ohio, the legislation was written with Goodyear's help. A companion bill, sponsored by Charles L. McNary (R) of Oregon, was introduced in the Senate as well. Together, the McNary-Crosser bill was designed to make American commercial airships economically viable by granting them the same benefits as the nation's merchant marine – such as carrying mail. The mail was critical to underwriting an airship's operating costs during their early days when passenger revenue would be slow to develop. Without it, Litchfield's plan didn't make economic sense.

Given airships could cut travel time from California to Hawaii from six days to two, the McNary-Crosser bill put them in direct competition with ocean liners. US-flagged steamships already carried mail to Asia but took at least a month to get there. American airships would deliver the mail to the Philippines, China and Japan in less than a week. But Litchfield needed the McNary-Crosser bill to get a slice of the business. Otherwise, commercial airships reliant solely on passenger revenue were a money-losing proposition.

In testimony before the House Interstate Commerce Committee, Litchfield urged speedy adoption of the Crosser bill. In his typically tortured syntax, Goodyear's CEO told the hearing, 'An airship industry is in existence in the United States and the construction art is advanced to the point that we may say that the establishment of Zeppelin airship passenger lines to Europe and the Orient, flying the American flag, is now entirely possible.'[10]

But nothing about Litchfield's crusade to pass the Crosser bill was easy. In their minority report, three congressmen on the House's Interstate and Foreign Commerce Committee called it a federal handout. 'This is not the time to engage in any new enterprise, which will increase the burden of taxes upon the American people,' they wrote.[11] This was a serious charge during the Depression given how much the country was suffering.

Having the bill termed a 'subsidy' must have rankled, given how much money Goodyear-Zeppelin was losing building big rigids for the Navy. Litchfield probably felt he was the one subsidising the American government, not the other way around. The House Committee eventually supported the Crosser bill, but its initial reluctance suggested congressional approval wouldn't be easy.

The truth is the McNary-Crosser bill wouldn't cost the American taxpayer a cent – not until Litchfield got his commercial airships up and running. According to Goodyear's best estimate, this would take at least three years once legislation was signed into law.[12] But passage of the bill was not a sure thing despite Litchfield leaving nothing to chance. To be clear, there is no evidence tying Litchfield, Hunsaker or Hugh Allen to the use of money, booze or women to influence congressional votes, but these incentives had been used by others to garner congressional support. Certainly, Congressman Crosser, who represented Goodyear's home town, knew on which side his bread was buttered. One can only assume others did, too.

In the meantime, the UK had surpassed the United States in commercial airship transportation. Given that the British Empire's far-flung colonies included Canada, Australia, Egypt and India, as well as parts of Africa, passenger-carrying airships were a commercial necessity. In the summer of 1930, the Vickers-built *R100* successfully crossed the Atlantic to Canada in only seventy-eight hours.

The *R100* was the fourth big rigid to cross the Atlantic, the UK's *R34* being first in 1919 followed by Germany's LZ-126 in 1924 and the *Graf Zeppelin* in 1929. But the *R100*'s sister looked to change everything. Lauded for her palatial trappings, the *R101* made her maiden voyage on 5 October 1930. Bound for India, she never got there, as she crashed into a French hillside, killing forty-eight of her fifty-four passengers. The British may have built the first big rigid to cross the Atlantic, but the *R101*'s casualty rate of 88 per cent was too high for public opinion to stomach.* The UK abandoned commercial airships altogether, leaving the market open for Goodyear.

But Litchfield was getting antsy. When 1932 dawned, it marked two years since the McNary-Crosser bill had been introduced in Congress, yet it still hadn't come up for a vote. The delay was not to Litchfield's advantage. The Depression didn't help. Litchfield's airship industry promised future jobs, but the country needed economic relief now, not later. In the meantime, Japan was looking at property in northern California for its proposed Tokyo–San Francisco airship service.**,13 Adding to the pressure, the *Graf Zeppelin* completed its 250th voyage that year with a 100 per cent on-time record.[14] Until Congress granted American airships the right to carry mail, Litchfield's plans remained grounded.

The House finally passed the Crosser bill (H.R. 8681) on 16 June 1932, by a fourteen-vote margin.*** The legislation granted the Postmaster General the right to pay a maximum of $20 per mile for any American-flagged airship carrying 10,000lb of mail 2,500 miles without refuelling.[15] Ten thousand pounds of mail was roughly ten times what most aeroplanes could carry. In contrast, the commercial airships Litchfield proposed could easily transport this amount earning a tidy sum of $50,000 per flight.

House passage of the Crosser bill was a victory for Litchfield. Importantly, Senate passage also seemed likely, given the Senate Commerce Committee had

---

*   By comparison, the *Titanic*'s casualty rate was 68 per cent.
** Japan's airship base was supposed to be located in Marin County but nothing ever came of it.
*** The final vote was 163 to 146, with slightly more Republicans voting in favour of the bill than Democrats.

reported favourably on the McNary bill. The next step was for a Senate vote to be scheduled.

The whole painstaking process had taken far longer than Litchfield preferred, but had his daughters been listening, their father was almost certainly playing a happy tune.

15

FOR WANT OF A NAIL

Six months after the House passed the Crosser bill, the normally staid *New York Times* waxed enthusiastically about Goodyear's proposed commercial airship. The article claimed it would include 'startling features such as an observation deck along the top of the great hull … passenger planes … and roomy cabin accommodations'.[1] Goodyear said its airship would soon be flying non-stop from New York to Los Angeles using its planes to pick up and drop off passengers along the way – an expansive vision for aviation in 1932. But with the *Akron* flying, and the *Macon* only six months away from completion, it didn't seem fanciful.

The McNary bill was finally scheduled for a Senate vote in March 1933.[2] In the meantime, airship competition was heating up. Ralph Upson's Aircraft Development Corporation announced a proposal to build a metal-clad airship carrying passengers between the United States, Puerto Rico and South America with stops along the way. The plan was speculative, but not unreasonable. Pan American Airways was eyeing a similar route for its clipper service. Additionally, the *Graf Zeppelin* was making monthly scheduled flights between Frankfurt and Rio de Janeiro.

One way to think of the *Graf* is as the Concorde of her day. The steep cost of a round trip made her a status symbol, but the real reason people paid such an exorbitant price was for speed not luxury. The *Graf* could travel from Germany to South America in fewer than three days, when the fastest ocean liner took nearly a week. In contrast, no aeroplane could come close to the *Graf* in terms of distance covered – though the gap was narrowing. Meanwhile, Litchfield had waited four years for the McNary bill to be voted on in the Senate – a long time to wait for what he wanted. Until it did, the *Graf* had the market to herself.

History suggests Litchfield's desire to build commercial airships was misguided but that's not totally fair. For one thing, airships made economic sense. According to Hunsaker's analysis, an airship's operating cost per passenger mile was comparable to those of a first-class ocean liner. Importantly, an airship could cross oceans more economically than an aeroplane. Of course, American commercial airships would be dependent on revenue from airmail and cargo until passenger traffic picked up, but Hunsaker estimated it would take only a few years before there was enough demand for twice-weekly flights across the Atlantic.[3]

If this seems optimistic, consider Hunsaker's analysis of transatlantic steamship travel. Between 1924 and 1932 an average of a million passengers per year crossed the Atlantic by ocean liner. About 100,000 of these, or 10 per cent, travelled first class. Of these, more than half paid extra fares to travel on the fastest liners, while 43 per cent paid a premium for superior accommodation. Additionally, 5 per cent of first-class passengers suffered severe sickness, while another 5 per cent wanted to get to their destination in a hurry.[4] These were ideal targets for airship travel.

According to Hunsaker, if the International Zeppelin Transport Corporation could siphon the cream from first-class ocean liners it could keep three airships flying at 75 per cent capacity with a fourth in reserve.[5] Additionally, Hunsaker's estimated profit margin of 14.5 per cent was enticing. These were reasonable assumptions so long as airships flew a heavily trafficked route such as America to Europe. But the McNary bill had to pass to make this plan work. Without it, the entire scheme collapsed.

Obviously, an airship ticket would not come cheap. In the case of the *Graf*, passengers paid nearly $600* to fly from Germany to Brazil – more than twice the cost of a first-class ocean liner berth. But Hunsaker believed the elite class of airship traveller wouldn't be price sensitive.**

If economics, luxury and speed were one aspect of a commercial airship's appeal, the other was their safety record. As both Goodyear and the Navy repeatedly pointed out, Zeppelins were the safest form of transportation in the world. Airship technology and operating practice had reached a point by 1933 that people thought them both proven and reliable.

---

*   Approximately, $11,000 in today's dollars.
**   There was only one class of travel aboard an airship, just as there was only one class of travel on Concorde: premium.

Germany's flagship, the *Graf Zeppelin*, was already in her second year of regularly scheduled passenger service. She'd not only managed to circle the world in twelve days, twelve hours and thirteen minutes* but had crossed the ocean 144 times.[6] Despite hurricanes, typhoons, Atlantic squalls and fierce thunderstorms not one passenger had been injured.[7] In 1932 alone, the *Graf* made nine round-trip voyages between Germany and Brazil. By the time she was taken out of service in 1937, the *Graf* had racked up 590 flights, carrying paying passengers over a million miles.[8] No wonder rigid airships were seen as the future of long-distance transportation.

Goodyear's commercial blimp fleet had an equally admirable safety record. From 1925 to 1932, Goodyear blimps carried 93,000 passengers more than a million miles without incident.**,[9] Even when taking into account the total number of people who'd died flying aboard either a commercial or military airship between the end of the First World War and the *Hindenburg* in 1937, the number was only 329.[10] For perspective, far more Americans die in automobile accidents over a holiday weekend than they did in the entire history of LTA flight.

It's also important to note that while the *Graf* was busy chalking up firsts, aeroplanes, trains, cars and ocean liners were involved in one disaster after another. One of the more horrific sinkings, the *Morro Castle*, killed 134 people in 1934 – far more than any single airship disaster. Railroads experienced similar catastrophes. A single train crash in Nashville, Tennessee, killed 101 passengers in 1918. This is twenty-eight more than died aboard the *Akron* and one quarter of all recorded airship fatalities. Yet people continued boarding trains and ocean liners without hesitation.

People forget that aeroplane crashes were far more common in 1933 than ship or train disasters. The only reason planes didn't kill more people is that

---

*   It's important to note that this was time spent in the air. The flight itself was broken into legs, with time spent on the ground in between. As a result, the total length of the voyage was twenty-one days, five hours and fifty-four minutes – still an amazing accomplishment.

**   In a speech in 1933, Goodyear-Zeppelin's Vice President, J.C. Hunsaker, claimed Goodyear blimps had made 43,201 flights, flying 1,336,723 miles while carrying 104,671 passengers without a single injury. Of course, he neglected to include the *Wingfoot Air Express* in these statistics. As a result, one shouldn't lend total credence to either Hunsaker, Arnstein or Rosendahl's safety stats. All three's livelihood depended upon their defending airship safety, resulting in bias. This may explain why their numbers don't always add up and almost never include deaths incurred by the ground crew that serviced airships. Nevertheless, rigid airships had a remarkable safety record compared with other modes of transport, so their safety statistics can be taken as directionally accurate.

that they couldn't carry that many. Road safety fared little better: nearly 30,000 people died in car accidents in 1933.[11] In fact, no mode of transportation killed more people than the automobile, and yet many preferred travelling by car.

Of course, even the casual observer will note that, despite their impressive safety record, there was no shortage of airship disasters. By 1930, these included the UK's *R38* (forty-four dead), the United States' *Roma* (thirty-four dead), France's *Dixmude* (fifty-two dead), the United States' *Shenandoah* (fourteen dead) and the UK's *R101* (forty-eight dead). Yet Litchfield continued to pursue airship development. The question is why?*

The history of transportation is riddled with failure. This is as true for trains, ocean liners, automobiles and aeroplanes as it was for the Apollo Moon programme, NASA's Space Shuttle and SpaceX. Litchfield planned on learning from the mistakes of others to build the safest airships ever flown; that's why the crash of the *R101* in 1930 didn't hinder him one bit. If anything, it removed the UK from the playing field, leaving Germany as his only competitor.

Goodyear's CEO was not known for taking chances. 'I do not think anyone would write me off as a hare-brained dreamer,' he said. 'I got into the field because I believed … the passenger-carrying airship … [have] great possibilities in international commerce and trade.'[12]

One should take Litchfield at his word but there was a tendency, both at Goodyear and in the Navy, to file previous airship disasters under 'lessons learned'. Whether due to structural deficiency or poor operating practice, disasters were viewed as painful interruptions along a path of continual progress – problems to be solved, not harbingers of disaster. In the case of the *Shenandoah*, her airframe was too weak to endure the rigours of a Midwestern thunderstorm. The *R38* was similarly deficient. In both cases, safety concerns were thought to have been addressed until the next calamity proved the designers wrong.

---

*   Some critics say the reason rigid airships never caught on was the spectacular nature of their crashes, but the *Titanic* sinking was no less spectacular than the *Hindenburg*, yet ocean liners dominated long-distance travel for another forty years. Other critics point to the public's fear of flying as a reason for airships' failure, yet commercial airline travel has operated successfully for more than sixty years. The real reason the rigid airship did not succeed wasn't their spectacular crashes but their poor economics. In the long run, they could not compete with alternate forms of transportation. This is why they continue to struggle today.

The *Los Angeles'* unprecedented flight record reinforced Litchfield's confidence. Not only had the *Los Angeles* been flying for eight years, but she'd completed a transatlantic voyage and two transcontinental flights: one east–west to California, the other north–south to Panama.

Unfortunately, a certain amount of confidence was endemic to airship design. Neither Litchfield, Moffett nor Arnstein realised there were conditions an airship might encounter in flight that lay beyond their understanding. Their hubris, mixed with equal measures of courage, determination and stubbornness, would prove a deadly combination.

Litchfield must have breathed a sigh of relief when the McNary bill was finally scheduled for a Senate vote on the morning of 2 March 1933. Although the lame-duck Congress would break for recess two days later, it was plenty of time to win approval.

The first order of business the day of the vote was for the Senate chair to recognise the bill's author, Senator McNary. But the usual chair was absent that morning. When his stand-in recognised a different senator, McNary lost his opportunity to call for a vote. This left only one more day before the Senate recess. But when Senator Thomas J. Walsh (D, Montana) died unexpectedly, the Senate adjourned a day early,[13] ensuring the McNary bill never even came up for a vote.

You'd think Litchfield would have been furious. After all, he'd been trying to get the McNary bill through Congress for four years. And yet it's odd how he glosses over it in his autobiography, saying the McNary bill 'slipped the mind' of the temporary chair.[14] That the temporary chair would make this mistake given he was the Senator from Goodyear's home state of Ohio beggars belief. After all, Goodyear officials had travelled to Washington specifically to oversee the vote.[15] What the heck went wrong?

Litchfield had been pursuing his commercial airship dream for twelve years. He'd spearheaded negotiations with Luftschiffbau Zeppelin, staffed up Goodyear-Zeppelin at considerable expense and competed twice for the Navy's rigid airship business. Six years later, he still found himself without the linchpin legislation he needed to make commercial airships a success.

As it turned out, this was the least of Litchfield's problems; for one month after the Senate failed to pass the McNary bill, the *Akron* crashed off the coast of New Jersey. Suddenly, Litchfield's dream of building commercial airships, indeed his dream of building any airships at all, hung by a thread. Given the many obstacles he'd overcome, it must have been a bitter pill to swallow.

You don't get to be head of an industrial colossus without experiencing setbacks, which is why Litchfield's resiliency was as remarkable as his determination. But Litchfield was not a patient man. He was determined to build commercial airships no matter what. And nothing, not the defeat of the McNary bill, nor the *Akron*'s astronomical death toll, was going to stop him.

16

AIRSHIP FEVER

Litchfield could have given up his quest after the *Akron* disaster. But instead he remained convinced that commercial airships could do for the twentieth century what railroads had done for the nineteenth. He may also have suffered from sunk cost fallacy, meaning he was reluctant to abandon his airship strategy after investing so much money. Still, it's remarkable how Litchfield refused to take his foot off the gas pedal. To understand why, you have to appreciate the environment he was operating in: the world was suffering from a serious case of airship fever.

One reason people were so enthusiastic about airships was their steady drumbeat of firsts. These included the first airship to cross the Atlantic (1919), the first airship to reach the North Pole (1926) and the first airship to circumnavigate the globe (1929). In some but not all these cases, an airship achieved its first before an aeroplane. In those instances where an airship came second, it appeared a more robust technology, travelling farther, staying aloft longer and carrying more passengers than fixed-wing aircraft.

For example, Alcock and Brown were first to fly across the Atlantic, doing so in an aeroplane. But three weeks later the *R34* crossed the Atlantic both ways carrying passengers, while Alcock and Brown's plane could only carry the two of them, took the shortest route possible (Newfoundland to Ireland) and crashed upon landing. No aeroplane would come close to replicating the *R34*'s round trip from the UK to the United States for another twenty years.

Airship fever was not only fuelled by big rigids crossing the Atlantic but by efforts to reach the North Pole as well. Several aeronauts had tried conquering the Pole by balloon*, the most famous being S.A. Andrée. Andrée, a Swedish

---

*   Including Walter Wellman, whose epigraph appears at the beginning of this book.

adventurer, made his attempt in 1897, only to disappear without a trace. Thirty-three years later the bodies of Andrée and his two companions were discovered on a remote, fog-shrouded island south of the Arctic Circle. A journal found on one of the men's bodies explained what happened. Andrée not only didn't reach the Pole; he was airborne for fewer than three days before his leaky balloon crashed on the ice cap. Incredibly, a camera was also recovered. When its photographs were developed they showed Andrée standing next to his deflated balloon in an ice-filled wasteland.

The US Navy announced its own attempt to reach the North Pole in 1923 using the *Shenandoah*.[1] However, the expedition was cancelled when President Coolidge deemed it 'too dangerous'.[2] Three expeditions claimed to have been first to reach the North Pole: one led by Frederick Cook (1908), another by Robert Peary (1909) and the third by Navy Commander Richard E. Byrd (1926). But all three claims have been called into question. The first undertaking to indisputably reach the North Pole was the Amundsen-Ellsworth-Nobile expedition, which did so by airship.

Flying in the semi-rigid *Norge*, the Rome to Nome expedition was even more surprising given how temperamentally different its three leaders were. Roald Amundsen was a Norwegian explorer who'd led the first expedition to reach the South Pole in 1911. Reserved to the point of being chilly, Amundsen was a man of few words. In contrast, Umberto Nobile was an excitable Italian general who insisted on travelling with his little dog, Titina. Meanwhile, Lincoln Ellsworth, the young, handsome and fabulously wealthy American socialite, was the perfect blend of Jazz Age sophisticate and Indiana Jones adventurer. The difference in the three men's temperaments led to a number of disagreements, exacerbated by Titina's non-stop yapping in the control car. How they co-operated long enough to succeed was an achievement in itself, but succeed they did. Early the morning of 12 May 1926 they dropped the Italian, American and Norwegian flags out the *Norge*'s control car window, making theirs the first verified expedition to reach the Pole.

It's important to remember that a trip to the Pole was as exotic in 1926 as a rocket trip to Mars. Hollywood capitalised on the event by releasing *The Lost Zeppelin* three years later. Advertised as, 'The Greatest Thrill Picture Ever Made', the early talkie features a fictitious Navy airship, the *Explorer*, crashing at the South Pole – a prime example of how airship fever fed popular culture.

In addition to crossing the Atlantic and reaching the North Pole by air, another important first was circumnavigating the globe. The US Army Air Service belted the earth in 1924 when four of its aeroplanes making seventy-four stops took 175 days to do it. In 1929, however, Germany's *Graf*

Zeppelin circled the world carrying fifty passengers, setting both speed and distance records on each of the journey's five legs. All three of these big rigid firsts reinforced Litchfield's belief that airships were a viable means of long-distance transportation. They also whipped up public enthusiasm.

It's difficult to appreciate today just how thoroughly airships permeated the American consciousness, but from the mid-1890s through most of the 1930s, airships dominated popular culture in the same way NASA's effort to put a man on the Moon did in the 1960s, with one important caveat. Airship fever lasted twenty-five years *longer* than the Mercury, Gemini and Apollo programmes.

Strangely enough, little remains of America's national obsession today. Except for a few giant hangars in Lakehurst, New Jersey; Akron, Ohio; and Mountain View, California, the Goodyear blimp is the only vestige of a craze that once captured the American imagination.

Airship fever may be in the past, but it was an essential part of the American zeitgeist even before they began flying. Take for example an 1849 illustration by Nathaniel Currier. It depicts a group of gold miners travelling to California by dirigible. The only problem is the first airship to cross the American continent didn't do so until 1924. And yet popular media was already imagining airships as the future of transportation seventy-five years before they delivered.

The early days of science fiction played an important role in fuelling this fever. Authors such as Jules Verne and H.G. Wells penned immensely popular books about LTA flight inspired by the Montgolfier brothers, whose experiments with hot-air balloons captivated eighteenth-century France. Verne's *Around the World in 80 Days* (1870) and Wells' *The War in the Air* (1907) both featured fanciful LTA craft. As the nineteenth century melted into the twentieth, prognosticators helped spread airship fever. In 1900, *The Ladies Home Journal* predicted that by the year 2000:

> Air-Ships ... will be maintained as deadly war-vessels by all military nations. Some will transport men and goods. Others will be used by scientists making observations at great heights above the earth.[3]

That same year, *The New York World* published an illustrated supplement, *New York City as it will be in 1999*, showing no fewer than three airships crossing the East River. An even more optimistic forecast appeared in 1908 when Moses

King published *King's Dream of New York*. One of its illustrations depicts the New York City skyline teeming with airships bound for such exotic places as the North Pole and the Panama Canal. Even *Little Nemo*, one of America's first comic strips, dreamt of dirigibles during his multi-year slumber. Though none of these predictions bore any relation to reality, they reflected the public's fascination for all things *dirigeable*.

Like many popular crazes, airship fever had its loopy side. Nineteenth-century Americans spotted airships well before they existed, much like UFO sightings today. One newspaper headline in 1896 summarised the craze:

WINGED SHIP IN … SKY
CLEAVES AIR … LIKE … HUGE CONDOR
ALL SACRAMENTO SEES … NEW WONDER[4]

The only problem is there weren't any dirigibles in California during the late nineteenth century, certainly none capable of what the *San Francisco Call* reported. But just as one barking dog incites another, a wave of mysterious dirigible sightings swept the nation. Between 1896 and 1897, airship sightings appeared in such respectable papers as the *Omaha Bee*, *St Louis Post Dispatch* and *Dallas Morning News*. Some reported them as having wings, while others claimed they travelled impossible distances. Attempts to explain the sightings ran from a secretive inventor conducting tests to alien pilots from another planet. So many people were convinced the inventor Thomas Edison was behind the phenomena that he was forced to issue a statement denying it.

The most likely explanation is that journalists, more interested in selling newspapers than telling the truth, made up the stories. One article about a Kansas farmer who reported a mysterious dirigible lassoing his cow before sailing off proved to be a hoax.[5] It also marks the first time a cow being abducted by aliens was reported by a newspaper.

Evidence of our love for dirigibles can still be found if one knows where to look. There were musical theatre productions such as *The Air Ship*, which played in New York City in 1898, and *An Aerial Honeymoon* (1914), a farce about a newly married couple's wedding night aboard a big rigid. There were also popular songs with names such as 'Come Take a Trip in My Air Ship' (1904), 'Papa, Please Buy Me an Airship' (1909) and 'In an Air Ship Built for Two' (1920), mimicking the romantic possibilities on a tandem bicycle. There were Dirigible-branded oranges from California, Zeppelin bread from Ohio and a 1907 toy from Cracker Jack snack box depicting a family of bears in an airship dropping Cracker Jack boxes on hungry humans below.

The big rigid, which overlapped with the art deco movement, can be found in many of its design elements. Zeppelins not only influenced graphic artists in Germany, Russia, Japan, Canada, the UK and France but also the design of cars, buses and trucks. Additionally, people could send illustrated greeting cards with airship themes for virtually every holiday including Halloween, Thanksgiving, Christmas, New Year, Valentine's Day, Easter and St Patrick's Day. One postcard, presumably from the First World War, shows a French airship crew defecating over Germany. Not to be outdone, there's a German version as well.

As airships became more common, they began appearing on a variety of objects. There were dirigible-shaped lamps, silver-plated desk sets and Zep-patterned wallpaper. Even Jazz Age flappers wore dresses with airships on them.

Beginning with a silent film called *The Airship Destroyer* in 1909, more than fifty movies have been made featuring dirigibles. The subject proved so popular that at least five airship movies were released between 1929 and 1933, with three appearing the same year. These early films included Britain's *High Treason* (1929), depicting airships bombing New York; *The Sky Hawk* (1929), about a cowardly British pilot redeeming himself by downing a German Zeppelin; *Madam Satan* (1930), about a hedonist masquerade party aboard a big rigid; and *Dirigible* (1931), about a competition to reach the South Pole by airship. *Dirigible*, directed by Frank Capra and starring Fay Wray of *King Kong* fame, included scenes filmed aboard the *Los Angeles*. One Hollywood studio, Monogram, even featured a dirigible in its logo. Moffett could not have asked for a better advertisement for his LTA programme.

You'd expect aviation-related publications to take an interest in airships, but magazines for a general audience did as well. *The Saturday Evening Post*, *The New Yorker*, *Fortune*, *Boy's Life* and *Amazing Stories* all featured airships on their covers, often more than once. There was even a 1920s pulp called *Zeppelin Stories*, which carried nothing but airship tales for a quarter.

There was also no shortage of airship-related toys for children. A variety of tin dirigibles were sold by American, German and Japanese manufacturers including versions of the *Shenandoah*, *Los Angeles*, *Akron* and *Graf*. The real-life *Akron* even used a tin toy version of itself to weight its radio antenna in flight.

By 1924, boys could make their own dirigible using a Gilbert Erector building set whose hole-punched metal pieces resembled tiny airship girders.

Airship-shaped harmonicas, pull-toys and piggy banks were found under many a Christmas tree, as was a Zeppelin-inspired bicycle sold by Sears. There were any number of airship-related board games as well including *Zippy Zepps* and *To the North Pole by Air Ship* (which included an Italian version), and several versions of a manual dexterity game in which a child flew a tiny Zeppelin from Friedrichshafen across the Atlantic to an equally tiny mooring mast at Lakehurst. Needless to say, illustrations soon began showing Santa travelling by airship rather than a sled. Is it any wonder that 'Z for Zeppelin' began appearing in children's reading charts?

Kids weren't the only ones enchanted by airships; adults were fascinated, too. One item that continues to be popular are Zeppelin-shaped cocktail shakers. There were also airship-themed lighters, cigar cutters and ashtrays, not to mention Aero Crepe toilet paper (1911) with a dirigible on its package.

Advertising was just beginning to emerge as a mass medium when airships began flying, which is why one of the blimp's earliest applications was as a flying billboard. The UK's Mellin's Food built an airship to advertise its infant formula in 1902. *Le Petit Journal*, one of France's largest newspapers, boasted two non-rigids bearing its name. In 1909, suffragette Muriel Matters flew over London in an airship with 'Votes for Women' stencilled on its side. One year later, a Parseval airship began flying over Germany with illuminated advertisements for such products as Meyer's Coffee, Lang-Nese Cakes and Palmin coconut oil. When Boston-based Poole Piano Company couldn't afford its own airship, it printed up a series of postcards showing a blimp delivering its pianos around the city.

It didn't take long for dirigibles to graduate from billboards to print ads. Though many of these relied on airships for borrowed interest, it was hoped their cutting-edge technology would reflect positively on the product being advertised. This was the same thinking that eventually led Madison Avenue ad executives to promote a powdered orange juice substitute called Tang, associated with the US space programme.

Many manufacturers used airships to burnish their corporate image. Packard advertised its engines used by the *Shenandoah*, while Texaco and Prestone boasted its motor oil and anti-freeze kept the *Los Angeles* flying. Even a Seagram's whisky ad showing the spectacular view from a passenger airship touted: 'Luxurious air cruises of the future by men who plan beyond tomorrow.' One can only assume Litchfield drank whisky.

In addition to all this ballyhoo, airships were occasionally used to sell real estate. In 1929, the Hotel Jefferson in Birmingham, Alabama, built a dirigible mast atop its roof, as did the Rand Building in Buffalo, New York, despite neither city being on an airship route. When the Empire State Building announced its dirigible docking station in 1931, its mooring mast was already considered impractical. This may explain why the equipment necessary for operating a mooring station was never installed in the world's tallest building. Nor did any airship ever dock there, but it sure sold office space.

Airship fever wasn't limited to America. It was also rampant in countries with their own LTA programme. The UK, France, Germany, Italy, Spain, the Soviet Union, Argentina, Brazil and Japan all suffered some version of it. Naturally, Germany led the way since it had the most airship manufacturers, including Zeppelin, Parseval and Schütte-Lanz. There was Zeppelin-shaped jewellery for ladies of distinction and a 1911 ice ballet in Berlin featuring skaters dressed as dirigibles. Japan also incorporated airship motifs in its traditional crafts, including kimonos and woodblock prints.

As airship enthusiasm reached its peak during the late 1920s and early '30s, America could boast Zeppelin-shaped diners as far apart as California and Massachusetts; a Zep-themed petrol station in Los Angeles;* and a variety of Zeppelin-inspired hood ornaments from Buick, Chevrolet and Oldsmobile. Any number of airship-related souvenirs could be found, including *Graf Zeppelin* pocket watches, and *Akron* ashtrays and bookmarks made from the same Duralumin as her girders. Germany even had a Zeppelin-shaped train complete with propeller that set a land-speed record in 1931. The question remains, however, why was America fascinated by airships for so long?

There are a variety of explanations. One is that airships promised a better future – something Americans anticipated during the 1920s and longed for in the '30s. In the beginning, airships were sold to the public not just as railroads of the sky but as the key to relieving traffic congestion and pollution in cities caused by horse manure. This contributed to making dirigibles a powerful symbol of modernity. They not only promised a range of benefits; they represented the technological ascendance of America. Obviously, the public's love of airships went hand in hand with its fascination for the growing field of aviation, but something about dirigibles made them special.

---

*   The petrol station was owned by Goodyear.

The *Shenandoah*, *Los Angeles* and *Akron* especially fanned the flames. Not only did they make regular promotional appearances over major American cities, newspapers, newsreels and magazines followed their every move with bated breath. But what impressed most people about airships was their tremendous size. Big rigids weren't like anything the American public had ever seen before. Larger than most buildings, their immensity was awe inspiring. That's why they had nicknames such as 'Flying Ocean Liner', 'Dreadnought of the Skies' and 'Leviathan'.

That something so big could fly suggested man had finally conquered the law of gravity, or so he believed. In the days when large crowds regularly congregated to witness news-making events, airships not only fed a hunger for novelty, they promised a better tomorrow. Few people forgot the first time they saw an airship pass overhead for the simple reason that no other man-made moving object blotted out the sun. This made seeing a big rigid the greatest contributor to airship fever. That is until the *Akron* crashed. After that, no one in America would view airships in quite the same way again. No one that is, except Litchfield.

17

CONSEQUENCES

The year 1933 should have been a celebratory one for Litchfield, since it marked the sesquicentennial of LTA flight. But the Senate's failure to pass the McNary bill, followed by the *Akron* crash punched a gaping hole in his plans.

Most men would have scrapped Goodyear-Zeppelin as a money-losing venture, but Litchfield refused to budge. As CEO of one of America's largest, most influential companies he was used to getting his way. Still, the only means of recouping all the money he'd invested was to add commercial airships to Goodyear-Zeppelin's product line. Without them, he'd be left holding the proverbial bag.

Since the Goodyear blimp was synonymous with the tyre manufacturer, it was difficult for Litchfield to back out of the big rigid business without tarnishing the brand.* There was just too much invested financially, strategically and image-wise to cut and run. And so, like a gambler on a losing streak, Litchfield planned on winning back his losses.

It's also important to remember that Litchfield never bet the parent company on LTA flight. He was too shrewd for that. Goodyear's core business was the manufacturing and sale of tyres. The company didn't need LTA revenue to survive.

Finally, there's something to be said about the power of Litchfield's vision. A world knit together by silver-backed behemoths gliding silently across the sky was easy to fall in love with. Why else would he stick to the LTA business despite all the warning signs?

---

*   Even today, airships remain an important part of Goodyear's communications strategy.

Before the *Akron* crash, global confidence in airship travel had been on the upswing, peaking around 1929. Now the national mood soured. Newspapers rehashed every problem that had ever bedevilled Moffett's big rigid programme. They even had a name for it, 'the *Akron* jinx'.[1] Although Litchfield's dream had turned into a nightmare, it made little difference. Quitting wasn't in his nature.

When Wiley lost his uniform in the *Akron* crash, he had to file an expense report to recoup its cost.[2] However, the Navy wouldn't reimburse him until its Court of Inquiry had assigned blame for the crash.[3]

But Wiley's trials weren't over. Congress began its own investigation into the *Akron* crash the same month as the Navy released its findings. Congress didn't usually hold hearings on transportation disasters unless they were egregious but the *Akron* crash, like the *Titanic* sinking, received special attention because of its record number of fatalities.

The Joint Committee to Investigate Dirigible Disasters was not only determined to get to the bottom of why the *Akron* crashed, but parse the future of airships. The committee's five senators and five congressmen claimed the hearings would be free of Navy influence. Maybe, but eight of its ten members were known to be hostile to airships including its Chairman, Senator William H. King, a Utah Democrat.

The hearings began on 22 May 1933 and lasted for two and a half weeks. The *New York Times* barely covered the proceedings as a steady stream of grim economic news pushed them off the front page. Yet, the congressional hearings generated far more sparks than the Navy's Court of Inquiry.

The King Committee, as it was known, called fifty-six witnesses – far more than the naval proceedings. Wiley, Arnstein and Hunsaker were among those who testified. One witness, Fred S. Hardesty, a consulting engineer with an interest in airships, said the *Akron* was too heavy, which made her unsafe. He also claimed, 'Dr Arnstein never designed an airship until he came [to the United States].'[4] But charges of structural weakness were lost in a haze of conflicting testimony. As it turned out, Hardesty had a point about the *Akron*'s structural integrity. But his credibility was undermined because of a patent dispute he was involved in between Schütte-Lanz and Luftschiffbau Zeppelin. No one took him seriously.

In contrast, Charles Lindbergh, first to fly solo across the Atlantic, was more optimistic about the future of airships.[5] Telling the committee that, 'HTA and LTA development is comparatively new,' Lindbergh went on to say, 'I do not believe that we can expect, in a single generation … to be able to decide … which one will … be most advantageous … The major portion of development lies ahead.'[6]

The King hearings generated 2,500 pages of testimony. When it issued its findings on 14 June 1933 airship naysayers were stunned. The report not only gave rigid airships a clean bill of health but called upon the Navy to build a bigger replacement for the *Akron*. Additionally, the report recommended recommissioning the *Los Angeles* as an LTA training vessel until such time as a moderately sized, rigid airship could be built to replace her. The committee also recommended keeping Lakehurst Naval Air Station open even though the Chief of Naval Operations had announced its impending closure. In other words, the committee saw a far more robust future for the American airship than Congress or the Navy.

When it came to assigning blame for the loss of the *Akron*, the report was even more surprising. Agreeing with the naval Court of Inquiry that weather played an important role, the committee called into question the professionalism of the *Akron*'s senior officers. 'Had there been more experienced and better trained men in command the disaster probably would not have occurred,' the report stated.[7] The findings also criticised the Navy for its high turnover of airship captains, citing the *Akron*'s three COs in eighteen months and the *Los Angeles*' seven in eight years as examples.

This was a glaring problem for Moffett's LTA programme. Terming the rotation of airship officers to sea duty 'mistaken', the report called for the Navy to correct the policy or be penalised.[8]

Although the findings didn't address whether the *Akron* was structurally deficient, the report blamed the crash as much on the Navy as the weather. This was progress when compared with the Navy Court of Inquiry. Importantly, the committee believed in the future of the American airship, implying the loss of the *Akron* was the price the country paid for innovation.

In a surprising show of unanimity, eight of the ten committee members signed the final report. One member, Representative Dow W. Harter (D) of Ohio, said he was 'more than pleased' with its findings.[9] This makes sense given Harter's home district was Akron, Ohio. If implemented, the findings would mean more money for Goodyear, one of his district's biggest employers.

However, not all committee members were happy with the findings. Neither Chairman King nor Senator Hiram Johnson (R) of California would sign the report. They not only doubted that the Navy's big rigids were safe but questioned the need for airships.

One wonders how the committee's findings could have been so out of step with prevailing opinion. Many in the Navy, Congress, media and the private sector were sure the *Akron* loss spelled the end of big rigids but the committee's report was a stunning turnabout.

One explanation is that the government needed to keep money flowing to regions hard hit by the Depression. This included Akron, Ohio, and Lakehurst, New Jersey, both of which had representatives on the committee. The Navy's sunk cost of approximately $40 million in its LTA programme was probably another consideration.[10] It's also possible that committee members were swayed by the testimony they heard, deciding naval airships deserved another chance. Whatever the reason, the findings granted airship supporters a new lease on life.

Advocates for Moffett's LTA programme were found where you'd expect them. Both Goodyear and the BUAER continued to be ardent supporters. After Roosevelt appointed Rear Admiral Ernest J. King (no relation to Senator King) to replace Moffett as Chief of the BUAER, King called for a new airship to replace the *Akron*. It's hard not to imagine Litchfield rubbing his palms together at the prospect. But Secretary Swanson stood in his way. 'For the present, there are more important matters … receiving attention,' he told reporters.[11]

The King Committee's report was encouraging, but the zeitgeist had changed. This is why Goodyear-Zeppelin struggled to find its footing in the aftermath. Less than five months after the *Akron* crash, Goodyear-Zeppelin VP, J.C. Hunsaker, gave a talk in Chicago that was mostly spin. Blaming the *Akron* loss on operator error, Hunsaker told his audience, 'Safety is already of a high order. The compartmentalization of the buoyant gas, the large dynamic lift, the adequate ballast supply, the division of power plants, [and] the redundant hull structure … give an airship a unique immunity from material or mechanical troubles.'[12] You can almost hear the eye rolling.

What's surprising is how little Goodyear executives recognised the ground beneath them had shifted. This explains why Hunsaker kept evangelising on behalf of big rigids. His safety claims were true up to a point, but his speech was tin-eared at best. Airship firsts may have captured the public's imagination but their catastrophes were equally captivating, which is why the *Akron* crash was all anybody talked about.

Despite pockets of support, the American big rigid had more foes than friends by June 1933. In response to Admiral King's desire to tap Industrial Recovery Act funds to build more airships, Carl Vinson, Chairman of the House Naval Affairs Committee, advised Secretary Swanson against it. Swanson hardly needed coaching. In a letter he sent President Roosevelt, Swanson made his opposition clear:

> In view of the sharp division of opinion in Congress … it would be unwise to request funds for building another airship. It is possible that funds may be available … but … I am strongly of the opinion … they should be applied to supplying … [aeroplanes] rather than being put into lighter than air ships.[13]

Roosevelt was more focused on alleviating the Depression than funding an unproven weapon the Navy couldn't afford. This left the future of the American airship in serious doubt. With Moffett dead, hostile elements in Congress and the Navy were determined to snuff out the programme. In other words, the future of the American rigid airship came down to its sole surviving representative, the USS *Macon*. The question remained, however: was she up to the task?

PART III

A GIANT IN TROUBLE.
USS *MACON* (ZRS-5),
1933–34

18

BUILDING THE *MACON*

The *Macon*'s crew was staying at the Anthony Wayne Hotel in downtown Akron when they heard news of the disaster. They awoke early that morning expecting to be transported by bus to the Goodyear–Zeppelin air dock, where they were preparing the *Macon* for her maiden flight. The night before, they'd receiving a blistering lecture from their captain, who reprimanded them for the naked woman found wandering their floor.[1] The last thing they expected was waking up to a tragedy.

As the *Macon*'s crew gathered in the hotel lobby, newsboys across the country were already hawking headlines that read, 'Akron Downed At Sea',[2] 'Hope Abandoned'[3] and '74 Feared Lost'.[4] Word of the disaster spread quickly among the men as they fought to read the newspaper over one another's shoulders. One enlisted man, exiting the elevator, stopped short when he saw his colleagues.

'What's happened?'

When told the news, he slipped his sailor's cap off his head and collapsed in a chair repeating, 'Oh, God, oh, God.'[5]

When the *Macon*'s watch and materials officer, Lt (jg) George W. Campbell, heard what had happened, he rushed from the hotel to the newsroom of the *Akron Beacon Journal* hoping to read the ticker-tape updates.[6] Initial reports were confusing. No one knew why the airship had crashed. The local paper reported the *Akron* had been struck by lightning.[7] This proved incorrect, but the only thing early reports agreed on was that there'd been a heavy loss of life.

The LTA community was small and tight knit. Many of the *Macon*'s crew had served aboard the *Akron* with those that had died. The men not only lived near one another on base or in Lakehurst; they socialised, married into each other's families and watched their children play together. Since lighter-than-air flight was the centre of their world, the loss not only stunned them, but gave them survivor's guilt.

Litchfield was in Arizona when reporters caught up with him. Expressing sympathy for families of the *Akron* crew, he said Goodyear would co-operate with any investigation. Then he hurried back to company headquarters.

President Roosevelt issued a statement that day saying he 'grieved with the nation' over the loss of the *Akron*.[8] In contrast, Dr Arnstein was so dazed by the news he avoided reporters. Finally emerging that afternoon, he told them in a quavering voice, 'We are at a loss to understand what might have caused the wreck … Naturally I cannot indulge in speculation.'[9]

Dresel, the *Macon*'s commanding officer, was surprisingly fatalistic in his response, especially since he'd once skippered the *Akron*. Refusing to second guess the reason for the crash, he told reporters, 'These things must happen …'[10]

Although Litchfield's hometown newspaper praised him for striving 'mightily to advance the progress of Goodyear in the lighter than air field', the editorial read more like a eulogy than a compliment.[11] What it didn't say was that the *Akron* crash changed everything.

A joke allegedly went round after the *Akron* crash: 'Don't worry. There's another one.'[12] If true, it wasn't funny. Still, it's fortunate the *Macon* had been christened by the time the *Akron* was lost otherwise she might have been cancelled. As things stood, the future of Moffett's rigid airship programme was in serious doubt, as were Litchfield's carefully laid plans to build commercial airships.

The *Akron* crash cast a long shadow over the *Macon*, which had been playing second fiddle to her first-born sister from the start. For example, assembly work couldn't begin on the *Macon* until the *Akron* vacated the Air Dock. This didn't happen until October 1931. In the meantime, Goodyear-Zeppelin started manufacturing girders for the *Macon*'s airframe that summer. The process commenced with feeding Duralumin sheets, 6 to 9in wide, into a giant press that punched up to three different-sized holes in them. The holes reduced weight by up to two-thirds, while the press flanged their edges (i.e. turned them inward) for added strength. Next, the metal was anodised and varnished to resist corrosion. After that, four sheets were riveted together to form a box-shaped girder.[13] The *Macon*'s four-sided girders were an Arnstein innovation. He'd used a three-sided version for the *Los Angeles* but had come to realise that four-sided girders were stronger.

The *Macon*'s twelve main rings (or main frames as the Navy called them) were the first part of the airship to be assembled. Acting like the bands of a barrel, they held her hull together. Building the rings was no small task given the central one was fourteen storeys tall and so heavy it had to be built lying on the floor.[*,14] This highlights the contradiction at the heart of a big rigid. They have to be built strong enough to carry the aerodynamic loads encountered in flight, but not so heavy they can't get off the ground. This means strength and weight are in constant conflict with their need to be lighter than air. In the *Macon*'s case, she weighed an astonishing 400,000lb, yet when filled with helium was still light enough to fly. That something as big as the *Macon* could float in the air struck some people as miraculous, but it was nothing more than science, chemistry and smart engineering.

Once the *Macon*'s first ring was assembled it was hoisted upright on to scaffolding. Next, a second main ring was raised approximately 74ft from the first. Then, three intermediate rings were placed between the two main rings after which thirty-six longitudinal girders were used to connect them. Since the *Macon*'s construction was modular, a two-ring bay had to be completed before the next ring could be hoisted into place and the whole painstaking process repeated.[15]

The numbering of the *Macon*'s main rings could be confusing. Goodyear-Zeppelin used metres instead of feet to measure the space between main rings; a practice Arnstein had used when building Zeppelins in Germany. Importantly, a main ring's number was based on its distance from the 0 ring, which was by the rudder post in the stern.[**] For example, main ring 17.5 was 17.5m (or 57ft) from the 0 ring, hence its designation.[16] The closer a ring was to the bow, the larger its number.

The *Macon*'s rings were so large her crew used them like a giant ladder to climb about the airship, except in the bow and stern where the narrowing of her hull made the diameter of her rings much smaller.

Hundreds of men swarmed over the *Macon* as she was assembled bay by bay. Whether dangling down her hull on rope chairs suspended from the ceiling

---

*   It weighed 4,000lb.
**   The numbering of the *Macon*'s twelve main rings from stern to bow was: 0, 17.5, 35, 57.5, 80, 102.5, 125, 147.5, 170, 187.5, 198.75, 210.75.

or scrambling across scaffolding built up from the floor, the Air Dock hummed with activity as the airship's oval-shaped silhouette began to emerge.

Among the more unusual aspects of building the *Macon* was the impossibly long ladders used to reach the outside of the ship. Each ladder, 85ft in length, was made in Germany out of Oregon spruce.[17] Dubbed 'pie racks' because of their resemblance to the cooling shelves found in bakeries, the extension ladders were mounted on a four-wheeled wagon for easy movement. The ladders never rested against the side of the airship, as she couldn't support their weight. Instead, the wagon wheels were locked and a wooden brace extended to hold the ladder in place. These ladders were not only steep, however, they also had a tendency to sway. But this didn't bother Goodyear workers. At a time when Akron's unemployment rate was a staggering 60 percent, they were grateful to have a job.

Goodyear-Zeppelin employees took pride in their work not just because they were skilled, but because they were building something special. They shared Litchfield's vision for a fleet of American-flagged airships spanning the globe. Better yet, they were building one with their own hands.

Assembling the *Macon* could be as tedious as it was exhilarating – exhilarating because few men had built anything as magnificent; tedious because the work was so exacting, inspectors used a magnifying glass to spot imperfections.[18] For example, each one of the 6.5 million rivets[19] used to hold her girders together had to be heated before being squeezed into place using a specially built tool that looked like a conductor's ticket punch.[20] If a rivet cooled before being pressed into place, its alloy crystallised, rendering it useless. When this happened, the rivet was melted down, recast and the installation process repeated.[21]

One important difference between the *Macon* and her sister was the amount of ballyhoo she received. Since the *Akron* was the first of her kind, Moffett drove a gold rivet in front of 30,000 people, as part of her ring-laying ceremony. For perspective, 30,000 people was greater than a capacity crowd watching the Dodgers baseball team play at Ebbets Field. The event was even broadcast live to a nationwide radio audience.[22] But the *Macon* never had a ring-laying ceremony, which helped cement her status as second in line.

If the *Macon* had been a person, she'd probably have resented all the attention her older sibling got. For instance, the Air Dock was open on weekends so the public could watch the *Akron* take shape. By comparison, the *Macon*'s ring-raising ceremony was so spare the public wasn't even invited. It wasn't that the *Macon* didn't get publicity. Hugh Allen's PR machine worked overtime pumping out short films, articles and press releases promoting her. Many of these items made such good copy they were reprinted verbatim in newspapers. Additionally, Moffett and Arnstein gave speeches and wrote articles for leading newspapers and magazines promoting rigid airships. Despite all this, the *Macon* suffered from middle-child syndrome.

On the positive side, construction went faster on the *Macon*, in part because Goodyear-Zeppelin had already cut its teeth building her sister. For example, it took only forty-five minutes to hoist the *Macon*'s first ring into place, compared to three days for the *Akron*, despite the latter having twice as many workers.[23]

By the time the *Macon* was ready for her bow-raising on 4 July 1932, she was three-quarters complete.[24] Fifteen thousand people attended the ceremony. Among those gathered was a delegation from Macon, Georgia, including the city's mayor and a female reporter from the *Macon Telegraph*. After the reporter blew a whistle, workmen hoisted the airship's bow into place, the last step in assembling the *Macon*'s airframe before interior work began. It had been a year since work had started, but more surprising than the speed with which the *Macon* was built was that she almost never got built at all.

A clause in the Congressional Appropriations Act of 1929 allowed the Navy to cancel the *Macon* any time before her sister ship was commissioned. A 1930 memo to Moffett from Commander Garland Fulton, Chief of BUAER's LTA design section, said, 'so far as is known, there is no intention on the part of the Secretary [of the Navy] to cancel the second airship'.[25] But enough rumours were swirling by 1931 that Litchfield and Moffett were worried. As Commander Rosendahl put it, 'There was emphatic agitation, both open and undercover, to cancel the contract for the second [airship] … Only great effort and ingenuity on the part of … Admiral Moffett kept the (*Macon*) from being cancelled.'[26]

One reason Litchfield was keen to build the *Macon* is that it enabled him to keep a nucleus of airship workers employed on the Navy's dime. These men could be redeployed to design and manufacture commercial airships for the private sector. But Litchfield faced a quandary. If he began construction on the *Macon* and the Navy cancelled her, he would be stuck with part of the cost. If he delayed too long, however, Goodyear couldn't enjoy the economies of scale that came from building two airships, one right after the other.

Moffett faced the opposite dilemma. If Goodyear didn't delay building the *Macon*, he wouldn't be able to apply what was learned from the *Akron*'s flight

operations to improving the *Macon's* design. But the longer Moffett waited
to build the *Akron's* sister, the easier it would be for Congress to cancel the
project. He was damned if he did and damned if he didn't.

Moffett chose to build the *Macon* as quickly as possible, but conflicting pri-
orities put a strain on the Goodyear-Navy partnership. For example, Litchfield
cut the *Macon's* workforce in half to reduce costs during the Depression but
this contributed to Moffett feeling Goodyear was dragging its feet.[27] Some of
the staff reduction can be attributed to efficiencies gained by building a dupli-
cate ship, but it was also important for Goodyear to reduce expenses when
revenue was plummeting.

At the same time the *Macon* ran the threat of being cancelled, Moffett was
lobbying to increase her size. In April 1931, he sent a memo to Secretary of
the Navy, Charles F. Adams III, proposing a 74ft section be added to increase
the *Macon's* range by 25 per cent and lifting capacity by another 40,000lb. This
made sense for a long-range scout but meant construction would take longer
than planned.[28]

Arnstein was confident he could accommodate the size increase, but his boss
was less than enthusiastic. Litchfield had grown impatient watching Goodyear-
Zeppelin bleed red ink. Enlarging the *Macon* not only meant further delays
but going deeper into the red.

The issue came down to cost. The size increase, estimated at between
$300,000 and $400,000, was no small change for 1931. When it crept up to
$500,000 a year later, both the Secretary of the Navy and the Chief of Naval
Operations baulked at the price. This meant Moffett had to find another way
to fund the increase if he wanted to make the airship bigger. One idea was
to give the *Los Angeles* to Goodyear as a passenger airship in exchange for
making the *Macon* bigger.[29] Another was to sell the *Los Angeles* to the city
of Chicago for its 1933 World's Fair. Even Howard Hughes telegraphed the
BUAER expressing interest in buying the airship.[30]

Moffett considered $500,000 a fair price for the *Los Angeles*, but nobody
wanted to pay that much. And so the *Macon* remained her original size.

These were just some of the dilemmas Moffett and Litchfield faced building the *Macon*, but the greatest threat came from congressional budget cuts.
These were so severe the Navy mothballed the *Los Angeles* in June 1932 as a
cost-savings measure. Her helium alone (always an airship's biggest expense)
saved the Navy $250,000 a year.[31] Since the *Los Angeles* trained airship crews,

her mothballing didn't bode well for the future of big rigids in the Navy. There were even rumours the *Akron* would be laid up to save money once the *Macon* was commissioned.

Big rigids may have been cheaper to build and operate than the heavy cruisers the Navy used for scouting, but Moffett felt the squeeze. As the *New York Times* noted, 'With Naval aviation appropriations severely curtailed ... the immediate future of the flying fleet is not considered bright.'[32]

After the *Akron* was commissioned, Dr Arnstein wrote, 'Any man who has built a house is apt to think afterward of a number of things he would have done differently.'[33]

Arnstein was putting a good face on the situation. The truth was, not everything worked as planned on the *Akron*, meaning they had to be fixed on her sister. The *Macon* required enough modifications that it put a strain on the two organisations. This was especially true when the Navy nickel and dimed Goodyear over who paid for the changes.

There were close to 100 differences between the *Macon* and her sister, proving that even identical twins have their oddities.[34] Most were minor, but it still meant that new parts had to be designed, new stress calculations done, new tests conducted and new schematics issued. The biggest fights involved anything that increased the weight of the airship, since the BUAER approved the design of every girder, grommet and gusset. Goodyear usually lost these battles, making for a painful, time-consuming and expensive struggle.

Fortunately for Goodyear, the *Macon*'s construction followed so quickly on the heels of the *Akron* that no major alterations could be made to her design. Nevertheless, cost overruns were inevitable. Group Change Order No. 1 issued on 1 August 1932 listed fifty-eight individual changes to the *Macon* totalling $86,267.50.[35] There were to be nearly two dozen such change orders.[36] Goodyear, like many contractors, ended up eating some of these costs, which is why it considered the BUAER's approval process both burdensome and unfair. But Goodyear–Zeppelin had to accede to its client's wishes if it wanted to be in the airship business, which made for an uneven power dynamic.

Almost everything about the *Macon* was political, including her naming. The public had its own ideas about what to call her. A lady from Dayton, Ohio, suggested the airship be named *The Lindbergh* after the famous flier, while a man in Albuquerque, New Mexico, wanted to call her the *Palo Alto* because that's where President Hoover once lived. Other suggestions included the *Washington, Mount Vernon, Edison, Zenith* and *Fechet*.[37] *Fechet* was a particularly unusual choice since it was the name of Major General James Edmond Fechet, Chief of the Army Air Corps. Given the intense rivalry between naval aviators and Army flyers, the moniker was dead on arrival.

Protocol dictated that cruisers be named after cities, but many were bewildered when Representative Carl Vinson announced *Macon* as her name[38] since many larger, more influential cities had vied for the honour.[39] The reason was political. Macon, Georgia, was the largest city in Vinson's district. Since Vinson was Chairman of the House Naval Affairs Committee, which oversaw funding for Moffett's airship programme, it was a way of currying favour with the man who held the purse strings. It also didn't hurt that Vinson was up for re-election.

Once the *Macon*'s airframe was assembled, twelve giant gas cells, each shaped like a lozenge, were hung inside the ship. The cells varied in size depending on where they were located. The largest, in the centre of the ship, contained 980,000 cu ft of helium; the smallest, near the bow and stern, contained a tenth as much. Hung between two main rings for support, the *Macon*'s gas cells were made out of 55,000 sq yd of canvas impregnated with a gelatin-latex to keep them from leaking. Had they been made out of the intestinal lining of cattle, as they were on the *Los Angeles*, more than 1.5 million cows would have had to be sacrificed.[40]

Filling the *Macon*'s gas cells with helium was akin to a ship being launched at sea; it proved she could fulfil her most basic function – to float. During this time, the *Macon*'s cotton canvas covering was laced into place. After being tightened several times, it was painted with multiple layers of dope, making it waterproof. The last two layers, mixed with aluminium pigment, gave her a silver hue to reflect the sun's rays. This was necessary because if her helium became too warm its molecules expanded to the point the airship became too light to control.

Although construction of the *Macon* went faster than her sister, she missed her contract delivery date by three months. She might have been finished sooner had it not been for all the change orders, but at least she hadn't been cancelled. By the time the *Macon* was ready for christening, her sister had less than a month to live. She wouldn't have to play second fiddle much longer, but when she was finally cast into the national spotlight it would be for the worst possible reason.

19

CHRISTENING

When the *Akron* was christened in August 1931, 100,000 people turned out to watch despite the sweltering heat. In contrast, only 5,000 people attended the *Macon*'s official naming ceremony – proof the second child never gets the same fuss made over it as the first.[1]

Admiral Moffett and his wife travelled from Washington to Ohio by train, arriving in Akron for the festivities on the morning of 11 March 1933. Litchfield hosted a lunch for the admiral and his wife that afternoon, grateful for everything he'd done to support Goodyear's rigid airship aspirations. It quickly became apparent that the day-long festivities weren't just to celebrate the *Macon* but Moffett as well. Given the admiral was only six months from retirement it was as much his day as Goodyear's.

Still, the christening was a decidedly threadbare affair. A fierce wind[2] blew snow flurries[3] outside the Air Dock as cars lined up in front of the main gate. Invited guests bought hot coffee from a concession stand before filing inside the gigantic hangar, where they stamped their feet to keep warm. As small boys, surprisingly conversant in the *Macon*'s technical details, chased each other around the hangar, shivering guests, some wrapped in blankets, gawked at the giant airship as she floated overhead.[4]

One oddity people noticed were the double-decker 'sky cars' in the far corner of the Air Dock. Made of metal with a bright orange stripe, the gondolas were intended for the aerial tramway at the Chicago World's Fair.[5] Not exactly lighter than air, they were a means of generating revenue, which Goodyear-Zeppelin badly needed.

While naval officers in dress blues mingled with civilians in heavy overcoats, a smattering of well-behaved Boy Scouts roamed through the crowd. In addition to a number of US Army officers, military attachés from the UK and

Japan were also present.[6] A Japanese naval officer was a surprising guest given the *Macon* was meant to prevent an attack by Japan. But the Imperial Japanese Navy had long held an interest in LTA flight, which was his excuse for being there.

There was a tradition of first ladies christening the Navy's rigid airships. Calvin Coolidge's wife had christened the *Los Angeles*, while Mrs Herbert Hoover christened the *Akron*. But Eleanor Roosevelt wasn't christening the *Macon* despite the tradition. Instead, Goodyear had Jeanette Moffett to sponsor the airship. This was a tip of the hat to Moffett for his many years of service,[7] but it was also Litchfield's way of saying thanks for the airship business.[8] Some of the Georgia delegation felt Eleanor's absence was a snub, but it didn't stop them from enjoying the festivities.[9] In fact, the citizens of Macon were so pleased at having an airship named after their city they'd sent eight 'Georgia peaches', the finest of southern womanhood, to serve as Jeanette's escort.[10]

A 300-piece brass band played 'Anchors Aweigh' as invited guests studied the *Macon*. If she looked as if she'd been assembled from a child's construction set when being built, what stood out now was her tremendous size. As one attendee put it, there was 'a feeling of pride that ... puny men had ... created the immense ... structure'.[11] But that wasn't the half of it.

Everything about the *Macon* was impressive, including her statistics. Composed of 10 million parts, 6.5 million rivets and 1,500 miles of wire to hold her Duralumin airframe together, more than 7 acres of fabric were used for her outer covering[12] and 1,000 miles of thread to stitch it all together.[13] Her blueprints alone ran to more than 1,000 pages, including schematics for every one of the 25,000 individual parts that went into her construction, making her the most complicated aircraft ever built. Each one of these parts had to be designed by Goodyear-Zeppelin's engineering team before being approved by the BUAER's LTA design section. Once fabricated, they were weighed one by one on a butcher's scale before being installed to make sure the airship didn't exceed her contract weight.

Weight was always a concern with lighter-than-air craft for the simple reason that an airship can't get off the ground if it's too heavy. Since the *Akron* was heavier than her contract allowed, the Navy mandated that the *Macon* be slimmer. This required an extraordinary attention to detail. Not only was every part fabricated from the lightest weight material available, but measures were taken to ensure that the interior parts of the airship that required painting received only a single coat.

Nevertheless, everything else about the *Macon* was oversized. For example, each one of her fins was 105ft long, 40ft high and weighed 2 tons. With the same surface area as three tennis courts,[14] a fin was so large a man could easily walk around inside of one without having to stoop. [15]

The reason the *Macon* was so breathtakingly big was she needed to contain 6.5 million cu ft of helium to stay aloft. Helium was first discovered in Kansas in 1905. First extracted in Kansas in 1905, helium was a by product of natural gas wells. Given its rarity and expense, the United States considered helium a strategic resource and refused to sell it to Germany, which is why Zeppelins relied on hydrogen as their primary lifting gas.

The Navy had initially used hydrogen for its LTA craft until 1921, when it began switching to helium. This was an improvement because helium wasn't flammable. It also meant a dirigible's engines, once located on the outside of their hull to prevent sparks from accidentally igniting their hydrogen, could now be safely located inside the airship, as on the *Akron* and *Macon*. Now, only the drive shaft, propeller, cooling and water recovery systems were housed outside the hull, greatly reducing wind resistance. This not only made the *Akron* and *Macon* faster than previous rigid airships but increased their range as well.[16]

Six and a half million of anything is a lot, but if it's hard to visualise just how much space an invisible gas takes up, 1 cu ft requires the same amount of room as a square block with 12in sides. Since 1,000 cu ft of helium is needed to lift 69lb, it's easy to understand why the 400,000lb *Macon* needed 6.5 million cu ft of the stuff to get off the ground. Incredibly, she had enough lift left over to carry an additional 173,000lb.[17]

Helium had its drawbacks. Besides being far more expensive than hydrogen, it had 7 per cent less lifting capacity.[18] This is why the Navy was obsessively weight conscious where the *Macon* was concerned. A good example of thriftiness was the custom-built signal light the *Macon* used to communicate with ships at sea. Large enough to be seen 30 miles away, it only weighed 11lb, including its shell, glass covering, light fixture and shutters.[19] This type of innovative engineering seemed more like science fiction than science fact in 1933, but it was necessary if the *Macon* was to fulfil her mission as a long-range scout.

The complexity of the *Macon*'s interlocking systems was equally mind-boggling. These systems included propulsion, exhaust ventilation, cooling, heating, water recovery, electrical generation, ballast control and steering, plus elaborate piping and pumps to move all of its ballast water and fuel.

Take the *Macon*'s flight controls. The *Macon* used two methods to steer: a rudder on her upper and lower tail fins governed her port and starboard movement, while elevators on her horizontal tail fins controlled her altitude. Both of these flight controls were connected to the bridge by cables hundreds of feet long running through a series of pulleys and sheaves to prevent them from getting slack.

The *Macon*'s propulsion system was also complicated. Composed of eight Maybach VL-2 engines imported from Germany, each one of these twelve-cylinder behemoths were nearly as tall as a man and weighed 2,500lb. Capable of generating 560hp, they were considered superior to any American-made engine on the market, much to the Navy's chagrin since it preferred American suppliers.

Given four of the *Macon*'s engines were on the port side and four on the starboard, each one required its own fuel, lubricating, cooling and exhaust system. These systems needed to work regardless of whether the airship was flying on an even keel. Since the *Macon* carried 62 tons of fuel spread across 110 tanks, electric pumps were used to keep it flowing even when the airship was flying at a nose-up angle – which she often was. Fuel tanks varying in size from 120 to 400 gallons were located near each engine compartment in pods of three. The centre tank was suspended by a single wire that could be cut, dropping it overboard when the ship needed to be lightened in an emergency.[20]

Adding to this complexity was the *Macon*'s water recovery system. The system was designed to convert engine exhaust into water to offset the weight lost from burning fuel. This was critical because the longer a dirigible flew the lighter she became. If the decrease in fuel weight wasn't offset, she'd have to vent helium, which was too expensive to waste. And so the *Macon* relied on converting engine exhaust into water ballast to compensate.

A technical innovation in its day, the water recovery infrastructure consisted of four bands of condensers, looking like solar panels, climbing up the outside of the hull. Unfortunately, the Rube Goldberg contraption never worked as planned. Not only did it make the *Akron* slower, it leaked like a sieve. In theory, the system should have recycled 145lb of water for every 100lb of fuel burned, but the reality was that only 90 to 110lb of water was recovered for every 100lb of petrol consumed.[21] Additionally, the water recovery system often stained the airship's canvas covering with long black streaks of carbon. This problem was more pronounced on the *Akron* than the *Macon*, but that didn't prevent scrubbing it off being assigned as punishment duty.

The *Macon's* ballast control was equally complex. Once the water recovery system converted engine exhaust into water, it was channelled into ballast bags throughout the ship. These bags, made of rubberised fabric, were connected by piping both to the water recovery system and to one another. This was necessary because the water had to be evenly distributed across the airship so she wouldn't be thrown off kilter. Some of the ballast bags contained a whopping 4,500lb of water, only a little less weight than the average SUV. Each bag also had a quick discharge valve operated by a wire pull in the control car in case they needed to be emptied in an emergency.[22]

Since wind, rain, snow, temperature, heat and humidity directly affected how light or heavy the *Macon* flew, the water recovery and ballast systems were critical to maintaining her equilibrium. This made for a constant balancing act as fuel was burned; its exhaust fumes converted into water; the water shifted into ballast bags; and the ballast bags emptied, filled or their water moved as needed. Add to this, the venting of helium when the airship was too light, or water ballast dumped overboard when she was too heavy, and the officers on the bridge were engaged in a never ending series of adjustments.

The crew's living quarters were functional if spartan, to keep the weight down. Concentrated in the front third of the airship – extending from the aeroplane hangar to the control car – the crew's living area took up a surprisingly small amount of space compared to the rest of the ship. The captain and first officer were the only ones to have private cabins. They were located on the port side of the airship near the control car. There were also separate sleeping quarters for officers, chief petty officers and enlisted men. The officers' quarters were located amidships near the captain's cabin, while the enlisted men's bunkrooms were on the opposite side off the starboard catwalk.

The largest of the enlisted men's bunkrooms contained twenty bunks (called racks), the smallest only eight. A rectangular piece of fabric stretched across the bunk beds' bare Duralumin frame served as a mattress. A second piece of fabric was sometimes laced between bunks for privacy. Men slept in sleeping bags, but were allowed a pillow for comfort, presumably because it didn't weigh much. Hot bunking was common, meaning two enlisted men shared the same bunk with one sleeping while the other was on duty.

The most noticeable thing about the crew's quarters was how the *Macon's* airframe divided up the space. The airship's girders cut diagonally through the bunkrooms, making the crew feel they were roosting in the metal rafters of a truss bridge. There was also a washroom containing sinks and toilets (called heads) but no showers.

The corridors in some of the crew quarters included downward-facing windows that provided a spectacular view of the earth below. A few aluminium chairs, with three of their four legs cut off at an angle so they'd conform to the curvature of the hull, were stationed by these windows and secured to the airframe so they wouldn't move in flight.

Furniture on the *Macon* (and there wasn't much) was not only durable but so lightweight you could lift it with a finger.[23] Made of Duralumin, it included desks and tables bolted to the floor, with only a few chairs and stools allowed to move freely.

Given that the *Macon* was the Navy's newest airship, everything about her was state of the art. The latest fire prevention system used carbon dioxide to protect her engines and generators, while a customised telephone system connected the control car to the duty stations on each of her three catwalks. The *Macon's* telephones had a rotary dial and a neon light to signal when someone was calling. When a crewman couldn't get through because the line was occupied, it was called 'camping on busy'.

The Navy was so weight conscious that crewmen were only allowed to bring one small footlocker regardless of how long the flight was.[24] The rectangular box was big enough for a razor, cake of soap, change of socks and underwear. Weight may have been a constant concern, but no consideration was given to how heavy a crewman was. Some of the *Macon's* enlisted men tipped the scale at over 200lb. So long as they passed their physical they were deemed fit to fly.

The *Macon* had a well-equipped galley turning out complete meals three times a day for her eighty-man crew. Sandwiches and coffee were always available for those on late-night duty, and since the food was good, no one complained. The galley was modern if tight. It included a propane-fuelled range and oven made from stainless steel, an 8.5-gallon water heater and a 7-gallon coffee urn. Given the Navy's concerns about weight, the oven, water heater and coffee urn were a single unit weighing only 140lb. There was also a refrigerator (the price of which the BUAER complained about) that used solid carbon dioxide to keep things cold. Plates and cups were made out of a new lightweight plastic called Beetleware that was advertised as unbreakable. Rubbish was sometimes dumped at sea, but there's no mention of where the sanitary tanks were emptied.

The *Macon* had not one but two generators for electricity. One powered her overhead lights, electric outlets, desk lamps, telephones, fuel pumps, ventilating fans and water and oil heaters, while the other powered her two radio transmitters. The *Macon's* interior lighting, dependent on 40-watt bulbs, was generally yellowed and subdued. At times it could be downright spooky when its hole-punched girders cast cubist shadows against the inside of her canvas covering.

Nearly 800 suppliers[25] including General Electric, Westinghouse, DuPont, Sherwin-Williams, The Republic Steel Corporation, Revere Brass and the Winchester Repeating Arms Company contributed to the *Macon's* outfitting.[26] Manufacturers took such pride in supplying the Navy's big rigids that they advertised their involvement. As one example, the Thomas A. Edison, Inc. of Orange, New Jersey, requested permission to photograph the toaster it had provided for promotional purposes. None of this was a surprise given that manufacturers benefited from their association with the most modern airship in the world.

An impressive amount of redundancy was designed into the *Macon*, all of it safety-minded. Instead of having one keel like the *Los Angeles*, the *Macon* and her sister ship had three: two in the bottom half of the airship (one portside, the other starboard) and a central keel in her upper reaches. These three keels were the airship's backbone. Running the length of the *Macon*, they were used by the crew as catwalks to traverse the ship. Impossibly narrow, they required some getting used to. Given the *Macon* was 785ft long, inspecting all three of her keels, twelve main rings, twelve gas cells and all the nooks and crannies in between easily covered half a mile.[27]

The *Macon* also had eight engines, compared with only five for the *Los Angeles*, so it wasn't a problem if one or two failed in flight. And though the *Macon* had only twelve gas cells compared to the *Los Angeles'* fourteen, they contained more than twice the helium. Importantly, the *Macon's* gas cells were designed like the watertight compartments on a ship. In the unlikely event two of her twelve gas cells failed, she could still remain aloft.[28] The *Macon* even had an auxiliary bridge in her lower tail fin in case her control car became disabled. Only 3ft wide and 15ft long, it had a back-up helm and elevator control wheel to steer the ship. It also afforded a spectacular view of the world below. No one hoped they'd ever have to use it.

Another important safety feature was Dr Arnstein's 'deep ring' structure. Used to construct both the *Akron* and *Macon*, each main ring was composed of three separate rings riveted together. The design not only made the *Macon*'s rings far stronger than those on the *Los Angeles*; they helped her endure the aerodynamic forces she encountered in flight.

In addition to all the safety-minded redundancies, the *Macon* was tested within an inch of her life. Wind tunnels estimated the load-bearing capacity of her airframe, while diffusion tests ensured her gas cells didn't leak. At one point, a wooden stand was erected in the Air Dock upon which a mighty Maybach engine was kept running for days to determine its reliability. As far as building the safest airship in the world was concerned, nothing was left to chance.

Telling the difference between the *Akron* and *Macon* was like sexing a chicken. It was hard to tell them apart. Although the *Akron* and *Macon* looked alike, there were some differences. For instance, the *Akron* had a long-standing problem with her gas cells bulging at the top. This not only made it difficult to inspect them for damage but put undue stress on the main rings between them. As a result, the ramie cord netting used to hold the *Akron*'s cells in place was redesigned for the *Macon* using a smaller, tighter mesh. This not only reduced the bulging; it gave the *Macon*'s khaki-coloured gas cells a distinctly quilted look. To reduce weight, the *Macon* also dispensed with the photo lab the *Akron* had carried, while adding additional rip panels to her outer envelope for dropping her slip tanks in an emergency.[29]

The *Macon* may have been second in line after the *Akron*, but she was faster than her sister. To improve speed, the *Macon* swapped out her two-bladed propellers made of wood for three-bladed ones made from metal. Each propeller was so long it had a 16ft diameter, making them look more like the blades of a wind turbine than a standard prop.

The propellers were an innovation in their own right since the shaft on which they were mounted could be swivelled 90 degrees like a gondolier's oar. This enabled the airships to move up or down, forward or reverse, or simply hover in place six years before Sikorsky invented his first helicopter.

The *Macon* was also streamlined to improve speed. This included changing the ventilation hoods on her roof to reduce wind resistance, adding cowling to her outriggers and moving her engine's eight radiators flush against her hull.

Not all changes to the *Macon* were an improvement. For example, the gelatin-latex used to coat her gas cells prompted mould growth, which ate away at the lining. Additionally, engine vibration in the *Akron*'s stern was so severe it not only shattered light bulbs; it was said to rattle a man's fillings right out of his mouth. Arnstein would try reducing the vibration by adding additional bracing to the stern engine rooms.[30] The problem was never eliminated, however, which is one reason why the Navy considered removing the *Macon's* No. 3 and 4 engines.

One of the oddest-looking things about the *Macon* was the cloth-covered bumper on the bottom of her control car. Used to absorb the shock of landing, it looked like a swollen blister. Its framework was made of rattan, ideal for absorbing shocks since it was strong, lightweight and flexible. Other notable features included the mooring station in her bow. This was essential to docking the airship. It included an annunciator to let the control car know how fast or slow to go, a winch to lower the mooring cable through a hatch in the bow and a gangplank the crew used to disembark. The *Macon* also had eight machine-gun emplacements: three along her upper gangway, one in the furthermost part of her tail, two in her bottom fin near the auxiliary bridge and two in the aft compartment of her control car.[31]

The *Macon* and her sister were the largest aircraft in the world when completed, but size had its benefits. One of them had a cruising range of nearly 10,000 miles. This meant she could carry her eighty-man crew for days at a time without needing to land – a remarkable achievement in 1933.*

But the most amazing thing about the *Macon* was that she carried fighter planes inside a hangar in her belly. The hangar was located in the bottom of her hull just forward of amidships. Some 76ft long, 58ft wide and 16ft high, it was capable of carrying five aeroplanes suspended on an overhead monorail – one in each corner with a fifth in the middle.** Planes were lowered through a T-shaped hatch in the hangar floor that could be slid open. The ability to house, deploy and retrieve aeroplanes in mid-flight made the *Akron* and *Macon* the world's first flying aircraft carriers. There was nothing like them in the world.

---

*   The *Macon* could easily carry more than 100 men and did so on several occasions.

**   Although the *Macon* comfortably carried four aeroplanes, she often carried only two. The fifth aeroplane made the airship hangar too crowded to easily deploy and retrieve aircraft.

When the *Macon* was finally finished she was nothing short of an engineering marvel. And now after twenty-one months of construction she was finally ready to be christened.

As the high-school band played 'Dixie', Jeanette Moffett was escorted to the viewing platform by the eight Georgia peaches, some of whom wore fur coats to keep warm. Mrs Moffett, wearing a cloche hat and carrying a large bouquet of roses, was accompanied by her husband and Litchfield. Meanwhile, a publicity-shy Dr Arnstein trailed somewhere behind.

The viewing stand, far smaller than the one used for the *Akron*'s naming ceremony, was draped in red, white and blue bunting. Two microphones were prominently positioned at the front of the platform. With the *Macon*'s bow jutting 75ft over the dais, its control car a dramatic backdrop, the scene was set for the ceremony to begin.

The Ohio Governor had cancelled at the last minute, leaving a second string of government officials to speak at the event. Litchfield served as master of ceremonies. Stumbling over the introductions, his face looked pinched, his nose reddened by the cold.[32] The Mayor of Akron's welcoming remarks were thankfully short. Then, Litchfield read a message from President Roosevelt congratulating Moffett on the *Macon*'s christening and his many years of loyal service. The Secretary of the Navy, never an airship fan, sent a telegram in place of attending. Next, the Mayor of Macon presented an enormous silver punch bowl on a serving platter. Engraved with the city's seal, it bore the inscription: 'Presented to USS *Macon* by the City of Macon, Georgia March 11, 1933.'[33] The mayor didn't realise it at the time, but his gift was too heavy to be carried aboard the airship.

Finally, at 1330 hours, Jeanette Moffett reached up to grasp the tasselled end of a red, white and blue cord hanging from the airship. As the crowd began to roar its approval, Mrs Moffett intoned the words, 'I christen thee the United States ship *Macon*.'[34]

Almost nobody heard her above the din, but it made little difference. As Jeanette pulled the rope, two hatches in the airship's bow flopped open releasing forty-eight white racing pigeons. While the pigeons made for the Air Dock's open doors, the *Macon* was allowed to rise 6ft or so before being cranked into place. Moffett, standing erect and stern-faced, saluted as the band played 'The Star-Spangled Banner'. By then, two of the forty-eight racing pigeons were on their way to Georgia bearing the message, 'The *Macon* has been christened.'[35]

The entire ceremony lasted only ten minutes, a blessing given the bitter cold. In a photograph showing Litchfield just after Mrs Moffett pulled the rope, the most noticeable thing is the huge grin on his face. Not known for smiling, Goodyear's CEO would have even less cause a few weeks later when the *Akron* crashed.

This wasn't the end of the festivities, though. A reception was held that night at the Mayflower Hotel honouring Admiral Moffett and his wife, followed by a banquet and fancy-dress ball. Nearly 500 people attended the dinner, where Moffett made a speech. Broadcast coast to coast over a radio hook-up, Moffett took the opportunity to promote commercial airships.

'The Navy's constant object has been to build the *Akron* and the *Macon* not only for naval purposes but to show the way for the commercial uses of airships,' he told his audience. 'We feel we have done our part and that it is now up to Congress to pass legislation that will make it financially practicable to build and operate commercial airships.'[36]

This was a blatant pitch to Congress to pass the McNary-Crosser bill, but Moffett didn't stop there. Refuting complaints that airships were too expensive, he noted they were far cheaper than a Navy's surface cruiser, adding, 'like all new things [airships] are received with suspicion and … ridicule'. He concluded his remarks by imploring the country not to surrender its leadership position.[37]

Moffett didn't stick around for the ball; he and Jeanette had a train to catch, so they left after the admiral finished his speech. That Jeanette Moffett should christen the same kind of airship that would kill her husband is rife with irony. That Litchfield had never been closer to achieving his dream only adds to the sting. Nevertheless, three weeks later Admiral Moffett would be dead, Jeanette Moffett a widow and the Navy's rigid airship programme fighting for its life. That night, however, all anybody wanted to do was enjoy the party.

20

TRIAL FLIGHTS

There's no denying the loss of the *Akron* cast a funereal pall over the *Macon*'s trial flights. If that wasn't bad enough, the *Macon* was not only late being delivered; she was overweight and over budget. The *Akron* had been dogged by the same issues. She even faced accusations of sabotage and poor-quality workmanship, although these were later refuted. Given the *Akron*'s tail-smashing incident, doubts about her viability had been increasing. Now that she'd crashed, those doubts shifted on to her younger sister. The *Macon* was now in a fight for her life and she hadn't even flown yet.

It didn't help that her first trial flight kept getting postponed. Originally scheduled for 21 March 1933, it was put off until 10 April because of construction delays. When the *Macon* was finally completed on 12 April (more than three months late*), her inaugural flight was set for the next day. But the landing field's soggy condition caused this to be rescheduled. Wind gusts on 14 April made for unfavourable docking conditions, while rain, fog and low visibility caused a further postponement until the 20th.

The delays may have been a blessing in disguise. It had been less than three weeks since the *Akron* crashed. As a result, newspapers were filled with accounts of the Navy Court of Inquiry and the upcoming congressional hearings. This made poor optics for the *Macon*'s trial flights, especially because no one could say why the *Akron* had crashed until the investigations were over. In the meantime, it was possible a design shortfall might plague her sister. But the Navy had no intention of grounding the *Macon*, despite the bad publicity. Eighteen days after the *Akron* was lost, the *Macon* made her first trial flight.

---

*   Her contract called for her to be completed by 21 January 1933.

The Goodyear-Zeppelin Air Dock hummed with activity in the pre-dawn hours of 21 April. Even at that early hour a wide variety of Goodyear personnel, Navy officials, newsreel cameramen, reporters and curious onlookers gathered to witness what promised to be a historic occasion. An unfortunate mishap occurred when one of the *Macon*'s ground crew lost his footing atop the mooring mast and fell 76ft to the ground. Breaking both his legs, he was rushed to hospital for X-rays.[1]

The Air Dock's twin, 600-ton doors slowly rumbled open at 0510 hours. Since the Navy would be operating the *Macon*, it assumed temporary possession of her from Goodyear. Fifteen minutes later, the giant, motorised mast began towing the airship out of the 'shed'. More than 100 men held a spider's web of handling lines as they walked the behemoth to her mooring-out circle 1,500ft away. It was so chilly you could see their breath. Meanwhile, the voice of her mooring officer, amplified by a sound truck, boomed instructions across the field.

Once the *Macon* reached the mooring-out circle, her stern was allowed to swing free. Then, at 0602 hours, with the sky beginning to redden, the *Macon*'s captain, Commander Dresel, issued the order everyone had been waiting for, 'Up ship!'

As the *Macon*'s ground handlers released the landing lines, the airship with 105 souls on board slowly rose into the sky.[2] In addition to her sixty-man crew, the *Macon* bore Goodyear's CEO, Paul W. Litchfield, as well as thirty-one employees of the Goodyear-Zeppelin Corporation, including J.C. Hunsaker and Dr Karl Arnstein. Navy representatives included the eight-man Board of Inspection and Survey. Led by Rear Admiral George C. Day, the board would determine over the course of four trial flights whether the *Macon* was ready to be commissioned in the US Navy.

Relying on static lift (e.g. helium) rather than engine power, the *Macon* floated free of her earthly constraints like a balloon released by a child. But a temperature inversion at 400ft stopped her in her tracks. Ordering four of the *Macon*'s propellers rotated downwards, Dresel used their vertical thrust to punch through the layer of warm air. Next, he began testing the *Macon*'s flight controls, beginning with the elevators on her horizontal tail fins. These were critical features, along with helium and her engines, in the airship's ability to rise or descend.

As the *Macon* flexed her elevators, the airship's stern pitched up and down. Satisfied he had attitude control, Dresel took the *Macon* up to 2,500ft, where he levelled off. After piping down landing stations, he steered the airship over Lake Erie, where he completed a series of turn manoeuvres to prove the airship could be steered. Now he brought all eight of her engines online and headed towards Cleveland.

With the sun shining overhead and Lake Erie glistening below, the *Macon* had near perfect conditions in which to perform. A ship's shakedown cruise is serious business, especially since things are expected to go wrong. Stress gauges speckled the *Macon*'s fins and airframe to measure the aerodynamic loads she experienced in flight while her crew kept a close eye on each one of her complex systems, making sure they functioned properly.[3] Meanwhile, Cleveland's morning commuters were treated to the spectacular sight of the silver-skinned goliath cruising overhead.

Big rigids were such low-flying aircraft that city sounds could be heard inside the control car. It was even possible under the right conditions to hear conversations on the ground, although the crew was under strict instruction never to hail anyone or drop a message overboard as some had in the past.[4]

As the *Macon* passed overhead, her giant shadow brought traffic to a halt. Pedestrians, feeling the sun blotted out, suddenly stopped in their tracks to stare heavenwards. At the same time, a biplane, hired by Goodyear's PR factotum, buzzed around the airship filming her inaugural flight.

As the day warmed, the air became bumpy, so Dresel kept the airship over Lake Erie. Later that afternoon, he conducted a high-speed run and achieved 80mph, just shy of the *Macon*'s contractual obligation.

Following a twelve-hour flight, Dresel headed back to the Air Dock. As the *Macon* circled the Wingfoot Lake Airship Base, her landing lights flashing in the dusk, Dresel had to wait more than an hour for the wind to die down before making a landing. By 1850 hours, the *Macon*'s bow was 'locked in the cup' and her bottom tail fin restrained to keep from banging on the ground. After that, she was towed into the Air Dock, where the Navy returned responsibility for the airship to Goodyear-Zeppelin.

News coverage of the *Macon*'s maiden voyage was overwhelmingly positive. Thanks to Hugh Allen's masterful press relations and the goodwill Moffett engendered even in death, *The Washington Post* hailed her inaugural flight as a 'striking demonstration of [the] ideals of Rear Admiral William A. Moffett'.[5]

Maybe, but the *Macon*'s trial flights had as much to do with sunk cost and face saving as Moffett's lofty ideals. No one was ready to cancel the Navy's rigid airship programme just yet; it would cause too much embarrassment given all the money that had been spent. Meanwhile, Moffett's programme hung in the balance.

The *Macon's* second flight took place two days later. It included more ascent and descent trials as well as a climb to pressure height. Among the 106 people on board was Lt Cdr George W. 'Tex' Settle, who'd supervised every aspect of the *Macon's* construction while embedded at Goodyear-Zeppelin, and the BUAER's chief airship designer, Commander Garland Fulton. Fulton was Arnstein's opposite number at the BUAER but significantly more powerful since he had the authority to approve or deny Arnstein's suggestions.

The most famous person on board that day was undoubtedly Lt Commander Wiley. 'Doc' Wiley had been unable to make the *Macon's* first trial flight because he'd been testifying at the Navy Court of Inquiry. Still, his 'temporary' assignment as a member of Admiral Day's Board of Inspection and Survey was a bit of PR wizardry.[6] If the sole surviving officer of the *Akron* crash was confident enough to fly aboard her sister ship then surely nothing was wrong with her.

Wiley kept a characteristically low profile, arriving in Akron at 0300 hours on Sunday morning. But given his celebrity he was quickly spotted at the Air Dock.

'That's him,' someone in the crowd whispered, straining to get a better look. 'That's the *Akron* officer they rescued!'[7]

One can't help but wonder what went through Wiley's mind as he boarded the *Macon*. Just three weeks earlier an icy wave had pushed him out the *Akron's* window. Now he was about to fly on her twin. Typically reticent, Wiley kept his thoughts to himself.

The *Macon's* second trial flight proceeded smoothly. Except for the occasional bumpy intermezzo caused by warm air rising from the ground, she performed admirably. After a flight of nearly thirteen hours, 75,000 people gathered to watch her land – a remarkable showing for a second outing.[8] Locked in the cup shortly after 2000 hours, the *Macon* was towed inside the Air Dock, where she was put to bed.

Admiral Day called the second flight 'very successful', while Dresel, always conservative in his pronouncements, reported the airship 'handled satisfactorily'.[9] But newspapermen were more interested in what Wiley had to say. Cornering him after the flight, they bombarded him with questions about the *Macon's* performance.

Wiley was unstinting in his praise. 'Very nice ship, very enjoyable flight,' he told the *New York Times*. 'Seems a little handier than the *Akron* and apparently is speedier,' too.[10]

Wiley was more comfortable on the bridge of an airship than talking to reporters. One newspaper described his prematurely grey hair as looking 'a shade whiter' following the *Akron* crash.[11] But there was little doubt Wiley considered the *Macon* superior to her predecessor.[12] Asked whether the *Akron*'s loss had changed his opinion about airships, Wiley answered, 'No, it has not altered my faith in lighter-than-air.'[13] The next day, he left Akron to attend the Navy Court of Inquiry at Lakehurst.

The *Macon*'s third trial flight couldn't be scheduled right away. The Navy needed to review the data it had collected from the first two flights while Goodyear made adjustments to the airship. In the meantime, Dresel travelled to Lakehurst to testify at the inquiry.[14] The *Macon* could hardly fly without her captain, but it was a reminder the jury was still out concerning the cause of the *Akron* crash.

The *Macon* remained in her air dock for nearly a month as data was studied, fixes made and inclement weather caused further delays. Finally, on 15 May, she was ready for her third trial flight.

Air conditions were exceptionally smooth that day – perfect for flying the ship at full power. At one point, the *Macon* flew 2 knots faster than she was contractually required – an encouraging sign.[15] But reports of an approaching thunderstorm cut the flight short. No one wanted to risk the *Macon* flying in the same kind of weather that had downed the *Shenandoah*. By the time rain began falling, she was safely locked in the cup.

Although no official statement would be made until her trial flights were over, members of the Navy's Inspection Board and Survey hinted to the press that the *Macon* was an improvement over her predecessor.[16] Still, pressure for her to turn in an outstanding performance was high.

Eight days after the *Macon*'s third trial flight, Admiral King sent a memo to the Chief of Naval Operations:

> While it is desirable the USS *Macon* proceed to the Pacific coast as soon as conditions warrant … in view of all the circumstances now prevailing, it seems desirable to send her first to base temporarily at the NAS Lakehurst for a shaking down period during which she could be kept under close

observation by the Navy Department and by the contractor so as to insure that she will be in better material readiness to take up Fleet operations immediately upon arrival in Sunnyvale.[17]

King was Moffett's replacement at the BUAER. Whereas Moffett had a reputation of being gruff, King had a reputation for being angry. As his daughter once said, 'He is the most even tempered person in the Navy. He is always in a rage.'[18] Even President Roosevelt thought King 'shaves every morning with a blow torch'.[19] Nevertheless, King had to be politic in his approach since he'd inherited a troubled programme from Moffett. What his memo makes clear is that he wanted the *Macon* close at hand so that Goodyear and the Navy could keep an eye on her. Since the loss of the *Akron* had freed up space at the Lakehurst hangar, the *Macon* would take up temporary residence until King was confident she was ready to travel to her new base in California.

The decision was both cautious and wise, suggesting King was giving the *Macon* every opportunity to succeed. An extended shakedown period would help dispel any concerns about the *Akron*'s sister. King wasn't taking any chances.

The *Macon*'s fourth trial flight was held on 12 June, nearly a month after her third. Designed as an endurance flight, it was the perfect excuse to fly over the Chicago World's Fair. Some 60,000 people turned out daily for what was billed as the Century of Progress. This made it just the kind of hand-waving flight Moffett would have favoured. The fact the *Macon* would be the first rigid airship to fly over the fair not only helped polish the programme's tarnished image but provided bragging rights since the Navy would beat the *Graf Zeppelin*'s appearance by four months.

The biggest complaint about the *Macon*'s forty-eight-hour flight was that the cigar lighter in the control car's aft compartment stopped working. After the flight, Secretary of the Navy Swanson pronounced the *Macon* 'OK' – hardly a ringing endorsement.

A bigger surprise was in store after the *Macon* returned from Chicago. That's when the *New York Times* announced that Wiley had put in for sea duty 'at his own request'.[20] This meant Wiley, second only to Commander Rosendahl in national notoriety, was leaving Moffett's LTA programme. Assigned to the USS *Cincinnati* as navigation officer, he would be serving aboard the very kind of scout ship the *Macon* was intended to replace. The irony was so thick you could cut it with a knife.

After the *Macon*'s fourth trial flight, Admiral Day's Board of Inspection and Survey agreed to accept the airship on behalf of the US government. But this was only a 'preliminary acceptance', meaning the *Macon* would have to undergo additional trials at Lakehurst before being judged ready to assume her duties. In the meantime, Goodyear was issued a receipt for the vessel, an important formality when transferring ownership.[21]

The *Macon*'s commissioning ceremony took place in the Goodyear-Zeppelin Air Dock on Friday, 23 June 1933. After the *Macon*'s executive officer mustered her crew, Admiral King read the order placing the *Macon* in commission. Next, Dresel read his orders naming him commanding officer, after which the airship's colours and commission pennant were hoisted, and her first watch set.[22] Six hours later, she departed for her temporary home at Lakehurst.

A more cautious BUAER chief might have distanced himself from Moffett's LTA programme, but King wanted to demonstrate his support, so he boarded the *Macon* for her eight-hour flight to Lakehurst. The airship flew through the night crossing over Ohio and Pennsylvania before turning north at Philadelphia. Arriving over Lakehurst shortly after 0300 hours, Dresel ran into trouble when a tailwind caused him to overshoot the mooring mast. To complicate matters, the airship's mooring cone didn't fit in the mooring cup atop the mast, requiring it be filed down. Finally, locked in the cup at 0423 hours, the *Macon* was towed into the Lakehurst hangar, where she sat alongside the USS *Los Angeles*, scheduled to be decommissioned the next week for lack of funds. If the *Los Angeles* symbolised a proud past, the *Macon* represented an uncertain future. What might happen next was anyone's guess.

21

LAKEHURST

If the *Macon* was born under a cloud, it's surprising how many people wanted to build another airship just like her.

Admiral King, BUAER's new chief, wanted to replace the *Akron*. But Secretary Swanson nixed the idea, saying, 'For the present there are more important matters which are receiving attention.'[1]

King wasn't the only one arguing for a replacement. The King Committee's stunning endorsement of Moffat's LTA programme helped stir up interest. Still, King's desire to replace the *Akron* was not easily realised, given the anti-airship climate. Moffett had also felt the pressure. Less than a month before the *Akron* crash, Rep. William H. Sutphin, a member of the House Committee on Naval Affairs, sent Moffett a letter warning him his LTA programme was losing popularity:

> Dear Admiral Moffett … I am sure that you … are not aware of the ever increasing antagonism of the taxpayers of our country toward lighter than air service. The Department fails to capitalize [on] its greatest asset which is good will. What the department needs is a salesman who will go out and sell [to] the people because after all they are the ones who pay the bills.[2]

No one worked harder to sell the Navy's rigid airship programme than Moffett, hence his plethora of speeches and hand-waving flights. But congress was losing faith in the *Akron* even before she'd crashed. Making matters worse, the Depression had drastically reduced defence spending. Given a choice between funding the surface fleet or Moffett's LTA programme, the Navy's battleship admirals favoured the fleet. The truth is, plans were being discussed to lay up the *Akron* as a cost-saving measure once the *Macon* was commissioned.

Now that she had crashed, majority opinion turned against any more rigid airships for the Navy, which is why King faced an uphill battle keeping the programme alive.

The summer of 1933 proved a happy time for the *Macon*'s crew. Since the airship's stay at Lakehurst lasted four months they were able to spend time with family and friends who lived on base or nearby. The Jersey shore, only a few miles distant, offered a pleasant diversion, and though the future of NAS Lakehurst looked dim, the *Macon*'s arrival had forestalled its closing – a welcome reprieve for the civilians who worked on the base.

If there was a cloud in the silver lining, it was the terrible grief that still pervaded Lakehurst following the *Akron* crash. The *Macon*'s busy flight schedule helped to dull the ache but couldn't erase it. And yet the tragedy resulted in at least one happy event when an enlisted man aboard the *Macon* married the widow of one of his colleagues who'd gone down with the *Akron*.

During this time, Dresel took the *Macon* out on numerous training flights. In a 6 July memo to the Chief of Naval Operations, he outlined how he planned to employ her. 'The mission of the *Macon* during the period of 1 July to 1 October, 1933 is to operate in a manner as will best fit her to … join the Fleet.'[3] But the *Macon*'s commanding officer drew a hard line when it came to hand-waving excursions:

> It is believed that the shake-down period of the *Macon* can best be accomplished by continuing the policy of 'Rigid Airships working at sea', and it is therefore recommended that requests for the vessel to appear over cities, participate in celebrations, or carry passengers other than naval personnel and contractor's representatives, be disapproved when possible.[4]

Dresel's memo is a reminder that the *Macon* was as an ocean-going scout, not a promotional device for the Navy. This distinction was sometimes lost under Moffett, but Dresel was determined to remind those above him that the *Macon* should be employed as a military aircraft. This was wise counsel given how many people hoped she'd fail. Nevertheless, it disappointed many local politicians who viewed a visit by the *Macon* as proof of their clout.

The *Macon*'s aeroplanes flew aboard the airship for the first time on 7 July.[5] Part of the dirigible's heavier-than-air unit, the Curtiss F9C-2 fighters were critical to her defence. Called Sparrowhawks after the small but nimble bird of prey, each carried twin .30-calibre machine guns to repel an aerial attack. Their pilots spent the day hooking on to the airship's trapeze. Once snared, their biplane was cranked on board, removed from its perch and the trapeze lowered to catch another one.

Despite Dresel's plea to minimise hand-waving flights, the *Macon* was drafted to celebrate the arrival of General Italo Balbo, Mussolini's Air Minister, and his armada of twenty-four flying boats on 21 July. General Balbo had flown across the Atlantic from Italy to Chicago, marking a milestone for heavier-than-air flight. Although the *Macon* could easily cross this distance, the feat suggested aeroplanes were rapidly catching up. As General Balbo's sleek, doubled-hulled, seaplanes floated on Jamaica Bay, the *Macon*'s Sparrowhawks dived in salute, yet another promotional stunt that did nothing to further the airship's mission.

Additional training flights, conducted mostly at sea, were held in July and August.[6] Dresel and his crew acquitted themselves well, causing confidence in the *Macon* to improve. Soon they'd be ready to voyage across the United States to their new home in Sunnyvale, California. Once on the west coast, the *Macon* would engage in fleet exercises, giving her an opportunity to demonstrate she had the right stuff. Meanwhile, her officers, crew and heavier-than-air pilots continued familiarising themselves with their new airship.

Not everything went smoothly, of course. Owls nesting in the steel rafters of Hangar No. 1 defecated constantly on the *Macon*'s canvas cover.[7] Since bird faeces contained acid that could damage the envelope, frequent scrubbing was required. And owls weren't the only nuisance; rat infestation had always been a problem. Mice had even taken up residence in the *Shenandoah*, attracted to the cattle intestines lining her gas cells. But these were minor problems. In every important respect the *Macon* was performing as intended. Besides, every Navy had its share of rats.

One problem that continued dogging the *Macon* was her being overweight. The *Akron* had weighed more than 20,000lb than intended.[8] The *Macon* was meant to be lighter and she was, but still heavier than planned.

The *Macon*'s weight was a sensitive issue. Fulton and Arnstein often danced around it during construction. In Goodyear's defence, J.C. Hunsaker noted that any weight overage was 'due to our decision to remove every possible risk of failure of parts or apparatus where it appeared that close adherence to weight estimates involved some risk of ultimately unsatisfactory operation'.[9] Simply put, Goodyear wanted to make its airships as safe as possible.

But Fulton had trouble seeing the forest for the trees when it came to excess weight. In the meantime, Navy change orders, some of which increased how much the *Macon* would weigh, continued piling up. Fulton may have had the Navy's best interests at heart, but he could be a bully where Goodyear-Zeppelin was concerned. Every time Dr Arnstein requested a weight increase in the name of safety, Fulton held his feet to the fire.

Dr Arnstein wanted to deliver the safest airship possible, but safety issues weren't the only area where he felt stymied. Goodyear was forced to absorb many of the cost overages related to the weight increase. In a contrite letter Arnstein sent to the Inspector of Naval Aircraft, he sounds almost beaten down. 'In view of the fact that the [*Macon's*] weight has been exceeded by over 5,000lb the contractor agrees to the impost of the full penalty in accordance with the contract.'[10]

It's not hard to fathom why the *Akron* and *Macon* were overweight and over budget. Goodyear was building the world's largest airships and there were few benchmarks to guide cost estimates. Those provided were just that, estimates: they represented Goodyear's best guess for something that had never done before. And yet Fulton forced Goodyear to absorb the cost overruns despite being responsible for many of them. The weight penalty ended up costing Goodyear-Zeppelin $25,000 – twenty times the average annual income of a US worker in 1933.[11] Although the *Macon* ended up significantly faster than required, no commensurate bonus was paid for her increase in speed, only penalties were meted out.

As the *Macon* prepared for its fourth trial flight, the Navy still owed Goodyear-Zeppelin $220,000. Some $200,000 of this would be held back for another six months as part of the airship's warranty period.[*,12] Given that business was bad at Goodyear-Zeppelin, this kink in its cash flow could only hurt its solvency. But Litchfield had little recourse when it came to collecting monies owed by the Navy. And so, Goodyear-Zeppelin kept quiet thanks to Fulton's short-sighted bullying, Arnstein's polite demeanour and Litchfield's refusal to antagonise Goodyear-Zeppelin's most important client.

The *Macon's* final trial flights took place on the last two days of August. Admiral Day and his Board of Inspection and Survey were on board for both flights, as was the BUAER's Admiral King. Admiral William V. Standley, Chief of Naval

---

*   The *Macon's* warranty expired on 23 December 1933.

Operations, also attended even though he was about as ardently anti-airship as they came.

A new perch had recently been installed on the *Macon*'s belly near her stern. There a Sparrowhawk could await its turn to snag the airship's trapeze. The trapeze was also new, having been upgraded by Goodyear-Zeppelin, and this made it easier for the *Macon*'s planes to hook on. The HTA unit practised catching the trapeze during the airship's last two trial flights. The *Macon* even set a new speed record, proving Arnstein's streamlining was successful. As a Navy report summarised, the 'USS *Macon* … was found to be in all respects an airworthy airship … the work being well performed and … in strict conformity with the contract, drawings, plans, and specifications.'[13] She was now an officially recognised vessel of the United States Navy.

Litchfield had hoped the Navy's big rigid business would lead to the private sector hiring Goodyear to build commercial airships, but after the *Akron* crash, American demand for big rigids dried up. Now only the *Macon* could help Litchfield realise his dream of a fleet of American-flagged, passenger-carrying airships spanning the globe. But if the *Macon* represented the hopes and dreams of Litchfield, it was up to Dresel, her captain, to prove the naysayers wrong.

One thing in Dresel's favour was his crew: many of them veterans of the *Akron*, *Los Angeles* or *Shenandoah*. They not only knew what they were doing, they believed in the future of rigid airships. But neither Goodyear nor the Navy could afford another mishap. One mistake not only risked the cancellation of Moffett's big rigid programme, but jeopardised the American airship as the future of long-distance transportation. Everything depended on what Dresel did with the *Macon*.

The *Macon* had become the Navy's last best hope for proving big rigids airworthy. There was only one problem. Her designer, Dr Arnstein, had serious doubts about her safety, and no one was listening.

22

DR KARL ARNSTEIN: A GIANT DISPLACED

The man with the most acute grasp of how safe the *Akron* and *Macon* were was their chief designer, Dr Karl Arnstein. Arnstein was every bit a giant as Litchfield and Moffett in the field of lighter-than-air flight, although he was far too modest to consider himself one. Frequently hailed as one of the world's foremost experts on stress analysis, Arnstein was credited by the *New York Times* with contributing to the design of 100 lighter-than-air craft over the course of his career.[1] This included doing the stress analysis for Germany's Zeppelins as well as his contributions to the design of three of the US Navy's five big rigids – the *Los Angeles*, *Akron* and *Macon*. The other two, the *Shenandoah* and ZR-2 (the UK's *R38*), were based on Zeppelins Arnstein had worked on.

The total number of airships Arnstein contributed to is open to debate. He wasn't Luftschiffbau Zeppelin's chief airship designer; that was Ludwig Dürr. Nevertheless, between 1915 and 1924 Arnstein did the critical stress calculations for more than fifty military and commercial Zeppelins. Given he was the chief designer for the *Akron* and *Macon* as well as the L, K, M and N-type blimps Goodyear built for the Navy, the number of airships Arnstein worked on is probably between sixty and eighty. What's clear is that no one understood the aerodynamic loads a rigid airship might encounter in flight better than Dr Arnstein.

It shouldn't come as a surprise that the *Akron* loss devastated Arnstein. But even when the Navy Court of Inquiry and the joint congressional committee investigating airship safety attributed the *Akron* crash to operator error, Arnstein wasn't so sure.

The *Akron* included several unique design features Arnstein pioneered. These included her box-shaped girders, her deep ring structure and eliminating the traditional cruciform bracing in the *Akron*'s stern in favour of a new method of anchoring her fins. All of these changes were a departure from previous practice. But they were backed by rigorous stress analysis and supported by data from wind tunnel tests. That's why Arnstein believed his innovations improved the *Akron*'s safety, not undermined it.

There's no denying the *Akron* was an experimental aircraft, but if anything was wrong with her design, Arnstein was to blame. One thing that concerned him was the strength of main ring 17.5 where the *Akron*'s tail fins were anchored. Specifically he was worried the redesign of the *Akron*'s fins, undertaken to make her bottom fin visible from the control car, had changed the location of her aerodynamic stress loads in flight. Arnstein was conservative by nature, so he'd designed frame 17.5 to be strong. Nevertheless, he worried the fin redesign might lead to unforeseen consequences. Importantly, if there was a problem with the structural integrity of the *Akron*'s frame 17.5, the *Macon* shared it as well.

Arnstein was greatly respected for his expertise, but he was never part of Litchfield's inner circle. Hunsaker ran the business side of Goodyear-Zeppelin, which gave him clout. In contrast, Arnstein focused on design and engineering. Although important, it wasn't the same powerbase as being in charge of the balance sheet.

There's also evidence Litchfield didn't treat Arnstein with the respect he deserved. For instance, Litchfield referred to Arnstein as 'the little doctor' even though at 5ft 8in Arnstein wasn't particularly short.[2] This could be interpreted either as paternal (Litchfield was over 6ft tall himself) or condescending. As it was, Litchfield rarely treated his employees like equals.

Furthering the divide, Arnstein was a lot of things his boss was not. Not only was he multilingual, his old-world poise, continental charm and exquisite manners contrasted with Litchfield's brutish style. Of more concern, Arnstein's European formality could be mistaken for deference. That Litchfield was his boss's boss only widened the gap.

Arnstein was unquestionably brilliant. Bald and bespectacled with owlish features, his unusual ability to calculate abstract stress coefficients made him a leader in the field. But he was also cultured, religious and a devoted family man, none of which held much appeal for Litchfield. Quiet and self-effacing,

Arnstein's hobbies included collecting fine art, stamps, graphology* and gardening – all lone pursuits.[3] So fond was he of roses, Arnstein was said to have had 400 bushes around his home.[4]

More a product of pre-war Europe than razzle-dazzle America, Arnstein was not used to the rough and tumble ways of American business. His hazel eyes and Mona Lisa smile imbued his features with kindness, while his cultivated upbringing (which included wearing a fur-collared overcoat) must have seemed exotic in the Ohio heartland.

Arnstein became famous in America for building airships, but he shunned publicity. He particularly hated meeting reporters, whom he felt twisted his words.[5] An engineer's engineer, Arnstein didn't make grand pronouncements or exaggerated claims. He preferred sticking to the facts.

Born in Prague, Bohemia,** on 24 March 1887, Arnstein grew up Jewish at a time when it was increasingly dangerous to do so. He attended the University of Prague, where he studied engineering, graduating with the highest distinction in 1910. While earning a Doctor of Technical Sciences degree (which he was awarded in 1912), Arnstein served as assistant to the head of the university's Bridge Engineering Department, where he also taught classes.

There's little doubt Arnstein was a pioneer in the field of stress analysis. After leaving academia to become chief engineer for a Strasbourg construction firm, he designed the longest single-span bridge in the Alps. His design soon became the model for European bridges of this type. He was also responsible for reinforcing the main tower of Strasbourg Cathedral. The thousand-year-old monument held such cultural importance that Arnstein's repair work added to his reputation.

Arnstein might have remained a civil engineer, but the First World War intervened. Soon he found himself goose-stepping in the Austrian infantry.[6] Hearing of Arnstein's reputation as a genius in stress analysis, Count Ferdinand von Zeppelin arranged for his release from the Army in 1915. Shortly thereafter, the count put Arnstein to work at Luftschiffbau Zeppelin working on rigid airships for the war effort.

Stress analysis was new to aircraft design, but Arnstein had a knack for it. He not only pioneered the use of Duralumin in building big rigids, he would hold

---

*   The study of handwriting.
**   The Czech Republic today.

more than thirty patents related to their design. Arnstein's stress calculations enabled Zeppelins to double in size, allowing them to travel farther for longer periods of time. His contributions also proved critical to a new type of Zeppelin nicknamed 'height climbers', which could reach the then unheard altitude of 20,000ft.

Arnstein had several innovative ideas when it came to airship design that he wanted to implement at Luftschiffbau Zeppelin. But the company's chief airship designer, Dürr, was conservative and stymied some of his innovations. This frustrated Arnstein, who wanted to be the chief designer. Since Dürr wasn't going anywhere, Arnstein focused on stress analysis.

Arnstein met his future wife, Bertha Jehle, at a tea party hosted by her brother-in-law, who worked at Luftschiffbau Zeppelin. Eleven years Arnstein's junior, Bertl (as she was known) was a high school student who found the serious-minded engineer the perfect target for practical jokes. One day she snuck into Arnstein's rented room while he was at work, filling his coat pockets with rocks. Typical of his good-natured demeanour, Arnstein accepted the joke with grace.[7]

Two years later, Bertl and Arnstein were married. Prior to the ceremony, Arnstein converted to Catholicism, Bertl's religion, remaining an ardent Catholic the rest of his life.[8] By all accounts the two were happy.

Had Count von Zeppelin not plucked Arnstein from the military, he might have been killed during the war, drastically pruning, if not uprooting, the Zeppelin family tree. But Germany's surrender put an end to Arnstein's airship work. The Versailles Treaty forbade the country from building big rigids for the military. Five years after the war, Arnstein was reduced to designing kitchen spatulas for the German market.

Prospects looked grim for Luftschiffbau Zeppelin, but Litchfield changed all this when he arrived in Friedrichshafen to cut a deal. Litchfield wasn't just interested in patents. He'd heard about the company's up-and-coming expert in stress analysis. As he recalled, 'One man I particularly wanted was Dr Karl Arnstein.'[9]

Luftschiffbau Zeppelin knew Arnstein was important. The company had even tried hiding him from the US Navy when building the *Los Angeles*. The ruse failed, however, when Commander Garland Fulton identified Arnstein as making important contributions to the project.[10] But when Litchfield offered Arnstein the chief engineer position at Goodyear-Zeppelin, the doctor hesitated.[11] Despite the hardships Arnstein and Bertl were suffering in Germany, they were reluctant to uproot their two daughters to a country they'd never visited.

Prospects in Germany were bleak in the 1920s. When Arnstein paid a visit to Akron to suss out Litchfield's offer, the Roaring Twenties were well under way. Arnstein was particularly struck by the bounty of American life. At a dinner held in his honour, Arnstein observed, 'It was an impressive evening for me coming from starving Europe to see the table sagging under the load of a fish and chicken dinner.'[12]

Given Arnstein aspired to the position of chief airship designer, the move made sense. America was one of the few countries prepared to fund big rigids but it would also prove an enormous adjustment. Twenty-one years later another German engineer named Werner von Braun would make a similar deal with his former enemy, just like Arnstein.

In November 1924, Arnstein set sail for America aboard the SS *George Washington*. Accompanied by twelve engineers handpicked from Luftschiffbau Zeppelin, he bunked alone since Bertl and their two daughters wouldn't join him until spring the following year.[13]

In an on-board photograph taken shortly after the ship docked in New York City, the thirteen men are shown standing in a lifeboat looking happy and relaxed. Most of the men are wearing caps, while Arnstein wears a homburg like the prosperous burgher he intended to be. Kurt Bauch, the youngest of the group, stands in the front row not far from his boss with the ship's life ring draped around his neck. This may be why so many of the men are smiling.[14] Or perhaps they were just excited by their grand adventure.

Litchfield needed Arnstein in Akron right away, so there was no time for sightseeing. Before he could visit the Statue of Liberty (the Empire State Building hadn't been built yet), the future of rigid airship design in America was hustled aboard an Ohio-bound train.[15]

Hugh Allen, Goodyear-Zeppelin's PR Director, dubbed Arnstein's engineers the 'twelve disciples'. Like Litchfield, Allen spoke of Arnstein in a condescending manner, calling him 'the little German professor', which the media soon picked up.[16] As we know, Arnstein was not especially small, nor was he German. He wasn't even a professor. His twelve engineers, who revered him, knew better and called Arnstein by his correct title, '*Herr Doktor*'.[17]

One would assume Arnstein suffered from culture shock upon arriving in Ohio. Although Akron had been a town of only 40,000 when Litchfield first moved there in 1900,[18] the world's rubber capital had since become the fastest-growing city in America. Fuelled by immigrants attracted by factory jobs, Akron's population had swelled to more than 200,000 by the time Arnstein arrived.

Ohio means 'beautiful land' in the Chippewa language, but there was nothing beautiful about the Akron Arnstein encountered. The city was heavily industrial. Its many rubber factories, their smokestacks stretching towards the sky, spread a coarse black dust over everything from sheets hung to dry to a baby left in its pushchair. The unmistakable stench of rubber could be smelled for miles. Still, Akron was the Promised Land compared to post-war Germany. Arnstein and his men didn't have to be photographed in a lifeboat to understand Litchfield had rescued them. But Litchfield hadn't done it out of kindness. He expected them to deliver. The future of Goodyear-Zeppelin depended upon it.

The American press compared Arnstein to Albert Einstein, which embarrassed him.[19] Although he spoke English fluently, he did so with a heavy accent at first, robbing him of confidence. Arnstein eventually grew comfortable with the language, but it made for an awkward start. Litchfield would later claim Arnstein and his men had little difficulty integrating into Goodyear, but that's hard to believe given America had been at war with Germany only six years earlier.[20] Not only did enmity still exist between the two countries; their cultural differences were profound.

Unfortunately, the promised contracts to build big rigids were slow to arrive. Neither the military nor the commercial market was ready to commit when Arnstein moved to America. The delay didn't bother Litchfield; he was playing a longer game. But Arnstein and his twelve disciples had been working at Goodyear-Zeppelin for four years before the company won its first contract to build big rigids for the Navy. Now, Arnstein finally had the opportunity to build an airship that would showcase his revolutionary design.

Arnstein had a lot to learn when it came to working for Americans. For example, he was used to autonomy at Luftschiffbau Zeppelin.[21] Not even the German military would contradict his decisions. But when it came to building the *Akron* and *Macon*, nothing got done without approval by the Bureau of Aeronautics. The Navy even embedded an inspector of aircraft in the Goodyear-Zeppelin Air Dock who second-guessed Arnstein at every turn, strong arming him when it suited the Navy's purpose.

Arnstein was surprised at how much control the Navy exerted. Nor did it help that Litchfield had a 'client is always right' mentality. Too gracious to challenge his boss, Arnstein preferred a more collegial approach, which is why the confrontational style of American business frustrated him. But so much was riding on the Navy contract that Goodyear-Zeppelin frequently bent to its customer's will, which didn't always result in better design decisions.

There's no doubt Arnstein and his men were under pressure to deliver. They'd worked sixteen-hour days, six days a week designing and building the *Akron*.[22] But despite their best efforts, Arnstein's worst nightmare came true when the airship crashed. There was a basic decency to Arnstein that's hard to miss. He was as conscientious as he was precise; he did not jump to conclusions. Nevertheless, he could not shake the feeling that the *Akron* suffered from a hidden design flaw. If so, he knew her sister shared it, too.

As Congress and the press debated the future of the American big rigid, Goodyear-Zeppelin's chief engineer launched a discreet investigation into the safety of his creation. What he soon discovered would leave him shaken. In the meantime, the future of the American airship was at stake.

23

DOUBTS

When Dr Arnstein told the Navy Court of Inquiry the *Macon* was 'intended to excel all previous airships', he spoke the truth as he understood it.[1] Arnstein wasn't prone to exaggeration. He was as careful in his public statements as he was in his engineering. He'd done everything within his power to make the *Macon* the safest airship in the sky. It was his paramount concern.

In contrast, Goodyear's master of spin, Hugh Allen, felt no such compunction to temper his pronouncements. The *Akron* has 'the accumulated experience of thirty years of airship building and flying', an Allen puff piece proclaimed. 'Extensive research into the most exact measurement of the stresses that will be encountered by any portion of the ship' in flight has been undertaken. Allen even boasted Goodyear had 'developed its own science of gauging the strength of the materials which encounter such stresses'.

Allen's claims were true up to a point, but they did not tell the whole story. No one had ever built airships as big as the *Akron* and *Macon*. This meant Goodyear–Zeppelin's engineers were working on the edge of the unknown. Arnstein insisted on building redundancy into his two airships to increase their safety, but what he couldn't foresee was that some of the assumptions he used in designing them were either incomplete or inaccurate. As time passed and Arnstein learned more, his doubts about the *Akron*'s structural integrity increased.

The field of stress analysis was relatively new when Arnstein designed the *Akron*. This meant he didn't have a large body of historical data to draw upon. Arnstein was intent on correcting this, but much was still unknown about the aerodynamic loads an airship might encounter in flight. These loads put stress on a big rigid's airframe that, under severe circumstances, could collapse.

This is why two of the Navy's big rigids, the *Shenandoah* and ZR-2 (*R38*), had suffered catastrophic failures in flight.

As Jeffrey Cook notes in his landmark engineering study of the *Akron* and *Macon*, 'The history of rigid airship technology is a progressive one, in which successive designs were based upon the successes and failures of previous designs.'[2] But past learning didn't necessarily prevent future failures, as six major airship crashes between 1921 and 1933 proved.

Arnstein had conducted wind tunnel tests on a scale model of the *Akron* to determine where aerodynamic loads would occur on the airship. Still, the tests were only as accurate as the assumptions they were based upon. As Arnstein and the Navy would soon learn, some of their assumptions were incorrect.

Arnstein's original design called for the *Akron*'s tail fins to be long and slender, similar to those on the *Los Angeles*. But the Navy asked Arnstein to change their shape. The request was precipitated by an accident the *Graf Zeppelin* suffered in 1929 when the airship's 15-degree, nose-up angle at take-off was so severe it nearly drove her tail fin into the ground. Commander Rosendahl, who was aboard the *Graf* at the time, described the incident as 'just about the … most hair-raising experience of my life',[3] which is saying something given Rosendahl had piloted the bow half of the *Shenandoah* to safety after the airship was ripped in two during a thunderstorm over Ohio.

But Arnstein's original design placed the *Akron*'s control car so close to her bow that the curvature of her hull blocked the view of her tail. After the *Graf* incident, Rosendahl insisted the *Akron*'s bottom fin be made visible from the control car. Commander Fulton, the BUAER's senior airship designer, shared Rosendahl's concern and a similarly overbearing personality. As a result, Fulton made sure Goodyear-Zeppelin addressed Rosendahl's concern.

Arnstein explored several options, including a double-decker control car and rear-view mirrors,[4] all designed to make the bottom tail fin more visible. After much discussion, it was decided the *Akron*'s bottom fin should be extended downwards to ensure it could be seen. The result was Change Order No. 2 issued on 22 July 1930.

Change Order No. 2 fundamentally altered the design of the *Akron*'s four fins; despite the fact the airship was already under construction. It not only shortened their length; it increased their height and width. Arnstein knew this change might alter where the fins experienced their greatest aerodynamic loads. The problem was he didn't know exactly where those loads might occur on the new design.

If it's hard to appreciate just how big the *Akron*'s fins were, the March 1933 issue of *Universal Engineer* describes just one as being 'large enough to accommodate a six-room house with plenty of front, rear and side yard and a double garage for good measure'.[5] Although the *Akron*'s bottom fin was slightly smaller than the other three,[6] the combined weight of all four was nearly 8 tons. Despite this weight, the *Akron*'s fins had to be secure enough to withstand the tremendous aerodynamic strain they encountered in flight, especially when buffeted by powerful winds.

In addition to redesigning the *Akron*'s four fins, Change Order No. 2 moved her control car approximately 8ft closer to her stern, while lowering its floor 1 to 2ft.[7] This provided the officers on the bridge a clearer view of her bottom fin. But Change Order No. 2 not only altered the shape of the *Akron*'s tail fins; it reduced the number of places where they were anchored. Arnstein's original design called for the *Akron*'s tail fins to be anchored at frames 0, 17.5 and 35. Change Order No. 2 eliminated the anchoring at frame 35, which left the fin's forward leading edge unsupported for 34ft.[8]

Arnstein had originally anchored the *Akron*'s fins to three of her main frames because he felt his innovative 'deep ring' design was strong enough to support them. But the reason he anchored the fins to three main rings in the first place was because he'd eliminated the traditional cruciform structure in her stern as a weight-saving measure. Basically a giant girder running through the middle of the airship's aft section, the cruciform tail structure anchored one fin to the fin on the opposite side, forming a giant cross, hence its name. Previous Zeppelins had relied on this design to anchor their tail fins, but Arnstein dispensed with it, believing his 'deep rings' strong enough to handle the load.

In a speech about the factor of safety used in airship design, Arnstein acknowledged the trade-off between designing an airship with an adequate safety factor versus the need to accommodate its operator. 'The real safety of a structure depends … as much on how the engineer's "best estimates" are made … as it does on the value of the "factor of safety" which he uses,' Arnstein stated. 'But engineers are not magicians and when radical changes in size or details of structure are embarked upon, either a larger factor of safety with its attendant reduction of efficiency should be used, or else the risk attendant upon such a pioneering venture must be realised by the users.'[9]

Arnstein's words are telling. What he was saying is that a large safety factor should be employed when designing airships like the *Akron* and *Macon*, even if it reduced their efficiency. However, if operators such as the Navy demanded design changes that reduced the factor of safety, then the responsibility for future problems lay with the operator not the designer.

Commander Fulton, the Navy's LTA design expert, was satisfied that changes to the *Akron*'s fins could be made safely, but he would have done well to heed Arnstein's advice. For, as later events would show, the manner in which the *Akron*'s redesigned tail fins were anchored was shockingly inadequate.

Not everybody was comfortable with Change Order No. 2. Kurt Bauch, Arnstein's youngest disciple, 'strongly objected' to the redesign of the fins.[10] Bauch had worked on the fin's original stress analysis, so knew a redesign would change his load-bearing calculations. Arnstein understood Bauch's concerns but Litchfield wanted a happy customer, so Arnstein redesigned the fins based on the data he had at hand. Since the data was incomplete, Arnstein, who was nothing if not conscientious, worried about the fins.

Arnstein knew the redesigned fins altered his assumptions in ways he couldn't foresee. He was especially unhappy about reducing their anchor points from three to two. That's why he was anxious to put the revised fin structure through additional wind tunnel tests. Unfortunately, it wasn't until seven months after Change Order No. 2 was approved that the National Advisory Committee for Aeronautics (NACA) was finally retained to conduct wind tunnel tests on Arnstein's new fin design. Using a giant 1:40 scale model of the *Akron*, pressure measurements were taken at nearly 400 points on the hull, including eighty-four locations on each side of her horizontal fins. The model was then subjected to some of the most severe aerodynamic conditions ever tested on an airship.[11]

It took another five months before Arnstein got the test results, and by then the *Akron* was only two months away from her first flight. The good news was the tests showed Goodyear-Zeppelin had accurately forecast where most of the aerodynamic loads on the *Akron*'s tail fins would occur. One thing stood out, however. There was an unusually high load concentration on the forward third of her upper tail fins' leading edge , which extended from where it was anchored at frame 17.5 to intermediate frame 23.75, where it was not well supported.[12] The concentration was most severe when the airship flew at a 20-degree, nose-up angle, but since this was unlikely to occur, the BUAER wasn't worried. Still, the load concentrations on the forward third of the fin's leading edge were about twice that on the rest of the fin. This was significant because it meant the load factor had shifted closer to where the fins were anchored at frame 17.5, significantly reducing their factor of safety.[13]

When Dr Arnstein presented the NACA test results to the Navy, Fulton rejected them out of hand. Arguing that the results conflicted with data collected from previous wind tunnel tests, Fulton was confident Arnstein's main rings were strong enough to support the *Akron*'s tail fins.[14]

For perspective, frame 17.5 was vital to the *Macon*'s structural integrity. Located near her stern, it not only had to be strong enough to hold the airship's hull together, but bear part of the aerodynamic strain her tail fins encountered in flight. Since Arnstein would not sacrifice safety in the name of weight saving, he would insist Fulton allow him to strengthen frame 17.5. Fulton, on the other hand, wasn't going to approve strengthening the frame if it meant increasing the *Akron*'s weight. If anything, he wanted Arnstein to reduce the airship's tonnage, not add to it.

But Arnstein didn't see it that way. The NACA results led him to recommend reinforcing frame 17.5 where the tail fins were anchored, thereby increasing the airship's weight.[15] Fulton was already annoyed that frame 17.5 was heavier than he thought necessary, so he rejected the recommendation.[16]

To be clear, Arnstein didn't lack confidence in frame 17.5. He believed his proprietary 'deep ring' structure made the *Akron*'s main frames strong enough to support any aerodynamic load the airship might encounter. But Arnstein, like most engineers, didn't take chances. Given the NACA test results, he wanted to be sure frame 17.5 would support any increased loads the *Akron* might encounter on the forward edge of her fins.

Arnstein was especially concerned because the NACA test results suggested the *Akron*'s fins might be vulnerable if broadsided by a gust.[17] Since the fins weren't designed to be driven sideways, Arnstein recommended that cable bracing be added to support them. But cable bracing also increased the airship's weight. Arnstein felt this was an acceptable trade-off if the *Akron* were to be the safest airship ever built. Fulton did not.

Arnstein was so concerned about the NACA tests results that he insisted they be repeated.[18] When the second test came back, Fulton again refused to accept there was a problem. Arnstein tried persuading him, but eventually acquiesced (at least initially) to keep the peace. But once the *Akron* crashed, everything changed. Arnstein became so concerned, he once again urged Fulton to add cable bracing to support the *Macon*'s fins. Knowing the Navy flew its big rigids aggressively, putting additional strain on their airframe, Arnstein complained, 'In America they want to fly airships the way they drive automobiles, any time … anywhere.'[19] In contrast, Luftschiffbau

Zeppelin only flew its commercial airships in good weather, while Navy airships bulled their way through adverse conditions. This highlights the fundamental difference in operating practice between the US Navy and Germany's commercial Zeppelins. But nobody, least of all Moffett, wanted a weapon that only flew when the sun shined.

Fortunately, Moffett's penchant for severe operational practices was not shared by the BUAER's new chief. Admiral King felt 'airships should avoid bad weather'[20] if possible. But weather forecasting was primitive in 1933. Add to this that no one knew the conditions under which it was unsafe for the *Macon* to fly, and Arnstein thought it smart to play it safe. Fulton disagreed, thinking they were playing it plenty safe already.

After the *Akron* crash, Dr Arnstein's concern grew to the point of urgency. He didn't want his airship flying if it suffered from a design flaw. But there was little time to fix the problem before the *Macon*'s first trial flight, especially with Fulton standing in the way.

Arnstein was so worried that less than ten days after the *Akron* crashed he took it upon himself to have Goodyear–Zeppelin order and pay for cable bracing to anchor the *Macon*'s tail fins.[21] He even had eyelets installed for anchoring the cables.[22] However, when Fulton found out, he was furious. And so, much to Arnstein's dismay, his cable bracing was never installed.

Although the Navy Court of Inquiry found the *Akron* crash was caused by severe weather, Arnstein was concerned enough that a structural failure might have been involved that he sent a personal letter to Lt Cdr Wiley. Arnstein's letter asked Wiley whether the big rigid 'broke in the air or failed after striking the water'.[23] This shows just how concerned he remained about the *Akron*'s structural integrity. When Wiley replied to Arnstein nine days later, he wrote, 'It is my personal opinion … the damage to the *Akron* was caused by the ship striking the water.'[24]

Arnstein might have found Wiley's letter reassuring if it hadn't differed greatly from what Wiley had told the House's Subcommittee on Aeronautics. On the first day of the hearing, Wiley testified he thought the *Akron* had broken in two, causing it to strike the water.[25] Wiley would change his testimony in a dramatic reversal four days later when he told the naval Court of Inquiry he thought a severe downdraught had pushed the *Akron* into the sea. But one has to wonder why Wiley radically reversed himself? Was he legitimately confused as to what happened that night, did he change his mind upon reflection or was he protecting Moffett's rigid airship programme because admitting a structural failure had caused the *Akron* to crash might force the Navy to ground the *Macon*, casting doubt on the future of the rigid airship programme? This left the fate of the Navy's big rigids almost entirely on what Wiley had to say.

As previously mentioned, the most striking about Wiley's testimony is just how muddled it was given that he was in the *Akron*'s control car the night she crashed. The only person to survive from the bridge, not to mention the airship's sole surviving officer, Wiley was the Navy's most important witness. The *Akron*'s other two survivors, Deal and Erwin, had been on duty inside the airship, so weren't privy to events on the bridge. Additionally, Erwin and Deal were enlisted men, which meant naval higher-ups tended to discount their opinion when compared with a senior officer's. And yet Wiley's testimony was surprisingly vague as to what happened. This helps explain why Arnstein was concerned about the *Macon*'s safety.

Hugh Allen once wrote that the *Macon*'s fins 'were rigid enough … that … little external bracing is required'.[26] Arnstein knew better. He'd been pestering Fulton about shoring up the *Akron*'s fins for two years. After the *Akron* crash, he redoubled his efforts.

Travelling to Washington, DC on 19 May 1933, Arnstein met Fulton to present a revised plan for adding cable bracing to the *Macon*'s fins. Fulton didn't refuse Arnstein's proposal outright. Rather, he 'deferred' making a decision until a later date.

But Arnstein refused to back down. Continuing to raise the issue every chance he got, he sent Fulton a letter two months after their Washington meeting:

> I wish to get unofficially your comments on the subject of bracing Frame 17.5 which I had mentioned to you sometime ago. At that time we had studied quite an extensive bracing which would have required some reinforcement on members of Frame 17.5. The weight of 500 to 600lb was considered by you as prohibitive and we had dropped the proposition.[27]

Arnstein was sensitive to Fulton's concern about a weight increase, which is why his revised proposal recommended cable bracing instead of reinforcing frame 17.5. As Arnstein's letter explains:

> I am submitting this idea for your personal consideration since the weight … does not seem to be prohibitive. The general idea is to provide additional reinforcement for the forward part of the fins, which is the part that may get high loads when going into a turn. Unless I hear from you we will not raise the subject any more officially.[28]

Fulton's response, which came two days later, could only have disappointed Arnstein:

> I have your letter about the possibility of reinforcing the forward edge of the fins, and wonder if you will be good enough to tell me more in detail just why you think this reinforcement would be a good thing. Although the weight of the scheme you now propose is not excessive, it involves quite a lot of work … In other words, I feel the additional brace wire … unless it is actually necessary from a standpoint of safety in flight … is something to be avoided.[29]

The two men's correspondence is steeped in a veneer of politeness. Nevertheless, one can't help but feel Fulton's intransigence. Meanwhile, Arnstein's letters smack of an inability to overcome his deference to authority. Despite this shortcoming, Arnstein kept pressing his concerns, if not frantically then with an increasing urgency.

It's also important to note that the letter exchanges between Arnstein and Wiley, Wiley and Arnstein, Arnstein and Fulton, and Fulton and Arnstein were handled in a back channel manner. This is an odd way of dealing with an important issue unless you wish to avoid scrutiny, embarrassment or both. The most remarkable thing is how firmly Fulton resisted fixing an issue the *Macon*'s chief designer thought serious enough to raise time and time again.

One problem is that Arnstein was far too polite to raise his voice. If he had, it might have had an impact on a bully like Fulton. Still, Fulton knew of Arnstein's concerns, especially since they'd been raised so often they'd begun to irritate him. And yet, such was the dysfunctional nature of the Goodyear–Navy relationship that Fulton refused to heed Arnstein's warnings despite their increasing frequency if not decibel level. All because Fulton thought he knew better than the man who had designed the *Macon*.

24

FULTON

The question naturally arises: why would Fulton remain so intransigent given the Navy had already lost the USS *Shenandoah* and *R38* to structural failure? After all, Fulton had gone along with many of Arnstein's innovative designs, including his box-frame girders, 'deep ring' design and eliminating the cruciform tail structure. Why then wouldn't he acquiesce when it came to an important safety issue?

One reason was that the *Akron* loss was chalked up to weather, not structural deficiency. No one thought frame 17.5 was responsible. Additionally, it would be difficult to ground the *Macon* for expensive repairs given the anti-airship climate. If they did, there was a chance the *Macon* would be scrapped and the rigid airship programme cancelled. It's also possible that Fulton and Arnstein simply had a difference of opinion. Having said this, there was an unmistakable conflict between weight, cost, profit and safety when it came to building the *Akron* and *Macon*. The Navy and Goodyear wanted a safe airship, but only the Navy had final approval when it came to the design. When Arnstein recommended a change that increased the *Akron*'s weight, cost or delayed its completion, he either lost the battle or Goodyear paid a penalty. This led to compromises rather than improvements in the *Macon*'s design.

It's clear the Navy's approval process had built-in disincentives when it came to fixing problems. It is to Dr Arnstein's credit that he refused to back down despite these disincentives. He took every opportunity to argue the need to reinforce frame 17.5 and/or add cable bracing. When he complained that Fulton wouldn't permit him to fix the problem, Litchfield brushed him off saying, 'the customer is always right'.[1]

An important part of Fulton's job was approving the *Akron* and *Macon*'s design but getting BUAER approval when a change was recommended was never an easy task. Before he'd say yes, Fulton had to be satisfied Arnstein's stress, weight and cost estimates were correct, and that the change didn't significantly delay completion. When Fulton did approve a change, the Goodyear-Zeppelin staff considered it 'a small miracle'.[2] This was typical of Fulton's high-handed approach towards his vendor. No one had built an airship as complicated as the *Akron* before, yet Fulton penalised Goodyear for 'mistakes' the Navy had an equal hand in making.

It wasn't as if Goodyear didn't know what it was doing. If anything, its airship brain trust was a dream team. In addition to hiring Dr Arnstein from Luftschiffbau Zeppelin and twelve of his most talented engineers (some of whom held doctorates), Goodyear employed Dr Jerome C. Hunsaker, who'd enjoyed a distinguished career as a naval constructor, and C.P. Burgess, who'd worked at the BUAER as an aeronautical engineer. Simply put, Goodyear had more in-house expertise designing big rigids than the Navy. When it came to disagreements, though, the customer was always right.

If it's true every vendor must curry favour with their client, Goodyear's cultivation of the Navy's LTA division was no exception. But there's a fine line between keeping a client happy and allowing bad decisions to be made. While Fulton lorded his power over the company, Arnstein, Hunsaker and Litchfield were reduced to taking orders. Arnstein found it particularly galling that Fulton dismissed his safety concerns. After all, he'd spent his entire career estimating the external forces bearing down on bridges, cathedral buttresses, air docks and dirigibles. But Fulton wouldn't budge.

Of all people, Fulton should have known better. As he wrote in a 1929 paper for the *Journal of the American Society of Naval Engineers*:

> Much thought and experimental effort has been applied to the engineering problems connected with airships … There is still lack of agreement as to what conditions represent the worst that may be encountered … Turbulent air … represents the most severe conditions … [but] our present knowledge is far from complete … For the present, however, the airship designer must … rely on judgment and such lessons as the past have taught, trying to err always on the side of safety.[3]

This is a surprising concession in light of what happened. What's even more revealing is that Fulton admitted: 'There will always remain certain storm disturbances that will wreck any airship … [therefore] we must … avoid dangerous conditions.'[4]

Clearly, Fulton knew there were circumstances in which a rigid airship should not fly. He also knew Moffett pushed his airship captains to fly in weather that grounded most aircraft. And yet he repeatedly dismissed Arnstein's pleas to strengthen the *Akron* and *Macon*.

Fulton once wrote that his relations with contractors were 'cordial … mutually profitable and contributed to the advancement of aeronautical technology'.[5] Nevertheless, the record shows he could be stubborn, demanding, arrogant and condescending. No wonder he was the bane of Arnstein's existence.

A letter from Arnstein about the *Akron*'s teething problems captures the doctor's attempt to placate the imperious Fulton:

> My Dear Commander Fulton, I am very sorry indeed that I have not had an opportunity for a long while to have a more personal talk with you on all the problems connected with airships … I was also very sorry to learn from a few remarks … that you rather felt that we are not having a great deal of interest in the problems connected with the performance of the *Akron*. As a matter of fact there isn't anything that occupies our minds more than these problems. It seems to me however that we have been following a rather unwise policy by trying not to develop into a 'nuisance' by staying outside and eagerly awaiting information from you which might give us an opportunity to approach you with suggestions … It is our desire just as much as yours to help to correct, or at least to understand all deficiencies of our ship.[6]

Arnstein's deference is painfully clear. You can feel him walking on eggshells. If Fulton had listened to Arnstein when the doctor first expressed concerns about the *Akron*, there would have been enough time, money and goodwill to fix the problem. But the data was thin, so Fulton chose not to act. When more data confirmed there was a safety issue, the *Akron* was over budget, overweight and behind schedule. Further delays were unwelcome.

Arnstein wasn't the only person to worry about how securely the *Macon*'s fins were anchored. A member of the *Macon*'s Board of Inspection and Survey also expressed 'astonishment' at the way the fins were attached.[7] Additionally, Kurt Bauch's concerns never went away. When it became clear the *Macon* could fly faster than contractually required, Bauch worried it would put a greater aerodynamic load on the fins than forecast. Before the *Macon*'s final trial flight, he mentioned to Arnstein that there might be 'an opportunity to suggest again to the Navy the addition of some sort of fin brace cables at main frame 17.5'.[8] But Arnstein told him that Fulton had already said no.

Bauch's recollection confirms that bracing the *Macon*'s tail fins was still being discussed as late as 30 August 1933, five months *after* the *Macon* had begun flying. Yet Fulton continued to stand in its way.

Later, Fulton would claim that the Board of Inspection and Survey did not express concern about the *Macon*'s fins during her trial flights.[9] This is disingenuous at best; the trial flights were planned in such a way as to ensure the fins didn't experience excessive wind loads. Fulton would also claim Goodyear's list of uncompleted items for the *Macon* did not 'contain any references to any projected fin brace cables at frame 17.5'.[10] Of course not, he'd prohibited it.

We don't know how 'Froggy' Fulton got his nickname, but it's likely he earned it at Annapolis. Although handsome enough, Fulton's senior photograph in the 1912 edition of *The Lucky Bag* yearbook shows a slight bulging around the eyes, but it's the description underneath that's more revealing. Calling Fulton a 'fusser', it described his personality in uncomplimentary ways:

> An unlooked for determination, a solemnity that at times is almost painful … and there you have … our great enigma, Fulton. He has been with us for four years, but who of us can say that he knows him.[11]

Fulton was a bright student, graduating second in his class from Annapolis. After two years of sea duty he joined the Navy's Construction Corps. During this time, he was sent to the Massachusetts Institute of Technology (MIT) to pursue a graduate degree in naval architecture. There, Fulton took a course in aeronautical engineering from Commander Jerome C. Hunsaker, who would eventually join Goodyear as Vice President of its airship division. Fulton was inspired enough by Hunsaker's course that after graduating MIT, he transferred to the aeronautical division of the Bureau of Construction and Repair. When the Bureau of Aeronautics was formed in 1921, he quickly followed.

When BUAER decided to purchase what would become the *Los Angeles* from Luftschiffbau Zeppelin in 1922, Fulton participated in the negotiations. He spent the next two years supervising her construction in Friedrichshafen, where he met Dr Arnstein. The two were said to become 'friends',[12] but friendship is hard to believe given the power imbalance that existed between them.

While at Friedrichshafen, Fulton developed a reputation among the German staff as intrusive and overbearing, in part because he demanded to see proprietary information the company was reluctant to surrender.[13] Dr Eckener tried smoothing out the differences, but many of the Germans refused to trust Fulton. When Fulton returned to the BUAER, it was as the Navy's leading expert on lighter-than-air design. For better or worse, the pupil had become the teacher.

One reason for Fulton's success is that he had a habit of cultivating powerful men who could help his career. He'd not only studied under Lt Ernest J. King at Annapolis (who'd later become his boss at the BUAER),[14] he'd briefly served as Commander Hunsaker's assistant at the Bureau of Construction and Repair.[15] Neither Moffett nor King knew enough about airship engineering to overrule Fulton. In fact, Moffett considered Fulton so indispensable he relied on him to resolve issues with Goodyear. In other words, no one at the BUAER was in a position to question Fulton's judgment.

By 1933, Fulton had spent nearly ten years as the Navy's top LTA design expert. He may not have had as much experience as Hunsaker or Arnstein, but being their client made him top dog.

When the *Macon*'s first Quarterly Hull Inspection report was issued at the end of September 1933, it was deemed in 'excellent' condition.[16] Nothing could be further from the truth. But the reports would continue to describe the hull as excellent right up until it wasn't. In the meantime, Arnstein seemed powerless to change things. As far as the *Macon* was concerned, Fulton would have a lot to answer for.

25

SUNNYVALE

As the *Macon*'s crew readied their airship for her first transcontinental voyage, they looked forward to their new posting in Sunnyvale, California.[1] However, the *Macon* faced an uncertain future. Neither Admiral David F. Sellers, Commander in Chief of the US Fleet, nor Admiral William H. Standley, Chief of Naval Operations, were favourably inclined towards her.[2] Still, the *Macon*'s crew were too excited to worry about politics as they scrambled about the airship. Believers convinced of their purpose, they would prove the naysayers wrong despite the deck being stacked against them.

Lakehurst was an unseasonably warm 73°F as the *Macon* floated in her hangar on the evening of 12 October 1933. Big rigids generally took off in the early morning when the sun's rays helped to increase their lift, preferring to land in the early evening when temperatures were cooler and the wind had died down. This voyage was the exception, however. It would depart at night.

The *Macon* needed to keep her weight at a minimum for the 3,000-mile journey, so a reduction in flight personnel had been approved. Five of her 'white hats' (Navy slang for enlisted men) were permitted to drive to California.[3] To further lighten her load, the *Macon* would carry only one of her six aeroplanes: the N2Y-1 trainer used to ferry passengers to the ground. Her five Sparrowhawks would fly separately to the Golden State.

When Dresel gave the 'Up Ship!' command at 1805 hours, the *Macon*, with seventy-four souls aboard, lifted slowly into the sky.[4] Rising gracefully through low, scattered clouds, a light wind blew warm air through the open bridge windows. As the airship assumed a gentle upwards slope, Dresel instinctively adopted the spread-legged stance of a sailor at sea. Once she reached 1,000ft he waited for the N2Y-1 to fly aboard before setting course for Richmond, Virginia.

Airships preferred the southern route when crossing the United States because it allowed them to skirt the higher parts of the Rockies and Sierra mountains. Hugging the eastern seaboard, they flew south to Georgia before crossing Alabama, Mississippi, Louisiana, Texas, New Mexico and Arizona. After that, they turned north heading for California.

The crew lived in a relatively small area of the *Macon* compared to the vast size of her interior, but duty stations were spread throughout the ship. Wide-ranging inspections were conducted every four hours. These ranged from the mooring station in the tip of her bow to the inside of her four gigantic fins and everything in between. This included the *Macon*'s gas cells, which were inspected for leaks, her girders for wear, her outer cover for tears and the 1,500 miles of wire holding it all together for their prescribed tension. This endless cycle of inspections kept the bosun's mates, electrician's mates, first- and second-class seamen and aviation machinist's mates (who tended the engines) plenty busy.

Dresel made it a point to fly over the Georgia town where Carl Vinson, the Chairman of the House Naval Affairs Committee, lived since he paid the bills.[5] Next, he passed over the *Macon*'s namesake city. Everything seemed to be going smoothly until the *Macon* encountered her first real test over western Texas.

Airships frequently experienced difficulty over Texas. The *Shenandoah*, *Graf* and *Akron* had all run into trouble there. The west Texas Mountains, ranging from 5,000 to 8,000ft, sometimes forced an airship above pressure height. The state's thunderstorms, which were outsized and obnoxious, were also infamous. Knowing there was never enough room to manoeuvre in its narrow mountain passes, and no place to land in an emergency, airship captains loathed flying over the Lone Star State, but they had little choice. It was the only route that circumvented the mountains, which were too high for an airship to fly over.

Shortly after reaching the Texas border, the *Macon* ran into a thunderstorm. Dresel's aversion to thunderheads was well known, so he tried skirting the front. But he soon found his airship buffeted by winds and torrential sheets of rain. Given the *Macon*'s surface size, thunderstorms could add as much as 8 tons of water to her outer covering, forcing a loss in altitude.[6] Fighting powerful headwinds, Dresel threaded through the painfully narrow canyon, watching mountain peaks pass at eye level. As lightning flashed, rain drummed so loudly on the airship's cover it drowned out conversation on the bridge. When the outside temperature suddenly dropped, the *Macon* shot over pressure height, where she began automatically venting helium. Dresel dumped ballast to compensate, but it was a tense moment. No one could forget both the *Akron* and *Shenandoah* had been lost in similar storms, but three hours later the tempest passed.[7]

After seventy hours in the air, the *Macon* arrived over Sunnyvale, California. True to the town's name, it was a beautiful day. The sky was a spectacular blue, the orchards drenched in sunshine.

A Goodyear blimp greeted the *Macon* over NAS Sunnyvale. Thanks to the press wizardry of Hugh Allen, her gondola was jammed with newspaper reporters to record the *Macon*'s historic arrival. As the *Volunteer* circled the *Macon*, the newsmen were awed by the size of the Navy's airship, which looked as if it could gobble them up and still be hungry.

Dresel wanted to show off his airship, so he flew the 38 miles north to San Francisco. San Francisco was a relatively small city in 1933. With a population just over 500,000, she not only failed to make the list of America's ten largest cities, she was half the size of Los Angeles. But what she lacked in size she made up for in spirit. When the *Macon* arrived, thousands of people crowded the city's rooftops, cheering at the top of their lungs as she flew lazily by.

When the *Macon* returned to Sunnyvale, the reception awaiting her was even more impressive. The South Bay was rural and sparsely populated, but you wouldn't have known it from the turnout. Hundreds of cars lined the Bayshore Highway as 30,000 people gathered to watch her arrival. Men in suits accompanied by women in calf-length dresses gathered along the chain-link fence marking the base's perimeter. In keeping with the historic occasion, parents brought their children, adding a carnival-like atmosphere.

Since airships require a large, unobstructed area for take-off and landing, the crowd had an excellent view of the 1,000-acre base. This included one of the *Macon*'s two gigantic mooring-out circles, which was twice as large as a major league baseball field. Directly behind the mooring-out circle stood the *Macon*'s hangar. Twenty storeys tall, it was the biggest structure between San Jose and San Francisco.

As the *Macon* flew over her new home, the crowd's murmur turned into a roar. Dresel idled the airship's eight engines, ordering smoke flares be dropped to gauge the wind direction. Then he conducted a weigh off.

Landing was always a delicate procedure for a big rigid. Their size, weight, and constantly changing buoyancy made it difficult, especially when the wind was blowing. Dresel reduced speed as he approached the mooring mast. At an altitude of 200ft, he ordered the engines backed down to check their progress. Shortly thereafter, the airship dropped her landing lines, which were snapped up by ground handlers. Ground crews had shrunk dramatically since the days when 200 men were needed to land the *Shenandoah*, but it was still a tough job. Not only were they engaged in a tug of war with an object immeasurably bigger and stronger; they often got soaked when an airship, needing to lighten its load, dumped its water ballast directly on top of them.

One of the *Macon*'s trail ropes accidentally landed on a sightseer's car, damaging it, otherwise the landing proceeded smoothly.[8] As the *Macon*'s bow approached the mast, her mooring cable was lowered through a hatch in her bow. A half dozen sailors balanced precariously atop the mooring mast, grabbed the cable and attached a line. Then a winch at the base of the mast began reeling in the airship. Shortly before 1630 hours, the *Macon*'s mooring cone was safely 'locked in the cup'.[9]

With the airship officially secured, her stern was moored to a railroad flat car. Next, the stairs in her control car's aft compartment were lowered to the ground. Dresel stepped out looking tired but was gracious enough to smile at reporters. Calling the *Macon* a 'splendid ship', he said, 'Each officer and man performed his duties in a commendatory manner.'[10] What he didn't say is how relieved he must have felt to safely deliver the Navy's last-surviving rigid airship to her new home.

The next day's headlines were enthusiastic. The *San Francisco Examiner*, a pro-airship paper given its owner, William Randolph Hearst, had sponsored the *Graf*'s round-the-world voyage, screamed the loudest. 'Macon Makes Pygmies of Skyscrapers', it read.[11] The account of her arrival was equally effusive: 'Biggest. Strongest. Fastest. Safest. The USS *Macon*, pride of the Navy, is all of these. Among all the lighter-than-air craft in the world, America's newest dirigible is supreme.'[12] As far as San Francisco was concerned, the *Macon* could do no wrong.

The heart of Moffett's big rigid programme now shifted from Lakehurst to Sunnyvale. Dozens of west coast communities had vied for the honour of hosting the airship, with Moffett leading the search. Camp Kearny, an Army post near San Diego, had been the inside favourite, leaving the Bay area an underdog. But when the mayor of San Francisco heard about the search, he found the idea of a new naval base so economically enticing he issued a public appeal for land to house it. Laura T. Whipple, a local real estate agent, heeded the call. Hearing that Ynigo Ranch in the South Bay was up for sale, she paid it a visit. The ranch seemed ideal given it was situated on a flat, treeless plain, so Whipple helped recruit four local counties to raise money to buy it.* They were joined by the San Jose Chamber of Commerce and several local newspapers, which eventually raised the majority of the ranch's $476,077 purchase price.[13]

Even after the land was bought it wasn't clear the Navy would accept it. Critics claimed the region was too foggy, while Sunnyvale supporters countered Camp Kearny was vulnerable to attack. It wasn't until the Bay Area deeded the land to the Navy for a dollar that it clinched the competition.[14]

Sunnyvale was so excited by the news, it closed its schools for a day and held a parade.[15] It's not hard to understand why. The Navy promised to spend $5 million building the airship base.[16] Combined with 500 new construction jobs as well as the revenue generated by the servicemen who'd be housed there, NAS Sunnyvale was an economic godsend in the bleak days of the Depression. As one Chamber of Commerce member told Moffett in a telegram, 'Santa Clara … appreciates your efforts more than any other man in the US Navy.'[17]

The airship base was an anomaly amidst the region's orange trees, almond groves and dairy farms, but aviation-related firms soon sprang up to serve it. Fed by a thriving military-industrial complex, the peninsula's aeronautics industry would evolve into such giants as Lockheed, the Martin Company and NASA – many with branches near NAS Sunnyvale. When the aerospace industry fell on hard times, it eventually morphed into the hi-tech field, becoming Silicon Valley in part because the greatest white elephant technology in aviation history had been based at NAS Sunnyvale.

The name NAS Sunnyvale was surprisingly misleading. The base actually spanned two towns: Sunnyvale to the south and Mountain View to the north, with the majority of the base in Mountain View. But Navy officials thought it a mistake to name the base Mountain View, given the natural antipathy airships had for mountains.[18] The name didn't last long, though. Commissioned only eight days after the *Akron* crashed, NAS Sunnyvale had its name changed one month later when the Secretary of the Navy renamed it Moffett Field in honour of the man responsible for its creation.[19]

The *Macon*'s crew soon became local celebrities. Bay area newspapers wrote about her flights, while her take-offs and landings usually drew a crowd. Given the airship was visible from many vantage points around the bay, people

---

*   The participating counties were Santa Clara, San Mateo, San Francisco and Alameda.

jumped in their cars whenever she appeared and sped towards Sunnyvale to watch her land. Things could have been far worse for the *Macon's* crew in the midst of the Depression. Sunnyvale, true to its name, was not only a delightful post, but a Navy safe harbour. In short, Moffett Field was the bay area's version of Cape Kennedy, with the *Macon* a stand-in for the Saturn V rocket and her crew the glamorous astronauts.

Hollywood even got into the act when Warner Brothers' biggest star, Jimmy Cagney, portrayed a sky sailor aboard the *Macon* in the feature film *Here Comes the Navy*. Shot on location at Moffett Field and featuring scenes of the airship in flight, the movie received an Academy Award nomination for Best Picture. The airship's crew couldn't have been prouder.

Moffett Field may have been an ultra-modern, state-of-the-art airship base, but when it first opened it looked like a new housing development plopped down in the middle of a broccoli field.* Composed of buildings in the Spanish adobe style with red clay-tiled roofs, the base sat on a vast, open plain bordered by San Francisco Bay to the east and the Bayshore Highway to the west. Its one- and two-storey administration buildings arranged around a quadrangle looked like a child's play set next to the huge hangar and helium storage tank that towered above them. The hangar, built in the art deco style of Streamline Moderne, was so huge it could accommodate three *Titanic*-sized ocean liners side by side, with room to spare.[20]

In a memo written eleven days after the *Macon* arrived in Sunnyvale, Admiral Standley made it clear the *Macon* had a limited grace period in which to perform:

> The department desires that the *Macon* be employed to the fullest extent practicable in fleet operations in order that her military value as a unit of the fleet may be ascertained. Submit a report by 30 September 1934, giving conclusions reached, together with recommendations as to future policy of the Navy Department in regard to the continued operation and new construction of rigid airships.[21]

---

*   The Ynigo ranch grew broccoli, cauliflower and hay on the site.

In plain English, Standley was giving the *Macon* a year to prove herself. A year isn't long for a new weapon to demonstrate its value, but the Navy's patience had worn thin. Dresel, the *Macon*'s captain, was aware of the situation. But asking battleship officers to give the *Macon* a fair chance was unrealistic. Simply put, the judges were biased.

There was another problem, however, one that had nothing to do with whether the *Macon* was a useful addition to the fleet. It was the question of whether Dresel was the best man for the job. The answer is, he wasn't.

26

UP TO THE TASK?

The question about Dresel had more to do with temperament than ability. Other officers had more hours flying in airships, but Dresel was the only one to have captained three of the Navy's five big rigids. Forty-four years old when he took command of the *Macon*, he'd been captain during her trial flights as well as her shakedown at Lakehurst. It's fair to say Dresel knew the *Macon* better than anyone else. Nevertheless, it would take more than familiarity to prove her a worthy addition to the fleet.

A graduate of the US Naval Academy, Dresel had spent nearly twenty years in the surface Navy. He'd not only commanded five Wickes-class destroyers (which he referred to as 'four-stackers') but a Yangtze River gunboat in China.[1] Then Dresel did something unusual. In 1929, he volunteered for Moffett's LTA programme.

Why Dresel would give up two decades in the surface fleet to join an experimental aviation programme is unclear. One reason may be that the new generation of airships presented more opportunities for advancement than the fleet. Or, maybe he was looking for a new challenge. What's clear is that Dresel took a left turn in his career.

Dresel was old for LTA school, but that wasn't the only problem. His quick advancement rubbed some of the old guard the wrong way. After serving a year as first officer aboard the *Los Angeles*, he was put in command and helmed her for eleven months. In spring 1932, he was ordered aboard the *Akron* to serve as executive officer on her first transcontinental flight. Five weeks later, he was put in charge.

Career airship officers such as Wiley and Rosendahl felt that experience not rank should earn a command. But Dresel had the rank of Commander, allowing him to jump ahead of more experienced airship officers, leaving Wiley and Rosendahl to grumble.

Dresel gained important experience commanding the *Akron* but had trouble figuring out how to best use her heavier-than-air unit. Having said this, there were disagreements in LTA circles on how to employ the airship's aircraft. Lt Ward 'Crash Helmet' Harrigan, Squadron Leader of the *Akron*'s HTA unit, believed her planes should be used to increase the airship's scouting range. Commander Rosendahl, who'd captained the *Akron* before Dresel, thought her planes would be best used to defend against attack. Then again, Rosendahl thought the *Akron* could be used for bombing – an idea that should have been put to rest after the Zeppelins' mixed record during the First World War.[2]

Dresel came down somewhere in the middle. He favoured using the airship to locate the enemy but then letting her aeroplanes develop the contact once she'd retreated to safety.[3] Deciding how to use the *Akron*'s planes was an important strategic question because they were essential to the airship's effectiveness. If aerial navigation had been more advanced, or radios and radio direction finders more sophisticated, Dresel might have used his aeroplanes to scout more effectively. As it turned out, he was fairly unimaginative.

Described as a 'modest man who loathed publicity',[4] Dresel could look dashing when he wore his white scarf and leather aviator's jacket, but he usually kept a low profile. As proof, he resisted many of the requests the *Macon* received for hand-waving flights,[5] choosing to train his men at sea – a far more appropriate use of an ocean-going scout than building goodwill for the Navy.

Additionally, Dresel was one of the LTA programme's most popular skippers.[6] Firm but fair, he treated his crew with respect regardless of rank. His jumping to the front of the line may have instilled grumbling among his peers, but Dresel's men appreciated his benevolent command style. For example, he preferred flying only on Monday through Thursday, giving his crew a long weekend off. If a sailor on liberty got into trouble in town, Dresel would look the other way so long as the man was back on base before midnight Sunday.

What's clear is Dresel was unusually solicitous of his men.[7] Popular author John Toland, whose ability to tell an entertaining story occasionally gets in the way of the facts, recounts the time Dresel found a rigger aboard the *Akron*, asleep at his post. The sailor was understandably terrified given it was a court martial offence. According to Toland, Dresel calmed the sailor by saying, 'I hear your little girl was pretty sick last night. You'd better cork off a few hours. I'll stand your watch till you get someone to relieve me.'[8] If true, this is a remarkable story. If not, Dresel's decency was still plain for everyone to see.

If the man had a weakness, it was in being too cautious. As he told the Navy's Court of Inquiry into the *Akron* crash, 'My ideas of the operation of rigid airships are probably very conservative … I do not concur in statements which I have often heard that these ships can stand by any kind of weather.'[9]

The *Macon's* crew found Dresel's conservative approach reassuring, knowing their commander was unlikely to fly in the kind of weather that might get them killed. This made Dresel the ideal commander if you didn't want to lose your airship in a crash. But his conservative approach was the opposite of what the *Macon* needed. Moffett's big rigid programme was in its eleventh hour and everything was riding on the *Macon's* performance. Was Dresel capable of the kind of out-of-the-box thinking necessary to prove the *Macon* worthy? Specifically, could he develop the kind of strategy and tactics needed to show the *Macon* was an effective long-range scout when many in the Navy were ready to condemn her?

Dresel may have been loved by his crew, but a cautious approach was not what was needed. The *Macon* required a commander who could hit a game-winning home run in the bottom of the ninth. Dresel was more likely to bunt. In the meantime, the umpires were rooting against him.

If training cruises and hook-on drills were the *Macon's* 'required reading', her final exam was the Navy's fleet exercises held several times a year to measure performance. Fleet exercises were simulated war games based on real-world scenarios. The exercises divided the fleet into two opposing forces (e.g. Blue and Black) each assigned a task such as attacking or defending the Panama Canal. The results were used to refine naval strategy necessary for countering a variety of threats.

Unfortunately, the Navy's big rigids had never distinguished themselves during fleet exercises – not that they'd participated in many. The *Shenandoah* had flown in only one and though she'd found the enemy, she was forced to drop out due to mechanical problems.[10]

Since the Treaty of Versailles forbade the *Los Angeles* from participating in military activities, an exemption had to be obtained before she could partake in Fleet Problem XII. Held off the west coast of Panama in 1931, the *Los Angeles* found the opposing fleet but was ruled 'shot down' shortly thereafter.*

---

*   In one of those quirks of fate, Dresel was the umpire aboard the *Los Angeles* who ruled her shot down.

That airships were vulnerable to being shot down was not wasted on Moffett. That's why the *Akron* was designed to carry aeroplanes to defend against attack. By using her planes to repel enemy fighters, an airship could increase its chances of survival. But the *Akron* carried none of her planes when she participated in a scouting exercise with the fleet off the east coast in January 1932.[11] Instead, they used lookouts.[12] By the time the *Akron* got close enough to spot the enemy, she was ruled 'shot down' again.

It's important to note that no airship was actually 'shot down' during a fleet exercise. They were just ruled so by on-board umpires who, looking out the windows of the airship's control car, judged whether a surface ship blinking its signal light to simulate anti-aircraft fire had hit the target.

In addition to deploying planes to defend the airship against attack, the *Akron* had machine-gun nests that, during war games, used camera guns to repel air attacks. If it sounds like an airship bristled with defensive weapons, they did. But that didn't stop them from being shot down. So long as captains like Dresel used the airship rather than her planes to find the enemy, they were vulnerable to attack.

Fleet Problem XIII, held in the waters around Hawaii in March 1932, simulated an attack on Pearl Harbor by enemy aircraft carriers. Unfortunately, the *Akron* missed the exercise because her tail-smashing incident had put her in the repair shop. This was a missed opportunity since the fleet problem was ideal for showcasing the *Akron*'s ability to scout large areas of ocean. Had she been successful it would suggest she might have been useful in preventing Japan's attack on Pearl Harbor. Since she didn't participate, we'll never know.

The *Akron* performed only slightly better during the June fleet exercise off the California coast. Although she succeeded in finding the enemy, she was not carrying her planes and therefore unable to defend against attack. When enemy planes found her she was judged shot down.

The commander of the scouting force thought so little of the *Akron*'s performance he recommended against spending more money on big rigids, at least for the foreseeable future.[13] Admiral Standley didn't need much convincing. He was already sceptical.

Admiral King, Moffett's successor, fought hard to get the *Macon* a 'square deal',[14] but his influence was limited once she was operating with the fleet. It was up to Dresel to change opinions, but he had never commanded an airship during a fleet exercise before the *Macon*. This meant he had little practical experience in airship scouting. Nor was there much precedent to follow, making Dresel's task more difficult.

Fleet exercises D, E, F and G, held over a three-month period beginning in late 1933, was an alphabet soup of failure for the *Macon*.

There's no denying Dresel got off to a slow start. Exercise D, held in November, was one of the largest war games in US naval history. The *Macon* took up position off Point Arguello, California, searching for the Brown fleet, but Dresel stumbled from the beginning. He wasn't two hours into the exercise before the *Macon* was shot down by an enemy cruiser. Since there was no point in returning to Sunnyvale, the *Macon* was reincarnated as the ZRS-6 and continued the exercise. Later that day, she was shot down again, this time becoming the ZRS-7.[15]

Dresel turned in another desultory performance the next day for Exercise E. At one point, so many enemy fighters swarmed his airship it was described as a bee attack. Once again, he was ruled shot down.[16]

In his defence, Dresel had good reason to limit use of the *Macon*'s planes. He didn't want to risk them getting lost while searching for the enemy. Sparrowhawks had radio sets and homing equipment, but neither were reliable,[17] so there was a constant fear a Sparrowhawk might never find its way back to the airship. Both the *Akron* and *Macon*'s HTA units worked hard to overcome this limitation, developing a navigation method that allowed them to journey out of visual range, but Dresel never fully grasped the role aeroplanes could play in the *Macon*'s scouting missions, so they continued to be underused.

It didn't help that the fleet exercises were formulated in such a way as to put the *Macon* at a disadvantage. Her strength was surveying broad swaths of ocean, not small areas crowded with the enemy. Since Moffett knew scouting a congested area was a problem for airships, he'd explored ways of camouflaging them. Various paint schemes designed to make a big rigid blend in with the sky were investigated, but finding an aerial analogue for battleship grey proved difficult. An aerial smokescreen dropped by aeroplanes was considered, but the smoke proved so acrid the Navy worried it would burn a hole in an airship's outer covering. The real problem wasn't camouflage; it was that airships needed to get so close to the enemy to spot them – they were big, fat targets.

Dresel fared little better during Exercise F held in January 1934, in which the *Macon* flew over the enemy fleet at night with her lights illuminated.[18] The results were predictable. To be fair, its amazing Sparrowhawk pilots could spot the enemy at all given everything they had to do in the cockpit. Not only were they subject to wind, rain, cold and the spray of hot engine oil; they had to control the stick with one hand, operate a telegraph key with the other and work the rudder pedals with their feet, all while reading a navigation chart and keeping an eye on the fuel gauge.[19]

Concerned about the *Macon*'s weak performance, Admiral King sent a letter to Dresel after Exercise F:

My Dear Dresel:

This is a crucial year for airships with the *Macon* carrying practically all the hopes for the future of airships in the Navy. The attitude of certain influential members of Congress as unfolded at our recent appropriation hearings is not favourable … I understand that Admiral Standley told the Committee 'off the record' that the *Macon*'s performances to date had not been impressive.

The whole situation is one that calls for the most strenuous work during the next nine months, to the end that a positively favorable report may be forthcoming from Fleet authorities. I am fearful that a neutral sort of report will not be sufficient.

It is too much to expect that special Fleet problems will be framed to suit the *Macon*'s special capabilities. Likewise, major Fleet exercises will be few and far between. It seems to me that intervening periods ought to be employed on special problems framed to suit the *Macon*'s capabilities as a scout, and executed by the *Macon* independently or in conjunction with Fleet units … I am writing a personal letter to Admiral Halligan as a plea for the wider use of the *Macon* and a square deal for her so that at the end of the year no one can say she has not had a fair deal.[20]

One reason King was so concerned about the *Macon*'s performance is that she'd recently been transferred from the Rigid Airship Training and Experimental Squadron to the aircraft division of the US Fleet's Battle Force (COMBATFOR). This was a crucial difference because it meant the *Macon* had graduated from being an 'experimental' aircraft to taking her place amidst the fleet. The coddling was over.

But getting the *Macon* a 'fair deal' was as much a political challenge as a military one. King's letter requesting Dresel show more initiative was only half the battle. The other half was getting the Navy to tailor fleet exercises to showcase the *Macon*'s strengths.

King delivered on his promise to pen a letter to Rear Admiral John Halligan, Commander Aircraft, Battle Forces. In it, he asked that the *Macon* receive special consideration:

Dear John:

I don't know to what extent you get in on planning the tasks which are being set for the *Macon* to execute but I hope that at every opportunity you will personally and officially advocate her employment to the maximum possible extent.

This is to be a critical year for airships. We have only one ... We must not be reckless, but if airships are to justify themselves the *Macon* has got to show more than she has shown.

The more I see of airships the more I can visualise a useful field for them in searching operations, especially in conjunction with their airplanes, provided we can get the airships to perform ...

Most of the problems will be close to shore for reasons of economy, and this factor will probably prevent the long range characteristic of the airship from showing up to best advantage ... but I never would consider an airship as of much use in tactical scouting.[21]

King recommended Halligan set up special scouting problems for the *Macon*, such as 'searching for any vessels that may be passing between Hawaii and the coast,'[22] to show that she could find a needle in a haystack. The challenge was persuading the fleet to co-operate. But the surface Navy was happy to rely on its heavy cruisers as ocean-going scouts, so pleas to employ the *Macon* in ways for which she was designed fell on deaf ears. Meanwhile, Dresel continued to flounder.

Bad weather delayed the *Macon*'s arrival at Exercise H in February 1934. Visibility was so poor she accidently flew over two enemy battleships, which quickly shot her down.[23] When the weather continued to deteriorate, Dresel high-tailed it back to Sunnyvale, missing Exercise I altogether.[24] As far as the fleet was concerned, the *Macon* was a flying white elephant.

Some officers in the LTA programme accused Dresel of treating the *Macon* with kid gloves, including Rosendahl, who didn't think he flew her often or aggressively enough.[25] One reason Dresel's caution was understandable is that he didn't want to be the third Navy commander to lose a big rigid. Some thought the loss of an airship acceptable in wartime once she'd reported on the enemy's location, but others preferred she never be given the chance.

March 1934 marked the one-year anniversary of the *Macon*'s christening. Admiral Moffett's widow, Jeanette, sent a telegram commemorating the event:

> Just a year ago, I christened you. In the 12 months since then much has happened; but you, under the guidance of Capt. Dresel, have triumphantly fulfilled every hope we held for you that day. I have sure faith that in the days to come continued success will follow you, and that you will splendidly justify the belief of Admiral Moffett in the dirigible. God speed you!

The next month, it was discovered the *Macon*'s aeroplane hangar had suffered a minor structural failure. Nobody had noticed because it was in a difficult place to spot. The failure was easily repaired, so no one paid it much attention,[26] but as it turned out, it was a harbinger of things to come.

Between November 1933 and April 1934, the *Macon* participated in five out of six fleet exercises, during which she was shot down six times, all under Dresel's command. Although she had moderate success finding the enemy, the *Macon* was dismissed early from two of the exercises, late to one and missed another altogether due to poor weather.

The *Macon* was blamed for this lackadaisical performance, but Dresel was responsible. Had he used her aeroplanes to find the enemy while keeping the airship safely out of reach, he would not have been shot down as frequently. Consequently, the naval exercises reinforced every poor opinion the surface fleet held about airships. Dresel might have learned his lessons faster if radio direction finders had been more sophisticated, but what-ifs are not the same as what happened. It wasn't that Dresel was incompetent, far from it. What he wasn't was inspired.

Harrigan's premature departure from the *Akron*'s HTA unit probably had as much to do with hampering the development of scouting techniques as Dresel's lack of imagination, but his over-reliance on the airship to do the scouting instead of her aeroplanes was the biggest part of the problem. Combined with his insistence on playing it safe, it's no surprise most minds were made up.

By the spring of 1934, it was clear the *Macon*'s days were numbered. Dresel had only one chance left to prove himself: Fleet Problem XV scheduled for the Caribbean in May. The future of the American airship lay in Dresel's hands, but not even Dresel could anticipate what happened next.

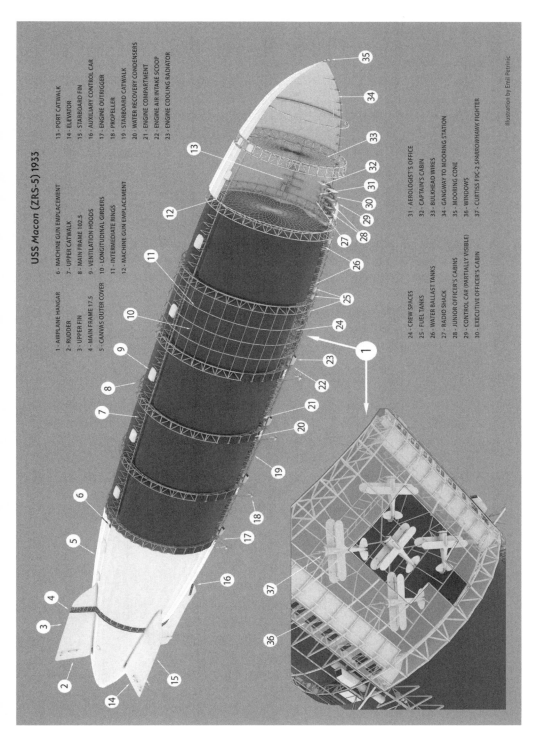

USS Macon (ZRS-5) 1933

1 - AIRPLANE HANGAR
2 - RUDDER
3 - UPPER FIN
4 - MAIN FRAME 17.5
5 - CANVAS OUTER COVER
6 - MACHINE GUN EMPLACEMENT
7 - UPPER CATWALK
8 - MAIN FRAME 102.5
9 - VENTILATION HOODS
10 - LONGITUDINAL GIRDERS
11 - INTERMEDIATE RINGS
12 - MACHINE GUN EMPLACEMENT
13 - PORT CATWALK
14 - ELEVATOR
15 - STARBOARD FIN
16 - AUXILIARY CONTROL CAR
17 - ENGINE OUTRIGGER
18 - PROPELLER
19 - STARBOARD CATWALK
20 - WATER RECOVERY CONDENSERS
21 - ENGINE COMPARTMENT
22 - ENGINE AIR INTAKE SCOOP
23 - ENGINE COOLING RADIATOR
24 - CREW SPACES
25 - FUEL TANKS
26 - WATER BALLAST TANKS
27 - RADIO SHACK
28 - JUNIOR OFFICER'S CABINS
29 - CONTROL CAR (PARTIALLY VISIBLE)
30 - EXECUTIVE OFFICER'S CABIN
31 - AEROLOGIST'S OFFICE
32 - CAPTAIN'S CABIN
33 - BULKHEAD WIRES
34 - GANGWAY TO MOORING STATION
35 - MOORING CONE
36 - WINDOWS
37 - CURTISS F9C-2 SPARROWHAWK FIGHTER

Illustration by Emil Petrinic

The *Akron* and *Macon* were the largest, most expensive and most technologically sophisticated aircraft of their day. The *Macon* in particular could carry up to five Curtiss F9C-2 Sparrowhawks in her belly hangar, which could be launched and retrieved in mid-flight, making her a flying aircraft carrier. (Emil Petrinic)

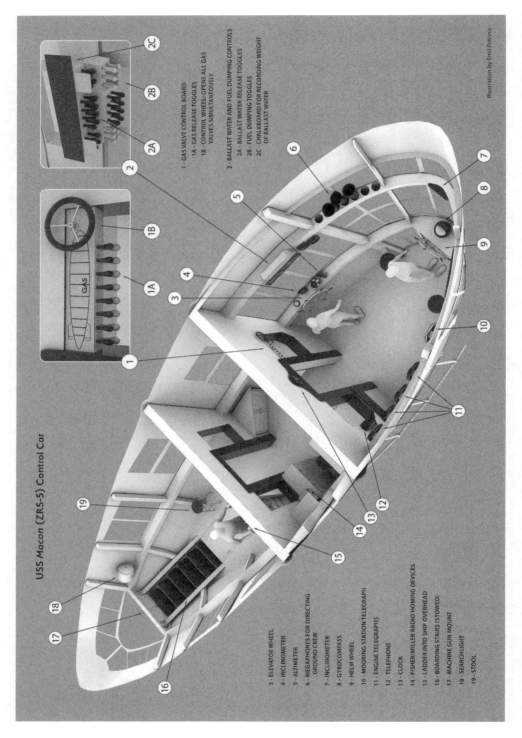

USS Macon (ZRS-5) Control Car

1 - GAS VALVE CONTROL BOARD
1A - GAS RELEASE TOGGLES
1B - CONTROL WHEEL: OPENS ALL GAS VALVES SIMULTANEOUSLY
2 - BALLAST WATER AND FUEL DUMPING CONTROLS
2A - BALLAST WATER RELEASE TOGGLES
2B - FUEL DUMPING TOGGLES
2C - CHALKBOARD FOR RECORDING WEIGHT OF BALLAST WATER

3 - ELEVATOR WHEEL
4 - INCLINOMETER
5 - ALTIMETER
6 - MEGAPHONES FOR DIRECTING GROUND CREW
7 - INCLINOMETER
8 - GYROCOMPASS
9 - HELM WHEEL
10 - MOORING STATION TELEGRAPH
11 - ENGINE TELEGRAPHS
12 - TELEPHONE
13 - CLOCK
14 - FISHER/MILLER RADIO HOMING DEVICES
15 - LADDER INTO SHIP OVERHEAD
16 - BOARDING STAIRS (STOWED)
17 - MACHINE GUN MOUNT
18 - SEARCHLIGHT
19 - STOOL

Illustration by Emil Petrinic

The control car was the *Macon*'s command centre. Roughly the same size as a single-decker bus, it was divided into three compartments: the forward compartment contained the bridge where the elevator and helm stations were located; the navigator's room in the middle compartment; and the aft compartment where the crew liked to smoke. (Emil Petrinic)

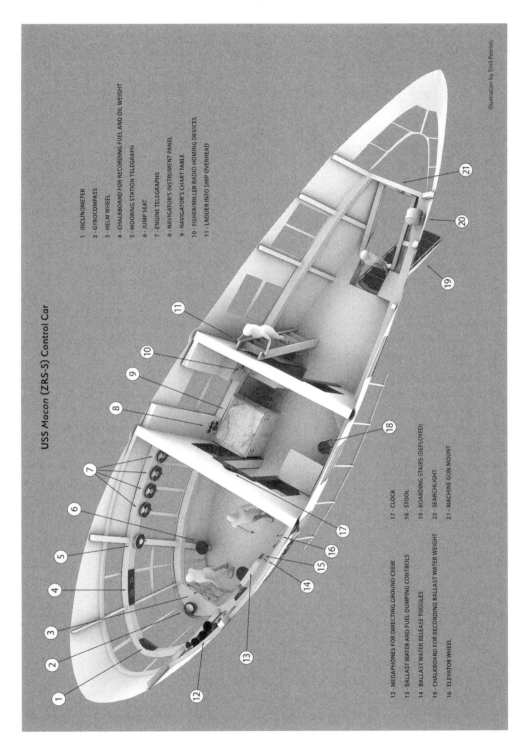

USS *Macon* (ZRS-5) Control Car

1 - INCLINOMETER
2 - GYROCOMPASS
3 - HELM WHEEL
4 - CHALKBOARD FOR RECORDING FUEL AND OIL WEIGHT
5 - MOORING STATION TELEGRAPH
6 - JUMP SEAT
7 - ENGINE TELEGRAPHS
8 - NAVIGATOR'S INSTRUMENT PANEL
9 - NAVIGATOR'S CHART TABLE
10 - FISHER/MILLER RADIO HOMING DEVICES
11 - LADDER INTO SHIP OVERHEAD

12 - MEGAPHONES FOR DIRECTING GROUND CREW
13 - BALLAST WATER AND FUEL DUMPING CONTROLS
14 - BALLAST WATER RELEASE TOGGLES
15 - CHALKBOARD FOR RECORDING BALLAST WATER WEIGHT
16 - ELEVATOR WHEEL

17 - CLOCK
18 - STOOL
19 - BOARDING STAIRS (DEPLOYED)
20 - SEARCHLIGHT
21 - MACHINE GUN MOUNT

Illustration by Emil Petrinic

When looked at horizontally, the *Macon*'s control car is shown with the bridge in the upper left corner (a man can be seen standing at the helm) and the aft cabin in the bottom right, with the ladder leading into the ship overhead, and stairs deployed for landing. The elevator station on the port side of the bridge can also be seen, with a man standing in front of its wheel. (Emil Petrinic)

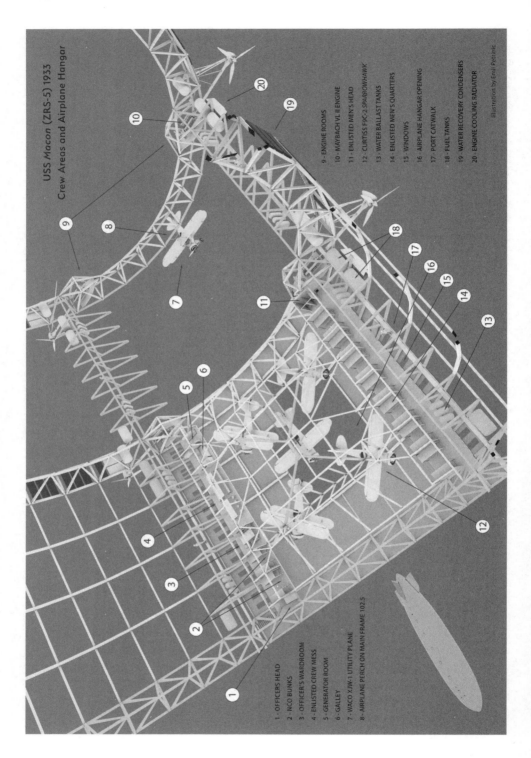

USS *Macon* (ZRS-5) 1933
Crew Areas and Airplane Hangar

Illustration by Emil Petrinic

1 - OFFICER'S HEAD
2 - NCO BUNKS
3 - OFFICER'S WARDROOM
4 - ENLISTED CREW MESS
5 - GENERATOR ROOM
6 - GALLEY
7 - WACO XJW-1 UTILITY PLANE
8 - AIRPLANE PERCH ON MAIN FRAME 102.5
9 - ENGINE ROOMS
10 - MAYBACH VL II ENGINE
11 - ENLISTED MEN'S HEAD
12 - CURTISS F9C-2 SPARROWHAWK
13 - WATER BALLAST TANKS
14 - ENLISTED MEN'S QUARTERS
15 - WINDOWS
16 - AIRPLANE HANGAR OPENING
17 - PORT CATWALK
18 - FUEL TANKS
19 - WATER RECOVERY CONDENSERS
20 - ENGINE COOLING RADIATOR

A close up view of the *Macon*'s belly hangar, showing five Curtiss F9C-2 Sparrowhawks hanging in place. The dark space underneath the aeroplanes indicates the hangar doors are open. (Emil Petrinic)

Called 'the father of naval aviation', Admiral William A. Moffett, Chief of the US Navy's Bureau of Aeronautics, was first to envision a fleet of dirigibles patrolling the Pacific to prevent a surprise attack by Japan. (Courtesy US Naval History and Heritage Command, Catalogue #NH50867)

One of America's leading industrialists, Paul W. Litchfield was President of the Goodyear Tire & Rubber Co. A giant in his field, Litchfield not only built the USS *Akron* and *Macon* for the Navy but was determined to launch a fleet of passenger-carrying airships that could span the globe. (Goodyear Tire & Rubber Company Records, The University of Akron, Akron, Ohio)

Dr Karl Arnstein helped design Zeppelins to bomb London during the First World War. When the war was over, he found himself working for his former enemy designing airships for military and commercial use. (San Diego Air & Space Museum Library and Archives, Catalogue #BIOA00275)

Lt Commander Herbert V. Wiley (shown here with his three children) was given the nearly impossible task of proving the USS *Macon* a worthy addition to the fleet, despite the many obstacles placed in his way. (Courtesy Wiley/Ross Family)

When Litchfield finally closed a deal to build rigid airships for the Navy, he thought his problems were over. Instead, they were just beginning. Litchfield is shown seated left at the 1928 contract signing ceremony next to Secretary of the Navy, Curtis D. Wilbur. Dr Karl Arnstein stands just right of Litchfield, with Goodyear-Zeppelin's Vice President, Jerome C. Hunsaker standing to Arnstein's left. Commander Garland Fulton, Moffett's lighter-than-air expert, is at the extreme right of the photo, hands crossed. (Goodyear Tire & Rubber Company Records, Archival Services, University Libraries, University of Akron, Akron, Ohio)

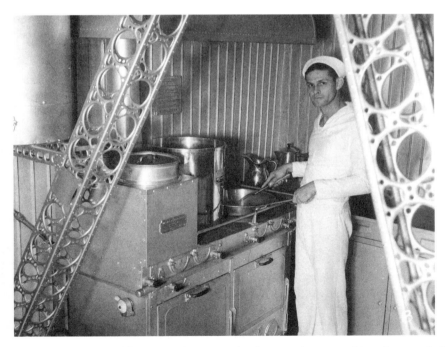

The *Akron* and *Macon* were self-contained cities in the sky, carrying everything they needed to support their eighty-man crew as they patrolled the ocean for days at a time without having to land. This included a galley, sick bay, radio shack, navigator and weather offices, telephones, electricity, running water, eight machine-gun emplacements and a sub-cloud car that could be lowered to spy on the enemy. (Goodyear Tire & Rubber Company Records, Archival Services, University Libraries, University of Akron, Akron, Ohio)

Both the *Akron* and *Macon* had three mess halls: one for enlisted men, one for the chief petty officers and the officers' wardroom (with a pass-through window to the galley, shown here). The food was so good, there was little complaining. (Goodyear Tire & Rubber Company Records, Archival Services, University Libraries, University of Akron, Akron, Ohio)

When the USS *Akron* crashed off the New Jersey coast in April 1933 it was the worst disaster in aviation history. Her bottom tail fin is shown being salvaged in an attempt to understand why the big rigid went down. (Official US Navy Photograph)

Only three out of seventy-six men survived the *Akron* crash: Lt Commander Wiley (seated), Aviation Metalsmith, Second Class, Moody E. Erwin (standing left), and Boatswain's Mate, Second Class, Richard 'Lucky' Deal. They are shown in NAS Lakehurst's Hangar No. 1 before testifying at the Navy Court of Inquiry into the *Akron* loss. (Official US Navy Photograph)

Dr Arnstein stands inside the Goodyear-Zeppelin Air Dock with a model of the company's proposed commercial airship. Goodyear aggressively promoted an American-flagged airship service that could transport up to 100 paying passengers in luxury on regular scheduled routes around the globe. (Goodyear Tire & Rubber Company Records, Archival Services, University Libraries, University of Akron, Akron, Ohio)

Left: The *Macon* under construction in the Goodyear–Zeppelin Air Dock around 1932. The *Akron* and *Macon* were the largest, most expensive, most technologically sophisticated aircraft of their day. Note the three workmen at the top of their respective ladders. (Goodyear Tire & Rubber Company Records, Archival Services, University Libraries, University of Akron, Akron, Ohio)

Below: If it's hard to appreciate just how huge the *Akron* and *Macon* were, each airship was fourteen stories tall and two and a half football fields long, earning them the nickname 'Leviathan of the Skies'. The three men standing to the right of the *Macon*'s bottom tail fin provide some scale. (Goodyear Tire & Rubber Company Records, Archival Services, University Libraries, University of Akron, Akron, Ohio)

Perennially in her sister's shadow, the *Macon*'s March 1933 christening ceremony was attended by far fewer people than the *Akron*'s. Litchfield appears at the extreme right of the photo with an uncharacteristic grin, while First Lady Lou Hoover pulls a cord, christening the airship. Litchfield's smile would turn into a frown once the *Akron* crashed three weeks later. (Goodyear Tire & Rubber Company Records, Archival Services, University Libraries, University of Akron, Akron, Ohio)

The bridge in the *Macon*'s control car was the airship's nerve centre. Its floor-to-ceiling windows offered commanding views but was not for the faint of heart. (Courtesy US Naval History and Heritage Command, Catalogue #NH82711)

A *Macon* crewman stands on one of the impossibly narrow catwalks while using a telephone to make a report. One false step on the 13in-wide catwalk could send a man plunging through the airship's outer cover to his death more than 1,000ft below. (Courtesy US Naval History and Heritage Command, Edward Morris Collection, Catalogue #UA 490.15.01)

Two of the *Macon*'s crew shown resting in the enlisted men's quarters. The crew slept in sleeping bags on tiered bunks with a piece of fabric stretched between the airship's Duralumin girders serving as a mattress. Hot bunking was common with two men sharing the same bed – one man slept while the other was on duty. (Lockheed Martin Tactical Defense Systems Records, Archival Services, University Libraries, University of Akron, Akron, Ohio)

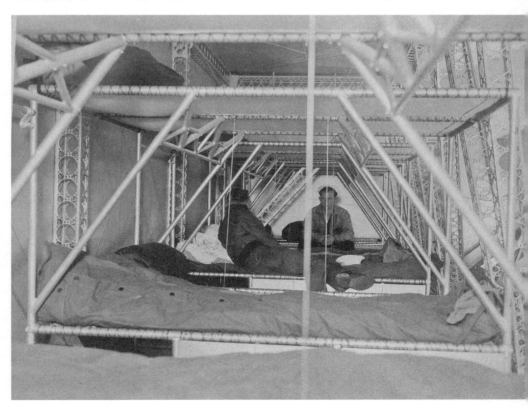

When it came to the design and construction of the Navy's airships, Commander Garland 'Froggy' Fulton was Admiral Moffett's right-hand man. He was also the bane of Dr Arnstein's existence, refusing to accept Arnstein's repeated warnings that the *Akron* and *Macon* contained a potentially devastating design flaw. (Smithsonian National Air & Space Museum Archives, Garland Fulton Collection, Catalogue #9A00593)

The USS *Macon* in flight. Note the control car near the bow with the aeroplane hangar just behind it. An N2Y-1 'air taxi' readying for deployment is also visible just inside the hangar. The propellers on the *Macon*'s eight Maybach engines could be angled to drive the airship up, down, forward, reverse or just hover in place. The four bands on the hull are the water recovery system; the row of black squares above the open hangar are windows. (Official US Navy Photograph)

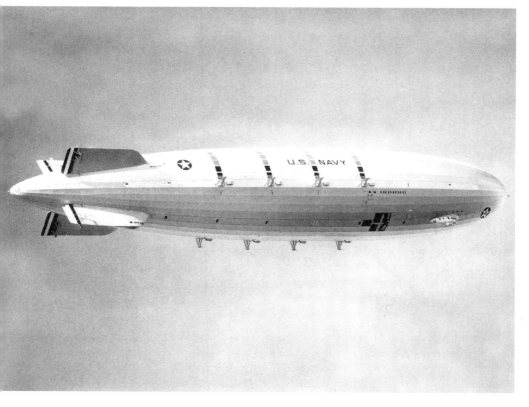

The *Macon* with three of her Curtiss F9C-2 fighter planes in mid-flight. The control car can be seen in the upper left-hand corner. Behind the control car is the hangar, which is open. A Sparrowhawk could rest on a perch just aft of the hangar while waiting its turn to hook on. (Official US Navy Photograph)

A Sparrowhawk dangles from the *Macon*'s trapeze circa 1933–34. The *Akron* and *Macon* could deploy or retrieve their aeroplanes in mid-flight. This not only increased the *Macon*'s scouting range but made the twin airships the world's first flying aircraft carriers. (Official US Navy Photograph now in the collections of the National Archives, Catalogue #: 80-G-441979)

The Sparrowhawks proudly wore the 'men on the fly trapeze' insignia until the Bureau of Aeronautics got wind of the breech in protocol and ordered its removal. The fat acrobat with his arms outstretched represents the *Macon* catching the skinny acrobat that represents a Sparrowhawk. (Wiley Collection, Museum of Monterey)

Lt Commander Wiley ('Doc' to his friends) was one of Moffett's most experienced airship officers. Catapulted to national fame by the *Akron* crash, he wasn't comfortable with his celebrity. Always a bridesmaid, never a bride, Wiley yearned for his own airship command. When the time finally came, the cards were stacked against him. (Courtesy Wiley/Ross Family)

The *Macon*'s crew, looking somewhat motley in their borrowed clothes, on board the USS *Richmond* after being saved. Left to right: Lt (jg) George W. Campbell (who Wiley saved from drowning); Sparrowhawk pilot, Lt (jg) Gerald L. Huff; the *Macon*'s meteorologist, Lt Anthony L. Danis; Sparrowhawk Squadron Leader Lt Harold B. Miller (who found President Roosevelt); Lt Commander George H. Mills; Lt Commander Calvin M. Bolster, the *Macon*'s Construction and Repair Officer; Lt (jg) Earl K. Van Swearingen; Lt Howard N. Coulter; Chief Boatswain William A. Buckley; and Sparrowhawk pilot Lt (jg) Leroy C. Simpler. (Courtesy Harold B. Miller, 1973, US Naval History and Heritage Command Photograph, Catalogue #: NH 77423)

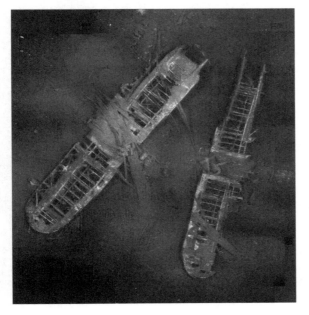

Several attempts were made to find the Macon wreck, but it wasn't until Lt Commander Wiley's grown-up daughter recognised one of its girders hanging on a restaurant wall that an expedition finally succeeded. This ghostly image shows two of the *Macon*'s Sparrowhawks resting upright and mostly intact off the Big Sur coast of California. (MBARI-NOAA/MBNMS-Ken Israel Integral Consulting, Inc.)

27

FLYING AIRCRAFT CARRIERS

Dresel's inability to capitalise on the gift he'd been given (i.e. the *Macon*'s aeroplanes) is not hard to understand since they were originally intended for aerial defence not scouting. Still, it's worth taking a moment to remark on the jaw-dropping ability of the *Macon* to launch and retrieve aeroplanes in mid-flight – a procedure that was critical regardless of how the planes were used.

Pilots used a three-step process to hook on to the *Macon*. The first step involved approaching her from behind, then reducing their speed to match that of the airship. The *Macon*'s top speed was around 85mph, but Sparrowhawks were considerably faster, which meant they risked stalling when slowing to the airship's speed. Careful not to drop below 63mph, a Sparrowhawk pilot aligned his plane with the *Macon*'s bottom tail fin before flying along the airship's starboard side, making sure not to collide with her hull. Once he passed her forward-most engine, the pilot skidded his plane directly beneath the hull, now only 25ft above him.[1]

Airships may appear slow moving, but it's hard to hold one steady in flight. Wind gusts, ground thermals and atmospheric conditions caused changes in altitude, especially in rough weather. The airship's engines also left a turbulent slipstream in their wake, which could cause a Sparrowhawk to rise or fall unexpectedly. This is why pilots chose not to fly directly beneath the airship until the last possible moment.

Using the trapeze to guide his approach, the pilot angled his plane upwards, slowly closing the distance between his skyhook and the trapeze.[2] A Sparrowhawk's skyhook was instrumental for landing. A large metal hook in the shape of a shepherd's crook, it was attached to the top of a small tower bolted on the biplane's upper wing. The skyhook also had a long, gently curving finger jutting out in front that helped to guide the hook on to the trapeze.

Since the hook was spring loaded, it locked on to the bar when the aircraft hit it just right. But that was easier said than done, especially for rookies hooking on for the first time.

The other ingredient necessary for hook-ons was the trapeze. Lowered from inside the hangar, it looked like a small crane hanging upside down from the airship's belly. Once a Sparrowhawk was 5ft below and 10ft behind the trapeze, the pilot nudged his throttle forward. When the skyhook reached the V-shaped bar, he throttled back, causing the hook to settle and catch in what can only be described as a delicate procedure.

But the pilot's job wasn't finished. He still had to centre his aircraft in the middle of the trapeze before being hoisted on board. The only way to do this was to apply enough rudder that his plane slid down to the middle of the V-shaped bar.[3] Meanwhile, his Sparrowhawk swung on its perch a thousand feet above the earth. Once his plane stopped swinging, the pilot idled his engine and was hoisted aboard.*

The procedure may seem terrifying, but once a pilot got the hang of it, they found hooking on to an airship easier than landing on an aircraft carrier.[4] Some even preferred it.

Once inside the hangar, a Sparrowhawk was transferred to an overhead rail system and shunted to one of the hangar's four corners for storage. The fastest the *Macon*'s crew could retrieve or deploy an aeroplane was fifteen minutes, slow for combat operations.[5] The reason for this was that the overhead rail system was a bottleneck, allowing only one Sparrowhawk to be launched or retrieved at a time.[6] To avoid overcrowding, the airship never carried more than four planes at once, even though the hangar could accommodate five. Nor did she carry aircraft during take-off because the excess weight reduced her buoyancy. Instead, her planes flew aboard the airship once she reached an altitude of 1,000ft.

The *Macon*'s Sparrowhawks were the first all-metal aircraft designed and manufactured by the Curtiss Aeroplane and Motor Company. Originally intended as fighter planes for aircraft carriers, they were small and lightweight, making them ideal for the *Macon*. With a top speed of 176mph they were more than twice as fast as the airship. But a Sparrowhawk's fuel capacity was limited, capping its range at 300 miles. This reduced how much scouting it could do before having to return to the airship for refuelling.

---

*   Lt Frederick M. 'Trap' Trapnell, one of the *Akron*'s pilots, designed a yoke that could be lowered from the crane supporting the trapeze to keep a Sparrowhawk's tail from swinging. Of note, Trapnell's life was saved the night the *Akron* crashed when McCord cancelled the flight of his N2Y-1 trainer at the last minute due to poor weather.

Pilots loved the Sparrowhawk's manoeuvrability. At times it seemed all you had to do to make a turn was stick your hand outside the cockpit. But they could be touchy during take-offs and landings. One pilot stood a Sparrowhawk on her nose while making a ground landing at night. Two months later a different pilot ground looped the same plane during take-off.*,7 And yet, the *Akron* and *Macon* launched and retrieved Sparrowhawks hundreds of times without losing a single plane.

Deploying a Sparrowhawk was similar to retrieving one in flight. While the plane hung in the *Macon*'s hangar, a set of twin-panelled doors embedded in the airship's belly were slid open by her crew.[8] Next, a Sparrowhawk pilot would attach a power cord to his plane's instrument panel to kick-start the engine. As the Sparrowhawk idled, it was lowered on the trapeze through the hangar's T-shaped opening. The fit was so tight the plane's 25ft wingspan cleared the doors by only a few inches.[9]

Once outside, the pilot pulled the skyhook's release mechanism, then eased the stick back to gently lift the plane's weight off the trapeze. Using the slipstream to help his plane drift free, he let gravity do the rest.[10]

Hook-ons were a three-dimensional exercise in nerve, timing and co-ordination. Sometimes, turbulence around the airship was so great it prevented a Sparrowhawk from reaching the trapeze. In that case, the pilot goosed his plane forward with a burst of power.[11] This could be tricky, though. If the pilot didn't apply the extra power delicately, his plane would leap forward, triggering the automatic release mechanism, allowing the skyhook to pass through the trapeze without catching.

Pilots hooking on for the first time tended to lunge for the trapeze, triggering the release mechanism, which they called 'jumping the bar'. As one Sparrowhawk veteran recalled, 'There were a couple of times when I thought I was locked on, and I'd sit back, fat, dumb and happy and just fall off.' But even this wasn't a problem. As the pilot explained, 'All I had to do was drop the nose … pick up a little flying speed and come back [to] hook on again.'[12]

The airship had to be at a minimum altitude of 800ft to perform hook-on operations. Sparrowhawk pilots needed at least that much height to recover in the case of a failed attempt.[13] A green signal flag flying from the control car indicated it was safe to hook on.[14] A red flag on the trapeze meant stand by, while a blue flag meant a plane should return to base.

---

* A ground loop happens when a plane's wing inadvertently catches the ground during take-off or landing, causing it to crash.

As if landing an aeroplane on to a moving airship wasn't thrilling enough, the pilots also made hook-ons at night. The hangar lights were dimmed to protect their eyes while floodlights illuminated the trapeze. Otherwise, the procedure was the same.

Technically, Sparrowhawk pilots needed ten successful hook-ons to qualify for airship duty,[15] but according to Lt Harold B. 'Min' Miller, Squadron Leader of the *Macon*'s HTA unit, it took at least fifty before the procedure was second nature.[16]

Interestingly, no Sparrowhawk pilot washed out of the *Akron* or *Macon*'s HTA units, for the simple reason those assigned were accomplished aviators. That's not to say there weren't close calls. On one occasion a plane's release mechanism failed, trapping the plane underneath the *Los Angeles*. This was a serious problem because the airship couldn't land with a plane hanging from its belly. Dresel, who was captain at the time, gave permission for an officer to climb down the trapeze's metal lattice work without benefit of a parachute and, using a wrench, hammer on the release mechanism until it finally gave way.[17] After that, Goodyear redesigned the skyhook to work better.

Another time, a Sparrowhawk pilot hit the trapeze so hard he sheared off the guard tube protecting his skyhook. If he tried flying off the trapeze, he risked damaging his propeller. While the pilot assessed the situation, a second Sparrowhawk circled the airship waiting to hook on. Low on fuel, the second plane couldn't land at an airfield, because its wheels had been removed to accommodate an auxiliary fuel tank. This meant the only place the second plane could land was the airship. Disaster was averted when the pilot stranded on the trapeze figured how to wriggle off without damaging his plane. The second Sparrowhawk hooked on in his place, barely avoiding disaster.[18] No wonder Admiral Moffett acknowledged Navy pilots had a 'shorter life'.[19]

Catching and releasing an aeroplane in mid-flight was so daring, Sparrowhawk pilots had their own nickname. They called themselves 'belly bumpers' aboard the *Los Angeles*. On the *Akron* they were 'little oaks' – a play on the expression 'little oaks from great *Akrons* grow.'[20] Various mascots representing the airship and her Sparrowhawks were also considered, including a shark surrounded by pilot fish and a kangaroo with a pouch. At one point Miller, the Sparrowhawk Squadron Leader, suggested their insignia be a horse's rear with flies buzzing round it.[21] No one took him seriously.

By the time Sparrowhawk pilots were hooking on to the *Macon* they were known as 'the men on the flying trapeze'. Their colourful insignia showed a fat man, symbolising the airship, hanging by his knees from a trapeze while catching a thin man, representing a Sparrowhawk, in mid-air. The insignia captured the unit's *esprit de corps*, as did the individual paint schemes for each of the six Sparrowhawks. The BUAER eventually caught wind of this in the autumn of 1933 and ordered the insignia and paint schemes removed.[22] Typical of the unit's independent mindset, they were slow to comply.

There's no denying the *Macon's* HTA pilots harkened back to an earlier time. Cut from the same cloth as Santos-Dumont, Thomas Baldwin and Roy Knabenshue, their youth, confidence and brashness made them the daring young men in their flying machines. Their courage and daredevilry were truly impressive.

The 'men on the flying trapeze' may seem like a novelty act, but hooking on to an airship had a storied past.

The first time a lighter-than-air craft carried an aeroplane aloft was in 1905 when a California college professor, John J. Montgomery, successfully released a man-carrying glider from a balloon. Montgomery conducted several demonstrations but was forced to stop when his glider pilot became tangled in the ropes suspending his glider and was accidentally killed. The next year, Santos-Dumont used his No. 14 dirigible to lift his home-built aeroplane, the 14-*bis*, into the air for testing.[23] Dumont never repeated the experiment since the combination prove unstable.

After Zeppelin raids pummeled London during the First World War, the British got into the act. It was thought a fighter plane lifted into the sky by a blimp could engage a Zeppelin in aerial combat longer. The theory was tested in 1915 when a Sea Scout blimp lifted a B.E.2c fighter above the English countryside. But when the aircraft's pilot pulled the release mechanism, the suspension cables tethering his plane to the blimp failed to let go at the same time. The resulting jerk threw the pilot to his death, hence bringing the experiment to a conclusion.[24]

The UK, Germany and the United States all dropped aeroplanes from lighter-than-air craft in 1918. There's a big difference, however, between an LTA craft dropping an aeroplane and the far more difficult task of catching one in mid-flight.

The US Army was first to tackle the problem. In September 1921, Lawrence B. Sperry proposed the Army attach a giant hook to the upper wing of an aeroplane that could be used to snag a trapeze suspended from an airship's belly. Sperry Aircraft won the contract to build the device and delivered a prototype to the Army for field testing in 1924.[25]

Over the course of two days, Lt Clyde V. Finter tried five times to hook his Sperry Messenger on to an Army blimp, all of them unsuccessful. It wasn't until his sixth attempt in December 1924 that he became the first pilot to successfully land on an airship in mid-flight.[26]

That next year, the Royal Air Force experimented with hooking a de Havilland DH.53 on to the R33 over Pulham, United Kingdom.[27] The first attempt ended in near disaster when the de Havilland's propeller fouled one of the trapeze's bracing wires, causing the plane to dangle perilously from its perch. Fortunately, the skyhook's release mechanism still worked and the pilot glided safely to the ground. It wasn't until the third attempt later that month that the pilot, with the delightful name of Rollo Amyatt de Haga Haig, successfully hooked on to the R33. When de Haga Haig climbed up a rope ladder into the airship overhead he became the first HTA pilot to successfully transfer from his plane to an airship. Afterwards, he prophesied, 'There is no doubt that, given an airship suitably designed, aeroplanes can be released and hooked on ... with ease.'[28] True, but it never looked easy.

The US Navy didn't try hooking an aeroplane on to a big rigid until 3 July 1929. That's when Lt Adolphus W. 'Jake' Gorton lined up his Vought UO-1 with the stern of the *Los Angeles* and began closing the distance.[29] Only four of Gorton's fifteen passes succeeded in snagging the trapeze that day.[30] Even then his plane kept falling off its perch. Goodyear went to work modifying the skyhook's release mechanism. When Gorton made another attempt on 20 August, a less-sensitive device combined with a controlled stall allowed Gorton to successfully hook on – a feat he repeated the next day.[31]

Practicing hook-ons to the *Los Angeles* provided important learning for the Navy's next generation of rigid airships. As a result, the *Akron* and *Macon* were designed specifically as flying aircraft carriers with an interior hangar for aeroplanes and a retractable trapeze. Still, the *Akron*'s HTA unit was slow to organise. Lt Harrigan, who had hooked-on to the *Los Angeles* numerous times, oversaw the training. But the *Akron*'s HTA pilots didn't reach full strength until July 1932. Even then, only one of the *Akron*'s F9C-2 Sparrowhawks had arrived at Lakehurst. The unit wouldn't receive all six until September,[32] by which point it had more planes than pilots for training.*

'Crash Helmet' Harrigan was one of the first to realise the Sparrowhawks could serve as more than just defensive fighters – they could assist with the *Akron*'s scouting duties. His challenge was getting his superior officers to listen. With this in mind, he drafted a forty-two-page report, which he submitted to Dresel, laying out how to use the *Akron*'s HTA unit to expand the airship's scouting mission. Harrigan recommended adding the position of flight control officer to direct planes on searches, replacing the planes' landing gear with a reserve fuel tank to extend their range, and cited the need to improve the Sparrowhawks' radio communication with the airship.

The Harrigan report was spot on; Dresel even forwarded it to Fulton at the BUAER. But Dresel largely ignored its suggestions, using the airship as the primary scout despite Harrigan's recommendations.

Another important breakthrough for scouting came when Lt Donald M. Mackey developed a new navigation method that increased their range. This involved a Sparrowhawk flying away from the *Akron* at a 60-degree angle for a predetermined time, after which the plane made another 60-degree turn back to the airship. The 60–60 navigational method, with its reliance on geometry, required both the plane and airship to fly in a straight line at a predetermined speed, but it enabled the Sparrowhawks to venture out of visual range, increasing their scouting area while minimising the risk of never finding the airship.

Unfortunately, further advancements were cut short when the *Akron* crashed a month later. The only silver lining was that the weather had been so bad that none of the Sparrowhawk planes or pilots were on board when the *Akron* was lost.

After the *Akron* disaster, the *Macon*'s HTA unit grew even more proficient at scouting. This wasn't so much at Dresel's insistence as it was the Sparrowhawk pilots' belief that the proper role for the *Macon* was to serve as a flying aircraft carrier hosting aeroplanes to search for the enemy. To his credit, Dresel gave the *Macon*'s HTA unit a free hand in developing its scouting technique, but he still kept getting shot down during fleet exercises. Fleet Problem XV, scheduled for the Caribbean in May 1933, would give the *Macon*'s Sparrowhawks one more chance to show just how good they'd become at finding the enemy, but only if Dresel would let them. In the meantime, they'd have to make another cross-country trip to get to there.

---

*   See 'Principal Players' in the front of the book for the composition of the *Akron*'s and
     Macon's HTA units.

28

PERIL IN THE SKY

The giant orange-peel doors on the *Macon*'s Sunnyvale hangar slowly rumbled open early on the morning of 20 April 1934. Nearly 200ft tall and weighing 500 tons apiece, the doors were so heavy not even King Kong would have been able to budge them. Each door slid along a track on metal wheels requiring a dedicated motor to pull it open – never a quick procedure given how much they weighed.

Inside the hangar's vast floodlit interior, Dresel and his men prepared the *Macon* for her second transcontinental voyage, this time to the mooring mast at Opa-locka, Florida. Fleet Problem XV, to be held in the Caribbean, promised to be the Navy's largest war game of 1934. If it wasn't Dresel's last chance to turn the *Macon* around, he was knocking on its door.

The early morning sun crept over the Diablo Mountains across the bay as the crew scurried about their airship. Shortly after dawn, the *Macon* was towed out of Hangar One to her mooring-out circle. Soon the temperature of her helium, warmed by the sun, exceeded the temperature outside – a condition known as 'superheat'. This was an important trick often taken advantage of since the warmer the *Macon*'s helium grew, the lighter she became, making take-off easier.

No one looked forward to another bone-jangling journey across the country. According to a memo in the National Archives dated 26 December 1933, the *Macon* had been slated to travel via Panama, a flatter route tracing the canal. But the *Macon* was too big to dock at the Canal Zone's stub mast. Nor could she moor to the USS *Patoka*, an oil tender the *Shenandoah* and *Los Angeles* had used when docking at sea. Dresel had been aboard the *Los Angeles* when, moored to the *Patoka*, she'd dunked her tail in the ocean.[1] Since the *Macon* was far bigger, he decided not to risk another dip in the sea. And so it was agreed the *Macon* would retrace the same treacherous route she'd travelled to California.

Dresel knew the southern route could be trouble. Not only had the *Macon* encountered extreme turbulence on her way to Sunnyvale, but airship captains considered the conditions over Texas 'the most severe ... ever encountered'.[2]

Navigating the narrow mountain passes could be hair-raising for even the most experienced sky sailor. The *Shenandoah* had learned just how difficult it was in 1924, while hopping a mountain near Van Horn, Texas. Flying at 6,000ft, the airship's radio antenna (which didn't hang very low) had struck a telegraph pole and was sheared off. The *Shenandoah* was at maximum altitude, but the surrounding mountains were so high the airship only had 300ft of clearance.[3]

Commander Rosendahl had also been aboard the *Shenandoah* when navigating Arizona's Dos Cabezas pass. It was just one of many choke points along the southern route. As Rosendahl recalled, that trip had nearly ended in disaster:

> Sharp gusts in the canyons seemed ... to drive us perilously near the peaks ... In one place the wind, blowing around the end of a mountain ridge, set up a huge ... eddy ... The captain gave the order to turn left. The rudderman [complied] ... but instead of responding, the ship actually turned right! We were being carried directly at the mountainous wall.[4]

The *Shenandoah* averted tragedy, but 'Dos Cabezas' became the crew's code word for any unwelcome thrill.[5]

Dresel knew about these mishaps, so he requested an alternate route. As he penned in a memo to the Commander Aircraft, Battle Force, 'The writer has made three trips across this continent in an airship and considers the west to east passage the more difficult, due to the necessity of hopping the mountains.'[6]

The *Macon* was a low-flying reconnaissance aircraft meant for scouting the ocean; she wasn't made to fly over mountain peaks carrying 50 tons of ballast and fuel. As it was, she had to rely on 'dynamic lift' (e.g. flying with all engines at full power while the airship was in a nose-up attitude) if she wanted to keep aloft in the narrow canyons. Helium alone wasn't enough to keep her airborne in the high desert carrying so much weight.

The State Department obtained permission from the Mexican government for the *Macon* to fly a less dangerous route 360 miles south of Mexico City. Called the Tehuantepec passage, it avoided the west Texas mountains altogether.

But for some reason Admiral Sellers rejected the plan, leaving Dresel to take
his chances.[7]

The *Macon* got under way from Sunnyvale on Friday at 0937 hours. To lighten
her load, she shipped clothing and spare parts (including an extra Maybach
engine) ahead by train. Her five Sparrowhawk aeroplanes were also transported separately along with a spare set of wings, elevators and rudder. Despite
these measures, the *Macon* still carried 83,000lb of fuel and 17,000lb of water
ballast for the three-day trip.[8]

The *Macon* flew south over the orchards of Santa Clara Valley to the city
of Watsonville near the coast. Once she'd reached the Pacific Ocean, she
followed the central coast shoreline to Point Arguello before continuing to
Santa Barbara, Los Angeles and Long Beach. As the *Macon* motored in the
ocean breeze, she bobbed like a ship at sea. The movement was second nature
to her crew, who hustled along her narrow catwalks without giving it a
single thought.

Contrary to Hunsaker's claim that rigid airships were the antidote to sea-
sickness, the crew felt plenty of motion. Flying aboard the *Macon* may have
been smoother than a steamship fighting the waves, but air pockets and wind
gusts caused sudden changes in altitude. Despite what their promoters promised, catwalks flexed, envelopes fluttered and airships rolled.

The silent sentinels of the sky could also be noisy. It might have been eerily
silent inside the control car, but it was noisy as hell anywhere near her eight
engine compartments. In fact, the *Macon*'s engines were so loud they not only
deafened her crew, they could be heard from the ground.

Once the *Macon* reached Long Beach she turned inland, heading east over
the orange groves of Riverside. Dresel wanted to reach the San Gorgonio
pass, connecting the Los Angeles basin to the Coachella Valley, before sunset.
The deepest mountain pass in the lower forty-eight states, it separated the
San Bernardino Mountains to the north from the San Jacinto Mountains
in the south, making it a natural gateway. It was also one of the few places
an airship could cross these mountains without exceeding pressure height.
But Dresel had to be careful. Peaks 9,000ft high lined either side of the
corridor, which also funnelled powerful headwinds down its centre, making
navigation unpredictable.

Dresel's plan was to remain below pressure height while flying through the
pass, but when the *Macon* arrived at its mouth she was 17,000lb heavy.[9] It was

never desirable for an airship the size of the *Macon* to fly more than 10,000lb heavy in rough air.[10] But the distance from Sunnyvale to San Gorgonio was only 400 miles, so she still carried most of her fuel and ballast. This, combined with constant changes in atmospheric conditions, made the airship heavy when she most needed to be light. Complicating matters, Dresel planned to negotiate San Gorgonio pass at night, hoping for a smoother ride when the air was cooler.

If you've ever flown through unsettled air, you've felt the stomach-clenching sensation of a sudden change in altitude. This is similar to the up and down lurches the *Macon*'s crew endured in the San Gorgonio pass. The helmsman and elevatorman fought to keep the airship in trim but it was impossible given the conditions.

As Dresel recalled, 'the air was extremely turbulent both directionally and vertically'.[11] What he didn't say is that at least once during their passage the crew suffered momentary weightlessness, something the *Macon* was never designed to endure.[12]

After receiving a serious shake-up, the *Macon* finally exited the pass. Next, Dresel turned south-east towards the Salton Sea. By now, the airship was flying 20,000lb heavy,[13] which put a strain on her airframe. Dresel ordered 2,000lb of fuel dumped to lighten the load but it barely made a difference.

As the *Macon* flew through the night, she crossed the California border into Arizona, arriving over Yuma at 2030 hours.[14] There, Dresel picked up the Gila River and began following it towards Phoenix.[15]

Pilots in the early days of aviation had little to guide them across the United States. The *Macon* used a compass and navigational charts, but Dresel supplemented these with visual cues such as rivers, which acted as signposts along the way. If lucky, they might spot the name of a town painted on the roof of a barn, but that was difficult at night. The scattered lights of a town might guide them, but vast areas of the American south-west were uninhabited.

The *Macon* reached Phoenix, Arizona, at 2300 hours. Dresel began circling the city because he didn't want to negotiate yet another mountain pass in the dark, especially one little more than half a mile wide. When the sun crept over the horizon seven hours later, Dresel abandoned his holding pattern and headed for Tucson.

The *Macon* passed Benson on the second day of her voyage before continuing in serpentine fashion through the canyons of Dragoon pass. By the time she reached Willcox, Arizona, Dresel had dropped an additional 9,000lb of water ballast and 7,000lb of fuel, but the airship was still 20,000lb heavy.[16]

The *Macon* reached Bowie, Arizona, before crossing her second state line into New Mexico. The southern route was like a cross-country bus trip of obscure towns with names like Gila Bend, Casa Grande, Dragon, Lordsburg and Deming. But as plodding as the voyage was, the American south-west was spectacularly beautiful, particularly in the daytime. The *Macon*'s control car, with floor-to-ceiling windows, provided breathtaking views of the desert below. Elsewhere in the airship, off-duty crew stood on the port catwalk looking out the Cellon windows 'ooo-ing' and 'ahh-ing' at the soaring buttes, chiselled cliffs and ever-changing palette of red, tan, ochre and umber.

The desert wasn't just colourful, though. It was deathly hot. As the sun warmed the ground, great columns of super-heated air rose into the sky while cooler air from higher altitudes sank towards the earth, causing major turbulence.[17] Both dust devils and crosswinds buffeted the airship, resulting in sudden changes in altitude.[18]

The *Macon* followed the Southern Pacific's railroad tracks through New Mexico to El Paso, Texas, where she arrived shortly before 1100 hours on Saturday. There, Dresel picked up the Rio Grande, following the river southeast to Fort Hancock before making a port turn towards the notorious west Texas mountains. If all went according to plan, the *Macon* would cross the continental divide by noon, after which she could expect smooth sailing to Florida.

The journey was going reasonably well until everything fell apart over Van Horn, Texas. The *Macon* was flying 15,000lb heavy at full power while navigating a pass through the Sierra Diablo Mountains when she encountered what Dresel described as 'violently rough air'.[19] The description doesn't do it justice, given the crew thought it the worst motion they'd ever experienced on an airship.[20] As the *Macon* rose and fell more than 30ft per second, they grabbed hold of anything they could to keep from falling. The air was so turbulent the elevatorman had to be relieved every ten minutes because the job was too physically taxing.[21]

At one point, the *Macon* pitched so heavily her nose pointed upwards at a 19-degree angle. One officer inside her hull was shocked to see the forward section of the ship twist in one direction while the aft corkscrewed in another.[22] Meanwhile, the airship's roll was so pronounced[23] her navigator clung to his chart table so as not to be thrown on the deck.[24] Obviously, the officers on the bridge were concerned, but this wasn't the first time a Navy airship had encountered turbulence on the southern route. Still, Dresel had no choice but to run all eight engines at full speed. Not wanting to smash into the canyon walls, he needed every bit of horsepower to compensate for the airship flying heavy.

Suddenly, a powerful updraft drove the *Macon* to 6,800ft, causing her twelve gas cells to swell like puffer fish. Their automatic release valves instantly began venting the precious helium needed to stay aloft. Aware of the danger, Dresel dumped ballast, but the *Macon* had already dropped so much fuel he worried there wouldn't be enough to complete the trip.[25]

Then, at approximately 1155 hours, a severe downdraught forced the *Macon* into a nose dive. As the airship's elevatorman struggled to regain altitude, the entire ship was broadsided by a terrific gust, causing her to shudder.

Chief Boatswain's Mate Robert J. 'Shaky' Davis looked like a poor man's Clark Gable, right down to his pencil-thin moustache. Davis was the *Macon*'s chief petty officer. With twenty years in the Navy, seven of them on airships,[26] he had 7,000 hours on big rigids, making him highly experienced.

Davis regularly inspected every inch of the *Macon* as a matter of routine. This included her upper fin, whose leading edge had a tendency to wobble in flight. The motion was considered harmless except by first-timers, who found its creaking noise alarming.

Davis was on the port catwalk near frame 0 in the *Macon*'s stern when the airship took its sudden nosedive. Feeling an unusual jolt followed by a 'sharp report',[27] Davis hustled down the *Macon*'s catwalk looking for the source. When he reached frame 17.5, he spotted a truss girder snapped in half near where the port fin was anchored. Its ends rubbed together, causing a grinding noise that attracted his attention.

Once Davis realised saw the damage he reached for a nearby telephone and dialled the control car. Yelling to be heard over the engines, he shouted, 'We need to reduce speed!'

Dresel at the other end listened carefully to Davis describe the casualty between joints 8 and 8.5.* When he had finished, Dresel shouted back, 'Get it fixed!'[28]

Dresel ordered the engines slowed to relieve strain on the stern, but he could ill afford to do so since full power was needed to navigate the mountain pass. What happened next is open to debate. One account claims Dresel went to his cabin intending to fetch a wad of cash they'd need if the airship

---

 *   The Navy frequently used the term 'casualty' to describe damage to a ship, which can cause confusion since it also describes the injury or death of a person.

crashed.[29] No source is given for this claim, and no other account supports it. If true, it shows how close the *Macon*'s captain thought he was to losing his ship.

Shaky Davis had anticipated just such a casualty, which is why he kept a supply of wooden planks on board. Hoping to stave off disaster, Davis rushed towards the bow where the lumber was stored. Moments later, Lt Walter Zimmerman arrived at frame 17.5, where he discovered a second diagonal girder had sheered in two.[30]

Davis returned minutes later with a work crew. Carrying rope and wooden beams 8 to 10ft long, they set about repairing the damage.[31] But the two diagonal girders had broken in a spot that was difficult to reach. Improvising a splint, Davis lashed the planks to each of the girders' four sides, making sure to tighten the ropes.

As the work party feverishly made repairs, more girders in frame 17.5 showed signs of buckling, indicating a domino effect. One more gust and Davis worried frame 17.5 might fail, causing the entire airship to collapse.

Dresel knew the *Macon* needed babying but, given the turbulence, he had no choice but to resume top speed. Meanwhile, the girders in frame 17.5 groaned under the effort. Davis' temporary repairs fended off disaster, but nobody knew how long they'd hold. Making matters worse, the *Macon* still had 1,800 miles to go before reaching Opa-locka and no place to land before she got there.

The *Macon* didn't carry parachutes because they weighed too much. But Dresel didn't limp the rest of the way to Florida. By the time the *Macon* arrived at Opa-locka early on the evening of 22 April, he'd set a new transcontinental speed record – fifty-four and a half hours, the fastest an airship had crossed the United States west to east.[32] Given the circumstances, he was lucky to have reached his destination.

Arnstein had warned Fulton that excessive loading on the *Macon*'s tail fins might result in a structural failure where they were anchored. But Fulton had dismissed Arnstein's concerns even after the doctor pressed his case. Now, Arnstein had been proven right.

There's little doubt Shaky Davis' foresight and quick action prevented a worse calamity.[33] As Lt Calvin M. Bolster, the *Macon*'s construction and repair officer, later put it, 'It was a close call.'[34]

Given the circumstances, it's reasonable to ask why Navy airship captains insisted on pushing their big rigids to the limit. According to Rosendahl the answer was simple: 'We thought those ships were so strong they could take anything.'[35]

Perhaps, but Dr Arnstein, the man who designed them, knew better.

29

FLEET PROBLEM XV

The *Macon* reached Opa-locka early on the evening of 22 April 1934. A 120-man ground crew stood by to assist in her landing. Once the airship was secured to the expeditionary mast, Dresel granted liberty to his crew. Given the hair-raising experience they'd shared over Texas, he stood them all a drink.[1]

The day after the *Macon* docked in Opa-locka, a general foreman from Goodyear-Zeppelin flew down on the company plane with a mechanic to survey the damage. They were soon joined by Kurt Bauch[2] and two more Goodyear employees bearing repair materials. Bauch had expressed concern more than once about the load-bearing capacity of frame 17.5 now he was there to oversee its repair.[3]

The men worked sixteen-hour days to fix the damage. Gas cells No. 1 and 2 were partially deflated to gain access to the broken girders, an expensive proposition given that 400,000 cu ft of extra helium had to be brought in by railroad car to replace it.[4]

It took nine days to make repairs, showing just how extensive the damage was.[5] Although Fulton would later claim the *Macon* required only three days to be repaired, he was underplaying the seriousness of what happened.[6] Meanwhile, Goodyear-Zeppelin was in a race against time. If the *Macon* wasn't ready for Fleet Problem XV, it would be a black mark on her record, possibly the last.[7]

Opa-locka was a swampy, sub-tropical outpost 16 miles north of Miami. Hot, humid and rife with mosquitoes, it wasn't a comfortable spot to bivouac. The crew slept in tents in an open field near where the airship was docked. Food was prepared in a portable galley and served in a hastily erected mess tent.

Opa-locka wasn't a fully fledged airship base. There were only two of those: Lakehurst and Sunnyvale. Rather, Opa-locka was an 'advance operating base' with an obsolete stub mast and a mooring-out circle. The *Graf Zeppelin* had docked at Opa-locka in 1932, and Amelia Earhart would begin her round the world flight there in 1937, but the base provided few amenities in 1934.

Opa-locka was actually the shortened version of the Seminole phrase *Opa-tisha-wocka-locka*, meaning 'big island covered with many trees and swamps'. Glenn Curtiss, whose company designed the Sparrowhawk, had developed Opa-locka as a real-estate investment in 1926 but the development had recently been destroyed by a hurricane.

The Florida climate was sultry to begin with, but things grew more uncomfortable when a series of rainstorms, each more powerful than the last, deluged the region. As Dresel reported, 'This heavy rain was the first … of any consequence that the ship had encountered on the ground [and] brought out several poor features.'[8] Plainly put, the *Macon* leaked like a sieve.

It didn't help that due to the intense heat many of her hatches had to be left open, allowing rain to pour in. One torrential downpour leaked through the ventilation hoods on the airship's roof, turning her upper catwalk into a canal.[9] Water not only flowed along the gangway; it spilled over its edge, drenching the gas cells. At the same time, rain formed ponds on top of the ship, running down its sides and flooding the control car. Rain didn't only short out the airship's land-based power source;[10] it corroded the netting holding her gas cells in place. This was dangerous because broken netting caused chafing, which could puncture a gas cell. Additionally, 300lb of water was found to have collected inside the elevator on the *Macon's* port fin,[11] and pooled on the aeroplane hangar doors.[12] Needless to say, many of the crew got soaked, making for an unpleasant time.

While the storms raged, the *Macon's* bow remained rooted to the mast at the centre of its mooring-out circle. The mooring-out circle was defined by a loop-shaped railroad track. With her stern attached to a flat car to keep it from rising, the airship swung like a weather vane.[13] At one point, the wind was so strong the wheels of the flat car holding her stern in place lifted 18in off the track[14] – an astounding feat showing how much force a storm could exert on the world's largest airship. All that motion not only made repairs difficult; it resulted in a Miami Beach snooper being struck by the flat car when she got too close.[15]

As rain continued to fall, the *Macon* grew increasingly heavy. Ballast was dumped to counteract the increase, but this did little to improve the situation. When an officer checked the hollow space underneath the control car, several hundred pounds of water was discovered sloshing around. The officer had to use a hammer and chisel to poke holes in the control car's bottom to allow the water to drain.[16]

Repair work on frame 17.5 proceeded slowly, given the rain. Seven days after repairs had begun, Kurt Bauch sent a telegram to Arnstein in Ohio: 'Believe will finish Wednesday. Since ship wants me to pay all bills may need another 150 dollars.'[*,17]

It rained so incessantly that the ground turned muddy, sucking the canvas sneakers off the men's feet whenever they walked outside. Meanwhile, rattlesnakes seeking dry land were driven out of their lairs, making tent life difficult.[18] Despite these complications, the repairs were completed in time for the *Macon* to participate in Fleet Problem XV.

The BUAER Chief, Admiral King, was so pleased with the work he sent a telegram to Arnstein: 'Gentlemen the Bureau of Aeronautics wishes to express its appreciation of your quick response … in making repairs to the USS *Macon*.'[19] Dresel was also satisfied, deeming the airship 'as strong or probably stronger than it had been originally.'

Having barely survived her cross-country flight, the *Macon* prepared to depart for the fleet problem. Fleet Problems were much bigger and more complicated than fleet exercises, since they involved the Atlantic and Pacific fleet squaring off against each other. There were also more eyes watching. Everything came down to what the *Macon* would do. Would she continue to underperform, confirming expectations she belonged on the scrap heap, or would Dresel turn the situation around? Even if he succeeded, would it be enough to persuade Congress and the Navy to sheathe their long knives, or was it too late to make a difference?

Fleet Problem XV was designed to test whether the US could repel a foreign invasion of the Caribbean with control of the Panama Canal at stake. The fleet problem was broken into two parts. Exercise M was to begin on 6 May with the Atlantic, or Grey fleet, assigned the role of attacker, while the Pacific, or Blue fleet including the *Macon*, defended the Canal.

Goodyear-Zeppelin paid all the costs associated with repairing the *Macon* at Opa-locka.

Dresel topped off the *Macon*'s gas cells with helium early in the morning of 5 May in preparation for departure. That's when a crewman discovered an owl nesting above gas cell No. 8.[20] The owl was thought to have entered the airship the night before through a bow hatch. Unfortunately, the owl evaded capture, accompanying the *Macon* to the fleet problem. A crewman had to be detailed to watch it since there were concerns the owl's talons might puncture a gas cell.[21]

Exercise M opened with the *Macon* searching for Grey fleet forces between Panama and Jamaica. Once again, Dresel used lookouts to find the enemy.[22] When enemy fighters from the USS *Lexington* swarmed the *Macon*,[23] Dresel launched his Sparrowhawks to repel the attack,[24] but they were quickly overwhelmed and the *Macon* 'shot down'.

The *Macon* may have turned in a mixed performance, but at least the owl was captured on the way back from the exercise. A crewman using a flashlight temporarily blinded the creature, allowing it to be caught and released somewhere over Jamaica.[25]

The *Macon* faced considerable scrutiny during Fleet Problem XV. The *New York Times* reported almost daily on how she was doing. When Admiral King called the *Macon*'s performance at Exercise M 'a success', Secretary of the Navy Swanson countered his remarks, telling reporters the *Macon* was ineffective for war. Swanson was forced to walk back his comments the next day, calling them 'unwarranted', but nobody was fooled.[26] You could almost hear the axe being sharpened.

After replacing her No. 1 engine, which had failed, the *Macon* departed for Exercise N. Her Sparrowhawks tested a variety of navigation methods, venturing further from the airship than ever before. This enabled them to find the Grey forces at least once, saving the airship from being shot down.[27]

The *Macon* fared somewhat better during the exercise, but when her recently appointed flight control officer, Lt Mackey, filed a report outlining the Sparrowhawks' success, no one paid it much attention. The day after Fleet Problem XV concluded, a page one headline in the *New York Times* sounded an ominous warning:

STANDLEY … DOUBTS *MACON*'S VALUE[28]

Admiral Standley made clear … that to date the *Macon* had not proved herself to be of any particular value to the fleet. She was vulnerable, he said, and that vulnerability had been emphasized in every problem in which she had taken part [by being] 'shot down'.[29]

Standley's bias as a surface fleet officer was readily apparent. As he noted in the article, 'The outstanding lesson of the Problem is that when you strip down to the final battle the ... battleship is the ... arbiter'.[30] This wasn't surprising given that Standley was a member of the Navy's 'big gun' club, which favoured battleships. But his remarks, following so close on the heels of Swanson's, were alarming. As Standley made clear to the *Times*, he was not in favour of 'putting any more money into LTA craft until some definitive positive value ... has been assured'.[31]

Admiral King did what he could to counter Standley's anti-airship bias. He invited the admiral to Opa-locka to inspect the *Macon*, and even planned on having the airship fly to New York for a Presidential review of the fleet. Dresel didn't want to go, however, because it meant returning to California later than planned. 'A transcontinental flight by a rigid airship during thunderstorm period is extremely hazardous,' he cabled his boss. 'Accomplishment [is] doubtful.'[32]

Forgoing Roosevelt's review of the fleet seems like a missed opportunity, but it wasn't unreasonable. Both the *Shenandoah* and *Akron* had been lost during thunderstorms. Given his recent experience over Texas, Dresel didn't want the *Macon* to be next. But the airship's future was in doubt and she needed all the help she could get. Once the fleet problem was finished, King allowed the *Macon* to return to Sunnyvale, but it probably didn't endear Dresel to his boss.[33]

The *Macon* departed Opa-locka late on 16 May. Once again, she hit 'extremely turbulent air' along the way.[34] At one point, her port elevator threatened to jam – a potentially hazardous situation since she needed a functioning elevator to navigate the narrow canyon passes. The problem was eventually solved, but it made for another worrying moment.

On a lighter note, Shaky Davis is alleged to have heard a splashing in one of the *Macon*'s ballast bags while cruising over California. Upon investigation, he found a 2ft alligator swimming inside.[35] The story may not be true, but if it is, there's no mention of what he did with it. It's a known fact, however, that alligators can't fly.

After fifty-one hours in the air, the *Macon* moored at NAS Sunnyvale early on the morning of 18 May. She may have returned home safely, but her future had never been more in doubt. Her performance at Fleet Problem XV appeared as weak as frame 17.5, making her vulnerable on two fronts: her inability to find the enemy without being shot down and the question of her structural integrity. Yes, there were mitigating circumstances. Once again, she'd been used for tactical searches in a relatively small area where enemy ships were crowded together. But the fleet wasn't interested in excuses. Nor could her structural weakness be explained away.

The most important outcome of the Texas casualty was that Froggy Fulton finally admitted Arnstein had a point. Even then, it took a while. While the *Macon* was still in Opa-locka, Arnstein sent a letter reminding Fulton of his previous concerns. 'It is very probable that the loads on frame 17.5 were noticeably higher than one might expect from the original design specifications,' Arnstein wrote.[36] 'The repairs and reinforcements now under way should take care of conditions approximately equivalent to those which the *Macon* went through on this particular flight.'[37]

Using the Texas casualty to press his advantage, Arnstein told Fulton, 'If it is felt that flying the airship very heavy at full power through rough air is to be considered ... necessary, then the question of bracing frame 17.5 against the fins should be given renewed consideration.'[38] Reminding Fulton that flying the *Macon* in this manner 'has not been considered good practice',[39] Arnstein's letter politely asked him to revisit the assumptions they'd used in her design.

Even after he made a persuasive case for strengthening the airship, Arnstein closed his letter to Fulton by asking 'What do you think?'[40] It's an overly solicitous question given the damage the *Macon* had experienced over Texas. This is typical of Arnstein's deference, but the 'little professor' wasn't the only one who wanted to revisit the *Macon*'s design assumptions. Dresel also called for a re-examination. Writing to Admiral King, he urged, 'The entire question of fin strength should be carefully investigated in order that any possibility of failure in this portion of the ship ... may be prevented.'[41]

That's not to say there wasn't confusion over the severity of the damage. Dr Wolfgang Klemperer, one of Arnstein's twelve disciples, wrote a memo suggesting that the *Macon*'s broken girders were 'of no consequence for the coherence of the ship'.[42] But in a stunning admission of ignorance, a BUAER letter to Dresel admitted, 'There is no explanation in past theory or experience which will account for what actually occurred.'[43] That alone should have raised a few questions.

Arnstein was a pioneer in the field of stress analysis, but the science, though advancing, was still young. This doesn't absolve him of blame, but it's important to remember that Arnstein had been pushing to strengthen frame 17.5 for three years. The maths may not have supported all of Arnstein's concerns, but his gut told him something was wrong.

Arnstein undertook a new stress analysis of the *Macon*'s fins, with Fulton's blessing. This time the assumptions were revised to include the airship encountering more severe weather conditions. When Arnstein's calculations revealed the girders most likely to fail were the same ones that had broken over Texas,[44] Fulton had little choice but to concede frame 17.5 needed strengthening.

Minutes from the 17 July meeting at the BUAER's Washington headquarters make Fulton's capitulation clear:

> Item 10. Preparation of material necessary for reinforcement of Main Frame 17.5 and fins to be made immediately … Goodyear–Zeppelin to furnish all [materials] … and suggest the order of importance of the work.[45]

But even then, Fulton didn't consider strengthening frame 17.5 important enough to implement 'immediately'. As a 2 August memo from the Inspector of Naval Aircraft to Goodyear–Zeppelin states, 'Because the work is not urgent it is considered that it can be accomplished from time to time as opportunity offers.'[46] In other words, strengthening the frame need not be done in a timely manner.

Dresel struggled to put the best face on the *Macon*'s performance. When he finally delivered his report on how she performed during the past year he clearly equivocated. 'Before judging,' he wrote, 'the term "success" must be clearly defined.' After a lengthy paragraph exploring various definitions, Dresel concluded, 'It is believed that, taking all factors into consideration, the *Macon* was reasonably successful in carrying out the tasks assigned.'[47]

Dresel offered several explanations for why the airship hadn't performed better, including 'Personnel of this country have had comparatively little experience in the operation of rigid airships.'[48] He added, 'Until further experience is gained, I do not see how we can decide whether … the vessel is suitable.'[49] Given that the Navy had been flying rigid airships since 1923 you can almost hear the battleship admirals snicker.

Dresel's report also hedged its bets when recommending whether to build more rigid airships. 'One ship does not prove a type,' he wrote, 'but in view of the fact that this type of vessel is still in the experimental stage … it is recommended that the *Macon* be operated for about another year before the construction of another rigid airship.'[50]

Dresel's report fell short of a ringing endorsements. At the very least, he kicked the can down the road. Still, Dresel had a point. The Navy's rigid airships had been focused on training their crews since the *Shenandoah* was commissioned in 1923. This left relatively little time for developing scouting tactics. Indeed, such tactics weren't seriously investigated until the *Akron* was commissioned in 1931. But the rigid airship programme had been flying for eight years. Why hadn't it made more progress?

In contrast to Dresel's report, Admiral Sellers' memo to the Chief of Naval Operations was clear. The Commander in Chief of the US Fleet not only condemned the *Macon* for failing 'to demonstrate its usefulness as a unit of the fleet',[51] but added he was of the opinion that 'further expenditure of public funds of this type of vessel for the Navy is not justified'.[52]

Admiral King was furious with Sellers' report, but he shouldn't have been surprised. The *Macon* had been shot down nine times in seven fleet exercises.[53] The problem wasn't just being forced to search in confined areas chock-a-block with the enemy; it was Dresel's insistence on using the airship to find the enemy rather than rely on her aeroplanes for scouting.

On a more positive note, the *Macon*'s HTA unit had begun testing a new radio direction finder that used the airship's magnetic field as a compass. The revolutionary device was developed by Dr Gerhard Fisher, a German scientist who'd immigrated to Palo Alto, California. Fisher had built the device in his garage, a rite of passage that would become integral to the Silicon Valley success story.* A technological offspring of the metal detector Fisher had already invented,[54] the radio direction finder was a prime example of the ground-breaking innovation that would one day make the region famous. Importantly, it enabled the Sparrowhawks to range much further from the mother ship, an important step in turning them into successful scouts.

Sadly, it wasn't a development Dresel could capitalise on, for Admiral King had decided to make a change. Dresel would be replaced as the *Macon*'s skipper. But the question remained: would her next captain be any more able?

---

*   Hewlett-Packard and Apple also started in their founder's garage.

30

A GIANT IN WAITING

One has to wonder why Admiral King didn't replace Dresel sooner given the latter's performance. One explanation is that the Navy's rigid airship programme had been criticised for rotating airship captains too frequently. Another reason may have been that King was new to the BUAER and still feeling his way.

One obvious candidate to replace Dresel was Lt Cdr Wiley, but he had been granted sea duty, 'at his own request'.[1] As Dr Arnstein pondered the viability of his creation, and Litchfield struggled to make his dream of commercial airship travel come true, Wiley was solving navigation problems aboard the USS *Cincinnati* (CL-6), the very type of scout cruiser the *Macon* was intended to replace.

If Dresel's decision to join Moffett's LTA programme was unusual given his age, then Wiley's request for sea duty was equally odd.[2] Rotating aviation officers to sea was standard practice in the Navy, but Wiley had fulfilled this obligation in 1930, when he spent a year aboard the battleship USS *Tennessee* (BB-43). This meant sea duty was not a box he needed to check, especially with three motherless children at home. Why then did he choose to leave the Navy's LTA programme?

Wiley may have realised the Navy's LTA programme was a dead end. Serving aboard a white elephant, especially one on the endangered species list, made less sense than returning to the surface fleet. After all, the fleet was the heart and soul of the Navy; Moffett's LTA programme was a sideshow by comparison. It's also possible Wiley was suffering some form of post-traumatic stress disorder and needed a break. He'd not only lost the airship of which he was second in command; he'd personally survived a horrendous ordeal. It was understandable if he needed time to recover.

What's not clear is whether Wiley intended to permanently leave the LTA programme or just take a break. There'd been a tacit understanding when he'd served aboard the *Tennessee* that he would return to Lakehurst. But everything had changed since then. Moffett was dead, a new BUAER chief had taken his place, and the rigid airship programme was on the ropes.

Wiley was too experienced an airship officer to lose to the surface Navy. Even then, Wiley's memory of his time aboard the *Tennessee* couldn't have been pleasant. Wiley had been serving aboard the ship when his wife, Marie, entered California's Long Beach Naval Hospital in September 1930. After giving birth to a daughter, she'd developed toxemia,[3] slipped into a coma and died two days later at the age of 37.[4] Wiley was no stranger to death. His older sister, Zulah, had died of a heart problem when Wiley was three, followed by a second sister's death in 1913 when he was 22.[5] Wiley's mother had passed away the following year, and his older brother, Floyd, four years after that. This left Wiley, his younger sister, Minnie Fay, and their ailing father, the only survivors of a family once seven members strong. Surely Wiley, having suffered a similar loss, should have appreciated how difficult it was for three children to lose their mother at such a young age. Yet he'd sent his two sons to military school while leaving his infant daughter in the care of a nurse.

Wiley got to see his family a bit more when he was stationed aboard the *Akron* at Lakehurst. But, as Wiley's daughter later admitted, 'he wasn't home a lot.'[7] When he was, he could be distant and reserved. There were fond memories, of course. Gordon, Wiley's oldest son, remembered watching his father return to Lakehurst aboard the *Los Angeles* when his mother was still alive. As Wiley flew over the family home he'd lean out the control car window and drop his hat in the backyard, signalling Marie to pick him up at Hangar No. 1.[8]

Gordon was 13 when the *Akron* crashed; his brother David, 9; and baby Marie not quite 3. At first, neither boy knew whether their father had survived the disaster. Marie was too young to remember, but she recalls it as a 'traumatic time', especially following the loss of their mother.[9]

Although it was a time when fathers weren't home much, Wiley was particularly scarce, putting his naval career ahead of his family. Nevertheless, his request for sea duty following the *Akron* crash is hard to fathom given that he'd see his children even less. Gender roles were partly responsible (husbands worked outside the home, while wives were homemakers). But Wiley was a single father. This makes his decision to leave three motherless children alone for the second time in three years seem heartless. Nor could serving aboard a surface ship have been easy. The *Cincinnati*'s crew was well aware of

Wiley's background. This means he probably heard the Navy's newest airship disparaged as 'shit bag' and 'bloated sausage.' These were difficult jibes for a career LTA man to endure.

But there's another reason Wiley might have opted for sea duty. He'd inherited the same fatal heart condition that plagued his family. Avoiding the stress of the Navy's LTA programme made sense for someone with heart problems. Although doctors seemed unaware of Wiley's condition, indeed, it's unclear how much Wiley understood it himself, he ran the danger of being felled by a heart attack.

While Wiley plotted courses for the *Cincinnati*, a debate raged as to whether the *Macon* was safe to fly. Arnstein was in favour of grounding the airship while frame 17.5 was strengthened.[10] But Fulton worried that grounding the *Macon* for any length of time might result in her being cancelled altogether.

Litchfield pushed Arnstein to support Fulton's decision not to ground the *Macon*, but Arnstein resisted. He didn't oppose Fulton outright, as he couldn't risk angering Goodyear-Zeppelin's most important client, but he remained concerned about his airship's safety. And so it was decided the *Macon* would stick to ocean operations along the California coast where she was unlikely to encounter severe gusts like the one over Texas.[11]

In the meantime, the situation was growing desperate. Admiral King, believing the Navy's only big rigid was in her ninth inning with two outs, no men on base and zero runs on the scoreboard, decided to tap his best relief pitcher. To be fair, Dresel's cautious approach was fine if you didn't want to lose your airship, something the Navy was keen to avoid after the *Akron* debacle. But Dresel's learning curve had cost the *Macon* more than a year — a year that Moffett's embattled rigid airship programme could ill afford.

When King finally pulled the plug, Dresel didn't have far to go. He was assigned to command the *Macon*'s home base in Sunnyvale. The damage was already done, however, and nothing short of a miracle could convince Congress or the Navy the *Macon* was an effective long-range scout.

The person King tapped to replace Dresel was none other than Lt Commander Herbert V. Wiley. Now faced with the impossible task of proving the rigid airship worthy of the fleet, Wiley had every intention of doing just that if the political climate didn't sink him first. One thing was certain, though. Unless Wiley pulled a rabbit out of his hat, the 'Queen of the Skies' seemed destined for the scrap heap.

PART IV

A GIANT REDEEMED. USS *MACON* (ZRS-5), 1934–35

31

THE *HOUSTON* INCIDENT

The Navy's change of command ceremony is full of pomp and circumstance for a reason. It not only keeps a centuries-old tradition alive; it makes clear to a vessel's crew that the new guy's in charge.

The *Macon*'s change of command took place in Hangar No. 1 at NAS Sunnyvale on 11 July 1934. All hands were mustered to hear Dresel and Wiley read their orders aloud. Dresel, looking smart in his dress uniform with a ceremonial sword strapped to his side, stood in front of his crew, with Wiley, looking youthful despite his prematurely grey hair, facing opposite him. The cavernous hangar was cool and dark on the hot July morning. A narrow band of windows running its length allowed dusty beams of sunlight to cut through the shadows. In a performance as codified as a Noh play, seventy-plus men stood at attention as the *Macon* floated above them. After Wiley read his orders, he saluted Dresel saying, 'I relieve you.' Dresel saluted in return, responding, 'I stand relieved.'

The *Macon*'s new captain was a hard man to read. Unemotional and expressionless, he was not especially popular with his crew.[1] His colleagues respected him, to be sure, but that's not the same as liking him.

Wiley may have been a celebrity by 1934, but he was not exactly a hero. Through sheer luck (and his ability to swim), he'd been catapulted into the national spotlight. He wasn't famous so much for what he'd done as what he'd failed to do, which is drown. Yes, he was a meticulous airship officer, but he hadn't yet emerged as a giant in the field.

One thing was undeniable. Wiley had more flight hours in rigid airships than any officer in the LTA programme.[3] This may be why Admiral King chose him to command the *Macon*. Wiley had not only served aboard the

*Shenandoah, Los Angeles** and *Akron*; he'd worked closely with the latter's HTA unit, an experience that would help him hit the ground running when he took command of the *Macon*.

Wiley's reputation was mixed, however.[4] 'A strict disciplinarian who never hesitated to hand out extra duty', he was accustomed to dressing down his men for the slightest infraction.[5] Dresel might chew out his crew after finding a naked woman wandering their hotel floor, but he also stood them to a drink after their hair-raising experience over Texas. In contrast, Wiley was a taciturn bedrock of Midwestern values. Never outgoing, he was hard for the crew to warm up to.[6]

Wiley's character had something to do with this but so did his personal situation. He'd not only lost his wife during childbirth; he hadn't been promoted despite being in command of the *Macon*. How these hardships affected him is hard to know, but they may have contributed to his being so austere.

The *Macon*'s HTA pilots were particularly concerned about Wiley taking over. They considered him an 'old school' LTAer, 'lighter than air and thicker than mud'.[7] Afraid their new commanding officer would stick to established doctrine, the *Macon*'s HTA pilots were so worried that Lt Miller, the Sparrowhawks' Squadron Leader, remarked, 'we were ready to turn in our flying suits and prepare the [planes] … for … storage'.[8]

But Wiley didn't waste time getting started. The day after assuming command, he took the *Macon* on a flight over Los Angeles to watch her HTA unit perform. After hook-on drills, he sent the Sparrowhawks on a search exercise to see how well they employed the 60–60 navigation technique. Next, he had them test Fisher's experimental homing device designed to extend their scouting range.[9] Soon, Lt Miller, was singing his new captain's praises. 'The skipper was wonderful … he did everything possible. He realised that ship was a plane carrier and the planes came first at all times.'[10] Put simply, 'Doc Wiley took over with a bang!'[11]

Wiley's use of Sparrowhawks for scouting shouldn't have come as a surprise. He'd been the *Los Angeles*' XO when Lt Gorton hooked on for the first time. In fact, Wiley had more experience with HTA units than any other airship captain. Confident the Sparrowhawks could be used to extend the *Macon*'s scouting range, he flew back to Sunnyvale to hatch an audacious plan.

★   Wiley served as first officer aboard the *Los Angeles* as well as commanded her from
         May 1929 until April 1930.

While Wiley was observing hook-on drills President Roosevelt was vacationing aboard one of his favourite naval ships, the USS *Houston* (CA-30). Roosevelt had always loved the sea. Beginning with the small sailboat he'd skippered on Long Island Sound as a boy, he took every opportunity to sail the ocean. Although polio reduced his mobility, he not only kept a Presidential yacht on the Potomac; he travelled on Navy ships every chance he got.

Roosevelt boarded the *Houston* at Annapolis on 1 July for what promised to be a 5,000-mile voyage to Hawaii. Hoping to do some fishing,[12] the President was accompanied by his distant cousin, Henry L. Roosevelt, Assistant Secretary of the Navy, as well as a raft of newspaper men, his security team and a second heavy cruiser, the USS *New Orleans* (CA-32), for protection. The First Lady, who didn't care for ocean voyages, remained in Washington.

Roosevelt's trip was widely covered by the press, but details of his route were kept secret. Aware of the fleet's tendency to use the *Macon* for search problems ill-suited to her strengths, Wiley developed a search mission that was guaranteed to attract notice. He would find the President of the United States vacationing in the middle of the Pacific despite Roosevelt's location being classified.

Wiley's scouting problem was ideal. Since there was little information about the President's whereabouts, it perfectly mirrored the limited intelligence the *Macon* would have tracking an enemy during wartime.[13] If Wiley could find the President in the vast Pacific with only twenty-four hours' notice, it would demonstrate just how effective a long-range scout the *Macon* could be.

News reports indicated that the Presidential convoy had departed Clipperton Island off the west coast of Panama sometime on the afternoon of 17 July. Working with the *Macon*'s navigator, Wiley estimated the *Houston*'s course and speed, determining where she was most likely to be come 19 July. Then, he scheduled the *Macon* for a 'training cruise' at sea.[14]

It wasn't a lie exactly, but it wasn't the whole truth, either. Wiley knew he'd never receive approval from the Navy's battleship admirals if he revealed the true purpose of his mission, so he fudged the matter.[15]

Making a late morning departure on 18 July, the *Macon* 'up-shipped' from NAS Sunnyvale and headed north towards San Francisco. As the 'Queen of the Skies' passed the Golden Gate on her way to the Pacific, the crew could see the vermillion towers of the new bridge were still unconnected. Now, Wiley had only twenty-four hours to race 1,500 miles across a featureless ocean to a point where he'd calculated the President's convoy would arrive late on the morning of 19 July. If it would take a miracle to change the anti-airship bias in Congress and the Navy, Wiley would provide one.

The weather proved poor the first day of the flight.[16] Fog blanketed the ocean, rain squalls filled the sky and cloud cover reached 6,000ft. Flying blind, Wiley was forced to navigate by dead reckoning. But when the *Macon* arrived at her intended position early on the morning of 19 July she was only 22 miles off her mark – a truly impressive feat of navigation.[17]

At 1030 hours, Wiley ordered the *Macon*'s engines slowed before deploying two of her Sparrowhawks. The planes' landing gear had been replaced with an auxiliary fuel tank to give them an extra hour of flight.[18] It also made it easier to land in the ocean should they have to ditch.*[,19]

Wiley gave Lt Miller and Lt (jg) Fred 'Nappy' Kivette only an hour to find the President. Concerned the *Macon* wouldn't have enough fuel to make it back to Sunnyvale, he made it clear the pilots would have to return by noon.[20]

After Lt Miller settled into the cockpit, his Sparrowhawk was lowered outside the airship. When he was ready, Miller pulled the lever releasing his plane's skyhook from the airship's trapeze. A vertiginous drop lasting only a second or two followed, after which Miller gunned his engine and banked steeply away from the airship.

As the *Macon*'s twin Sparrowhawks disappeared south over the horizon, the lumbering dirigible followed in their path. Sixty minutes wasn't a lot of time to find the President, but at least no one would be the wiser should they fail.**[,21]

At 6ft tall and weighing 180lb, Miller could barely squeeze into the Sparrowhawk's cockpit wearing his winter flight gear.[22] Exposed to biting cold, drenching rain and a knife-sharp wind was hard enough, but searching for two grey ships painted to blend with the ocean was even more difficult. Despite cloud cover, turbulence and rain squalls, Miller spotted his quarry in less than an hour.[23] Wiley's estimate of where to find the President had been spot on.

Those aboard the *Houston* were initially shocked to see two fighter planes more than 1,000 miles from land appear out of nowhere. Since none of the Navy's aircraft carriers were in the Pacific,[24] there was concern an enemy might be launching an attack. Admiral Joseph M. 'Bull' Reeves, Commander in

---

* In the event a Sparrowhawk ditched in the ocean, the plane had an inflatable device under its wings to keep it afloat. Source: Mikesh, Robert C., *That Great Hook-Up in the Sky!*, *Wings*, February 1975, Vol. 5 No. 1, p. 25.

** Wiley later claimed he didn't reveal the true nature of his mission in case it failed. That way he wouldn't cause the programme any embarrassment.

Chief of the US Fleet, had promised Roosevelt there was zero chance anyone would ambush the Presidential convoy. Now two planes were buzzing the *Houston* with what appeared to be bombs hanging from their undercarriages. As Lt Miller recalled later, 'We gave those boys on the *Houston* a real thrill. Our belly tanks looked like bombs and some thought we were attacking the President's ship.'[25]

If there was genuine concern, it didn't last long; the distinctive shape of the Sparrowhawks' skyhooks made them easily identifiable. Fear of an attack soon gave way to a carnival-like atmosphere as off-duty crew jammed the *Houston*'s railings to watch the Sparrowhawks swoop and dive. Even Roosevelt came on deck to watch the *Macon* appear out of the clouds like a ghostly apparition.[26]

Tickled by Wiley's performance, Roosevelt sent his congratulations:

THE PRESIDENT COMPLIMENTS YOU AND YOUR PLANES ON YOUR FINE PERFORMANCE AND EXCELLENT NAVIGATION.[27]

Encouraged by the positive message, Wiley radioed the *Houston* for permission to drop two packages for the President. When permission was granted, Miller and Kivette returned to the airship, where they were each handed a parcel wrapped in waterproof rubber.

One account, written decades after the fact, claims Miller and Kivette had practised dropping the packages at Sunnyvale.[28] If true, their aim was lousy. They not only missed the deck of the *Houston*, both packages wound up in the drink.[29] Fortunately, their waterproof covering ensured they floated. The *Houston*, slowing to a halt, put a motorised whaleboat over the side. After retrieving both packages, they were delivered to the President.[30]

Wiley knew Roosevelt enjoyed reading the daily papers, which were impossible to get while at sea. Roosevelt was especially keen to follow the longshoremen's strike in San Francisco, which threatened to turn ugly. The packages not only contained a greeting from Wiley[31] but six San Francisco newspapers from the previous day and the latest issue of *Time*.[32] Additionally, Wiley included a sealed envelope addressed to the *Houston*'s mail orderly containing letters to be mailed. Wiley even included money for their postage.[33] One postcard commemorating the first delivery of mail by a dirigible at sea featured a silver foil cut-out of the *Macon*.[34] The postcard, stamped 'President's Cruise', read, 'USS *Macon* intercepted USS *Houston* – delivered papers for the President.'[35] Roosevelt was an avid philatelist, and would appreciate the commemorative covers. Indeed, Roosevelt signed one of the cards with its

18 July cancellation mark from Moffett Field and a 19 July postal mark from the *Houston*.

After receiving Wiley's packages, Roosevelt sent a second message:

WELL DONE AND THANK YOU FOR THE PAPERS THE PRESIDENT.[36]

If the point of dropping packages on the *Houston's* forecastle was to demonstrate the *Macon's* effectiveness as a bomber, it failed. But the larger point – that a rigid airship could quickly locate two cruisers in the middle of the ocean with a minimum amount of information – was made in the most sensational way, exactly as Wiley intended.

Reporters aboard the *Houston* scrambled to file stories about the *Macon's* dramatic arrival. While most accounts emphasised that an airship had delivered mail at sea for the first time, they missed the more salient point that Wiley had proven the *Macon* an effective long-range scout.* In fact, reporters seemed more interested in the course change the *Houston* made to avoid rough seas so that an emergency appendectomy could be performed on a crewman than Wiley's remarkable accomplishment.

There's no doubt that Wiley had proven the naysayers wrong. With minimal information, the *Macon* had travelled 1,500 miles in poor weather to find the most important man in the United States despite every attempt to keep his location a secret. And it took him only twenty-four hours to do it.[37]

That a sky-going scout located a surface one undoubtedly added spice to Wiley's accomplishment, but it was a finger in the surface Navy's eye. That Wiley had proven the *Macon* a worthy long-range scout in front of an unassailable witness like the President only added salt to the wound.

Wiley's needle-in-a-haystack mission should have made him a hero. There was only one problem: the Commander in Chief of the US Fleet was furious. Wiley's search may have been cleverly conceived and perfectly executed, but it infuriated Admiral Reeves. That Wiley had described the flight as 'a long-range scouting operation for a ship at sea' without disclosing the intended target was insubordination.[38] The sin of omission was as bad as a lie.

---

*   The 20 July 1934 report by Ontario's *Windsor Star* was one of the few accounts to grasp the significance of Wiley's achievement.

By 2030 hours the *Macon*'s radio room was buzzing with urgent messages demanding an explanation.[39] Had the *Macon* really made contact with the *Houston*? If yes, on whose authority?[40] Had she also delivered mail? If so, what was it?

In response, Wiley sent a cover-your-ass cable to Admiral King:

Made Contact Houston at Noon and Delivered yesterdays newspapers period Following received from naval Aide Quote The President Compliments you and your planes on your fine performance and excellent navigation unquote Wiley[41]

But a cable from COMBATFOR to King the next day indicates just how in the dark the Navy had been:

Macon requested and received from Commander Battle Force authority to make protracted flight to sea commencing Wednesday 18 July. There was no reference made in request from *Macon* to making contact with *Houston*. Commander Battle Force had no information regarding any papers carried by *Macon* on this trip. *Macon* directed to submit full report.[42]

When Wiley arrived back at Sunnyvale on 21 July, it should have been a triumphant moment. The airship had not only completed her longest flight yet, most of it over the Pacific; Wiley had done what previous *Macon* captains had failed to do. He'd shown the *Macon* could be more effective than a surface cruiser in finding the enemy. But it was a dangerous accomplishment in the eyes of some fleet admirals.

As one memo indicated, 'The Commander-in-Chief (i.e. Reeves) considers the flight, ill-timed, ill-advised, and conceived with disregard for proper Naval procedure.'[43] Admiral Standley, Chief of Naval Operations, was also not amused. As he told reporters, 'We consider it a publicity stunt … he had no business doing.'[44]

It must have felt to Wiley like the US Navy had ganged up against him. There were even rumours he'd be court-martialled.[45]

'They told me to show the *Macon* could scout,' Wiley protested. 'When I did, they want to court martial me!'[46]

In all fairness, Wiley should have been commended for his achievement.[47] Instead, his naval career appeared over. The *Macon* had finally found a giant to guide her. The only problem was that the Navy wouldn't let him.

32

LT CDR WILEY:
A GIANT REVEALED

Wiley's roll of the dice might appear out of character, but he'd always been ambitious

The third child of Joel and Minnie Wiley, Herbert Victor was born at home in the small town of Wheeling, Missouri, on 16 May 1891. Steeped in the Midwestern values of hard work, self-reliance and emotional restraint, Wiley's early life was marked by his father's many business failures. In 1896, when Wiley was only 5 years old, his father closed his dry goods store, moving the family 275 miles south to the hamlet of Mountain Grove, Missouri. Situated in the Ozarks, Mountain Grove had unpaved streets, unnumbered houses and fewer than 900 inhabitants. There, Joel Wiley, who went by his initials, J.A., opened a general store, seeking financial success.[1]

Living in a white house with a picket fence, there was swimming in Beaney Creek, ice skating on Lake Lilly, and Sunday picnics. Wiley had many fond memories of the bucolic setting.[2]

Tragedy struck when his father's store was destroyed by fire. J.A. opened another one, only to have it fail in 1907.[3] The next year, Wiley's father moved the family yet again, this time to Chillicothe. There, J.A. opened Wiley's One Price Cash Store, hoping to find the financial success that had eluded him.[4]

If not exactly itinerant, the family's moves due to J.A.'s business struggles meant young Wiley was frequently uprooted. This lack of security would eventually drive him to escape his surroundings as he sought a chance to better himself. In the meantime, he was a handsome boy described as studious, cheerful and popular.[5] He enjoyed reading fictional accounts of the Wild West (the more lurid the better) but concealed his love of books by hiding them in a neighbour's barn.[6] One thing seemed clear. He was highly intelligent.

Wiley was also a strong swimmer.[7] An uncommon skill at the turn of the century, it would later save his life when the *Akron* crashed at sea. One newspaper account, written when he was an adult, claimed Wiley spent part of his childhood playing with a construction set, building 'derricks with which to hoist rocks and other objects'.[8] These entertaining if apocryphal stories indicate an early mechanical bent, but the first such set wasn't sold to the public until Wiley was 22 years old. Still, he enjoyed hanging out at the railroad depot watching the telegraph operator apply his trade.[9] One thing Wiley's boyhood friends all agreed upon: he was 'destined for high adventure'.[10]

Wiley graduated from Chillicothe High School with the highest honours in 1909.[11] He was already parting his hair in the middle by then, a popular style he maintained throughout his life. But prospects were limited for a bright boy in Chillicothe. Since J.A. could not afford to send his son to college, Wiley went to work 90 miles away at the International Harvester plant in Kansas City.[12] When the Honourable W.W. Rucker, congressman for Missouri's second district, was looking for a candidate to appoint to the US Naval Academy, Chillicothe's school superintendent passed along Wiley's name.[13] Rucker was impressed enough to select Wiley. Given the boy's humble parentage, it wasn't just a lucky break, it was a life-defining opportunity.

If Herbert Wiley dreamed of going to sea, he never told anyone. In fact, the first time Wiley saw the ocean was when he travelled to Annapolis to spend several months cramming for its entrance exam. But Wiley failed the exam along with 63 per cent of those who took it.[14] Embarrassed, he returned to Chillicothe to work in his father's dry goods store.

Family lore has it that J.A. also sought admission for his son to West Point. Wiley, being young, smart and ambitious, was probably more interested in the military's all-expenses-paid college education than any particular branch of the service. Whether or not the story is true, the *Macon's* future commander took the naval Academy's entrance exam a second time in April 1911 and passed. Sworn into Annapolis just six days short of being too old to qualify,[15] Wiley committed to serving in the Navy for eight years. That same month, his father closed his struggling store and retired.[16]

Wiley had little difficulty adjusting to military life. The third oldest midshipman in his class,[17] he was just under 5ft 9in and weighed 166lb, making him a bit stocky. His eyes were listed as dark (they were in fact, brown), his hair black (he wouldn't go prematurely grey until his 30s) and his complexion ruddy, with his hearing and eyesight deemed acceptable.[18]

When Wiley got into trouble at Annapolis it was for the type of things that challenge most young men: disorderly rooms or laughing in ranks.[19] This was not surprising given his youthful vigour.

Wiley was also close to his mother. Rarely did a Tuesday pass without her receiving a letter from Annapolis in her son's neat cursive hand.[20] But Minnie Wiley was not in good health. Suffering from congestive heart failure, her condition waxed and waned throughout her son's time at the Academy. In the summer before Wiley's senior year, she became so ill she wasn't expected to live. Wiley was granted emergency leave to visit her, but she survived that episode only to die a few months later.

The loss of a mother is a serious blow for any young man. As proof, Wiley carried the letters she'd written him at the end of her life for the rest of his own.[21] Three months after he'd buried her, Wiley ended up in the Annapolis infirmary with an undisclosed illness, causing him to miss a month of school. That didn't stop him from being popular. Like 'Froggy' Fulton, Wiley earned a nickname at Annapolis.[22] Known as 'Doc' to his friends, its pedigree is lost to time. Nevertheless, Wiley's senior entry in the Lucky Bag yearbook shows he was well liked:

> There is nothing narrow about Doc. His smile, his shoulders, and his mind are of the broadest. When you see a large and well cultivated pompadour … pushed back by a wide grin … sit up and take notice for it is the 'Doctor.' Herb has been known during his four years as a … reliable man. These qualities together with the fact that he does his best … have given him success at whatever he has turned his hand to … Those who have gained his acquaintance will back him against all others as a steadfast, unwavering friend.[23]

On 16 March 1915, just three months shy of graduation, Wiley received a bombshell. The US Naval Academy Medical Department informed him he was unqualified to graduate due to colour blindness.[24]

This was a serious matter. Wiley was so convinced he'd have to leave Annapolis without graduating he wrote a letter to his father outlining his career prospects in the private sector.[25] A follow-up memo from the Navy Department's Bureau of Navigation offered little comfort. Recommending Wiley be allowed to graduate, it said he should be discharged if a subsequent examination found him 'not physically qualified for continuance in services'.[26]

The week before graduation, Wiley appeared before a special medical board as a final court of appeal. After examining him, the board found Wiley's colour blindness was 'not considered sufficient to disqualify him for the service'.[27]

This was a surprising reversal, suggesting the board either cut Wiley some slack or the time he took to teach himself the difference between various shades of coloured yarn paid off.[28] Whatever the reason, Wiley was allowed to graduate on 4 June 1915, doing so near the top third of his class.

Young Wiley served on a succession of US naval ships including the USS *Colorado* (ACR-7), USS *San Diego* (ACR-6), USS *Denver* (CL-16) and USS *Montana* (ACR-13). In 1917, he married Marie Frances Scroggie, whom he'd met at an Academy social function. None of Wiley's family was able to attend the ceremony in New London, Connecticut.[29] Marie would die in childbirth thirteen years later, adding to Wiley's personal hardships, but there's nothing to suggest the marriage was anything but happy.

Wiley missed the First World War, serving stateside the entire time. Undoubtedly, this caused some frustration since he was keen to get ahead. Then, in May 1920, Wiley put in for submarine school.

The US Navy had been employing submarines for fewer than twenty years. Wiley had received torpedo training,[30] so his background was suitable. Since the school was based in New London it would be a convenient posting for the newly pregnant Marie, who had family nearby.[31] But sub school may have been more a means of advancing Wiley's career than something he pursued out of a special feeling. This favouring of ambition over personal preference would occur time and again in Wiley's career, eventually leading to the even more surprising decision to go into lighter-than-air flight. Wiley was deemed too important for the destroyer fleet to spare, so his request for sub school was never acted upon.[32]

In 1921, he was assigned as an instructor to the Naval Academy's Department of Electrical Engineering and Physics. When a request for volunteers to train aboard the Navy's first big rigid was made in December 1922, Wiley submitted his name for consideration.[33]

Something about getting in on the ground floor of the small but fast-growing LTA field must have appealed to Wiley. It not only offered a way to separate him from his competition but promised quick advancement. Attrition in the Navy's LTA programme was high, not just because it was demanding, but because the crash of the *R38* in August 1921 had wiped out some of the Navy's most experienced rigid airship personnel.[34]

Forty-one officers responded to the request for volunteers, but only nine were selected.[35] Among them were Wiley and Rosendahl, who reported to NAS Lakehurst in April 1923 as members of the Navy's rigid airship training class.[36] The two men would shadow each other in the programme for more than a decade.

Wiley's ground school courses included instruction in aerostatics, aerodynamics, aerology, engineering and navigation. He also accumulated flight hours in free balloons, kite balloons and blimps.[37] Since the Navy was assembling its first rigid airship at Lakehurst, Wiley assisted in her fitting out. When Fleet Airship Number One was finally commissioned as the *Shenandoah* in October 1923, he spent the next eighteen months serving aboard her.

Wiley was transferred to the Navy's second big rigid, the *Los Angeles*, in January 1925. He couldn't know it at the time, but the *Los Angeles* would become the Navy's most successful rigid airship. He served aboard her during many firsts, including the first time an airship was towed out of the hangar by a mobile mooring mast, the first time a plane hooked on to a big rigid and the first time an airship docked to an aircraft carrier. It was in many respects an excellent place to learn his profession.

Wiley was promoted to lieutenant commander in December 1925. But he was growing impatient, especially when he found himself reporting to Rosendahl, who'd been put in charge of the *Los Angeles*. Not long after, Wiley asked to be assigned to a surface ship, noting, 'I need battleship duty ... for my professional advancement.'[38] Wiley's request not only shows how ambitious he was but also suggests he wasn't yet wedded to Moffett's LTA programme since he made it clear he might not return to aviation.[39]

Rosendahl viewed his executive officer as someone who could get the job done, delegating much of the day-to-day responsibility of running the airship to him. But when the *Shenandoah* crashed, the Navy was short of LTA personnel, so Rosendahl refused to endorse Wiley's request for sea duty. 'This officer's services have been and will continue to be of very great value not only to the *Los Angeles* ... but to lighter-than-air activities of the Navy in general,' Rosendahl wrote.[40] It was a compliment, but it also meant Wiley wouldn't be allowed to leave the programme any time soon.

Wiley was given temporary command of the *Los Angeles* in October 1928 when Rosendahl was invited to fly aboard the *Graf Zeppelin* for her first transatlantic crossing. That same month, Wiley skippered the airship on an 1,800-mile hand-waving flight to the American Legion convention in San Antonio, Texas. But Wiley planned a surprise during the voyage. Before the *Los Angeles* left Lakehurst, he sent his father a letter noting, 'Airships sometimes are driven out of their route by strong winds, and on this trip there will be a wind blowing our ship across the town of Wheeling. Watch for us and use a red fuse.'[41] As a local paper later reported:

An elderly father received a thrill tonight that comes to few persons when he saw the giant navy dirigible *Los Angeles* glide through the night over this village. The liner cruised over Wheeling at exactly 10:30 with J.A. Wiley watching its progress … With nearly the entire population of this country town assembled at Mr. Wiley's home … a vigil for the first view of the onrushing liner was started soon after dark … Mr. Wiley had two gigantic red flares alighted … when a bright white light was flashed from the ship just as it reached Wheeling. [As] the searchlight … played over the assemblage … the father stood looking into the sky, moving a red flare. 'That's my boy,' he cried …. It was the first time that the father had … been so near his son in the last four years.[42]

Wiley successfully completed his round trip to Texas, but stepped down as the *Los Angeles*' captain when Rosendahl returned at the end of the month. If it was hard for him to relinquish command, he was characteristically silent about it. What's impossible to miss is his unauthorised use of the *Los Angeles* – something he would repeat six years later when employing the *Macon* to find the President.

After serving four years on the *Los Angeles*, Wiley was finally rewarded with her command in the spring of 1929. A year later, his request for battleship duty came through when he was assigned to serve aboard the USS *Tennessee* (BB-43). A year after that, Wiley was recalled to the LTA programme, in part because he was such a valuable player.

Relocating to Ohio, Wiley taught the fundamentals of LTA flight to the *Akron*'s crew using the airship as a classroom.[43] When the *Akron* was commissioned in October 1931, Wiley was appointed her executive officer, serving under Rosendahl for the second time.

But Wiley was frustrated. Always a bridesmaid never a bride, he'd served as executive officer under four captains on three different airships. He was tired of playing second fiddle. He wanted a command of his own.

After the *Akron* was lost at sea, Wiley's future in Moffett's LTA programme seemed in doubt, especially since he'd requested sea duty again. But after a year aboard the *Cincinnati*, Admiral King recalled Wiley to the LTA programme, putting him in charge of the *Macon*.

Wiley was 43 years old now – a bit long in the tooth for a lieutenant commander. He may have been in charge of the Navy's newest, most expensive aircraft, but few people expected him to succeed. Then he found the President of the United States in the middle of the Pacific and anything seemed possible.

If raising a family is difficult for naval officers, it was even more difficult for Wiley after losing his wife. He employed a series of housekeepers to look after his children as well as relying upon friends and cousins, but it didn't hide the fact he wasn't around much.[44]

After his wife died, their infant daughter, Marie, had gone to live with Roland and Nan Mayer at NAS Lakehurst. The couple were close friends of the Wileys. Lt Cdr Mayer had been in the LTA programme's airship training class along with 'Doc', where they got to know each other. Mayer's wife spent so much time caring for baby Marie she became her surrogate mother. When it was finally time to reunite the child with her father, Nan prepared an elaborate photo album of their years together to help ease the transition. Eighty years later, Marie still counted it among her most treasured belongings.

Wiley's only daughter was 4 years old when she moved back with her father.[45] One photo taken at NAS Sunnyvale a short time after their reunion shows a smiling Wiley in his blue naval uniform standing in front of one of the *Macon's* Sparrowhawks, cradling Marie in his left arm. Marie, casually draping her hand on her father's shoulder, looks unabashedly happy. Wiley's two sons are also in the picture: a serious-looking Gordon stands to Wiley's right, while David, in front, looks more relaxed.

'My Dad was very strict,' Marie recalls, explaining the family dynamic. 'Things were black and white with him. My brothers had to say, "Yes, sir. No, sir," but they respected him.'[46]

Wiley's children led a fairly spartan life but not every family moment was constrained by military decorum. Marie also remembers turning the inside of the *Macon* into her own personal jungle gym as she ran up and down its narrow catwalks joyfully giggling like the 4-year-old she was.

John Toland, author of *The Great Dirigibles*, claims Wiley developed a nervous tic after the *Akron* crash. Before disciplining a crewman he was said to giggle nervously, earning him the nickname 'Tee-hee'.[47] It's possible the story is true, though Toland doesn't cite a source. But it doesn't sound like Wiley. Either way, it wasn't meant as a compliment.

If our heroes are not always admirable that doesn't make their accomplishments any less heroic; it just makes them human. The truth is, men can do great deeds without being great themselves. Whether or not Wiley was a formidable leader, loving father or dutiful son, he was first and foremost an accomplished airship commander. Respected within the LTA programme, he was considered a good man to have in a tough situation. Yes, he'd worked hard to escape the lean years of his boyhood, but if he was emotionally cool it's not hard to understand the reason given his upbringing. Still, one wonders, given everything he'd accomplished, why would Wiley risk it all to find the President of the United States?

Wiley's decision to find Roosevelt wasn't the first time he'd placed a big bet. Switching from the surface Navy to airships was a gamble, as was applying to submarine school. Even taking the entrance exam for the Naval Academy was a risk, as Wiley discovered when he had to take it twice.

There's no doubt Wiley was ambitious. He regularly sought promotion, whether through repeated requests for sea duty or desiring his own command. He was particularly unhappy at being passed over by men of higher rank but less experience. Frustrated by the Navy's slow rate of advancement during the Depression,[48] Wiley looked for a way to stand out from the pack.

He also believed in his Sparrowhawks. He was confident that if employed as scouts, they'd prove the *Macon* superior to the heavy cruisers she was intended to replace. As proof, Wiley was already thinking of how aeroplanes could be used to extend an airship's scouting range two months before he assumed command of the *Macon*. In a May 1934 article for *Proceedings*, an influential magazine among Navy higher-ups, Wiley wrote, 'Scouting can be carried out efficiently when the airship lies back and sends in its planes.'[49] But he also knew the fleet admirals weren't going to give him a chance to prove it. This led to his radical decision to search for the President without asking permission. If fortune favours the bold, then Wiley had chosen the boldest path possible. Unfortunately, he miscalculated.

Wiley may have had more flying hours than any airship officer, but he'd crossed a line. When he sought to find the President of the United States without seeking permission, he was open to a charge of insubordination. And now they wanted to court martial him.

That the man the Navy had made responsible for proving the *Macon* an ocean-going scout was to be punished for doing exactly that is tinged with irony. But the organisation Wiley had unselfishly served for more than half of his life seemed determined to crush him. And no one, not Paul W. Litchfield, not Dr Karl Arnstein and certainly not Admiral Moffett (who'd been dead more than a year), was going to save him.

33

A GIANT EXCELS

Wiley's successful search for the President of the United States enabled the *Macon* to finally emerge from her sister's shadow. But the man who'd demonstrated an airship could do something most thought impossible was under attack. It made no difference he'd proven the *Macon* was a long-range scout in a dramatic enough way that people paid attention; the battleship admirals wanted his head.

Wiley put the best face on what he'd done in a report to the Chief of Naval Operations. Characterising his actions as of 'inestimable value in … demonstrating [the airship's] worth for naval scouting',[1] Wiley's words fell on deaf ears. Instead, Admiral Reeves accused Wiley of 'misapplied initiative'.[2]

Wiley could ill afford to antagonise such a powerful man as Reeves, so he sought the protection of Admiral King. Even then, Wiley was reluctant to admit his mistake. 'I may be guilty of misapplied initiative,' he wrote his boss, '[but] I still think the only error was not telling where I was going.'[3]

Wiley had been counting on promotion to commander,[4] but as he confided to King, 'My personal apprehension is that … I am "cooked" for selection.'[5] Of more concern, he added, 'I am now afraid to use any initiative whatever [sic],[6] despite a show of initiative being exactly what the *Macon* required.'

Wiley resolved to take his punishment like a man. 'I do not write this to you in the spirit of crying over the situation,' he told King in closing. 'I admit I bungled, and have something coming to me.'[7] But a handwritten comment scrawled across the bottom of Wiley's letter is telling. 'I understood doctrine was to encourage rather than discourage initiative,' it reads.[8] Although the handwriting may be King's, whoever wrote it had a point. Wiley may have been guilty of 'misapplied initiative', he may even have been insubordinate, but he'd shown the *Macon* could find a needle in a haystack whether or not the fleet admirals liked it.

Discussion of Wiley's punishment took place behind the scenes. King was sympathetic, and he wasn't the only one. Wiley's oldest son, who grew up to be a naval officer like his father, told an interviewer that Admiral Reeves intended to have his father court-martialled, but that President Roosevelt intervened.[9] The President knew Wiley, having hosted him at the White House following the *Akron* crash. He was also said to have been tickled when the *Macon* appeared over the *Houston* out of nowhere. Whether the President put in a good word for Wiley isn't known for sure, but Admiral King certainly did. Wiley not only wasn't brought up on charges, he retained command of the *Macon*. In the meantime, his long-sought-after promotion to commander remained in doubt.

With an experienced crew under Wiley's command, the *Macon* was positioned for success. Once the smoke cleared, he began designing long-range search problems to showcase his airship's strengths. Although this is what had got him into trouble in the first place, he made sure to inform COMBATFOR of each flight's destination.

Wiley didn't have to wait long before a real-life scouting problem presented itself. The SS *Naitamba*, a 34ft yawl, had been missing for a month after departing Hilo, Hawaii. Her three-man crew didn't have a radio, so the *Macon* was directed to search for the sailboat. The *Naitamba* eventually sailed into California's port of San Pedro under her own power. Wiley had been sent too far north to find her anyway. But the *Macon* had searched 50,000 square miles of the Pacific – yet another impressive demonstration of her scouting ability.

Wiley had more success the next month devising his own search problem. He decided to find the SS *Lurline*, a luxury ocean liner travelling from Hawaii to San Francisco. Departing Sunnyvale on the evening of 26 October, the *Macon* launched her Sparrowhawks the next morning. They soon found the passenger ship despite poor weather.[10] Once again, Wiley showed he could find a target with limited information.

Wiley's command of the *Macon* was both aggressive and forward thinking. Between July and December 1934 he made twenty flights, logging nearly 800 hours in the air[11] – the most any rigid airship had been flown by the Navy.[12] During this period, he conducted several experiments designed to make the *Macon* self-sufficient. He tested rescue gear to save a Sparrowhawk pilot forced to ditch in the sea.[13] He also experimented with a device to scoop ballast water from the ocean,[14] and using a plane for in-flight refueling.[15] Although the pilot rescue gear worked well, the latter two plans never panned out.

The most unusual device Wiley experimented with was the sub-cloud observation car. Also called the spy basket, periscope and angel car, the contraption looked more like a children's ride at an amusement park than a device used to spot the enemy. Lowered from the *Macon*'s aeroplane hangar on a steel cable 3,000ft long, the spy car had an open cockpit and just enough room for a single occupant to observe the enemy. A key-type radio (which never worked very well) enabled an observer to report their findings to the *Macon* overhead hidden in the clouds.

Originally pioneered by Zeppelins during the First World War, the sub-cloud observation car was an unstable contraption that Germany quickly abandoned. The first and only time the *Akron* conducted an unmanned test of the spy basker, the officers in her control car were surprised to see it suddenly appear at eye level. Swinging like a giant pendulum, the spy basket threatened to wrap itself around the airship. When it was Wiley's turn to test the spy car, he didn't take any chances. He loaded it with 200lb of sand rather than risk a human occupant.[16]

In addition to being unstable, there was concern the spy car might be struck by lightning. There were also worries its ¼in cable might break. At one point, discussions were held about installing a parachute to float the contraption to safety, but this was rejected in favour of its occupant wearing one instead. Still, there were doubts it could be deployed given how close to the ocean the spy basket hung.

Even after a stabilizer was added to make it safe for human occupancy riding in the angel basket demanded courage and a cast-iron stomach.[17] More than one pilot experienced an existential crisis as they trailed 1,000ft below and 200ft behind the airship.[18] Lt Miller, who rode in it at least once, recalled you were, 'for the most part alone and unhappy.'[19]

Getting shot down during war games was a constant problem, so Wiley worked hard to improve the *Macon*'s defensive tactics. He drilled her lookouts in spotting enemy fighters, and her gun crews in how to repel dive bomb attacks. He also practised evasive manoeuvres designed to bring enemy fighters within range of the *Macon*'s machine guns.[20]

Clearly, Wiley was a man in a hurry. Working tirelessly to prove that the *Macon* was everything Moffett, Litchfield and Dr Arnstein wanted, he was respected by his crew if not always loved. Nevertheless, Wiley faced a number of obstacles. When Lt (jg) Harry W. Richardson crashed his unit's N2Y-1 trainer, the *Macon*'s newest pilot not only totalled their only air taxi but broke both his ankles.[21] The Navy wouldn't replace Richardson for another four months, reducing the *Macon*'s HTA unit to two pilots. This was a problem, given Wiley wanted his Sparrowhawks to do the airship's scouting.

There were other problems as well. The *Macon* may have been built as 'the eyes of the fleet', but the fleet was on the east coast when Wiley took command and remained so for the next five months. This meant he had zero opportunity to demonstrate the gains he'd made to the fleet. Worse, Wiley didn't have enough fuel to keep the *Macon* flying. Petrol prices had nearly tripled during the Depression, threatening to curtail the *Macon*'s flight operations.[22] The only way Wiley could keep his airship flying was to beg the BUAER for an extra $700 to buy fuel.[23] 'My plans for extensive flying are knocked into a cocked hat by the limit on the amount of fuel I can have,' Wiley told Fulton.[24] Three days later, Wiley cut short the *Macon*'s southern California trip because he worried they wouldn't have enough fuel to get home.[25]

The situation was so dire NAS Sunnyvale laid off civilian personnel to fund the *Macon*'s operating costs. On 20 August, Admiral King personally approved an increase in the *Macon*'s fuel allotment, without which she would have been grounded.

If a reduction in pilot strength and fuel shortages weren't frustrating enough, the Navy kept sending the *Macon* on promotional flights. These included a trip to San Francisco for the American Legion parade and a flight over Sacramento during the State Fair.[26] Wiley found these hand-waving trips galling. They not only consumed precious petrol, they failed to advance the *Macon*'s scouting mission. Typical of these were the festivities for Navy Day. The *Macon* could hardly avoid making an appearance on the Navy's birthday, but she was not only required to drop confetti over the Mare Island naval base; she had to visit towns in the San Joaquin Valley as well. That same day, she conducted hook-on demonstrations over San Francisco while hosting an NBC radio broadcast from her control car. Afterwards, she headed south to Palo Alto to take part in the half-time show at the Stanford–USC football game. As 50,000 people watched the *Macon* pass over the Stadium, Wiley made a five-minute radio broadcast, after which he deployed one of his Sparrowhawks to wow the crowd.[27]

Wiley can be forgiven for wondering whether anyone was taking the *Macon*'s scouting mission seriously. King, wanting the *Macon* to succeed, sought to have her assigned from COMBATFOR to the scouting fleet hoping they'd devise search problems better suited to her strengths. But the scouting fleet was no more anxious to have her than COMBATFOR.

In the meantime, reinforcement of frame 17.5 dragged on. Wiley knew the main ring needed strengthening. He'd even had Lt Bolster, the *Macon*'s construction officer, draft a letter for him requesting the BUAER render an opinion on the matter.[28] But Wiley also knew he had to keep the *Macon* flying. Time spent in the hangar would not only prevent him from proving she could scout but reinforced the airship's reputation as undependable.

Given the *Macon* would mostly be flying over the ocean, the BUAER thought the repairs were not urgent. This is why Wiley didn't regard them as 'important enough' to be rushed.[29] And so, it was decided that frame 17.5 would be reinforced in stages over an eight-month period. This way, the repairs wouldn't interfere with the airship's operating schedule.[30]

Arnstein didn't agree, however. He knew the near fatal casualty over Texas, combined with the subsequent wind tunnel tests, showed the *Macon*'s fins experienced higher loads than originally predicted. He also knew the Navy was accustomed to flying her in an extremely aggressive manner, putting further stress on her tail fins.

Arnstein wasn't one to take chances; he viewed safety as paramount. Still, all of his back and forth with Fulton had got him nowhere until the casualty over Texas. Arnstein was so convinced reinforcing frame 17.5 should take place as soon as possible, he prepared two boxes containing 600lb of parts, plans and instructions for strengthening the *Macon*. Shipped to NAS Sunnyvale by train on 14 September, they didn't arrive until early October. Unfortunately, there were delays in getting the shipment to the right officer. When C.P. Burgess visited NAS Sunnyvale at the end of October, he was surprised to see repair work had not yet begun.[31]

One reason Wiley didn't want the *Macon* laid up for a long period is that a fleet exercise was finally scheduled to take place off the California coast in November. This is why he wanted repairs spread out over seven overhaul periods. Phase one would reinforce where the bottom tail fin was anchored at frame 17.5. After that, repairs would progress to where the horizontal fins were attached, leaving the upper fin to be strengthened last.

The repair work had still not begun by early November.[32] Arnstein lobbied for the Navy to move faster, but Goodyear-Zeppelin had little sway since the *Macon* was past warranty. When Arnstein heard repairs had been delayed because the officers at NAS Sunnyvale preferred playing golf on the weekends, he was furious. The Navy 'just didn't give a damn!' he exclaimed in an uncharacteristic display of anger.[33]

Arnstein grew so concerned he wanted to send his own men to repair the *Macon*, but Litchfield would not hear of it.

'It's not our airship,' he told Arnstein. 'It's the Navy's responsibility.'

When Arnstein refused to give in, Litchfield ordered him to 'Stop insulting Fulton.'[34]

Litchfield would later say that, had he known of the *Macon*'s weakness, he'd have insisted on grounding her.[35] This sounds like an after-the-fact rationalisation. As it was, repair work on frame 17.5 didn't get under way until 10 November 1934. Even then, the work wouldn't be complete for another five months.

Although Wiley was making progress in proving the *Macon* an effective scout, the fleet hadn't been paying much attention. That changed in November when the *Macon* had her first fleet exercise with Wiley as commander. Despite yet another tactical scouting problem, two of the *Macon*'s Sparrowhawks managed to find the enemy early on the first day. When the USS *Saratoga* (CV-3) spotted the *Macon*, she launched six of her dive bombers for attack. This is when Wiley's training of the crew paid off. As the *Saratoga*'s aircraft dropped out of the sky, he ordered 'hard right rudder', bringing all six planes within reach of the *Macon*'s camera guns. They were promptly 'shot' down. Not long afterwards, the *Macon*'s Sparrowhawks found the *Saratoga*, tracking her without being spotted.[36] One account even suggests the spy car was used to direct the airship in dropping rolls of toilet paper to simulate bombing.[37]

The *Macon*'s scouting performance was so encouraging that Admiral Henry V. Butler complimented her even though he wasn't a fan of airships.[38] The sharks were still circling, however. That autumn, Admiral Reeves testified before the Navy's General Board that, 'For one dirigible at a cost of $4 million you could have 26 … patrol planes … If you ask me whether I would have one dirigible or 26 patrol planes, I would answer patrol planes.'[39]

Aeroplanes were catching up with big rigids by 1934. Although scouting cruisers such as the *Houston* and *Cincinnati* were the *Macon*'s competition, seaplanes had improved to the point they'd become a significant threat. And since aircraft carriers transported aeroplanes to places they couldn't reach on their own, they too vied to render the *Macon* obsolete. Ironically, Wiley's race against the clock wasn't just against anti-airship forces in Congress but the BUAER'S own rapidly improving aircraft.

Then, on 7 December 1934 something happened that showcased the *Macon*'s scouting progress. The airship was participating in Fleet Exercise Z off the California coast. She'd been shot down the previous day but was doing a bit better when the exercise was suddenly suspended because two of the *Cincinnati*'s seaplanes had got lost. Running out of fuel, they'd been forced to ditch in the ocean.

Wiley sent two of the *Macon*'s Sparrowhawks to search for the missing planes. Finding both planes within thirty-five minutes, the Sparrowhawks dropped smoke flares to mark their location.[40] Finding two downed aeroplanes during a fleet exercise wasn't as spectacular as finding the President of the United States in the middle of the Pacific, but it was difficult to ignore the progress the *Macon* was making. Once again, Wiley had demonstrated what the airship could do. In the process, he'd shown up his former shipmates aboard the *Cincinnati* – the very same crew that had made fun of the *Macon* during a previous fleet exercise. Even the *New York Times* praised 'the greatly expanded area which the dirigible and her fighting planes are able to cover'.[41]

On 11 January, the *Macon* was told to stand by while Amelia Earhart attempted to become the first person to fly solo between Hawaii and California. The airship was ready to begin the search on two hours' notice should Earhart ditch in the Pacific.[42] Although Earhart completed her record-making flight the *Macon*'s search capabilities were at least being recognised.

Later that month, Wiley took the airship on a two-day flight over the Pacific. There he tested the Sparrowhawks' homing and radio transmission equipment with encouraging results. A Sparrowhawk was now able to get a bearing on the airship from a distance of 185 miles, making it easier to find their way home.[43] This advancement would enable the Sparrowhawks to range more freely when searching for the 'enemy' during the upcoming fleet exercise in February.

Admiral King was so pleased with Wiley's progress he sent a congratulatory memo:

It is noted there has been a gratifying increase in the activities of the USS MACON. All scheduled requirements appear to have been successfully met and a great deal of additional development work has been proceeded with … It is also noted that the recent activities of the MACON have apparently been well received by those Fleet units with which the MACON has co-operated. All of the foregoing shows that progress is being made in determining the utility of airships of the MACON type to the Fleet … It is realised that this condition of affairs has not been brought about easily … The Chief of Bureau of Aeronautics wishes to record his appreciation of accomplishments thus far and to express the hope that the good work will continue.[44]

King's praise must have pleased Wiley, especially after being accused of 'misapplied initiative'. And that wasn't the only good news. That same month, Roosevelt's Federal Aviation Commission (FAC) came out in support of the Navy's rigid airship programme, stating, 'It should be the policy of the United States to undertake further construction and operation of rigid airships in naval and commercial service.'[45]

Echoing many of the King Committee's findings, the FAC recommended the Navy build two big rigids along with a moderate-sized metal-clad. It also called for a training airship to be constructed replacing the *Los Angeles*, which had been mothballed to reduce costs.[46]

This must have made Litchfield happy after the damper the *Akron* crash put on passenger-carrying airships. In other words, Wiley's efforts to prove rigid airships a worthy addition to the fleet, combined with Litchfield's patient promotion of commercial airship travel, were finally bearing fruit.

In the meantime, Admiral King had achieved an important breakthrough. King had been lobbying the surface Navy for more than a year to develop search problems suited to the *Macon*'s strengths. In December 1934, the acting Chief of Naval Operations finally issued a memo supporting King's request:

The Department desires that plans be made to … develop the strategic scouting potentialities of the *Macon* by long distance flights over the open sea. Specific consideration should be given to a flight … from the West Coast to Hawaii and return.[47]

Importantly, Admiral Reeves sent a memo to King on Christmas Eve stating: 'Hawaii is a logical place from which to operate a large dirigible and the

Commander in Chief [of the fleet] desires that complete preparations be made to operate the *Macon* frequently from the mooring mast at Ewa, Oahu.'[48]

This was a major vote of confidence, which is why the *Macon* was scheduled to make three round-trip flights to Hawaii beginning in March 1935.[49] The first trip would take her from Sunnyvale to Oahu and back, a distance of 5,000 miles. The second would take her even farther to Midway Island with a third trip to Pearl Harbor.[50]

Wiley had already published an article describing how a fleet of airships using Sunnyvale and Hawaii as a base could prevent a surprise attack by Japan:

It has been calculated that 12 rigids could cover continuously any possible [enemy] fleet approach to our Pacific coasts. Thus we find the airship the only scouting vessel within our means that might cover these vast areas in which a hostile fleet might be proceeding.[51]

The article might seem prescient, but a surprise attack by Japan had been one of Moffett's biggest concerns. The best news of all, however, was that Fleet Problem XVI would be held in the Pacific in May. This would allow the *Macon* to scout a vast triangle bounded by Hawaii, the Marshall Islands and Alaska.[52] Since this represented tens of thousands of square miles it was an excellent opportunity to demonstrate the airship's long-range scouting ability.

If that wasn't enough, the *Macon*'s skipper was also cooking up another bold plan to sway the opinion of battleship admirals – one designed to show his airship's offensive capabilities. Wiley knew the Navy's aircraft carriers couldn't conduct flight operations at night. But darkness wouldn't hinder the *Macon*; she had ample experience launching and retrieving her aeroplanes at night. Wiley would use this advantage during the May Fleet Problem, when he planned to launch a night-time attack against the *Lexington*. If all went well, the *Macon*'s planes would dive bomb the carrier until referees determined she'd been sunk.[53] If nothing else, the scheme suggests Wiley still had plenty of misapplied initiative left.

The *Macon*'s Hawaiian trips were also a boon for Litchfield. His Pacific Zeppelin Transport Corporation had been poised to launch a commercial airship service between California and Oahu for several years. A few successful flights by the *Macon* would help erase any bad taste investors still had about airship travel improving Litchfield's chances for launching a commercial airship service to Hawaii.

Meanwhile, reinforcement of frame 17.5 was almost complete. The area where the bottom tail fin was anchored had been strengthened along with the section where the horizontal fins were attached. The last part of the frame to be reinforced was the top half, where the *Macon*'s upper fin was anchored. This repair had been left for last because it required her No. 1 and 2 gas cells being deflated, which would ground the *Macon* for at least a week. Given Wiley's desire to participate in the February fleet exercise, the repairs had been put off until the major overhaul scheduled for March.

But there was a cloud amidst all the progress. Five days before the *Macon* was due to join the fleet, Wiley received news that his father had died. J.A. had not been well for some time. In fact, his health and finances were so poor he'd had to move in with his daughter. Still, his death from a heart attack at age 79 came as a blow. Unfortunately Wiley had to miss his father's funeral.[54] He could not miss the upcoming fleet exercise upon which so much depended. As usual, Wiley suffered his misfortune without complaint.

34

A GIANT IN DANGER*

Things were finally looking up for Wiley as the *Macon* cruised north along California's rugged coastline. It was the afternoon of Tuesday, 12 February 1935, and the *Macon* was returning from a successful two-day scouting exercise with the fleet. It was her fifty-fourth flight since being commissioned. She had flown nearly 1,800 hours, 100 more than her ill-fated sister.[1] As Wiley stood looking out the control car window he must have felt a sense of satisfaction about what he'd achieved.

The *Macon*'s crew had been rousted from their warm beds for General Assembly at 0600 hours the previous morning. A siren followed by the master at arms yelling, 'Hit the deck you cloud busters!' did the trick.[2]

As Hangar One's twin, orange-peel doors rumbled open, the *Macon*'s crew filed in through the first grey streaks of dawn. Shortly thereafter, all eight of the airship's engines were warmed up, filling the hangar with a cacophonous roar. Once all the crew had boarded the ship, the *Macon*'s mooring officer blew his whistle. Then, lifting his megaphone, he shouted, 'Walk the ship out!'[3]

The *Macon*'s mobile mast slowly towed the airship through the open doors to the south mooring circle, where she swung in the wind. After conducting the weigh off, the officer of the deck reported, 'All departments ready for flight.'

'Get ready aft! Get ready forward!'[4] Wiley commanded.

---

*   Author's note: Some eyewitness accounts are occasionally inconsistent or conflicting; some even contradict themselves if told more than once. Given this, I've tried to draw on only those accounts that can be confirmed by more than one person, or seem reasonable given the known facts.

Lt Bolster, in the control car, pulled the toggles releasing water ballast until the 200-ton *Macon* was lighter than air. Moments later, Wiley gave the order, 'Up ship!'[5] after which the giant dirigible slowly rose into the sky.

The *Macon* departed Moffett Field carrying eighty-three officers and crew, plus a few passengers. Her cabins may have been heated, but the upper and lower gangways inside the airship were freezing.[6] The winter weather was so miserable her enlisted men wore heavy flying suits to protect against the cold.

Wiley's mission was straightforward: he was to rendezvous with the fleet off the coast of Santa Barbara. Led by Reeves, the armada wouldn't be hard to find. It included ten battleships, seven heavy cruisers, four light cruisers, five submarines, a sub tender, an aircraft carrier and a hospital ship.[7] Wiley was supposed to track as many fleet units as possible, plotting their disposition and movements all while maintaining radio silence.

Given the confined search area, it wasn't the type of long-range mission the *Macon* had been training for, but Wiley was confident they could scout the fleet without being sighted. In preparation for the task, four Sparrowhawks' were landed aboard the airship as she flew south. Next, their landing gear was replaced by auxiliary fuel tanks to extend their range – a trick that had worked nicely when searching for Roosevelt. By noon on Monday, the *Macon* arrived off the coast of Santa Barbara, where she immediately picked up the fleet.

On the first day of the exercise, Radioman, First Class, Ernest E. Dailey was lowered in the spy car to observe the enemy. Pounded by prop wash, Dailey hung on desperately as the tiny car bounced in the slipstream.[8]

During the next twenty-four hours, the *Macon*'s Sparrowhawks proved amazingly effective. Venturing farther from the airship than they'd ever ranged before, they reported on the fleet's composition and speed while allowing the airship to remain safely out of sight.[9] As Lt Miller, the senior most Sparrowhawk pilot, described it, 'We did what was required and more. We tracked all outfits for the two days and were not seen … No question about it, we were getting someplace.'[10]

After a successful day of scouting the fleet, the *Macon* spent the night of 11 February blacked out to avoid being spotted. Even the flashlights the crew carried inside the vessel had dark blue cellophane taped over their lenses to reduce the light they shined.[11]

The airship spent the night cruising the Channel Islands near Santa Barbara, but gale force winds blowing over the Santa Ynez Mountains made the air so turbulent the crew had difficulty sleeping. Lt Cdr Mackey tried napping before his midnight-to-0400 watch, but the flight was so rough he gave up in disgust.[12]

The next day dawned just as miserable as the previous one, making it perfect for scouting. As the *Macon* remained hidden in the clouds, Wiley launched two Sparrowhawks, which had little difficulty monitoring the fleet. But Wiley was concerned about the forecast. Foul weather predicted for later that night could make it difficult for the *Macon* to dock at Sunnyvale.[13] At 1430 hours, Admiral Reeves, at Wiley's request, granted permission for the *Macon* to leave the exercise early.[14] Now, she headed north along California's central coast hoping to beat the bad weather home. In a few hours, she'd be locked safely in the cup of her mooring mast – plenty of time for her crew to buy their sweethearts flowers for Valentine's Day.

At 1452 hours, the *Macon* climbed to 2,700ft only to have a warning light alert her bridge crew that she was close to pressure height.[15] Typically, the *Macon* could climb to 5,000ft before the alarm was triggered, but the unsettled weather had caused a drop in barometric pressure, meaning the *Macon*'s operational ceiling was lower than normal. This was less than ideal because it prevented the *Macon* from flying over numerous squalls. In fact, the air was so turbulent she was running all eight engines, something she only did when the air was rough.*

Two of the *Macon*'s Sparrowhawks were out scouting when Wiley received permission to return home. Lt Miller was flying over the ocean near Point Buchon when he encountered a front lying directly in the airship's path.[16] As Miller flew through the squally weather, rain stung his face. A few minutes later, he emerged into a clear patch of sky, but the wall of dark clouds on the horizon promised more rain and turbulence.

As the *Macon* lumbered up the coast, Miller returned to the airship. After being secured aboard at 1549 hours,[17] he made his way towards the control car to report on the squalls he'd encountered.

Aviation Machinist's Mate, First Class, Wilmer M. Conover was on the bridge operating the *Macon*'s elevator wheel. It was not only the trickiest station on the bridge, it required considerable muscle and excellent flying instincts to anticipate the constantly changing conditions.[18] Considered a

---

★   Sometimes, the *Macon* employed all eight of her engines when a Sparrowhawk was hooking on, to make sure the plane didn't have to slow so much it risked stalling.

senior rigger, Conover had racked up more than 4,000 hours on big rigids including six years aboard the *Los Angeles*. Importantly, he was lucky, having missed the *Akron's* fatal flight because he'd been on his honeymoon.[19]

Coxswain William H. Clarke stood at the front of the bridge manning the helm. A relative newcomer, he'd been teased by his colleagues to watch out for the seaweed-covered ghost of an *Akron* crewman who was said to haunt the *Macon's* catwalks.[20] Conover and Clarke were joined on the bridge by the airship's executive officer, Lt Cdr Jesse L. Kenworthy, Jr; Lt Cdr Edwin F. Cochrane; and Lt Calvin M. Bolster, the ship's repair officer. Lt Cdr Scott E. Peck sat at the navigator's chart table in the compartment next door plotting their course.

Wiley was absent from the bridge, having retired to his quarters after the *Macon* was released from the scouting exercise.[21] He'd been on duty almost non-stop since they'd left Sunnyvale thirty-three hours earlier. Most likely, he needed a rest. Since the captain's cabin was located in the airship directly above the control car, he wasn't far away.

As Miller climbed down the ladder into the control car's aft compartment an Acey Ducey card game was under way.[22] You could still see the ring around his eyes where his flight goggles had been.[23] Lt (jg) Campbell was there as well, taking a smoking break.

Campbell was relatively new to airships; he'd only been serving on big rigids for three and a half years. Thirty-three years old, Campbell wasn't exactly inexperienced – he'd been with the *Macon* since her fitting out, but he was still considered junior. As a result, he occasionally bore the brunt of well-meaning teasing by his more senior airship colleagues.

'Right nasty out,' Campbell said, offering Miller a cigarette.

'If you think that's bad, you should see what those poor battle-wagon sailors are [putting up with],' Miller said referring to the fleet below.[24] 'Those ships are taking a pounding!'[25]

Miller briefed Campbell on the two squalls he'd encountered. Then Campbell headed to the bridge, where he was scheduled to serve as officer of the deck.

Miller remained in the aft compartment as eight bells sounded, signalling the watch change. While the rest of the crew settled into their duty stations, those relieved went to the galley seeking a warm meal, the smoking room for a 'coffin nail' or their bunk for some shut-eye. A few minutes later, the *Macon* broached the first squall exactly as Miller had predicted.

Entering the bank of roiling clouds was like penetrating a curtain of water. Heavy rain drummed on the airship's outer cover while blanketing the bridge windows in glassy sheets. Meanwhile, Miller wondered why Campbell hadn't heeded his advice to head west where the weather was more settled,[26] especially as turbulence, like a series of speed bumps, made the airship rise and fall.[27]

While the *Macon*'s airframe groaned in response, her crew grabbed anything they could to hold themselves steady. Then the *Macon* hit what Miller described as 'one good sock', causing the airship to soar upwards.[28]

The squally weather was nothing unusual for February. Airships had flown through far worse without a problem. Besides, if you didn't like the weather along the central coast, all you had to do was wait. It soon changed.

Wiley had returned to the bridge by now. As he conferred with his XO, the two men stood spread-legged absorbing the *Macon*'s sudden changes in altitude. A few minutes later, the ship emerged on the other side of the squall none the worse for wear.[29]

Tendrils of fog whipped past the outside of the control car as intermittent rays of sunshine crowbarred their way through the low-hanging clouds.[30] As the surf below pounded the shoreline, sending a zig-zag line of foam crawling up the coast, visibility shrank to 2 miles. A few minutes later it began to rain again, but at least the air was smoothing out.[31]

Wiley had planned to take the *Macon*'s usual route back to Sunnyvale. This would take them north along Big Sur's rocky coast to Monterey before turning inland at Watsonville. Next, they'd sail up the Gilroy pass to Moffett Field in Santa Clara Valley. But the *Macon*'s navigator, Lt Cdr Peck, was worried about the weather. Peck recommended they sail with the fleet all the way up the coast to the San Francisco lightship. There, they'd turn east, passing through the Golden Gate before heading south for the 40-mile journey to Sunnyvale.[32] It was a longer route, but the air over the ocean would be smoother than inland. It was also more prudent than trying to vault the coastal mountains with an unusually low 'pressure height' and even lower cloud ceiling.

The weather cleared again, but the outside air became choppy. Conover was having so much trouble holding the elevator wheel steady, a relief stood ready to lend a hand. Meanwhile, Shaky Davis was inside the airship on the port catwalk inspecting the fin that had caused such trouble over Texas.

Davis had made it a practice to inspect the fins whenever the air was rough. Opening a hatch on the port side of the hull, he eyed the enormous appendage extending from the stern.[33] He could see rain had loosened the fin's canvas covering, causing it to flutter.[34] This was normal, but Davis wasn't taking any chances. When the crewman on keel duty asked whether Shaky wanted him to inspect the upper fin, Davis responded, 'I'll do it myself.'[35]

Conover needed a break after the shake-up he'd received, so standing to one side, he let his relief take the elevator wheel. The *Macon* had been flying with all eight engines at standard speed for slightly more than two hours.[36]

'I think we're out of the worst of it,' Campbell told Wiley.[37]

The ship was still taking a beating, though. Flying at 60 knots, the combination of turbulence, engine vibration and prop wash kept those inside the hull on their toes. In the distance, seven Navy cruisers could be seen steaming through the white caps on their way north.[38] One of them, the *Houston*, was the same ship the *Macon* had found when searching for Roosevelt.

At 1704 hours, the *Macon* came abeam of the Point Sur lighthouse.[39] Wiley, wanting to stay clear of the Santa Lucia Mountains, remained 2½ miles off shore. The mountains not only ranged in height from 4,000 to 5,000ft, but gaps in between them were known to funnel powerful gusts out to sea. The air along the coast had calmed, but it was unlikely to last given the squally weather ahead.[40]

Shaky Davis' inspection of the upper gangway began at the bow and moved slowly towards the stern. Since it was against regulations for anyone to go into the upper keel alone for fear they might be overcome by a helium leak, Davis had brought along Aviation Machinist Mate, Third Class, Joseph E. Steele to help him.[41] The two men found several tears in the outer covering allowing rain to seep through as well as torn netting around one of the *Macon*'s gas cells.[42] Both were common problems easily repaired, but Davis, ever fearful of disaster, continued looking for trouble.

At the same time, fifteen enlisted men sat in the mess hall amidships eating a meal of roast beef and potatoes soaked in gravy.[43] As the men joked in between bites of food, they paid little attention to the growing turbulence outside. They'd flown so many times a few air pockets didn't bother them.

Nevertheless, Lt Bolster worried about the weather's effect on the *Macon*. Bolster was an engineer by training, having come up through the Navy's construction corps. This gave him a thorough understanding of the airship's strengths and weaknesses. Since Bolster knew the coastal mountains had delivered some 'nasty bumps' in the past, he was alert for trouble.[44]

Exiting the control car, Bolster climbed a series of ladders to reach the *Macon*'s upper catwalk, where he began inspecting the top half of the main rings. Not long after, he ran into Shaky Davis conducting his own inspection. Since Davis appeared to have the situation in hand, Bolster returned to the bridge.

After hanging a canvas bucket under a leak in the outer cover, Davis stopped by intermediate frame 23.75, near the stern. Here, he took a moment to closely inspect the area where the upper fin was anchored.[45] The leading edge of the upper fin was known to oscillate in flight, sometimes by as much as a few feet.[46] Since the *Macon* was flying close to her maximum speed, Davis wanted to check on how the frame was doing. A few minutes later, he slipped his hand between two transverse girders near where the upper fin was anchored. No doubt about it, he felt movement.[47]

The airship was in almost perfect trim as she approached Point Sur. Conover, at the elevator wheel, noticed the wind outside had become noisier as it increased in velocity.[48] Still, he'd flown through worse weather on the *Los Angeles* without a problem.[49] He wasn't concerned.

Bolster spotted a 'low black curtain' of clouds off the starboard bow.[50] Wiley didn't like the look of them, so ordered 'Left rudder'.[51] As the *Macon* began to turn, an unexpectedly violent gust hit the airship on her port side, shoving her bow towards shore while driving her nose down sharply.[52]

The roll was so pronounced the men in the control car grabbed something to keep from falling. Conover, who'd experienced more than his fair share of gusts, thought the ship's roll so severe as to be alarming.[53]

Lt Cdr Peck, the *Macon*'s navigator, was leaning out the control car window taking a drift observation when the ship began to tremble. Peck immediately knew something unusual had happened. Not only did the control car vibrate, the airship was knocked 20 degrees off course and her nose down by ten. As Lt Miller put it, it felt like 'a giant hand … swatted us'.[54] Of more concern, the *Macon* was pointing towards shore where the mountains loomed.[55]

Lt Cdr Peck started to tell the helmsman to steer away from shore. 'Better wait a minute,' Wiley told Peck, 'there seems to be something wrong.'[56]

The airship was flying at 1,250ft when the event occurred. Some people on the bridge say the gust, blowing in through the control car's windows, sent a blizzard of paper swirling to the floor.[57] Concerned the *Macon* was too close to the mountains,[58] Wiley finally ordered 5-degree left rudder. But as Clarke began turning the helm, the wheel spun out of his hands. As Clarke describes it, that's when 'all hell broke loose'.[59]

Wiley jumped in to help Clarke regain control,[60] but Conover was having similar problems with the elevator wheel. As soon as the bow began rising

Conover applied down elevator, but a 'tremendous force' ripped the wheel out of his hands.[61]

As the airship's nose inclined at a steep angle, Lt Bolster and Bos'ns Mate, First Class, Leonard E. 'Gene' Schellberg, jumped in to help Conover. The effect was negligible.[62] Within moments, the airship was climbing out of control.

Wiley thought the cables connecting the wheel to the elevators on the horizontal fins had broken, but when he asked Conover whether he still had control, Conover replied, yes. But something was amiss. The helm wasn't responding.[63] How could they control the airship if they couldn't steer?

Aviation Chief Machinist's Mate Andrew B. Galatian was enjoying the view from the window in the *Macon*'s bottom tail fin when the calamity struck. Galatian had been chatting with Aviation Machinist's Mate, Second Class, Matthew G. Fraas, Jr when they felt the airship begin to fall. At the same time, Galatian heard a noise that sounded like something being carried away overhead.[64]

Fraas felt the fall so unusual he waited to see what the airship would do. When the ship began trembling, he shouted, 'There's something wrong! I'm going up!'

'Wait a minute,' Galatian told him. 'Don't get excited.'

'I'm not but something has carried away.'[65]

Instinctively, both men looked up into the airship overhead. What they saw unnerved them. The No. 1 gas cell had begun to deflate.[66] Something was definitely wrong.

Lt (jg) John D. Reppy was in the smoking room inside the *Macon*'s hull when the gust struck, throwing him across the compartment.[67] Chief Machinist, Emmett C. Thurman, standing next to him, remarked it was the worst jar he'd ever felt on an airship, and that included their journey over Texas.[68]

The sudden lurch was so pronounced in the mess hall it threw three diners on to the deck along with their plates of food. A cook in the galley was also knocked off his feet.[69] Of more concern, stock from the roast slopped over its pan, causing a fire in the oven.[70] The flames were doused quickly, so the galley crew laughed it off. Then they returned to what they'd been doing.

Shaky Davis in the *Macon*'s upper gangway immediately knew something drastic had occurred. The violent lurch to starboard had been followed by an unusual noise in the stern. Heading aft to investigate, Davis encountered an invisible cloud of helium. He couldn't see the gas, but he could feel how cold it was. Seconds later he became dizzy.[71]

Helium may seem harmless, but it can easily render a man unconscious. In enough quantity, it can even kill him. Just one of the *Macon*'s gas cells contained more than enough helium to incapacitate anyone standing nearby. Once Davis regained his senses, he made an abrupt U-turn and retreated towards the bow.

Nobody on the bridge quite knew what had happened.[72] The control car was at least a city block away from the stern, so it was impossible to see the damage. One thing was certain. The helm was unresponsive. But the airship's nose-up attitude suggested some kind of casualty in her aft section. Worse, the airship continued climbing out of control.

Since helium is lighter than air, it naturally seeks the highest point within a contained space. This meant the escaping gas chased Davis and Steele up the now-slanting catwalk towards the bow. Davis pushed Steele as fast as he would go, concerned the man might lose consciousness, slip off the gangway and fall through a gas cell.[73] Pausing near frame 57, Davis picked up the telephone to report the helium leak but all the lines to the bridge were busy.[74] It was no longer safe for Davis and Steele to remain in the ship's upper reaches, so they climbed down to the lower keel to escape being suffocated.

As Harry Miller watched the silver giant sail up the coast, he was sure he'd never seen anything quite like her. Miller was the first assistant keeper on the 1400 to 1800 hours watch at the Point Sur Lighthouse. Situated 125 miles south of San Francisco, the lighthouse sat on a rocky outcropping on the remote cost of Big Sur, overlooking the Pacific.

After calling his boss to come take a look, Miller gazed through his binoculars as the *Macon* passed so close he could see the green lights on her starboard side blinking in the dusk.[75] Miller could also see the fleet on the horizon as it steamed towards San Francisco, but the *Macon* dwarfed them by comparison. As Miller watched the stately progression, the airship's nose suddenly plunged towards the sea. Moments later, her upper tail fin disintegrated like a paper bag exploding.[76]

The two men watched in disbelief as the catastrophe unfolded. The leading edge of the *Macon's* upper fin was first to separate from where it attached to the hull. Then, assisted by the airship's forward motion, the fin began peeling backwards, pausing for a moment before ripping away in stages.

As the fin tore free, it left a trail of debris cascading into the ocean. At one point, a large section of the fin's outer covering dangled off the airship's stern until it finally separated, slowly floating down to the sea. In its wake, a naked rudder post was left pointing skywards – the only sign of where the upper fin had once been. Now, the *Macon* began turning in confused circles leaking fuel, helium and water like a wounded animal. No longer able to steer, the leviathan began drifting southwards.

The first call to the control car warning of a casualty in the stern came less than a minute after the *Macon* lost control of her helm. Coxswain Joseph R. Connolly was on the starboard catwalk when he heard what he took to be girders snapping in frame 17.5. Heading aft to investigate, he was surprised to see two turnbuckles near the steering clutch box spin wildly.[77] This indicated the cables connecting the rudder to the bridge had been severed, hence the loss of steering.

As Connolly approached the stern, he heard pieces of Duralumin striking the catwalk.[78] More alarming, he saw gas cell No. 1 in the process of deflating.[79] It was easy to tell when a gas cell was losing helium: the bottom hung loose like the shirt tails of a ghost while its head ominously bulged.

Quartermaster, First Class, Theodore C. Brandes was standing watch on the lower port gangway when the *Macon* was broadsided by the gust. Like Davis, Brandes heard a worrying sound. Looking up, he saw the No. 1 gas cell nearly half empty.[80] The area above the cell, usually shrouded in darkness, seemed brighter, suggesting the roof of the airship had been torn open.[81] Brandes immediately rushed to the phone at frame 35 to report what he'd seen.

Around the same time, Galatian and Fraas were crawling up the ladder from the *Macon's* bottom fin to alert the control car that gas cell No. 1 was deflating. Fraas ran up the starboard catwalk, where he encountered Connolly already on the phone reporting the damage.

By now, Wiley knew there'd been a casualty in the *Macon's* stern. In addition to gas cell No. 1 deflating, an enlisted man reported the aft section was breaking up.[82] Wiley knew he had to quickly relieve the weight on the stern, so he ordered the engines slowed and all ballast dropped aft of amidships.[83]

While Lt Bolster began pulling the release toggles on the bridge, crewmen raced along the gangways, wire cutters in hand, snipping slip tanks as they went. As each tank fell, it tore a hole in the airship's outer cover before tumbling more than 1,000ft, splashing down in the ocean below.

But even as the *Macon* shed weight, her stern continued to sink. Wiley ordered the emergency signal sounded throughout the airship. Almost instantly, a siren began blaring from the twin horns atop each of the *Macon*'s eighteen telephones. Wiley hoped he could act fast enough to save the 'Queen of the Skies', but he ordered a distress call sent out just to be safe.

Since the radio shack was located inside the airship, Lt Campbell spoke to radio man Ernest Dailey via voice tube on the bridge. A native of Port Bend, Oregon, Dailey had served aboard the *Akron*. When his mother heard the airship had crashed at sea, she spent a few horrible hours thinking her son was dead. Only later did she breathe a sigh of relief when informed he'd transferred to the *Macon* a few days before.[84]

Dailey asked Campbell what the message should read. 'Tell the fleet the *Macon* is in trouble three miles off Point Sur and to stand by to aid us,' Campbell responded. Dailey repeated the message, making sure he understood correctly, then told Campbell he'd get it out, right away.[85]

The *Houston* was about 10 miles from the *Macon* when the airship lost her upper fin. The ship's captain saw the dirigible dropping ballast but didn't consider it unusual.[86] In contrast, a signalman aboard the *Houston* immediately knew something was wrong. As he described it, 'The upper fin seemed to be gone back to the rudder and there was a dark patch on the port side like someone had spilled ink.'[87]

Knowing an excessive loss of helium would doom the *Macon*, Lt Reppy raced down the tilting catwalk to repair the No. 1 cell before all of its gas escaped. Commandeering two crewmen along the way, Reppy told them to bring a cell repair kit, planning to patch the leak. As the three men approached frame 17.5, Reppy looked upwards only to see a huge hole in the hull where the upper fin had been. The entire top half of the frame was missing, taking part of the upper catwalk with it. All that was left was a gaping hole where a steady rain poured in. Complicating matters, wreckage from the fin had not only punctured the No. 1 and 2 gas cells, but the 0 gas cell as well.[88]

The *Macon* could stay aloft with two of her twelve gas cells emptied, but three was more than she could withstand. Suddenly losing 50,000lb of lift in her stern[89] created so much dead weight it risked collapsing her main rings in a chilling domino effect.[90] There were already signs frame 0 was weakening. If Wiley didn't do something fast, his airship would disintegrate.

Wiley's order to drop 16,000lb of ballast took stress off the stern, but it also contributed to the airship rising.[91] Wiley ordered a hard-down elevator to compensate for their nose-up inclination. He also began venting helium from the bow. But the inclination increased in severity. Off-duty hands were ordered to the bow, hoping their weight would bring her nose down, but as minutes passed, the runaway airship continued to rise.

Not everyone inside the *Macon* knew what was happening. Seaman, First Class, Arthur F. Glowacki thought they were having a drill.[92] As for the nearly thirty crewmen fighting their way up the canted catwalks towards the bow, they too wondered what was going on. Far removed from the decision making in the control car, they crammed together in the dim light of the airship's nose. Unfortunately, their combined weight did little to level out the ship.

In the meantime, Lt Bolster requested permission to redeploy the helm from the bridge to the auxiliary station in the *Macon*'s bottom fin – something that only happened in an emergency.

'Can I go aft and shift control?' Bolster asked the captain. 'We can steer from back there.'[93]

Wiley granted permission as the *Macon* continued to rise. Wiley knew if they exceeded pressure height, the valves on the airship's gas cells would automatically begin venting the helium they needed to stay aloft. If he didn't reverse the situation soon, the airship wouldn't survive. Meanwhile, she was coming apart at the seams.

Harry Miller watched from the Point Sur Lighthouse as fuel and ballast water streamed from the injured airship. He could see each slip tank send up a geyser of spray as it landed in the sea, followed by a thunderous report a few seconds later. When the *Macon* disappeared in a bank of low-hanging clouds, Miller was able to track her movements by the trail of ballast she left speckling the ocean.[94]

Wiley had hoped he could regain control of the situation, but as the airship climbed at 300ft per minute, he found himself in an impossible predicament. Unable to arrest her ascent, the *Macon* had passed 2,800ft, where she began venting helium. Knowing it was unlikely any of her eighty-three-man crew would survive a crash in the coastal mountains, he wanted to put his airship down at sea. But the damage to her stern limited his ability to manoeuvre.

At first, Wiley had ordered all eight of her engines slowed, then idled, to take the strain off her failing structure. Aviation Machinist Mate Julius E. Malak, in engine car No. 5, fought to keep up with Wiley's commands. In just a few minutes, engine speed went from standard to half, from idle to reverse, before returning to standard. It was hard work given the *Macon*'s engine compartments were small, cramped and hot, which is why Malak was copiously sweating.[95]

But the *Macon* needed engine power if Wiley was to steer out to sea. Unfortunately, engine power also risked driving her higher, given the 25-degree inclination. Still, Wiley had little choice. As the airship drifted south, bow first, he ordered her starboard engines idled, hoping her port engines would swing her out to sea.[96] What he didn't count on was the *Macon*'s tilt remaining so severe it drained water from the engine radiators, causing them to overheat. As smoke began pouring from her engines, the crew was forced to shut them down one by one. Thus Wiley was deprived of his only method of steering.

While all this was going on, efforts were under way to shift control from the helm on the bridge to the auxiliary station in the *Macon*'s bottom fin. Coxswain Worther M. Hammond had been drafted to assist in the procedure. At first Hammond thought the shift in control had been successful, but when he felt rain dripping down the back of his neck he looked up to see that the upper fin had been carried away, taking the top half of the rudder with it.[97] It was far from clear given the extent of the casualty whether he could steer with only the bottom half of the rudder remaining.

In the meantime, Wiley ordered his men to toss the deflated gas cells overboard to relieve strain on the stern. Wiley also ordered the hangar crew to dump the *Macon*'s four Sparrowhawks,[98] but the incline was so steep the aeroplanes jammed on their monorail.

Despite Wiley's efforts, the *Macon* continued to ascend. Twice he succeeded in reducing the airship's inclination to 10 degrees, only to have her tilt upwards again.[99] When she reached 4,600ft, he had no choice but to valve her three bow gas cells to level her out,[100] but it was helium he couldn't afford to spare.

Finally, at 1720 hours, the *Macon* paused just shy of 5,000ft. On the edge of her operational ceiling, her nose pointing towards the Moon, she'd been leaking helium at an alarming rate. Then the inevitable happened. Gravity took over.

Wiley now faced the opposite problem: how to prevent his airship from crashing back to earth. As the *Macon* began falling, the man who'd survived the worst disaster in aviation history appeared destined to repeat it, and nothing he did seemed able to stop it.

35

A GIANT IS LOST

Trapped inside a falling airship, especially one that didn't have many windows, was like being trapped inside a sinking submarine: the crew didn't know when the end might come, only that it would be over in an eye blink.

After sixteen minutes above pressure height, the *Macon* plunged like a runaway lift. Her crew prayed she didn't land in the mountains, but it was impossible to know where she'd come down since she was buried in clouds. Wiley hoped to land near the fleet,[1] but the wind had pushed the *Macon* several miles south, meaning he had only a rough idea of where they were. Given visibility was zero they'd have to be lucky.

After venting helium from the *Macon*'s bow, the airship's nose finally dropped enough that a few of her engines could be restarted. But the situation was still dangerous. The *Macon* needed her engines to manoeuvre out to sea, but running them put a strain on her crumbling airframe. Too much stress and the stern might collapse. The problem was, Wiley had no choice but to vent helium from the bow if he wanted her nose to come down enough so the engines could be restarted. But venting helium made the airship fall faster. If Wiley wanted to regain control he had to find a way to slow her descent, not increase it.

With the emergency siren blaring, Wiley made the decision to dump more ballast while ordering everything not nailed down thrown overboard. Gene Schellberg hurried down the catwalk, stopping at each engine car. Yelling at the mechanics, he told them to pitch their tool boxes over the side.

Back in the control car, Kenworthy began throwing everything he could find out the windows. This included the *Macon*'s signal light as well as the drawers in the navigator's table.[2] Even the *Macon*'s precious radio homing device, which the Sparrowhawks used to find their way back, was cast over the side.[3]

By now, Wiley had received reports that the three gas cells in the stern were more than two-thirds deflated. This led to a second attempt to throw the Sparrowhawks overboard. Lt Reppy, who seemed to be in all places at once during the disaster, pitched in to help along with Shaky Davis and the hangar crew. But the *Macon* was at such a crazy angle the aeroplanes remained jammed in place. Even if they succeeded in freeing one, the crew worried it might cascade through the hangar damaging the hull. Meanwhile, the ship was tilting so much that fuel ran out of the planes' belly tanks, threatening to ignite a fire. A mechanic mopped up the mess to prevent it from spreading, but the four Sparrowhawks wouldn't budge.[4]

The *Macon* continued to plummet despite attempts to lighten the ship. It wasn't until she reached 3,000ft that she began to slow. When the ocean became visible a minute or so later, Wiley was relieved to see they'd steered clear of the mountains.[5] But the fleet was nowhere in sight. Although the *Macon's* descent had slowed, she was still falling too fast. Up until then, Wiley had entertained the possibility of regaining control.[6] But when the airship reached 1,500ft, he realised the situation was hopeless. Now, it was a question of survival. If the crew was going to live through an ocean landing, he needed to find a way to slow her descent.

Accepting the inevitable, Wiley ordered the *Macon's* crew to 'Stand by to abandon ship.'[7] Turning to Lt Peck, he told him to spread the word. 'Never mind the communication tubes,' he said stone-faced. 'Make it a personal order.'[8]

Peck exited the control car, climbing into the ship overhead. Racing along the port catwalk, he yelled, 'All hands at landing stations!'

The crew, knowing the end was near, donned their inflatable life vests. There were plenty to go around and this was crucial given many of the crew didn't know how to swim. But the *Macon*, like the *Titanic*, didn't have enough life rafts for her eighty-three-man crew. In fact, the airship only carried eight inflatables,[9] the largest of which accommodated fourteen, the smallest only four. It was a surprisingly meagre number given the *Macon* spent most of her time at sea, but she couldn't afford the extra weight. Furthermore, the damage in the stern made the raft there inaccessible. When the *Macon* crashed, more of her crew were destined to end up floundering in the sea than could ever fit in seven tiny life rafts.

As Peck passed Wiley's order to the crew, Dailey was in the *Macon's* radio room tapping out a message on the transmitting key: 'We have had bad casualty. Will abandon ship as soon as we land on water.' He followed it with an alarmingly vague location: 'Somewhere within 20 miles of Point Sur, probably ten miles at sea.'[10]

When the *Macon* reached 800ft, Wiley gave the order to back down the engines.[11] This was intended to arrest the ship's forward momentum before she hit the waves.

When Aviation Machinist's Mate, Second Class, Jack F. Leonard, received Wiley's order he gleefully called out from the No. 3 engine car, 'We're going for a swim!'[12] But few crewmen were as jovial as Leonard at the prospect of landing in the Pacific.

At 500ft, Wiley ordered Lt Campbell to dump the emergency ballast from the airship's bow.[13] He'd been saving it to keep her nose down, but it was more important to soften the airship's landing than stay on an even keel.

Peck had returned to the control car by then, having personally spread Wiley's order through the ship. On the bridge, he found the captain wearing an inflatable life vest.

'Please put some air in it for me,'[14] Wiley asked.

Peck complied, blowing into each side before tightening the valves.

As the airship continued falling towards the sea, Wiley ordered everyone in the control car to pick a window, advising them to wait until the last possible moment before jumping.[15]

Kenworthy, the *Macon's* executive officer, had already removed the screens in the control car's aft compartment, making it easier to abandon ship. He'd also distributed flares from the navigator's locker, dropping a few out the control car window, hoping they'd guide the fleet to their location.[16] In the meantime, the Pacific rose rapidly to meet them. Moments later the *Macon's* stern hit the water.

Chief Boatswain's Mate, First Class, William A. Buckley, was in the *Macon's* stern when he saw the ocean 'coming up fast'.[17] Buckley had served on all four of the Navy's big rigids, so he was a confident sky sailor. Seeing that Hammond was still manning the auxiliary helm in the bottom fin, Buckley cried out, 'Hammond, for Christ's sake, get out of the fin!'[18]

Realising the bottom fin was going to be first to make contact with the ocean, Hammond climbed a ladder to the crazily tilting catwalk and began running forward. Elsewhere, someone in the *Macon's* bow was counting down the airship's altitude as she neared the ocean: 'Four hundred, three hundred, two hundred, one hundred, here she goes!'[19]

The *Macon* struck the water stern first at 1740 hours.[20] Wiley's backing down of the engines not only ensured the airship had little forward motion but made the shock of landing 'barely perceptible'.[21] Lt Miller thought, 'Wiley [gave] us the gentlest of landings,'[22] but not everyone agreed with this assessment. Lt Bolster felt the airship hit the ocean 'with considerable vertical velocity',[23] while Clarke, the helmsman, described it as a 'lurch'.[24] Regardless of how hard she landed, the next sequence of events seemed to occur in slow motion.

Once the *Macon*'s stern splashed down in the Pacific, the Navy's command structure was replaced by every man for himself.[25] Hammond hadn't got very far inside the airship before she'd struck the ocean. He was still racing towards the bow when main frame 35 collapsed, blocking his path. As girders buckled around him, Hammond retreated to frame 17.5, where water was flooding the stern.[26] Trapped, with no place to go, he kicked a hole in the airship's outer covering. Hammond was just about to jump when a girder pinned his leg.[27] As he struggled to free himself, water crawled up the gangway, threatening to drown him.

After a moment of panic, Hammond freed his leg and, jumping through the hole he'd made in the hull, plunged into the frigid waters of the Pacific. Anxious not to get tangled in the *Macon*'s wreckage, he swam furiously away from the ship. But long ocean swells caused the giant dirigible to wallow. Moments later, the elevator on her horizontal fin smacked down on the ocean, driving Hammond underwater. When the fin rolled up again, Hammond came spluttering to the surface, only to swim a few feet before the elevator forced him back under. Broaching the waves a second time, Hammond swam away from the ship as quickly as his arms and legs would carry him.[28]

Gene Schellberg had been trying to cut away the No. 1 gas cell when he heard the call to 'abandon ship!' He too sliced a hole in the *Macon*'s canvas cover, jumping out as water flooded her stern. But the *Macon* was tilting at a nose-up angle, meaning Schellberg jumped from a much greater height than he'd planned and he plunged so deep he ruptured an eardrum. When he finally resurfaced, the elevator on one of the *Macon*'s horizontal fins swatted him, too.[29] Coming up for air, Schellberg kicked off his shoes, shed his trousers and set out for an upside down life raft bobbing nearby. There he found Jack

Leonard trying to turn it over. Together, the two men flipped the raft, crawled inside and slunk down exhausted.[30]

It's important to remember that when the *Macon* hit the water stern first her bow remained high in the sky. Since engine car No. 5 was located roughly halfway between the bow and the stern, it too hung high in the air. Exiting the compartment, Julius Malak stepped on to the catwalk, marvelling at the quiet since all but two of the *Macon's* engines had been silenced.[31]

The No. 1 and 2 engines let out a loud hiss of protest as water lapped at their base, followed by a huge cloud of steam. Malak walked back into the No. 5 engine compartment, shed his shoes and coveralls, and climbed on to the outrigger outside the ship. Looking down, he could see Jack Leonard 20ft below standing on the outrigger.

'Let's go, Malak!' Leonard yelled, suggesting they jump into the water.

'You first,' Malak replied since his engine room was higher.

Leonard dived the 30ft into the Pacific. When he resurfaced he swam to an overturned life raft, which he struggled to flip over. Malak, deciding to let the airship sink a bit more before jumping, settled down to wait.[32]

Mess Attendants, First Class, Florentino Edquiba and Maximo Cariaso were best friends from the same part of the Philippines. Working as stewards in the officers' wardroom, the two men were setting the table for dinner when they felt the sudden shock in the stern. At first, they weren't sure what had happened. One rumour had the top fin carrying away.[33] But when they saw officers running up and down the catwalk they knew something was wrong.

'It looks like the end of us all,' one of the cooks joked, but Edquiba wasn't laughing.

'What's eating you?' Cariaso asked.

'I can't swim,' Edquiba confided.

'Stay with me,' Cariaso replied. 'I'm a good swimmer … I'll help.'

Cariaso told Edquiba to get a life belt while he went to find out what was going on. When Cariaso returned, Edquiba still hadn't donned his life preserver. Instead, he stood frozen in the galley looking panicked.

Cariaso grabbed a spare life vest, telling Edquiba to put it on. Then he went to find a knife, explaining he'd cut a length of rope to tie to his life jacket and giving the other end to Edquiba to hold when they jumped. When Cariaso returned the two friends exited the galley, hurrying up the catwalk towards the bow.[34]

While Malak waited for the airship to sink lower, he worked up the courage to jump. Not wanting to break his neck when he landed in the sea, he emptied the air from his lifebelt. When the moment came, Malak plunged so deeply into the ocean he thought he'd never come back up. Upon reaching the surface, he inhaled huge gulps of air, certain it was the best thing he'd ever felt.

The unmistakable shriek of anguished metal could be heard by the men floating in life rafts as the airship slowly sank. Those trapped inside faced a deadly maze of collapsing rings, twisted girders and bursting gas cells, all while climbing up hideously slanted catwalks to seek refuge in the bow. Each gas cell sounded a high-pitched note as helium was vented through its escape valve.[35] Seconds later, one of the *Macon*'s engines tore loose from its base, falling in the ocean before disappearing from view.

When the *Macon*'s stern hit the water her bow remained more than 250ft in the air.[*][36] This meant those trapped inside her control car had to wait for the bow to drop lower before abandoning ship.

Wiley was climbing out the control car's window when he noticed Clarke at the helm, seemingly frozen at the wheel.

'Get ready to jump!' Wiley barked.

Clarke snapped out of it, letting go of the helm. But instead of climbing out of a window, he decided on taking his chances inside the ship. Scurrying to the aft compartment, Clarke scrambled up the ladder and disappeared in the *Macon* overhead.[37]

---

[*]   For perspective, the *Macon*'s control car was higher than the Golden Gate Bridge's roadbed, which is 220ft above the water.

Wiley, perched on the control car's window, could see Kenworthy balancing on the handrail outside. As the Pacific rushed up to meet them, Wiley turned to Campbell, telling him, 'Boy, we better jump!'[38] With the water just 10ft beneath him, Wiley let go, followed moments later by Campbell.

By now, two-thirds of the *Macon* lay in the water. Seeing the airship's remaining gas cells would keep her temporarily afloat, some of her crew chose to stay on board. But as each ocean swell sent a shudder through the ship, the *Macon*'s airframe collapsed bay by bay.[39] As the accumulated weight of the ship pulled her under the water, it lifted her bow into the air until it towered above the waves like a gigantic headstone.[40]

Wiley spotted a life raft as he swam away from the control car. It contained his executive officer, Kenworthy, and Boatswain's Mate, Second Class, Charles E. Adams. Once Wiley reached the raft, he held on to its side and caught his breath. Campbell, who'd jumped right after Wiley, was unable to get out from under the airship before it landed on top of him. Stunned by the tremendous blow, he tried swimming only to find his arms and legs wouldn't move. Campbell sighted a raft seemingly miles away from the crest of a wave. Swallowing gallons of seawater, he fought to stay afloat.

Wiley spotted Campbell struggling in the water and called to see if he needed help.

'I can't make it!' Campbell responded.

Kenworthy and Adams told Campbell to hang on; they'd come get him. Then Adams tried hauling Wiley into the raft.

'Let go of me son,' Wiley told him. 'I'll get Mr Campbell.'

Wiley's skill as a strong swimmer came in handy that day for the second time in his life. Letting go of the raft, he struck out for the drowning man, fighting powerful swells along the way. When he reached Campbell, Wiley grabbed his shirt collar, told him to lie on his back and towed him to the raft, where Kenworthy and Adams pulled them aboard.[41]

After Wiley collected himself, he herded five of the *Macon*'s life rafts together and set about rescuing his crew.[42] When one raft became dangerously overloaded, Wiley transferred men to another.[43] Still, there were too many to accommodate, so survivors hung to the side of whatever raft they could find, treading water to keep afloat.

The Pacific was a chilly 54°F,[44] the outside temperature even colder. When a heavy drizzle began to fall, it increased the crew's risk of hypothermia. It was also getting dark. With no rescue vessels in sight and coastal fog hiding the shore, the men of the *Macon* were cold, wet and totally alone.[45] Soon the shallow rafts filled beyond capacity. As they did, the ocean waves began swamping them.[46] Worse, there was so much fuel in the water the seams of the rafts began to separate.[47]

Wiley knew some of his crew were inside the dirigible, so he kept his flotilla as close to the airship as possible. But it wasn't easy. The powerful swells conspired to separate the rafts, while the paddles were so small it was practically impossible to row. Despite Wiley's best efforts, two of the rafts drifted away.

While a number of crew took shelter in the bow, Seaman, First Class, Arthur F. Glowacki was trapped inside the airship. Using a knife to slice a hole in the *Macon*'s canvas hull, Glowacki climbed down the outside, cutting holes for grips as he went. But when Glowacki approached the stern he had second thoughts. He was sure he'd become entangled in the forbidding mass of floating wreckage if he jumped, so he climbed back up the outside of the ship towards the bow.[48]

Not everyone had difficulty escaping the *Macon*. A couple of her engine crew on the port side slid down a line into a waiting life raft without getting wet. Others jumped into the sea and were pulled into rafts without trouble. One officer, after climbing down a bow line, perched atop the forward part of the control car (the only part not submerged) and calmly waited rescue.[49]

Instead of jumping from the control car, Clarke had gone back inside the airship. There he ran into radio operator Ernest Dailey on the port catwalk near frame 170.[50]

Dailey had remained in the radio room until the last possible minute. Calmly tapping out an SOS message while chewing gum, he stayed until water could be heard swishing around the ship.[51]

Dailey and Clarke climbed up the main ring until they were above the curvature of the hull. Considered as safe a place as any to await rescue, Clarke kicked a hole in the outer cover so he and Dailey could look out. They were soon joined by Aviation Machinist's Mate Sydney Hooper, who stood next to them discussing the best time to jump. Since the *Macon*'s bow had taken on an upright position, their part of the ship was 175ft above water – far too high to jump safely. Dailey had lost his eyeglasses, so was unable to judge the height,[52] but Clarke argued they should wait.[53] The three men stood for a moment through the hole Clarke had kicked in the hull. They couldn't see much in the gathering darkness, but not a single rescue ship was in sight, just a handful of rafts clustered nearby. Cupping their hands, they took turns drinking the rainwater that slid off the airship's canvas cover.

'This sure hits the spot,' Hooper said. Then, without warning, Dailey made a move to jump.

Hooper, seeing what Dailey was about to do, yelled, 'Don't jump! We're too high!' But it was too late. Dailey turned over several times as he fell before landing on his back in the ocean with a tremendous crack. Moments later, a gas cell ruptured, releasing a cloud of helium inside the ship. Afraid of being gassed, Clarke and Hooper left Dailey to his fate, climbing upwards towards the bow as the *Macon* continued to settle.[54]

As the *Macon* sank, her gas cells failed one by one. After one main frame collapsed, its shattered girders punctured the gas cell next to it, causing helium to escape in a tremendous whoosh.[55] That in turn put more strain on the next main ring and caused it to fail, which punctured yet another gas cell and resulted in the *Macon* sinking faster. But so much helium had accumulated inside the ship that the crew in the bow were slowly being asphyxiated. Lt Reppy, realising the men were at risk of suffocating, disregarded his own safety and began making his way along the ship's upper gangway, tying shut the valves on each gas cell as he went. It wouldn't prevent them from bursting as the ship sank, but at least it stopped them from venting helium, buying them time.[56]

When the helium cell beneath Hooper exploded, he climbed through the hull opening where Dailey had jumped. Ripping holes in the *Macon*'s cover, he slowly worked his way towards the sea. But when the girder he was holding suddenly gave way, Hooper fell a considerable distance into the ocean. Surfacing unhurt, he made for the nearest life raft.[57]

After putting out the oven fire, Ship's Cook, First Class, William H. Herndon, Jr ran forward to frame 147.5, where he waited for the *Macon* to settle. When the time came to abandon ship, he tried jumping through one of the windows on the starboard catwalk, thinking it would give way. But Herndon was in for a surprise. The window was made of Duroplate, a high-strength plastic designed not to break. When he jumped head first, instead of shattering, the window bounced him back on to the catwalk, where he sat cradling his head and moaning.[58]

The two mess attendants, Edquiba and Cariaso, had succeeded in reaching frame 187.5 before escaping helium made it difficult to breathe. When the girders around them began buckling, the two men knew it was time to jump. After inflating a life raft with carbon dioxide, Cariaso dropped it through a hole in the hull. Handing Edquiba one end of the rope he'd tied to his life jacket, he told his friend to jump, promising to follow.

Cariaso bent down for a moment to coil the rope, but when he stood up Edquiba was gone. Panicking, the mess attendant had climbed up the girders disappearing into the bow. Left with no choice, Cariaso jumped into the sea leaving his friend behind.[59]

The Sparrowhawks' Squadron Leader, Lt Miller, was one of the dozen or so men remaining in the bow after the ship went vertical. At first, he thought he'd been crazy to stay behind, but some of the crew thought it a more secure situation than their colleagues in overcrowded life rafts adrift at sea. That feeling didn't last long. As each gas cell burst, the *Macon* sank a little bit deeper while the men in the bow found it increasingly difficult to breathe. With the sky darkening and no rescue ships in sight, the crew's chances of survival were quickly diminishing.

Realising they'd either suffocate or go down with the ship, Miller and his companions punched holes in the hull and began crawling on top of the *Macon*. They were happy to breathe fresh air, but the bow remained 125ft above the water – the same height as a twelve-storey building.[60] Too high to jump, the men had no choice but to wait for the *Macon* to sink further.

Seaman, First Class, Herbert R. Rowe, known as Monty to his friends, had climbed barefoot up the outside of the ship; his every step bloodied by the Duralumin girders' knife-sharp edges. Reaching one of the machine-gun emplacements on the *Macon*'s rooftop, he slid down a rope on the outside of the hull, burning his hands as he went. Forced by the pain to let go, Rowe fell 40ft and landed on the airship's partially submerged antenna. When he opened his eyes underwater, he could see the ghostly figures of empty flight jackets floating inside the control car. Shocked by the sight, he quickly resurfaced and swam towards a life raft.[61]

There were lighter moments amidst the chaos. When the men sitting on the bow realised they'd inhaled so much helium their voices sounded like Mickey Mouse, they broke out in laughter. Lt Cdr George Mills, intending to scold them for not taking the situation seriously, found that his helium-tinged voice lacked the proper command authority. Meanwhile, an enlisted man in one of the rafts jokingly called to those on the bow, 'What the hell are you doing up there? Come … in and get your feet wet!'[62]

By now the *Macon*'s nose was 75ft above the sea. An officer in a raft directed the men to stay put on the bow until the water reached a height where it was safe to jump. As the *Macon*'s port lights winked in the darkness, a dozen calcium flares flickered on the waves.[63] One officer, standing on the bow, shot signal flares from a Very pistol, hoping to alert the fleet to their location. Charles Adams, in the same life raft as Wiley, was grateful to see the distress flares light up the sky, but no ships were in sight.[64]

The men couldn't remain aboard the *Macon* forever, so Lt Clinton S. Rounds ordered lines rigged from the bow, allowing them to climb down to the water. As each man slid down his rope he shined a flashlight in the darkness hoping to attract a raft. As one *Macon* crewman described it, they looked like a string of fireflies in the night.[65]

Not all the lines reached the water. One man, who ran out of rope, hit the ocean so hard his life belt exploded. Another hung upside down, hopelessly tangled in the rope until the man above him cut them both loose and they tumbled into the sea.[66]

The men in life rafts blinked their flashlights, helping to guide those in the water to safety. One man swimming up to a raft clung to its side catching his breath.

'Get aboard,' someone said.

'Nope … Don't want to swamp you,' he replied.[67]

Despite the gallantry, it seemed like help was taking forever to arrive.

As the *Macon* sank another 25ft, fewer than a dozen men remained on the bow. Aviation Machinist's Mate, First Class, Edward R. Morris had waited inside the airship until the last possible moment, but when her final gas cell blew he knew it was time to leave. Feeling the girder beneath him collapse, Morris fled outside the hull, where a handful of men awaited him. Spotting a life raft, he jumped in the ocean and swam towards it.[68]

The *Macon* had dropped so many fuel tanks that a fuel slick coated the waves. Those that swallowed seawater soon found themselves vomiting uncontrollably. If that wasn't bad enough, a last-minute fire broke out inside the *Macon*, threatening the few who remained on her bow.[69]

Aviation Machinist's Mate, Third Class, Leonard E. Lehtonen was sitting atop the *Macon* when he suddenly felt a searing heat beneath him. The fire wasn't his only problem. With the ship moments away from sinking, Lehtonen knew the time had come to jump.[70]

Putting the best face on a grim situation, Lt Miller turned to the handful of remaining men, saying, 'Well, boys … Let's get in the water before this whole thing goes down.'[71] Kicking off his shoes, Miller used the hull like a slide to slip into the water. But halfway down he lost his balance, tumbling into the sea. Those left on board mistook Miller's fall for a panicked jump and, aborting their own slides, leapt into the sea after him.[72]

Clarke, the helmsman, jumped off the bow when it was only 15 or 20ft above the water. Swimming to a raft, he clung to its side, as he preferred to remain in the ocean because it was warmer than the air.[73]

Lehtonen was one of the last off the airship. When he landed in the water he became tangled in the web of ropes floating on the surface. Kicking his legs, he managed to free himself, but as he swam away the airship's vortex began pulling him under. Swimming for all he was worth, Lehtonen escaped the undertow but it was a close call.[74]

Just before the *Macon* slipped beneath the waves the fire inside her bow broke through the hull. The men in life rafts watched in wonder as the blaze ignited the Navy insignia – a huge red, white and blue star on the underside of the ship.[75] Then, at 1820 hours, the *Macon* sank from view, taking along with her any hope for Moffett's rigid airship programme as well as Litchfield's dream for a fleet of commercial airships; the age of the American big rigid had finally come to an end.

36

A GIANT IS RESCUED

Word spread quickly at NAS Sunnyvale that the *Macon* had gone down at sea. Fearing the worst, anxious relatives gathered at Moffett Field to learn what had happened. As the Associated Press reported:

> Navy wives whose husbands were aboard the *Macon* took news of the trouble with tight-lipped courage tonight. In twos and threes they gathered with their children … at the *Macon*'s base here. At the home of Lt Commander Edwin F. Cochrane in near-by Palo Alto, Mrs. Kenworthy, wife of the dirigible's executive officer … waited with their children. 'We do have our tragedies, don't we?' said Mrs. Cochrane nervously as word came that the crew was preparing to abandon ship.'[1]

The scene at the Bureau of Aeronautics in Washington was equally tense. Many of its officers knew men aboard the *Macon*. Meanwhile, a beacon atop Hangar One, switched on in anticipation of the airship's return, blinked optimistically through the night.[2]

The *Macon* had taken nearly an hour to sink. In that time, the fleet, alerted to the catastrophe, raced to her rescue. The problem was that nobody knew exactly where she'd gone down, even though all thirty-six ships were on the lookout after receiving Dailey's distress signals.[3] Additionally, the Standard Oil tankers *F.J. Luckenbach* and *J.S. Moffett* (no relation to the admiral) joined in the search, while six Coast Guard cutters were ordered out to sea.[4] But finding the *Macon*'s crew in the darkness would not be easy. Overcast skies, coastal fog and deteriorating weather contributed to making the search more difficult.

As the *Macon*'s survivors huddled for warmth in their overloaded life rafts, the brisk night air made them shiver in their wet clothes. Those less fortunate remained in the water, clinging to the rafts to stay afloat. Lt Bolster, with fourteen men in his eight-man raft, took turns slipping into the ocean to free up a place for those in the water.[5] The sea was cold, the wind, biting.

Hammond, who'd been swimming for nearly thirty minutes, was chilled to the bone.[6] In contrast, Lt Miller found the water invigorating. But that soon changed. Once a wave swept down the back of his neck followed by a cold breath of wind, Miller felt 'nearly frozen'.[7]

The sea was so rough Clarke swallowed copious amounts of saltwater[8] while clinging to the side of a raft.[9] Malak was so sick from all the petrol he'd ingested he didn't have enough energy to inflate his life belt, while Hooper's life preserver kept riding up his neck as he floated in the ocean, threatening to choke him.[10]

The rafts were so overloaded they risked sinking. Rowe's raft, built to hold eight, contained thirteen. In danger of capsizing, a good half foot of water sloshed around its bottom. The situation seemed dire until another raft appeared and took aboard some of the excess men.[11] Shaky Davis, his usual helpful self, was busy bailing but had swallowed so much seawater he paused regularly to vomit.

'Where the hell is the damn fleet?' an officer asked.[12]

Wiley kept his counsel but felt it was taking 'a considerable time' for the fleet to find them.[13]

Swimming ashore in the darkness was out of the question. Not only was the coast miles away, it was shrouded in mist. Big Sur was so mountainous there were few places to land safely. Plus, the breakers were huge. As Lt Miller admitted, 'We probably wouldn't have made it.'[14]

Lt (jg) Alfred B. Metsger was on the bridge of the scout cruiser USS *Richmond* (CL-9) when they received the *Macon*'s distress call. Only an hour before, Metsger had seen the *Macon* flying above the fleet as they made their way north on a goodwill mission to San Francisco. The *Richmond*'s captain immediately called for an additional boiler to be lit so they could raise enough pressure to race to the scene.[15] Breaking away from the ships around her, the *Richmond* began ploughing through the waves making for the *Macon*'s last known position 30 miles away.

The *Richmond* was an ideal ship to go to the *Macon*'s aid. Not only was she capable of doing 30 knots; she had a shallow draft, meaning she could get in close to shore without running aground.[16] Yes, she was the kind of ship the *Macon* was intended to replace, but nobody bore a grudge at least while the rescue was under way.

As the *Richmond* approached the crash site, she received a message from the USS *Pennsylvania* (BB-38): 'Have *Macon* in sight.'[17]

The *Pennsylvania* was the fleet flagship. First to reach the area where the *Macon* had sunk, the battleship reported spotting a light 4 miles off her port bow.[18] Possibly a distress flare, it faded quickly.[19] But the message was premature. The *Pennsylvania* may have seen lights in the distance, but she hadn't spotted the *Macon* because she'd already sunk. Nor had she found any survivors – at least not yet.

After receiving the *Pennsylvania*'s message, the *Richmond* switched on her searchlights, but the mist blanketing the ocean was difficult to penetrate. The long swells didn't help since their deep troughs tended to hide floating objects.[20] Still, it wasn't long before the *Richmond* began seeing calcium flares bobbing on the ocean.[21]

The *Macon*'s crew cheered when the first searchlights appeared in the distance. Initially, the beacons seemed close, but the men soon realised they were miles away. As time passed, it became apparent the ships were having trouble finding them. After a while, some of the searchlights appeared to be moving in the wrong direction.[22]

'They've turned away. Didn't see us,' someone in a raft said.[23]

Another man wiped tears from his face, blaming it on the rain.[24]

Two *Macon* crewmen dipped their oars in the ocean then began waving them overhead. They hoped the gleaming paddles would reflect the searchlights making it easier to find them. At the same time, a man in another raft took off his shirt and, tying it to an oar, began waving it like a flag.[25]

A signal man aboard the *Richmond* was first to spot two men in a raft frantically waving their paddles. Incredibly, they weren't found ahead of the ship but dead astern, meaning the *Richmond* had passed them in the dark.[26]

The ship's searchlight briefly lit up the raft before it disappeared behind an ocean swell. Captain Noyes immediately ordered the ship's engines backed down until he realised they were in danger of running the raft over.

Coming to a full stop, the *Richmond's* boilers let out a high-pitched screech of steam from their safety valves. When searchlights illuminated the scene, a half dozen yellow rafts chock full of men were seen floating on the waves. Blinded by the light, the *Macon's* survivors began shouting and waving. One raft had nine sailors lining its sides with three more lying on its bottom, all soaking wet and freezing.[27]

The *Pennsylvania*, being a battleship, was too big to directly assist in the rescue, but an officer on board described the calcium flares floating on the ocean as a 'sight never to be forgotten, sad … yet beautiful'. As the phosphorous burned brightly, leaving smoke trails in the air, the wave action made the flares appear to twinkle like the lights of a city at night.[28]

But the memorable scene quickly turned into a nightmare. As the rafts worked their way towards the *Richmond*, a huge patch of fuel ignited by the flares caught fire and began to spread.[29]

Rear Admiral Charles E. Courtney, aboard the *Richmond*, said his blood ran cold when he saw the fire break out. Describing the survivors silhouetted against the flames as looking like 'men on the brink of hell', Courtney was sure the fire would 'cheat us … all'.[30]

Wiley's raft with its eleven occupants was trapped between two pools of flame. Only 50yd from a rescue ship, the men paddled furiously to escape. It looked for a moment as if they might be burned alive, but after a few minutes the fires mercifully ran out of fuel and died.[31]

The *Richmond*, USS *Milwaukee* (CL-5) and USS *Concord* (CL-10) hurriedly lowered motor launches to rescue the *Macon's* crew. Wiley refused the first boat, telling it to rescue the men in two life rafts that had drifted away.[32] When a boat from the *Richmond* pulled alongside Miller's raft, his legs were so numb he had to be helped aboard.[33]

Most of the fleet had caught up by then, leaving the ocean packed with battleships, cruisers, an aircraft carrier and even a submarine. With the beam of their searchlights illuminating the fog it seemed as if the entire Navy had turned out for the rescue.[34]

The *Richmond* picked up sixty-four of the *Macon's* crew. The rest were divided between the *Milwaukee* and *Concord*. The men were understandably wet and cold. As Miller recalled, 'I could not keep still I was shivering so much. I thought I would crack all the enamel on my teeth.'[35]

Lt Kivette was in bad shape when he boarded the *Richmond* and the trouser-less Sparrowhawk pilot was so weak he had to be assisted to the wardroom. There, an officer helped him undress, sending for cigarettes, coffee and a towel. A few minutes later, Kivette revived himself under a hot shower.[36]

Once aboard the rescue ships, the survivors were taken to the sickbays, where they were examined by a doctor. The men were given blankets and some received a medicinal swig of whiskey.[37] The *Richmond's* officers lent the officers from the *Macon* some dry uniforms, while enlisted men received clothing from the ship's stores.[38]

In addition to the two Sparrowhawk pilots, Miller and Kivette, the *Richmond* rescued Campbell, Mills, Bolster and Clarke. Injuries consisted largely of hypothermia – quickly treated, as well as abrasions, contusions, lacerations and rope burns.

Once the *Macon's* officers felt better, the mood in the *Richmond's* wardroom took on a jolly tone. They kidded one another about their ill-fitting wardrobe while trading stories of what happened during the airship's final minutes. As laughter filled the cabin, their wristwatches were collected to counter the damaging effects of saltwater.[39]

The *Macon's* wild ride from casualty to splash down took approximately thirty-four minutes. It took another forty minutes before the airship sank, with rescue ships arriving forty-five minutes later. The time from structural failure to rescue was less than two hours, but it was two hours the *Macon's* crew would never forget.

President Roosevelt stayed up late that night being briefed on the rescue efforts. At one point he telephoned the Navy Department, so impatient was he for details.[40] The next day, the disaster generated headlines in every major newspaper in the country. A brief sampling shows just how alarming some of them were: '*Macon* Plunges In Sea';[41] *Macon* Sinks In Pacific';[42] and the terse, if accurate, '*Macon* Sunk'.[43]

Initial confusion over what happened was evident in an Associated Press story that ran shortly after the crash. 'The giant dirigible *Macon*, destroyed by a sudden mysterious disaster, lay at the bottom of the Pacific Ocean,' the story read. The exact cause of the disaster was apparently not known by the naval officers.[44]

At least one major newspaper mistakenly reported that the majority of the *Macon*'s crew had died in the disaster. *The New York Daily Mirror*, a Hearst tabloid known more for sensational stories than accurate reporting, published a front-page headline that read: '*Macon* Wrecked; Falls Into Pacific; Many Lives Feared Lost'.[45]

But that wasn't true. A message sent shortly after midnight from Admiral Reeves aboard the *Pennsylvania* to the Navy Department read:

Preliminary survey indicates that Dailey, radioman, and Edquiba, mess attendant, only missing members of *Macon* crew. Search continues.

Still, the survivor list in the *New York Times* inadvertently left off Shaky Davis.[46] The search for Dailey and Edquiba went on for several hours, but the only evidence of the *Macon*'s sinking was an oil slick and a single inflatable life jacket.[47] Their bodies were never found.

Despite a catastrophic structural failure, Wiley had managed to gently set his gravely wounded airship on the ocean, saving eighty-one of his eighty-three-man crew – a casualty rate of less than 3 per cent. There's little doubt the *Macon*'s death toll would have been far higher had the fleet not been in the area but Wiley's success in avoiding the *Akron*'s calamitous loss of life was nothing short of a miracle given the circumstances. The question was: would the Navy share that feeling?

The *Macon*'s survivors arrived in San Francisco Bay the next morning. By then, Wiley was on the front page of every major newspaper in the country for the second time in his naval career.

When the *Richmond* arrived at the entrance to the Golden Gate, the press boats were waiting. Some reporters had even pushed their way aboard the pilot boat sent to guide the rescue ships into the bay.

Before the *Richmond* had even dropped anchor, newsreel cameramen and press photographers boarded the ship to interview survivors. The *Macon*'s crew stood huddled together in celebratory fashion, bumming cigarettes from reporters as they recalled their last flight.[48]

When they were finally ready to go ashore, the crew made a tricky climb down a Jacob's ladder on the side of the *Richmond* into a waiting motor launch. As San Francisco's Navy Pier hove into sight the crew could be heard singing, 'Hail, Hail, the Gang's All Here'.[49]

Three cheers went up from the relatives waiting dockside as the men came into view. They certainly made for a motley crew in their mismatched clothes. As they climbed on to the pier the men were immediately swamped by wives, children and friends, who surged forward handing out hugs, kisses or hearty back slaps as circumstances warranted. One photograph shows a joyful woman throwing her arms around the neck of a *Macon* survivor. Nearby, Lt Campbell's wife, who initially heard everyone had died, greeted her husband with a huge smile. Campbell, wearing an open-neck shirt, smiles back, a cigarette dangling casually from his lips.

A phalanx of newspapermen shouted questions to the crew and then furiously scribbled their answers.[50] One of the first officers to speak to reporters was the *Macon*'s navigator, Lt Cdr Peck. 'There was no hectic storm,' Peck told newsmen as flashbulbs popped. 'The only way I can account for the fin being carried away is that it must have been pretty weak'[51] – an admission that was truthful if too candid.

Wiley, swamped by fedora-wearing reporters, was his usual reticent self. One photograph, appearing in the *San Francisco Chronicle*, shows him standing in front of a battery of newsreel cameras. Describing the scene, the caption reads: 'Heroic Lt Commander Herbert V. Wiley ... was as cool as the proverbial cucumber while ... jockeying his wrecked ship to an easy landing, but ... lost his ... courage when besieged by newsmen.'[52]

Wearing a borrowed pair of navy blue trousers and a cream-coloured sweater, his grey hair neatly parted in the middle, Wiley stiffly addressed the press about the crash.[53] 'I have some ideas as to the reason,' he told reporters, 'but I want to talk to the officers and men before I draw any conclusions.'[54]

Later that morning, the *Macon*'s crew were transported by truck to NAS Sunnyvale. There they were examined by doctors for a second time. Afterwards, a group photo was taken on the steps of the administration building. It was impossible to tell from the men's mundane expressions that their lives had hung in the balance just a few hours before. Later that day, the crew found time to autograph a piece of rubber torn from one of the life rafts.[55] Surprisingly, their captain's signature was the most prominent.

Wiley gathered his men that afternoon to listen to their first-hand reports of what had happened. Since a naval Court of Inquiry was forthcoming (not to mention another congressional investigation), he gathered vital information to clarify his thinking. The last thing Wiley wanted was to appear unsure about what happened in front of a naval review board, especially since he'd be called upon to explain his actions.

But controversy dogged the *Macon* in the days following her crash. The Associated Press distributed an illustration by one of its artists that ran on the front page of the *San Francisco Examiner*. The pen-and-ink drawing showed the dirigible floating on the ocean with a huge hole blown in her side. The caption reads: 'A roaring explosion preceded the airship falling into the Pacific, according to reports by ships speeding to her rescue.'[56]

This simply was not true. But rumours persisted that water had flooded the *Macon's* storage batteries, causing them to explode. Wiley and his officers thought the claim ludicrous, telling *The Washington Post* there'd been no such explosion.[57] But that didn't stop various theories from being published, including the old chestnut: the ship had been sabotaged.

Radioman Ernest Dailey's grey-haired mother had told a reporter, 'If he's dead, he died in [the] line of duty – but I don't think he is gone.'[58] His wife, Lucille, received a surprise on 14 February when a box of chocolates accompanied by flowers were delivered for Valentine's Day.[59] Dailey had made the arrangements before departing on his fatal voyage. Saturday, 16 February 1935, would have been his 28th birthday.

In contrast, the mother of Aviation Machinist's Mate James F. Todd was relieved to hear her 28-year-old son had been saved. 'I was always afraid that something would happen to him,' she told a reporter. 'He always tried to tell me that … dirigibles are as safe as automobiles.' Then she shook her head in disbelief.[60]

Wiley didn't have to wait long for the naval Court of Inquiry to be convened. Secretary of the Navy Swanson, Assistant Secretary Henry L. Roosevelt, Rear Admiral Ernest J. King and Admiral Standley met in secret on 13 February to discuss the court hearing.[61] Later that day, Admiral Reeves announced the Navy's investigation into the loss of the *Macon* would be held aboard the USS *Tennessee* anchored in San Francisco bay at 0930 hours the next morning. Only seventy-two hours had transpired since the disaster.

The speed with which Reeves announced the Court of Inquiry might suggest the Navy was eager to get to the bottom of what happened, but the *Macon* had been a thorn in the Navy's side for eighteen months. The more likely explanation is that Reeves and Standley wanted to put the whole embarrassing affair behind them as quickly as possible.

Although newspapers considered Wiley a hero, it wasn't clear whether the Navy would share this assessment. If they didn't, it could lead to a court martial and a premature end to Wiley's career. One thing seemed clear, however. The Navy was ready to shut down Moffett's problem-plagued big rigid programme as quickly as possible. Whether Wiley would co-operate was anyone's guess.

37

A GIANT ON TRIAL

Once again, Litchfield was quick to offer Goodyear's assistance. 'Every technical resource we have is at your command in any investigation the government may undertake in the loss of the *Macon*,' he said in a telegram to Secretary Swanson.[1] The move was a necessary act of self-preservation. One airship crash might be a fluke, but two within eighteen months was alarming.

Reactions to the disaster were overwhelmingly negative. Republican Carl Vinson, who had considered introducing a bill to the House Naval Affairs Committee authorising a replacement for the *Akron*, told reporters the *Macon* loss spelled 'the death knell' for the Navy's big rigid programme. Secretary Swanson concurred, saying there were many other things the Navy needed more than airships.[2]

Senator King, who'd chaired the congressional investigation into the *Akron* crash, told the press that rigid airships 'serve no useful purpose'. Calling them 'a menace to life', King added, 'To spend … more money for dirigibles would be criminal.'[3] Admiral Standley, never a fan, told a reporter, 'This should be a solemn warning to this country with respect to the use of LTA craft … for naval purposes.'[4] Even President Roosevelt thought the Navy should stop spending money on big rigids. Opening his press conference with mention of the *Macon*, Roosevelt told reporters there was no thought of asking Congress for another airship. Instead, he wanted to put money into long-range patrol planes.[5]

The loss of the *Macon* didn't just scuttle the Navy's rigid airship programme; it sank Litchfield's dream for a fleet of American-flagged passenger airships. As the *New York Times* noted:

Commercial development of dirigibles for transatlantic ... service ... was directly affected by the sinking of the [*Macon*] since all such plans have been based on a premise that the government would build one or more airships to rent for commercial operations.[6]

News of the disaster was so shocking that at least five congressional investigations were announced. In addition to the Navy Court of Inquiry, hearings were considered by the House Naval Affairs Committee, the House Patents Committee and the House Military Affairs Committee, as well as a joint congressional investigation similar to the *Akron* crash.[7]

The usual suspects continued to voice their support for big rigids. Commander Rosendahl, always an advocate, told the *San Francisco Chronicle* that if 'an adequate program is established airships will be found to be definitely useful to a navy such as ours and to our overseas commerce'.[8]

Rep. McLeod (R., Michigan) also endorsed the programme. The ranking minority member of the Navy Subcommittee on Appropriations, McLeod demanded a 'disaster-proof' airship be constructed to replace the *Macon*.[9] McLeod's call seemed out of step with majority opinion, but it makes sense once you realise he represented the district where Goodyear – the company that built the Navy's only metal-clad airship – was headquartered. Carl Fritsche, President of that company, hoped to turn a sow's ear into a silk purse by writing to President Roosevelt two days after the *Macon* sank:

Permit me to congratulate you on your calmness and courage in the face of the disaster to the USS MACON. It is most reassuring to observe the Commander in Chief of the Navy is not influenced by those who hastily condemn dirigibles for all time to come because of a failure which can be easily remedied. Having been jointly responsible for the construction of the Navy's Metalclad Airship, ZMC-2, which is now in its sixth year of successful operation with no demerits* against its record, might I not suggest that the Navy Department re-examine the possibilities of this type of craft before reaching any conclusion as to its permanent policy with respect to airships ... Having devoted the last fifteen years of my life without pecuniary profit to airship development, I feel you will agree I am not actuated by selfish motives in suggesting that consideration be given to the Metalclad.[10]

---

*   Not entirely true since the ZMC-2 had lateral stability issues when flying in rough air that made her crew seasick.

In an unusual turn of events, the Japanese ambassador conveyed his government's regret to the United States for the loss of the *Macon*, adding that the Japanese Imperial Navy was praying for the crew. This seems odd given the *Macon* was built to prevent an attack by Japan, but the reason Japan was so sympathetic is that she wanted her own airship fleet. As her foreign minister explained, 'The Japanese Navy would like to possess them, but it lacks the money.'[11]

Meanwhile, Litchfield had to sit by while Dr Eckener tried stealing market share. Able to boast that the *Graf Zeppelin* had made fifty-one ocean crossings carrying 6,000 passengers, Eckener sent a personal letter to President Roosevelt written on *Graf* stationary asking permission to lease the Navy's rigid airship facilities at Lakehurst and Florida, so the *Graf* could begin a regular scheduled service between the US, Europe and South America. Eckener wrote to the President:

> I am aware that several serious minded attempts have been made to establish airships on a sound commercial basis in the United States. I feel however that in the present economic situation, and with the prevailing skepticism as to the practicability of airships, some further demonstration through actual airship operation is desirable. I believe the Luftschiffbau Zeppelin is in the best position to make such a demonstration, and it is with reference to possible co-operation with the United States that I wish to outline a specific proposal for your consideration.[12]

These weren't the only voices in support of big rigids. Clark Howell, head of Roosevelt's Federal Aviation Commission (FAC), said the government should 'undertake further construction and operation of rigid airships in naval and commercial service'.[13] The FAC went so far as to recommend spending $17 million on commercial airships, including building a new airship passenger terminal on the east coast. As Howell put it, 'If the Germans can do it, we can.'[14]

Even Billy Mitchell, former Assistant Chief of the Army Air Corps and a fierce advocate for heavier-than-air flight, favoured big rigids. Calling their abandonment 'a sign of moral decrepitude',[15] Mitchell told the *Washington Post*, 'It would be very foolish to give up our airship development particularly in view of conditions in the far east ... If we continue to disarm we will be an easy target for any Asiatic country that comes along.'[16]

The *New York Times*' military editor, Hanson W. Baldwin, was also in favour. 'The *Macon*'s performance under Lieut. Commander Wiley had astonished even those skeptics who could see no need for lighter than air,' he wrote. 'There is still a considerable school of thought which holds that lighter than air craft can, if correctly built, perform services of which no other type is capable.' Baldwin concluded, 'Submarines have sunk, destroyers have capsized and planes have crashed, but these types have not been abandoned.'[17]

One suggestion tendered by a citizen supporter was that a public subscription be taken up to fund the *Macon*'s replacement, something Count Zeppelin had successfully done in Germany. But support for big rigids faced an uphill battle after the *Macon* crash. As the Mayor of Akron, Ohio, told the *New York Times*, 'I hope this accident may not affect the building of more ships here.'[18] He was whistling in the dark.

The Navy Court of Inquiry convened aboard the USS *Tennessee* on Thursday, 14 February at 0930 hours. The *Tennessee* must have held some painful associations for Wiley since it was the same ship he was serving on when his wife died. Anchored in San Francisco Bay, the *Tennessee* was a grey and imposing edifice, but she was still 200ft shorter than the *Macon* despite being one of the largest battleships in the Navy.

In contrast, the cabin where the hearing was held was a tight fit. Made entirely of steel with an oppressively low ceiling, its amenities included wood panelling and wall sconces that did little to soften the room's austerity. A leather-covered banquette ran along one side of the cabin with a mirror-backed credenza next to it. But the table in the centre was far too big for the cabin's small dimensions, making it feel claustrophobic. Adding to the feeling of closeness, the cabin was so overheated a curtained porthole had to be left open even though it was February.

Charged with investigating the loss of the *Macon*, the inquiry was intended to establish both cause and responsibility. Wiley was first to testify. Using notes to refresh his memory, he spread out a blueprint of the *Macon* on the table as well as a naval chart of the California coast to aid his testimony. Since the ship's log had gone down with the *Macon*, the only thing the court had to rely on was the quartermaster's notebook[19] and memories of the crew; Wiley's being the most important.

After recounting the *Macon*'s scouting exercise, Wiley gave a brief summary of the events off Point Sur. This included telling the court that he hadn't been concerned for his airship's safety, because the weather 'was not very turbulent'.[20]

Devoid of emotion, Wiley's account relied on formality to mask the inherent drama of his story.[21] The only time he got upset was when the Judge Advocate asked if he had any complaint about the crew.

'Complaint?' Wiley asked, clearly aggrieved. 'I should say not. Every man was splendid and all acted with a courage and efficiency that were astounding.'[22]

After Wiley completed his statement, the Judge Advocate questioned him:

Q. At any time during the rain squall did you surmise that the *Macon* was in danger?
A. No.
Q. Was there any undue strain on the structure at any time?
A. No, there was not.[23]

Wiley's testimony, though dry, contained a genuine surprise. As far as he was concerned, the *Macon* was structurally sound:

Q: I take it then that to your knowledge, there has been no indication of any weakness in the after part of the ship?
A: No, sir. No weakness that we were cognizant of.[24]
Q: Has the ship been injured in any way which might account for the casualty?
A: No, sir.[25]

It's hard to fathom how Wiley could neglect to tell the court the *Macon* had nearly been lost over Texas ten months before. But Kenworthy, the *Macon*'s executive officer, corroborated his captain's testimony. What's more surprising is how vague and confusing Wiley's testimony was.

Wiley knew the *Macon*'s fin had failed, puncturing three of her gas cells, but wasn't sure what had caused the fin to fail. Was it excessive aerodynamic loading caused by a gust, the turning of the elevator wheel, insufficient bracing or metal fatigue?

It's hard to understand what was going through Wiley's mind when recounting the loss of his airship. Was he truly befuddled or hiding what he knew about the *Macon*'s design flaw to protect Moffett's LTA programme? Or trying to cover up his mistakes? It was in many respects a repeat of his performance at the naval Court of Inquiry into the *Akron* crash.

One explanation may be that Wiley had to walk a thin line between telling the court what he knew and not casting aspersions against the Navy, Goodyear or himself. As events turned out, he succeeded. The court did not question his account but it made for confusing testimony.

The next morning Shaky Davis stunned the court when he filled in the blanks of Wiley's omission. When asked why he went aft to check on where the fins were anchored, he replied, 'Because when the *Macon* was over Texas two girders sheared off at 17.5 frame when [we] ran into squalls.'[26]

A 'startled silence' descended upon the court as the judges absorbed this new information.[27] Seeing their consternation, Davis tried reassuring them that frame 17.5 had been 'repaired and strengthened'.[28] But what he said next undermined any attempt to allay their fears:

> There's a transverse triangular girder at the point where the fin is secured to No. 17.5. I always put my hand there when it gets rough. I wanted to see how much it would lift.[29]

The judges had no idea the *Macon's* fins moved so much in flight. But when Steele, who'd accompanied Davis, told the court he thought it was the *Macon's* top fin carrying away that caused her to crash, it was clear something had gone drastically wrong.[30]

The lighthouse keepers' account of the *Macon's* fin 'exploding' confirmed Steele's contention.[31] But as Wiley sat on the banquette, grim-faced and with arms folded, the question hung in the air: what had caused the *Macon's* fin to fail?

Lt Bolster, the *Macon's* construction repair officer, testified after Davis. At first Bolster's testimony confirmed what the court suspected:

> I feel certain … that the cause was a failure of the structure either in the fins themselves or at the point where the fins were attached to the hull … It is hard to be certain of the exact location … but if I were told to say where I expected it would occur I would say at the diagonal girders at Frame 17, since a very similar failure had occurred on a previous occasion in April 1934 over Texas … These girders were reinforced and made stronger, but that was in the port fin. The girders in the top had not been reinforced although the work was ordered.

Once again the judges were surprised to learn that the fin that had failed had not been reinforced despite an agreement to do so. But what Bolster said next was even more shocking:

The orders ... stated that [the repairs] should be done at such times as to not interfere with [the *Macon*'s] operating schedules [so] the assembly and repair department at the NAS had been working on this reinforcement as opportunity between flights permitted. This reinforcement was not completed at the time of the accident ... [it] would have been made during the forthcoming overhaul.[32]

After the judges absorbed this news, the Judge Advocate asked Bolster a question:

Q. In your opinion, do you consider that sufficient internal strength was provided in the fins of the USS *Macon* to care for [the] unsupported overhang [created by the fins' leading edges]?
A. My present opinion is that it was not. Previous to the failure... I thought they were amply strong.[33]

The next day's headline in the *New York Times* said it all:

MACON'S LOSS LAID TO A BREAK AT FINS
San Francisco, Friday Feb. 15 – The testimony of Lt Calvin M. Bolster had a bombshell effect on the hearing ... The officer revealed that the weakness was known, that orders had been given for strengthening affected parts of the structure, and that material had been sent to the Sunnyvale base for that purpose but that the repairs had not been completed at the time of the fatal flight.[34]

Wiley disagreed with Bolster's testimony. He believed the *Macon* was structurally sound.[35] To admit otherwise would drive another nail in the Navy's rigid airship programme. Still, it was hard to ignore Bolster since he specialised in airship construction and repair.

Although the media credited Dr Arnstein with 'knowing more about the application of scientific principles to stress analysis ... than any man outside of Germany', court testimony made it clear something was wrong with the *Macon*.[36] This was reinforced by Dr Eckener, who attributed the *Macon* crash to 'faulty design.'[37] It must have distressed Arnstein to hear his former boss at Luftschiffbau Zeppelin blame his design for the crash, but if his feelings were hurt he kept it to himself.

The day after Bolster's testimony, a memorial service was conducted in the *Macon*'s hangar for Dailey and Edquiba. A second service was held the next day at All Saints Episcopal Church in Lakewood, New Jersey, this one offering thanks for the many survivors.[38]

If Wiley was worried that the crash of the *Macon* would hurt his chances for promotion, he needn't have been. On the second day of the inquiry it was announced he'd received his long-awaited promotion to commander. It was curious timing given the hearing was still under way. The announcement suggests the Navy considered it more expedient to label Wiley a hero than delve too deeply into his role in the crash. This seems a reasonable interpretation given the Navy wanted to bury Moffett's rigid airship programme with as little fuss as possible, which makes Wiley's testimony on 19 February all the more astounding:

WILEY NOT RUSH REPAIRS

Sunnyvale, Feb. 19 – Lt. Commander Herbert V. Wiley … told a Naval Board of Inquiry today he had not considered alterations intended to strengthen the girders in the airship 'important enough' to be rushed.[39]

Recalled for additional testimony on the last day of the hearing, Wiley admitted something he should have mentioned on the first day:

Q: You had no concern in operating the ship without these repairs being made?
A: I had no concern over it and I believe that none of my officers had any concern in this connection.
Q: Do you consider that the work authorised by the Bureau of Aeronautics had progressed as rapidly as possible consistent with the operating schedule of the USS *Macon*?
A. Yes, sir. I am primarily responsible for the precedence of the work that is done on the ship and considering other work and the operations it was done about as rapidly as possible. It might have been, sir, I think possible, that we could have concentrated upon this job a little more if we had considered it important enough to give it priority.[40]

This is a revealing admission given the *Macon* had almost been lost over Texas. What Wiley didn't say is that he'd been concerned enough about the ship's structural integrity when he took command that he asked Lt Bolster to draft a letter to the Bureau of Aeronautics requesting they look into the matter.[41]

To be fair, Fulton reassured Wiley the *Macon* was safe to fly, so long as she avoided severe gusts over land. But the *Macon*'s structural integrity was questionable enough that it remained a source of concern both for Shaky Davis and Lt Bolster, who took it upon themselves to regularly inspect her airframe during flight. Wiley's statement that he didn't consider the repairs important enough to make them a priority is damning, especially since plenty of people at Goodyear, not to mention his own crew, were concerned that the repairs should be made faster.

The reality is, Wiley thought proving the *Macon* an effective ocean-going scout was more important than reinforcing the area where her tail fins were anchored. He had to keep her flying if he wanted to achieve this goal. That meant spending as little time in the hangar as possible. Given the seriousness of the casualty over Texas, Wiley should have made reinforcing frame 17.5 a priority. His failure to do so cost him his airship. But the Navy Court of Inquiry was not going to find fault with his decision to delay strengthening frame 17.5 given the BUAER had reassured him the *Macon* was safe to fly.

That same day, the naval Court of Inquiry lined up the *Macon* survivors at NAS Sunnyvale to read them Wiley's account of their airship's loss. When asked whether they had anything to add, no one responded. As far as the *Macon*'s crew was concerned, 'God and Wiley saved our lives.'[42]

The court issued its findings slightly more than a month after the *Macon* crashed. They are worth reviewing despite their tortured syntax as much for what they don't say as what they do:

> The loss of the *Macon* was caused by a sudden lateral pressure from port on the upper fin, that this sudden pressure on … the forward part of the fin was transmitted through … frame 17.5 … causing a strain … under which one or more of [its diagonal girders] failed. That the loss of the *Macon* was owing to an inherent defect in design in that the forward part of the upper fin was not sufficiently secured against lateral pressure. That this defect could have been eliminated by external wire braces to the forward part of the fin,* by reducing the area of the forward part of the fins, or by a more substantial support to that part … In view of the state of the art of airship design at the time the *Macon* was designed, and in view of the fact that her design

---

*   Note: These were precisely the changes Dr Arnstein repeatedly recommended.

was made and approved by the most expert men in the county and was as thoroughly tested as possible, *this court can fix no responsibility for the loss of the Macon* [author's emphasis]. In conclusion ... the loss of the *Macon* ... should simply be charged to profit and loss ... if they ever build another airship they can build her a lot better.[43]

That neither Fulton nor Arnstein were called to testify shows that the court was more interested in what caused the *Macon* to crash than who was responsible. As a result, the court not only absolved Wiley and his crew, but the Bureau of Aeronautics and Goodyear-Zeppelin.

It's clear the Navy wasn't interested in apportioning blame. As King's assistant mentioned in a memo to his boss, 'It is regretted ... that important events were not more clearly established ... and that more of the experienced officers and men were not called up for testimony.' Importantly, he thought asking the crew to comment on Wiley's account 'was not sufficient' to reveal what really happened.[44] Nevertheless, he recommended King endorse the findings.

As much as King wanted to get to the bottom of what caused the *Macon* crash it was in the BUAER's best interests to do so discreetly. The Navy hardly needed further embarrassment where its LTA programme was concerned. So, King endorsed the findings with one important caveat:

> The Chief of the Bureau of Aeronautics proposes to endeavor through ... less formal means to seek additional information on the more technical aspects of the situation and is hopeful that eventually it will be possible to formulate a more complete technical picture of what actually did happen to the *Macon* ... Subject to the foregoing proposals for securing additional data now lacking, it is recommended the proceedings of the court of inquiry be approved.[45]

The *Macon* Court of Inquiry was a perfunctory affair. It was shorter than the *Akron* inquiry, much less thorough and its findings equally tepid. This should come as no surprise given the court's focus was more on what Wiley and his crew did right than what the Navy did wrong.

So why were the court's findings so weak? It appears the Navy wanted to put the whole affair behind it as quickly as possible. Since the Navy had no intention of building another big rigid, it served no purpose to find fault with the *Macon*'s design or operation. That's why the Navy swept any embarrassing revelations under the rug, choosing to celebrate Wiley for saving his men rather than blaming him for losing his airship. As the Judge Advocate wrote:

> During the last half hour of the life of the *Macon* her stern was one of the most unsafe places in the world; for not only was it filled with deadly gas, but there was danger that the unsupported tail might break away from the rest of the hull and fall like a rock. Every man aboard the *Macon* knew that; and yet we see men whose duty did not require their going to the stern deliberately going aft to see if they could possibly do anything to save the ship … The fact that a ship foundered at sea with a loss of but two lives out of 83 speaks more eloquently of the discipline of that ship than words could … The *Macon* is at the bottom of the sea, but this country may still be proud of her.[46]

It was bad enough that the Navy had lost two rigid airships in less than two years; what the Navy needed were heroes not guilty parties. But as Mackey, the *Macon*'s flight control officer, put it:

> If there were errors of design or faulty operation involved, it would have served the cause better to have forthrightly so stated. Instead, the loss is attributed, more or less to an act of God … selecting such testimony as supports this and ignoring equally valid and credible testimony at the contrary.[47]

After the Court of Inquiry released its findings, the Navy announced that NAS Sunnyvale would focus on heavier-than-air flight. *Macon* personnel who had not already been reassigned were transferred to NAS Lakehurst in New Jersey.[48] Soon, the *Macon*'s officers found themselves dispersed around the country, with many of them reabsorbed by the surface Navy.

In addition to being promoted to commander, Wiley was awarded a special commendation from Secretary Swanson, which read:

> At the time of the loss of the *Macon* you took immediate measures with a view to saving your vessel and crew. These measures were so effective that but two men out of a total of 83 were lost, this being by far the lowest percentage … ever known to have occurred in the case of a similar vessel.

You acted with the utmost coolness during the emergency and gave the officers and men an outstanding example of courage, resourcefulness, and morale. The department especially commends you for your heroic conduct and extraordinary achievement while in command of the *Macon* at the time of the loss.[49]

Forty-one of the *Macon*'s eighty-three-man crew also received commendations, including Kenworthy, Reppy, Cochrane, Mills, Peck, Bolster, Campbell, Buckley, Dailey and Davis. In Dailey's case, his commendation was sent to his widow.

Lucille Dailey had unveiled a plaque bearing her husband's name as part of a memorial honouring distinguished wireless operators in May. As sailors from the Brooklyn Naval Yard fired a three-volley salute followed by taps, all communications on the Navy's radiomarine were silenced for a minute in tribute.[50] Later, the Navy helped Lucille find a job in Washington – further proof they took care of their own.[51]

The *Macon* was stricken from the Navy's register of ships even before the Court of Inquiry issued its findings, but the airship continued having a profound impact on those associated with her. Chief among those affected was her father-creator, Dr Karl Arnstein.

The loss of the *Macon* shook Arnstein to his core. Sinking into a deep depression, he was unable to work. Arnstein blamed himself for the *Macon*'s loss, despite warning Fulton many times that the *Akron* and *Macon* were structurally weak. Worrying he should have done more to prevent the disaster, he found it difficult to reconcile himself to what happened. In reality, Fulton had ignored, gas lighted, bullied and condescended to Arnstein every step of the way. Now that Arnstein's worst fears had come true, he found himself mired in darkness.

Arnstein wasn't the only one affected by the loss of the *Macon*. Paul Helma, one of his twelve disciples, also became ill. When he couldn't return to work, Helma left Goodyear-Zeppelin, filing for disability. He never designed another airship again.[52]

Arnstein was so depressed, Litchfield sent him for an extended rest in Germany, including two weeks at the Glotterbad Sanatorium in the Glottertal.[53] In a handwritten letter from Germany, Arnstein addresses Goodyear's CEO as, 'My dear Mr. Litchfield,' confiding:[54]

Conditions of my health have made it necessary to go to a Sanitarium and I think it was not unwise to take advantage of the excellent facilities in Germany. I spent two weeks in … the Black Forest and will be happy to be on my way back in very much improved conditions …

faithfully yours, Karl Arnstein[55]

While Arnstein blamed himself for the *Macon*'s loss, Fulton was busy making sure no one blamed him. What unfolded next was tantamount to a cover-up.

38

ASSIGNING BLAME

The court's findings put the loss of the *Macon* to bed as far as the Navy was concerned, but the crash reverberated through the halls of the BUAER. Admiral King was determined to understand what went wrong with his airship long after the court released its findings. This was critical if he was to replace the *Macon*. A handwritten note soon landed on Fulton's desk:

> Is there anything of record in Bureau (or Navy Department) files or in the Court of Inquiry in case of *Akron* and/or *Macon*, which makes it appear that the Goodyear-Zeppelin Corp. at any time urged the Navy Dept. to agree to the strengthening in any way of any of the structure of the two airships which the Navy Dept. disapproved (1) while the ships were building (2) after they were in service? K[1]

Fulton's response was not long in coming:

> There is nothing I can find in the record which makes it appear that the Goodyear-Zeppelin Corporation at any time urged the Navy Department to agree to the strengthening of the structure of the *Akron* or *Macon*, which the Department disapproved.[2]

Fulton's reply is striking for its lack of honesty. In contrast, Arnstein drafted a concise, clear-headed letter to Litchfield providing a chronological accounting of his many attempts to reinforce frame 17.5.[3]

Arnstein's desire to build big rigids remained undiminished by his depression. As he told Litchfield six months after the *Macon* was lost, 'It is still my opinion that we can never hope to successfully develop airships in the United

States unless we (i.e. Goodyear–Zeppelin) undertake to build and operate commercial airships.'[4]

On the same day that Arnstein sent his letter to Litchfield, Fulton sent what can only be viewed as a 'cover your ass' memo to Arnstein. In it, Fulton outlined his recollection of events related to reinforcing the *Macon*'s fins:

> I felt there was considerable misunderstanding as to matters relating to fin reinforcements in the *Macon*. There have come to me from various sources … that point … to a campaign … designed to bring into question decisions made … I deplore the fact that in some quarters a remarkable degree of hindsight is being displayed and matters are represented now in a different way than they were represented formerly* … I would be particularly interested to know whether your Goodyear–Zeppelin records show anything that is in conflict with the memorandum … It seems to me that … less attention paid to gossip and vague allegations as to past history is a thing much to be desired.[5]

It's not surprising that Fulton's written recollection casts Goodyear in a poor light, while the Navy appears blameless. A senior executive at Goodyear–Zeppelin said Arnstein didn't like Fulton's memo very much. That it included a veiled threat ('The use to which this Memorandum will be put … has not yet been determined'[6]) must have given Arnstein pause since he took two months to reply. When he did respond his written reply was unusually curt: 'It is company policy to engage in no efforts to assess blame for what occurred,' Arnstein told Fulton. 'I hope that you will not interpret my silence on this subject as denoting agreement.'[7]

Arnstein's response reads like an aggrieved man who has been told to keep silent. Whether Litchfield ordered him to shut up, or he chose not to speak his mind can't be known. Either way, Arnstein's reason for remaining quiet was sensible. There was no profit in attacking a client, even if Arnstein considered Fulton partially responsible for the loss of the *Macon*, especially since Goodyear–Zeppelin continued to do business with the Navy.[8]

Fulton's memory would differ greatly from Arnstein's when it came to reinforcing the *Macon*'s fin. Fulton claimed in his memo to King that 'Dr. Arnstein had no real justification for the suggested fin bracings and did not indicate

---

*   Fulton's memo was probably triggered at least in part by Professor de Forest's claim that 'Arnstein begged the Navy to fix the *Macon*', but the Navy had been unresponsive.

any errors in the original load distribution [therefore] his suggestion was not favorably received in so far as the *Macon* was concerned.'[9]

This was patently untrue as the paper trail shows. Arnstein had been worried about the fins as far back as 1931. That's why he'd demanded the NACA wind tunnel tests be repeated. It also explains why Arnstein kept hectoring Fulton about reinforcing frame 17.5 for three years, going so far as to order cable bracing at Goodyear's expense.

Fulton's memo also insisted that the weight incurred by Arnstein's remedies was too great, but this contradicts his July 1933 letter in which he clearly tells Arnstein 'the weight of the scheme you now propose is not excessive'.[10]

Additionally, Fulton's memo claimed Arnstein did not recommend reinforcing frame 17.5 until much later than he actually did. This ignores the many well-documented times Arnstein fought to be heard on the matter. Equally revealing is Fulton's statement that the *Macon*'s strengthening of frame 17.5 where the fins were anchored was 'not an item that the G-Z Corp. was willing to include in their cost and weight allowances but was to be in the nature of a change for which the Navy Department would be expected to pay'.[11] OK, but did he ignore Arnstein's recommendations because they were unnecessary, too costly or excessively heavy? Fulton wanted it both ways.

Whether Fulton was covering his ass or misremembered his conversations with Arnstein, only Fulton knows for sure. What can't be denied is that he'd refused to do anything about Arnstein's concerns. Given the facts, Fulton's memo only obscured the truth.

So why did the *Macon*'s fin fail? Did a violent gust cause excessive aerodynamic loading, resulting in frame 17.5 collapsing and the upper fin being carried away, or did the fin fail of its own accord without any help from a gust?

THE VIOLENT GUST THEORY

One of the curious aspects of the *Macon* affair is how much disagreement there was among the crew over whether there even was a gust. Those subscribing to a violent-gust-caused-the-fin-to-fail theory included the *Macon*'s executive officer, Lt Cdr Kenworthy; her officer of the deck, Lt Campbell; her construction repair officer, Lt Bolster; Clarke, the helmsman; and Conover, the elevatorman. Since all five were in the control car at the time of the casualty their opinion carries weight.

Lt Campbell testified, 'The ship apparently received a side gust. One reason which makes me believe it was a side gust was the papers in the control car were flying … around which has happened many times before when we had side gusts.'[12]

Lt Bolster also subscribed to the side-gust theory. In a letter he sent Fulton a month after the *Macon* was lost, Bolster wrote, 'There is a no question but that a violent lateral gust hit the ship. All of us who were in the control car on the lookout for such a gust … distinctly felt it.'[*,13]

But one thing those subscribing to the gust theory could not agree upon was the direction it came from. Most thought it originated from the sea, striking the *Macon* on her port side as she headed north. Others thought the gust originated from the shore, funnelled through the gap between coastal mountains. Lt Roland G. Mayer, who'd 'had some very rough flights'[14] near the region where the alleged gust struck the *Macon*, speculated that it 'probably stream[ed] down from one of the canyons'.[15]

Powerful, land-based gusts undoubtedly occur where the *Macon*'s casualty took place, but it seems unlikely the gust (if there was one) came from the coast. That's because the *Macon* was pushed towards shore, not away from it. This could only happen if the gust struck the airship on her port side, which faced the ocean. If the gust had come from shore, it would have hit her starboard side pushing her nose out to sea. As it was, the opposite happened.

THE FIN FAILED OF ITS OWN ACCORD

Not everybody thought a side gust caused the *Macon*'s fin to fail. Lt Danis,[**] the *Macon*'s on-board weather forecaster, testified that he found the lurch puz-

---

[*] In a telling personal moment revealing how much the *Macon*'s loss disrupted the lives of her crew, Bolster closed his letter to Fulton by saying, 'I would appreciate learning as soon as you know when and where I am to go as I own a house which I must sell or rent.'

[**] Danis was one of the luckiest airship officers in Moffett's LTA programme. He not only survived the *Macon* disaster, but a delay in assigning him to the *Shenandoah* meant he had missed that crash by a few days. If that wasn't lucky enough, Danis was transferred off the *Akron* only a few weeks before she sunk in the Atlantic. When it came to escaping disasters, Danis had 'Lucky' Deal beat.

zling because air conditions were smooth at the time, suggesting they wouldn't 'encounter anything that would cause the ship to behave the way it did.'[16]

> Q: Do you believe the lurch was caused by a gust of wind?
> A: In my opinion, no sir.
> Q: What might have caused it?
> A: In my opinion, a structural failure might have caused it.[17]

The *Macon's* navigator, Lt Peck, also testified he didn't believe there was a side gust, noting, 'The ship suddenly, *without apparent reason* [author's italics], swung to starboard approximately 20 degrees and went down by the nose.'[18]

Lt Cdr Mackey, who was on board the *Macon* during her crash, revisited the circumstances of her casualty in 1965 when he wrote a response to a recently published book, *The Airships Akron & Macon* by Richard K. Smith. Smith's book contends that a gust triggered the fin loss, but Mackey disagreed: 'I maintain that what was attributed to cause [namely, the 'gust' striking the ship] was actually EFFECT [emphasis his].'[19] Mackey goes on to say:

> It was a well-known fact that the leading edge of the upper fin during flight, tended to oscillate or wobble through a considerable amplitude at its upper portion, particularly at the higher speeds.*,[20]

Although Mackey admits 'it would seem unlikely that a normal change of course could be the initiating cause of the casualty', he believes it was Clarke's turning of the helm that precipitated the failure. As Mackey noted, 'No one had ever experienced anything like it, nor had they ever experienced a bump without gustiness, therefore some assumed there was a gust.'[21]

Bolster attributes the confusion as to why the upper fin failed to one of three things: 'the individual's location in the ship ... his duties at that time and ... a lack of complete frankness on the part of some in giving their reactions.'[22] This last point suggests at least one of the *Macon's* officers wasn't saying what he knew, though Bolster never specifies who.

Whether or not a gust caused the casualty, Lt Mayer, an experienced engineer who knew the ins and outs of airship construction (but was not on board the *Macon* that fateful day), was confident it began with the failure of the frame where the *Macon's* upper fin was anchored.

---

*   Mackey says the leading edge of the upper fin oscillated 'a matter of feet during flight'.

'No ... doubt in my mind that the initial failure occurred in frame 17.5,'[23] Lt Mayer told Fulton. He was 'firmly convinced' that once frame 17.5 failed, the *Macon's* upper fin swung like a fulcrum, tearing away with 'explosive force'.[24]

Shaky Davis agreed with Mayer, telling the Navy Court of Inquiry, 'It has long been my contention that the upper fin, suddenly starting to collapse, acted as a massive rudder in the 65 knot slip stream and violently slapped the ship around, bow to starboard [causing] the lurch which seemed to many like a gust.'[25]

METAL FATIGUE

Another theory was that frame 17.5 failed due to metal fatigue, either exacerbated by a gust or simply of its own accord. Lt Bolster, who was knowledgeable about aerodynamic stress, rejected the metal fatigue theory, saying it was unlikely:

> It is possible that the structure which supported the fin might have failed without warning with no application of external force, however, due to the fact that this structure had been carefully watched and inspected, it seems to me that a complete breakdown ... without the application of some overload is extremely doubtful. I believe that there are cases where Duralumin has developed fatigue under long applications of varying stresses. However, I would expect such a failure to appear first in the form of cracks and would therefore expect careful inspection to find it before a complete failure occurred.[26]

The *Macon's* airframe was inspected every month for signs of weakness. Her hull inspection report for the month of January 1935 gave her a clean bill of health. Nevertheless, Lt Miller thought metal fatigue might have contributed to the casualty. As Miller noted in a March 1935 letter to former Sparrowhawk Squadron Leader 'Crash Helmet' Harrigan, 'An amazing fact is that both the *Akron* and the *Macon* had between 1700 and 1800 hours. That shows a lot to me in so far as possible metal fatigue goes.'[27]

Miller was a pilot not a structural engineer, but it's an interesting observation given the *Macon* was known to experience excessive vibration in her stern.[28] In fact, the vibration was so severe Goodyear had installed anti-flutter braces in her No. 1 and 2 engine compartments in an attempt to reduce it. When that didn't work, Dresel recommended removing two engines. Since the technology to locate microscopic cracks did not exist in the 1930s like it does today, it's possible frame 17.5 failed due to metal fatigue alone, or in combination with excessive aerodynamic loading.

It's important to remember that the section of frame 17.5 that failed was the only one that had not been reinforced following the casualty over Texas. This points to an inherent weakness in the frame where the fins were anchored. When the frame was reinforced, the defect was either moderated or eliminated. But the upper half of frame 17.5 wasn't scheduled to be reinforced until the following month, leaving it vulnerable to failure. It's possible metal fatigue contributed to the failure, but we can't know for sure.

About the only thing the varying explanations by the crew have in common is the conviction that their version was right. So what did Wiley believe?

Surely, the *Macon*'s captain, one of the most experienced big rigid men in the programme, had insight into what happened. In his written account, Wiley said that after ordering left rudder, 'the ship lurched suddenly as if in a powerful gust'.[29] But he dismissed the side gust theory in his court testimony. Instead, Wiley believed the *Macon*'s upper fin's collapse was triggered by his command to turn the rudder 5 degrees.

Normally, such a command would not be expected to have such a catastrophic result, particularly since it was given countless times in flight. But a turn of the helm could have triggered the fin to collapse if the fin (or its anchoring) was already excessively weak. Wiley didn't believe the *Macon* suffered any structural weakness, however, leaving his reasoning for the fin failure frustratingly opaque. In fact, Wiley's reasoning was remarkably jumbled, leaving Lt Bolster to wonder how his captain could be so confused. As Bolster bluntly told Fulton, 'I regret to say that about the only person on the ship who does not agree with [the gust theory] is Capt. Wiley, who for some reason none of us can understand, keeps talking about controls breaking, fabric tearing, rudder jamming and similar causes none of which could have explained the casualty as it occurred.'[30]

Wiley's explanation of the *Macon*'s casualty, like his explanation for the loss of the *Akron*, was all over the place. What's even more surprising is that many years later, Wiley changed his mind about the cause of the *Akron* and *Macon* crash. Speaking to Lt George Campbell (the junior officer he'd saved from drowning), Wiley is alleged to have said, 'You know George, the noises and behaviour of the two ships were almost identical when their fatal accidents happened. I am convinced that the same thing happened to the *Akron* as we know happened to the *Macon*.'[31]

It's important to note that this claim is controversial. We only have Rosendahl's second-hand account of the conversation presumably told to him by Campbell. Although it supports Erwin's contention that the *Akron* suffered a structural failure before hitting the water, no American court of law would accept it as evidence since it is hearsay. Still, it's intriguing that two of the Navy's most experienced airship captains, Rosendahl and Wiley, believed that the *Akron* and *Macon* crashed for the same reason: a catastrophic structural failure in frame 17.5.

So what caused the *Macon*'s fin to fail? Was it a side gust, a turn of the helm, or did it fail of its own accord either from metal fatigue, poor design or some combination of both? All four theories are credible, but it doesn't really matter. The bottom line is that frame 17.5 could not endure the type of aerodynamic loads the *Macon* encountered in flight. This left the area where the fins were anchored vulnerable to failure. Whether the casualty was caused by a side gust resulting in a sudden aerodynamic overload, metal fatigue or some combination can be endlessly debated. What's important is that the *Macon*'s design was at fault. Arnstein had been right all along.

THE CHAIN OF CAUSALITY

It may be impossible to know whether a side gust was responsible for the *Macon*'s casualty, but it is possible to draw a few conclusions about the cause. Like a lot of catastrophes, it wasn't a single event but a series of inter-related events that conspired to bring the airship down. As Arnstein noted in an address given just four months before the *Macon* crashed, 'The history of airships has shown that when disasters have occurred there has ... been some combination of circumstances ... which has magnified a series of minor failures into a major catastrophe.'[32]

When the top half of frame 17.5 failed, its upper fin tore away, puncturing three of the *Macon*'s twelve gas cells. This resulted in a critical loss of helium in her stern. Wiley tried compensating for the loss but dropped too much ballast too quickly.* This caused the *Macon* to ascend above pressure height, where she vented so much helium that gravity took over. This was the chain of causality.

---

* As Bolster told Fulton, 'We may have dropped weight faster than helium was lost.' Despite Bolster's soft pedalling, this is exactly what happened.

But these were not the only links in the chain. It's clear Arnstein did not make the correct assumptions when calculating the degree of aerodynamic loads the *Macon*'s fins would encounter in flight. Arnstein was hampered by the limits of stress analysis at the time, but he knew in his gut the *Macon*'s fins were insufficiently anchored. Although he did everything in his power to try and persuade Fulton to reinforce frame 17.5, including adding cable bracing to the fins, Arnstein was stonewalled every step of the way – another important link in the chain of causality.

Wiley's decision to stretch out repairs for frame 17.5 is also an important link. Had he reinforced the frame in a timely manner the *Macon* might not have crashed. Having said this, Wiley's delay in making repairs is understandable. First and foremost, he wanted to keep his airship flying to prove her an effective ocean-going scout in a Navy dead set against her. Nevertheless, his delaying of repairs contributed to her demise.

Additionally, had Wiley conducted a weigh off after the casualty occurred he might not have lost control of his airship.[33] A weigh off was standard procedure in such circumstances. His failure to follow protocol is another important link in the chain.

Again, Wiley's decision is understandable. Once he knew three of the *Macon*'s gas cells were deflating she was unlikely to stay aloft. As Lt Mayer later acknowledged, 'It is natural for one to drop ballast immediately … when acting under such conditions.'[34]

Obviously, Wiley wanted to avoid another *Akron* disaster, but that shouldn't obscure the fact that he overcompensated by dropping too much ballast too quickly. Wiley's actions may have been lauded for saving the majority of his crew, but it's possible two of his men would not have died had he conducted a weigh off, trimmed his airship and limped home. He either felt the situation so dire he had no choice but to drop ballast without conducting a weigh off, or he panicked. For this reason, as well as for taking more than eight months to complete the reinforcements to frame 17.5, Wiley bears responsibility for the *Macon*'s loss.

Of course, Arnstein is also guilty. It was his deep ring design that didn't prove strong enough to anchor the *Macon*'s tail fins. Twice frame 17.5 failed due to excessive aerodynamic loading, proof the *Macon* suffered a serious design flaw. Unfortunately, Arnstein's pleas to fix the problem fell on deaf ears, but that doesn't absolve him of blame.

The sad truth is, you can be an 'expert' in something and still encounter a problem so advanced that it's beyond your ability to solve. Much was unknown about the science of stress analysis when the *Macon* was designed. No one, not even Arnstein, had a complete understanding of the aerodynamic forces she might encounter in flight. Furthermore, Navy operating practices were such (flying heavy through turbulent air with all eight engines running at standard speed) they exacerbated the strain. Add to this excessive vibration in the stern and an inability to detect microscopic cracks in Duralumin girders, and Moffett's 'state-of-the-art' big rigids were asking for trouble. Arnstein knew there was a problem, however, and though he tried to fix it, was unable to persuade the Navy to follow his advice. For this, he too shares blame for the loss of the *Macon*.

Litchfield is also guilty since he ordered Arnstein to stop bugging Fulton about reinforcing frame 17.5. Even Litchfield admitted ten years later that the *Macon* 'should have been grounded' for repairs.[35] Hence, he, too, is culpable for her loss.

Wiley, Arnstein and Litchfield are not alone in sharing the blame, however. Fulton, who frustrated Arnstein's many attempts to reinforce frame 17.5, is also responsible, but the Navy Court of Inquiry didn't see it this way. It not only refused to assign blame, it more or less attributed the *Macon's* destruction to an act of God – as sure a way as any to avoid responsibility.

What the *Macon* crash really comes down to is Goodyear having had responsibility for designing the *Macon*, but none of the authority in ensuring its design (or the changes necessary to ensure its safety) was carried out. That was the Navy's responsibility. It made more sense for the Navy Court of Inquiry to dispense with the whole embarrassing affair than delve too deeply since both Goodyear and the Navy were to blame. By refusing to attribute the loss of the *Macon* to mistakes made by either party, the court absolved everyone involved.

On a positive note, the *Macon* benefitted from one important lesson learned from the *Akron* crash. She carried lifebelts. If she hadn't, more of the *Macon's* crew would have died since many couldn't swim. Having said this, the *Macon* could have done with more life rafts. As fate would have it, she was lucky to have the fleet nearby.

COULD THE *MACON* HAVE BEEN SAVED?

Five months after the *Macon* crash C.P. Burgess noted, 'It seems entirely reasonable to accept the … strength of the *Akron* and *Macon* as adequate with the reservation that adequate does not mean fool proof.'[36]

Clearly, the design of the *Akron* and *Macon* was far from foolproof, but the question remains: could the *Macon* have been saved had Wiley acted differently?

Aviation Chief Machinist's Mate Charles S. 'Chick' Solar, who'd been aboard the airship when she crashed, thought so. 'I personally feel that when the damage was first discovered if orders had been given to tilt the propellers of engines numbered 3, 4, 5, and 6 we could have flown to Moffett Field.'[37]

Solar was no expert, but Lt Mayer, who was, also thought the *Macon* could have been saved. Noting, 'It must be concluded that the ship did not lose the total amount of gas which it was, at first, thought that she did,'[38] Mayer told Fulton, 'had valving … begun forward, instead of dropping so much weight aft' the *Macon* could have 'regain[ed] the ship's normal attitude'.[39] This is why the first thing Wiley should have done after the casualty was to conduct a weigh off. Had he done so, he would have had a much better idea of how much ballast to drop, or gas to valve. Instead, his precipitous actions contributed to the loss of the airship rather than prevented it.

But not everybody believed the *Macon* was salvageable.

John Lust, a *Macon* crewman who was not aboard the ship the day it crashed, said flying her back to Moffett Field was 'a lot of baloney':

> As the fin broke off on the *Macon* a bunch of the gas cells were punctured. That made dead weight … Naturally, there's no helium in the stern end, so that kept breaking more girders as you went forward then the next cell would go and then the next. That's why they had to dump all of that ballast … The entire unsupported [stern] section was crumpling the rest of the frames … Like dominos.[40]

It's possible the *Macon* could have been saved if Wiley had conducted a weigh off, but given that three of her twelve gas cells had ruptured, it is unlikely. Having said this, there's no denying Wiley pulled a rabbit out of his hat when he gently set the *Macon* down on the Pacific. This accomplishment, given his airship was literally coming apart at the seams, was nothing less than extraordinary. For this, as well as showing the *Macon* was an effective long-range scout, he deserves to be called a giant.

Reasonable people can disagree over what caused the *Macon* to crash as well as whether or not she could have been saved. Some feel it was the loss of her fin that led to her demise, while others blame Wiley's response. The debate continues today. One thing reasonable people can agree on is that the Navy Court of Inquiry either glossed over or outright ignored these issues.

The Navy was acutely sensitive to the *Akron*'s high death toll. This explains why the court focused on Wiley's lifesaving efforts rather than questioning his judgment. It also explains why Wiley not only received his promotion but a letter of commendation. Had the Navy been determined to build another generation of big rigids it might not have let Wiley off so easily. As it was, it celebrated him as a hero. Under the circumstances, it was the expedient thing to do.

When it came to Fulton, the Navy circled its wagons. As Dr Theodore von Kármán, Director of California's Guggenheim Aeronautical Laboratory, told Arnstein, the *Macon* crash jeopardised Fulton's naval career.[41] Since Fulton was the BUAER's LTA design expert, he was indispensable, so the Navy shielded him from any consequences. And so, as far as the Navy was concerned, no one was responsible for the loss of the *Macon*. Arnstein, Litchfield, Wiley and Fulton got off scot free. As for Moffett, he'd already paid the ultimate price.

Regardless of whether one believes that fin failure caused the *Macon* to crash, or it was Wiley's precipitous actions, it's fair to say the Navy's ambitions for the *Macon* far exceeded her engineering. As talented and determined as Goodyear and the Navy were, they just couldn't build a big rigid robust enough to survive real-world circumstances.

As things turned out, neither could the Germans.

39

AFTERMATH

After the *Macon* crash the Navy's rigid airship programme appeared dead in the water, but looks can be deceiving. Litchfield refused to give up, continuing to lobby aggressively. The problem for Goodyear-Zeppelin was that there was very little money coming in after the *Macon*. Arnstein tried diversifying its product line. In 1935, he designed the *Comet*, a streamlined passenger train for the New York, New Haven and Hartford Railroad. But only one was built, so it wasn't successful.

With zero demand for big rigids, and the Depression tightening the nation's belt, Litchfield began laying off Goodyear-Zeppelin personnel. The company went from a peak of 800 employees down to ten.[1] The future of the American big rigid was never more tenuous.

Wiley, for one, was not ready to give up. Three months after the *Macon* was lost he authored a 230-page paper titled *USS Macon: Doctrines & Policies for Operation and Upkeep*.[2] The problem was there was no big rigid to which to apply it. In the meantime, he awaited reassignment.

Admiral King, like Litchfield, continued lobbying for rigid airships. He not only sought to replace the *Macon* but also the *Los Angeles*. However, Roosevelt's administration was deaf to his pleas. Secretary Swanson told the *New York Times* that he was prepared to resist any effort of Congress to appropriate money to build a ship to replace the *Macon*.[3]

In an artful bit of bureaucratic manoeuvring, Swanson announced a committee to study the future of the American airship. Forming a committee to study a problem was an age-old Washington trick to look like you're doing something when you'd prefer not to. Headed by Dr William F. Durand, a retired professor of naval engineering, the eight-man Durand Committee was a distinguished group of engineers. Drawn from academia and the private sector, it included Dr Theodore von Kármán, a leading aerospace figure of the day; Dr William Hovgaard, professor of naval design at MIT; and two members from the private sector: Frank B. Jewett, President of Bell Telephone Laboratories; and Charles F. Kettering, head of General Motors' research division.

The Durand Committee took its work seriously. It not only reviewed Wiley's written account of the *Macon* crash but transcripts from the Court of Inquiry.[4] Its members also travelled to NAS Sunnyvale to interview the *Macon* crew.

In July 1935, committee representatives attended a forum at the Guggenheim Lighter-Than-Air Institute in Akron, Ohio. The gathering read like a *Who's Who* of airship experts. It not only included Dr Durand and Dr von Kármán but Admiral King, Commanders Fulton and Rosendahl, and Arnstein, Burgess and Hunsaker. Even Carl Fritsche of metal-clad airship fame attended the meeting.

A brouhaha broke out during the conference when one of the Durand Committee members, Professor A.V. de Forest, told the gathering, 'The navy's refusal to permit reinforcement of the *Macon*'s ship structure at the vital point at which it gave way, was responsible for the crash.'[5] De Forest, an expert in metallurgy from MIT, blamed the 'obstinacy of certain navy officials who minimized the importance of putting on reinforcements',[6] adding, 'Dr. Karl Arnstein … repeatedly begged the Navy to allow him to strengthen the structure of that ship … [but] the navy refused … even after it was notified about it.'[7]

Bradley Jones, a professor of aerodynamics at the University of Cincinnati, agreed with de Forest saying, 'There has been too much of this hush–hush policy. Goodyear officials have been afraid to talk because the Navy is its best customer.'[8]

These were bombshell accusations, to which Arnstein's response inadvertently lent credence. 'Don't for heaven's sake, run down the navy!' Arnstein replied. 'Navy men are my best friends.'[9]

Swanson contacted Durand in a veiled attempt to muzzle de Forest,[10] but the Secretary of the Navy had no choice. He was forced to order an inquiry into the charges.[11] Predictably, nothing came of it.

Swanson may have hoped the airship issue would die a quiet death, but what he didn't count on was the Durand Committee endorsing the construction and operation of rigid airships both by the Navy and commercial sector. In a series of three reports, the first issued in January 1936, the committee said it could see no reason why airships as large, or larger, than the *Macon* could not be built:

> It is our recommendation that the Navy Department should continue with a positive, carefully considered program of airship construction including non-rigid and rigid ships of small or moderate size ... extending to a ship or ships of larger size.[12]

The Durand Committee specifically recommended the Navy build a training airship as a 'flying laboratory' to gain operational experience. The committee also recommended commercial airships be developed for passenger transport, even though aeroplane advances were rendering the airship obsolete.

The Durand Committee issued its final report in January 1937. Titled 'The Technical Aspects of the Loss of the *Macon*', the report focused on what had caused her catastrophic failure. Subscribing to the gust theory, even though it didn't credit the gust as particularly strong, the report made it clear that Arnstein had underestimated the aerodynamic loads the *Macon* would encounter in flight. Then it gave him a pass:

> It is of course true that in a structure so complex and with such a degree of redundancy as is found in airship framing, no method of mathematical analysis can give a complete account of the stress condition which may result from an assumed applied load.[13]

But Arnstein wasn't the only one to be handed a 'get out of jail free' card. The committee gave rigid airships one as well:

> We are firmly of the opinion that the lessons which are available from the experience with the *Macon* will furnish an abundant safeguard against any repetition of failure similar in character.[14]

This remarkable conclusion must have pleased Litchfield and Arnstein given everything they'd been through. Litchfield was quick to jump on the report's bandwagon, telling the *New York Times*, 'with this assurance from the scientists that airships can be safely built and operated, the government should take up the challenge and seek leadership ... in this field rather than sit back and leave [it] to other nations'.[15]

The Navy's policy committee, encouraged by Wiley's performance with the *Macon*, also recommended the Navy continue building and operating big rigids.[16] This encouraged Admiral King to develop an ambitious, five-year plan to build a training airship to replace the *Los Angeles*, two ZRS-type big rigids to replace the *Akron* and *Macon*, and another metal-clad, this one seven times bigger than the Navy's ZMC-2. But the $17 million price tag during the Depression ensured King's proposal was dead on arrival.[17]

This wasn't quite the end of the American rigid airship, however. In 1936, a series of design studies were undertaken by Goodyear for the Navy resulting in the ZRCV, a $10 million, 897ft-long big rigid with a gas volume of 9.5 million cu ft. The ZRCV was so large because she was intended to carry nine bombers.[18] Rather than pitch Congress on another scouting airship, the BUAER positioned the ZRCV as an offensive weapon akin to an aircraft carrier. Goodyear pushed the design as late as 1944, including print advertisements that asked the question, 'Will tomorrow's aircraft carriers FLY?' But nothing came of it.

Clearly, Litchfield wasn't giving up. Thanks to the lobbying efforts of Commander Rosendahl, who may have been lower in rank than Moffett but was no less persuasive, Congress authorised a new big rigid for training purposes in 1938. The $3 million ZRN was less than half the gas volume of the *Macon*, limiting its carrying capacity to two aeroplanes, but it put the Navy back in the game.

The good news didn't last, however. The House initially struck down the $3 million appropriation. Additionally, Admiral William D. Leahy, Chief of Naval Operations, told President Roosevelt that he did not believe the 'value of lighter than air ships for naval purposes justify … the expenditure of $3 million'.[19] Leahy wanted the money spent on battleships to counter the increasing strength of the Japanese Imperial Navy. Roosevelt concurred, saying, 'I made it perfectly clear, and have done so for two years, that I do not approve the construction of another large rigid airship for the Navy.'[20]

Admiral King was gone from the BUAER by then, replaced by Rear Admiral Arthur B. Cook. Cook, like Leahy, was a member of the Navy's 'big gun' club, which opposed airships. To be fair, Cook advocated government funding to build commercial airships that the Navy could then operate in times of war, but he opposed spending Navy money on big rigids, choosing to buy more aeroplanes instead.[21]

However, Litchfield continued lobbying Roosevelt to build big rigids. In a June 1939 letter on White House stationery Roosevelt's naval aide, Captain D.J. Callaghan, wrote to Litchfield:

I understand that you have recently held a conference with the President regarding the matter of airship design for the Navy. As a result of your conference I have been instructed to contact you and ascertain what your company now has to offer in the line of development for an airship which will meet the Navy's requirements.[22]

Roosevelt had grown wary of Litchfield's tactics, however. Ignoring the advice of the Navy's General Board, the President warned the public that pressure for a new rigid airship programme came 'from a very powerful lobby conducted by the rubber company which is seeking to salvage fairly heavy speculative investment'.[23] Neither the ZRCV or ZRN were built.

The *Los Angeles* was scrapped in 1940 for the paltry sum of $3,700.[24] Still, LTA advocates fought to be heard. Frank Knox, Swanson's replacement as Secretary of the Navy, endorsed building 'rigid airships as necessary to explore … their usefulness for naval purposes and to co-operate with other agencies in development of commercial airships'.[25] That same year Litchfield even succeeded in reintroducing a revised version of the McNary-Crosser bill, still hoping to get airmail contracts for American-flagged airships. However, with the Second World War on the doorstep, no one was listening.

Litchfield never stopped promoting big rigids for military and commercial use, but heavier-than-air's rapid progress put an end to his dream. In 1935, Pan Am's Clipper planes began transporting up to thirty passengers from California to Manila as part of a regularly scheduled air service. A year later, the Consolidated PBY flying boat assumed the *Macon's* scouting function, patrolling vast areas of the Pacific. There was no need for rigid airships to provide a similar service when aeroplanes could do it faster and cheaper. By 1936, the big rigid was obsolete.

America never did build another big rigid after the *Macon*. They were too expensive, unproven and problem-prone. True, surface fleet officers contrived to strangle the rigid airship in her cradle. The 'big gun' club not only deprived them of funding; they sent them on promotional flights and fleet exercises ill-suited to their strengths. On top of that, rigid airships had to compete with the surface fleet for scare funding during the Depression. It didn't help that aeroplanes bred like rabbits, while an airship's gestation period was akin to an elephant. After Moffett died, and King left the BUAER, the most powerful voices in favour of big rigids were silenced, leaving only Rosendahl, a mid-ranking officer, to argue the case.

If the Navy had gained more operational experience with the *Macon,* it might have delayed cancelling the programme, but replacing rigid airships with aeroplanes was inevitable. The *Akron* and *Macon* cost $8 million to build, compared with $20 million for a heavy cruiser. But $8 million could buy a lot of planes in 1935. Given the impending war with Japan, it was more important for the Navy to buy surface ships and aeroplanes than a problem-plagued fleet of airships. Even though Wiley managed to overcome many of these obstacles, the clock ran out when the *Macon* crashed. If aeroplanes hadn't made rigid airships obsolete, radar most certainly would have.

When the *Hindenburg* exploded over Lakehurst, New Jersey, in May 1937, the Navy's big rigid programme had been dead for two years. But it wasn't the crash of the *Hindenburg,* captured so dramatically on film for the world to see, that spelled an end to the American rigid airship.* It was the loss of the *Macon* two years earlier. Even though Germany had a *Hindenburg* replacement waiting in the wings, America had lost interest.

The last of her kind, the *Akron* and *Macon* were the end of an era. Their twenty-two-month operational window was not long enough to overcome their flagging reputation. When the Goodyear-Zeppelin Corporation was liquidated on 16 December 1940, it guaranteed Goodyear would never build a big rigid again.[26]

After the *Macon* crash Arnstein admitted, 'We now know pretty well how to design a rigid airship, but we did not before the *Macon.*'[27] As true as these words may be, it was too late to do anything about them. After 12 February 1935, 'pretty well' just wouldn't cut it.

★   It's important to note that the U.S. government was indirectly responsible for the *Hindenburg* crash. Since helium was considered a strategic resource, the Federal government refused to sell it to Germany. As a result, the *Hindenburg,* although originally designed to be filled with helium, had to rely on highly flammable hydrogen instead. The rest is history.

40

A GIANT IS FOUND

Marie Wiley, the daughter of Lt Cdr Wiley, was having lunch at Jeanne B's restaurant in 1989 when she noticed something unusual on the wall. Jeanne B's, located 20 miles north of Monterey, was favoured by the rough and tumble fishermen operating out of the commercial port of Moss Landing. It wasn't the kind of place Marie usually frequented, but the retired school teacher from Livermore, California, was hungry, so she'd stopped for a bite. What happened next made her serendipitous detour all the more surprising.

The object Marie noticed on the restaurant's wall was a 2ft section of Duralumin girder mounted on a wooden plaque. The punch-pressed holes with flanged edges were unmistakable.

'I recognised it immediately,' Marie recalled. 'I had walked among girders like that when I was a child. There was no question where it came from – my father's ship, the *Macon*.'[1]

It had been more than fifty years since the *Macon* had sunk. The general area of where she crashed was known, but since she'd floated awhile subject to the vagaries of wind, current and tide, her final resting place was a mystery. Although pieces of the *Macon* had washed up on shore, previous efforts to find her had failed.[2] The ocean was not only deep where she'd gone down but riddled with underwater canyons in which she could hide. Finding her would not be easy.

The first expedition to search for the *Macon* took place the year before Marie spotted the girder on Jeanne B's wall. Two amateur researchers, Ken Garner and Bill Walker, approached Steve Koepenick at the Port Hueneme naval base about finding the airship. The two sleuths had scoured naval records to develop a 2 by 3 mile search grid in which they thought the *Macon* might lie. A joint expedition was arranged using a side-scan sonar array from the Navy and a Remotely Operated Vehicle (ROV) from Monterey-based Western Instruments. Chris Grech, a contract ROV pilot, also joined the expedition.

Using side-scan sonar towed by the M/V *Independence*, Koepenick, Smith and Grech began 'mowing the lawn', but two-thirds of the way through the survey their sonar array collided with an underwater obstacle and was lost. However, the expedition wasn't a total bust. It proved the airship wasn't where the Navy thought it had sunk. Additionally, several sonar images looked like they could be debris from the wreck.[3]

Grech, the ROV pilot, had known virtually nothing about the *Macon* before being hired for the search. The more he learned, however, the more he became intrigued. When he joined the Monterey Bay Aquarium Research Institute (MBARI) later that year, he realised the non-profit organisation had just the right kind of sophisticated technology to search for the *Macon*.

Grech pitched MBARI about looking for the airship, but his idea was turned down. 'They're not in the treasure hunting business,' Grech explained. 'They're in the research business. It's a different mentality. They're not buccaneers.'[4]

But that didn't end the search for the *Macon*. At the same time Grech was pitching MBARI, Richard Sands, a retired naval aviator, approached David Packard about finding the wreck site. Packard had long held an interest in marine biology. The retired founder of Hewlett-Packard, he'd not only helped bankroll the Monterey Bay Aquarium but MBARI, its research arm. Furthermore, while attending Stanford in 1934, Packard had watched the *Macon* sail overhead. After Sands brought the idea to Packard's attention, Packard went to MBARI asking, 'Why don't we do this?'[5] Shortly thereafter, the *Macon* Expeditionary Group was formed.

Composed of Packard; Sands; Koepenick; Grech; Robert Rasmussen, Director of the National Naval Aviation Museum in Pensacola, Florida; and Marie Wiley's brother, Gordon, the *Macon* Expeditionary Group marked the second attempt to find the airship's wreck site. No one was quite sure where to look for it, though. Grech's solution was to investigate the targets the first search had identified, and so an expedition was planned for May 1989 using MBARI's boat, the *Point Lobos*, and its ROV, the *Ventana*.

Grech warned MBARI's management that finding the wreck 'was a long shot'.[6] It would be especially difficult since the *Point Lobos* was a day boat, leaving them only a few hours to conduct the survey before having to return to Monterey. Grech was also concerned that accommodation aboard the ship would be too spartan, and the ocean too rough, for Dave

Packard, who at age 77 walked with a cane. But it was impossible to tell the man funding the expedition he couldn't go. Nor could they turn away the numerous VIPs Packard invited to make the trip, so Grech was told to 'manage their expectations'.[7]

The 110ft-long *Point Lobos* was packed to capacity during the five-hour trip to the *Macon*'s crash site off Big Sur. Packard, naturally impatient, wanted to know forty minutes after the *Ventana* was dropped in the water whether they'd found the wreck.

The second expedition turned out to be a bust. Grech covered all the targets, but the *Macon* was nowhere to be found. If that wasn't disappointing, things took a turn for the worse when the *Point Lobos* accidentally ran over its ROV tether, wrapping it around the propeller. The boat's engine had to be shut down and a man in scuba gear put over the side to untangle the mess. Next, the boat's transmission broke, disabling the vessel. What was supposed to be a fun outing for Packard and his guests quickly devolved into MBARI's most notorious mission.

It had been a long day and Packard was tired. Since no one knew how many hours it would take to make repairs, Packard kept eyeing his beachfront home only a few miles away on the Big Sur coast.

'Just set me down over there,' he said, pointing to his house.[8]

The sea was too rough for a shore landing, which made Packard unhappy. That's when he hailed a commercial fishing boat working nearby. Telling the vessel's captain he'd pay to be transported to Monterey, Packard was told the trawler wasn't a taxi.

Some aboard the *Point Lobos* thought Packard might buy the fishing boat on the spot. Instead, Packard paid the boat's captain $1,500 to take him and his friends to Monterey. After that, MBARI was gun shy about doing any more searches for the *Macon*.

Grech was determined to find the airship's final resting place despite the second expedition's failure. He knew the best way to do this was to conduct a side-scan sonar survey to identify more targets, then return later with an ROV to investigate. But first he had to decide where to conduct the survey.

Grech's big break came when Marie Wiley recognised a piece of her father's airship on the wall at Jeanne B's. The *Macon* had made a strong impression on

Marie. She'd even hung the front page of the *San Francisco Chronicle* with the headline '*MACON* SUNK' in her home.[9]

After seeing the girder, Marie told her brother about the discovery. Gordon in turn shared the news with the *Macon* Expeditionary Group.[10] Grech thought the lead promising enough that he and Dick Sands decided to pay Jeanne B's a visit. If the piece was from the *Macon*, they hoped to learn where it was found. Sure enough, when they arrived at the restaurant the *Macon's* girder, corroded by sea water, hung on the wall.

Vincent Balestreri owned Jeanne B's along with his wife. A cranky character who'd worked on fishing boats as a cook, Balestreri was reluctant to answer Grech's questions. Commercial fishermen aren't known for their garrulousness; they prefer keeping their secrets rather than talking with strangers. As Grech recalls, 'They looked at us when we started asking where this piece came from like "who are you guys?"'[11]

Balestreri eventually divulged that a commercial fisherman named Stormy, who owned a boat named after a bug, had given him the girder. But Balestreri said he had no idea where Stormy was. Grech gave the story little credence, assuming they were being strung along.[12]

Grech refused to give up. Determined to find out if Stormy existed, he and Sands spent the next two months hanging around Moss Landing asking if anyone knew of a fisherman named Stormy with a boat named after a bug. Finally, they were told someone fitting that description had lunch every day in a restaurant across from Jeanne B's.

Stormy Harmon, a big, burly fisherman whose boat was named the *Hornet*, couldn't have been nicer. He told Grech he'd got the girder from his brother Freddy, who'd been given it by another commercial fisherman named David Canepa. Stormy gave Canepa's contact information to Grech. Now, all Grech had to do was contact Canepa and convince him to meet.

As luck would have it, Canepa was as co-operative as Stormy. Retired from commercial fishing, he told Grech he'd found the girder tangled in his net one morning after winching up a catch of black cod off Point Sur.[13]

'He'd lost a whole lot of rigging at [that] spot,' Sands recalled. 'He knew something was down there.'[14]

In fact, Canepa avoided the site for fear he'd lose his net. The eureka moment came when Canepa produced his logbook complete with LORAN co-ordinates pinpointing the spot where he'd found the girder.[15]

Within days of receiving Canepa's co-ordinates, Grech learned that the US Navy's deep-diving submersible, DSV *Sea Cliff*, was scheduled to conduct crew training in Monterey Bay. The *Sea Cliff* was sister to the *Alvin*, which found the *Titanic*. Capable of diving to 20,000ft, it was the ideal equipment for finding the *Macon*.

Grech contacted the commanding officer of the *Sea Cliff*'s support vessel, asking whether the Navy would be interested in searching for the airship. Fully expecting to be turned down, Grech was 'blown away' when the officer told him, 'Let's do it.'[16]

As it turned out, naval higher-ups knew all about efforts to find the *Macon*. The two amateur sleuths who inspired the first expedition had previously reached out to the Navy, as had Dick Sands. The requests hadn't got any traction because no one knew where to look. Now, armed with Canepa's co-ordinates, the Navy agreed to participate in a search, terming it 'training' for the *Sea Cliff*'s crew.

Grech felt conflicted, however. He knew MBARI could also lead the expedition, so he contacted Packard to ask for his blessing. When Packard told him, 'Go for it,' the third expedition to find the *Macon* was on.[17]

The *Sea Cliff*'s mother ship, M/V *Laney Chouest*, left port on 24 June 1990 to search for the *Macon*. Grech was nervous as the ship travelled south, as there was some speculation they were on a wild goose chase. Grech had already been 'snookered twice'.[18] Now, he worried Canepa's co-ordinates wouldn't hold up.

Using the retired fisherman's LORAN fix as 'X marks the spot', the *Laney Chouest* lowered the *Sea Cliff* over the stern. Inside, a three-man crew commanded by Lt Pat Scanlon watched through viewports made of thick Plexiglas as the submersible slowly descended.

Since it was a Navy training dive, Grech remained on the *Laney Chouest*. Given there was no video feed, he had to satisfy himself with listening in on the *Sea Cliff*'s voice communications, carried through an acoustic link to the mother ship.

Once on the bottom, the *Sea Cliff*'s crew used her long-range sonar to guide them to what everyone hoped would be the wreck site. It was a relatively shallow dive at 1,500ft, but sunlight has difficulty penetrating that deep, so the *Sea Cliff* switched on her powerful lights to pierce the darkness. In the absence of a visual, Grech had to imagine what was going on.

Within ten minutes of reaching the bottom, the *Sea Cliff*'s crew said they had something on sonar. As Grech listened in, his heart started pounding.

'I could tell from the sound of their voices they were excited,' he recalls.

As the *Sea Cliff* approached the target her crew was surprised to find four Sparrowhawks intact and sitting upright on the ocean floor. Despite the murkiness, there was no mistaking the planes' skyhooks, which stretched towards the surface waiting for something to grab.

The *Sea Cliff* located two debris fields during the five-hour dive. It also used its robotic arm to collect several artefacts, putting them in its metal basket for the return topside. But when the submersible accidentally snagged on part of the wreckage, the dive had to be scrubbed. After manoeuvring itself free, the *Sea Cliff* returned to the surface with a piece of the *Macon* wedged in her sled. Other than that she was fine.

'They were really jazzed when they came up,' Grech, who talked to the submersible crew, remembered. 'The best records were their personal accounts … They had video but it was … poor quality … They also had still cameras, but those pictures were also poor.'[19]

Using a fisherman's LORAN co-ordinates to find the *Macon* was not the traditional way of locating a wreck. 'It was a huge relief to find it,' Grech recalls. 'It finally got the monkey off our back.' Of note, the wreck was only 2 miles south of where the first expedition conducted its survey.[20]

Grech knew he wanted a more detailed survey of the wreck site. Fortunately, the *Sea Cliff*'s iconic image of a Sparrowhawk's arrester hook generated interest in a follow-up mission.[21]

Grech returned with an ROV the next year, the fifty-sixth anniversary of the *Macon*'s sinking. MBARI, no longer gun shy, led the fourth expedition. Packard watched the underwater survey on a video feed from the comfort of his living room, having learned his lesson. The survey revealed the *Macon*'s bow and mid-section were located in two distinct debris fields. Her tail section was nowhere to be found. It remains missing to this day.

The *Ventana*, MBARI's ROV, collected several artefacts from the wreck site. These included sections of Duralumin girder, beetleware dishes from the *Macon*'s galley and a skyhook, which went to the National Naval Aviation Museum in Pensacola, Florida.[22] There have been at least half a dozen expeditions to the *Macon* wreck site since then, sponsored by a variety of organisations including MBARI, National Geographic, the National Ocean and Atmospheric Administration (NOAA) and the Navy. There was even talk of a rogue expedition that planned on recovering one of the Sparrowhawks, hoping to display it in a purpose-built aquarium at Pensacola's National

Naval Aviation Museum. Since the *Macon* is a grave site, this unofficial undertaking was quickly nipped in the bud.*

The wreck resides in what has since been designated as the Monterey Bay National Marine Sanctuary, protecting it from salvagers. It's also been added to the National Register of Historic Places, reaffirming the *Macon*'s importance.

NOAA and MBARI returned to the *Macon* in September 2006 to test a new digital imaging technology. The author attended the week-long expedition, reporting on it for the *New York Times*. It was that indelible experience that led to the writing of this book.

The remains of what was once the world's largest aircraft rested on a sandy perch 1,450ft deep. It was fortunate the *Macon* didn't end up in one of the nearby marine canyons. If she had, she might never have been found. Amazingly, three of her four Sparrowhawks sat nestled together on the ocean bottom, and the bright yellow fabric on their wings (each with a white navy star in a circular blue field) stood out sharply against the ROV's powerful lights. The red objects swimming in a cockpit where Lt Miller once sat turned out to be rock cod. The 2ft-long fish circled the flight stick that Miller used to guide the plane, with its instrument panel as a backdrop. Meanwhile, a steady stream of marine debris illuminated by the ROV lights looked like falling snow.

As the ROV glided 20ft off the bottom, it sent images to its mother ship, the *Western Flyer*, on the surface. There, an ROV pilot with a joystick sat in a hi-tech cabin watching a video screen like he was playing a flight simulator game. One by one, the *Macon*'s silver mooring cone drawers from the navigator's table, an overturned metal chair, gas release valves, collapsed fuel tanks and massive Maybach engines appeared out of the green-tinged darkness.

Grech, now retired, says it's a little depressing how much the *Macon* has corroded over time. The airship's massive skeleton has long since flattened out and either been silted over, or eaten away. Sadly, the piece of the *Macon* that led to her discovery has also disappeared. Nobody knows what happened to the plaque after Jeanne B's closed. At one point Grech tried persuading

---

*   The *Macon*'s sole surviving Curtiss FPC-2 Sparrowhawk can be seen today at the Smithsonian National Air & Space Museum's Steven F. Udvar-Hazy Center in Chantilly, Virginia, where it's beautifully restored. A restored Consolidated N2Y-1 trainer, which was part of the USS *Akron* and *Macon*'s HTA squadron, can be found at the National Naval Aviation Museum in Pensacola, Florida. Both are worth a visit.

the Balestreris to donate it to a museum, but they wanted too much money. What matters most is not that the girder has disappeared, but that it led to the discovery of a giant that once ruled the sky. Without it, the *Macon* might still be missing.

EPILOGUE

After the *Macon* crashed, the Navy's LTA programme seemed destined for extinction. However, the Second World War proved a boon when the Navy finally stumbled upon a killer application for its blimps: conducting anti-submarine patrols along the coast. As a Goodyear ad in a 1942 magazine proclaimed, blimps 'Put the finger on U-boats!'

The military not only requisitioned Goodyear's blimps for anti-sub patrols and convoy duty; it also purchased 150 of them along with numerous barrage balloons. Sentries of the sea, Goodyear blimps became a familiar sight as they bobbed along the east coast searching for German U-boats, and the west coast looking for Japanese I-boats. The Second World War saved the programme's bacon.*

Whether rigid airships could have prevented Pearl Harbor is an intriguing question. The success of Admiral Nagumo's attack on the Pacific fleet depended on surprise. This was easier to achieve in the days before radar than it would be today. But as Rosendahl noted, 'Had Nagumo's force been sighted … by just one airship, or even by one plane from an airship, the attack on Pearl Harbor would not have come about.'[1] Litchfield concurred, saying, 'Two or three reconnaissance airships able to patrol the ocean from Alaska to Panama, might have prevented the tragedy of Pearl Harbor.'[2]

This is probably wishful thinking, but it is fair to say that a fleet of rigid airships patrolling Hawaii might have deterred Japan from attacking in the first

---

*   Not all Navy blimps fared well during the Second World War. The US Navy's K-74 was shot down by a German U-boat it was attempting to sink off of Florida in July 1943. In contrast, a Navy blimp had the honour of escorting the *U-858* when it surrendered off the New England coast in May 1945.

place, knowing their carriers could be sighted before reaching their target. As it happened, Japan was concerned enough about American airship activity that Nagumo sent a detachment of planes to destroy the mooring mast at Ewa.[3]

Litchfield, ever savvy about emerging markets, repositioned Goodyear's airship division before the war even started. In 1940, Goodyear-Zeppelin was reborn as the Goodyear Aircraft Corporation, focused on manufacturing aeroplane parts. Following Pearl Harbor, Goodyear Aircraft began building F4U Corsairs for the US Navy, becoming one of the nation's ten largest aircraft manufacturers.

But Litchfield wasn't satisfied with just building aeroplanes. In May 1942, he proposed a 10 million cu ft rigid airship for the Navy. The flying aircraft carrier would carry ten fighter bombers, which could be hung on the outside of its envelope for rapid deployment.[4] There was even discussion about using a rigid airship to attack Japan in much the same way Zeppelins bombed London during the First World War.[5] Nothing came of the idea, but a Goodyear-built blimp, the L-8, did deliver spare parts to Doolittle's raiders aboard the USS *Hornet* (CV-8) in April 1942.

Two years later, Goodyear Aircraft revived Litchfield's offer to build the ZRN training airship for the Navy along with a cargo-carrying big rigid with a helium capacity of 10 million cu ft.[6] If nothing else, it shows Litchfield remained committed to building big rigids even after the *Macon* crash.

Litchfield continued chumming the water for commercial airships, sponsoring a series of colourful print advertisements to stir up government interest. One such ad, appearing in leading magazines in 1945, depicted 'A day on board an airship'. The four-colour spread included illustrations showing an American husband and wife tucking their children into bed, an elaborately moustachioed English gentleman, a man wearing a turban and a young woman playing badminton. Litchfield was so determined to reignite interest in airship travel that he co-authored a book that same year with Hugh Allen, titled *Why Has America No Rigid Airships?*; neither the government, military nor private sector took the bait.

The Second World War revitalised Moffett's LTA programme, but once the war ended it was reasonable to expect the programme to wind down. Incredibly, it lasted another thirty years. The Cold War arms race had something to do with this. The Distant Early Warning (DEW) system designed to detect Russian bombers on their way to the United States with a nuclear payload needed an aerial platform that could hover in place while carrying a huge radar dish. Non-rigids turned out to be perfect for the job, resulting in eighteen N-class blimps entering service between 1952 and 1962.

Eleven times larger than the Goodyear blimp, the N-class series was enormous. Built by Goodyear and crewed by up to twenty-five men, the series culminated in the ZPG-3W, the biggest non-rigid airship ever built for the military at the time. The Arnstein-designed blimp remained on station for long periods, plugging radar gaps in the country's DEW line. But the crash of the ZPG-3W in 1960, killing eighteen of its twenty-one-man crew, contributed to the programme being shut down.

Proposals for commercial big rigids continued to be made throughout the 1950s. These included airships inspired by Eisenhower's 'Atoms for Peace' programme that were nuclear powered. Most of the designs were fanciful since the radiation hazard presented a significant obstacle. Not only was the shielding to protect the crew unrealistically heavy, any crash would have posed a serious safety hazard to the public.* Goodyear announced its own nuclear-powered airship in 1959, but it was mostly a fishing expedition to drum up customers.

PAUL W. LITCHFIELD

Litchfield never gave up pitching the benefits of an American airship – one reason the Goodyear blimps kept flying. But lighter-than-air flight takes up only fourteen pages in his memoir, which is surprising given how much effort he put into it.

Litchfield worked at Goodyear for fifty-eight years, growing the company beyond its core tyre business into plastics, electronics and nuclear energy. If anyone doubted the company was his life, Litchfield died six months after retiring in 1959.

Although he is little remembered today, there's a bronze statue of Litchfield on Goodyear Boulevard in Akron, Ohio. It shows him wearing a long overcoat and double-breasted suit with a roll of blueprints under his arm. A plaque on the pedestal lists his various titles at Goodyear as well as the epigraph, 'guided the company to world leadership in the rubber industry'. One might add the airship industry, too, even if it was only briefly.

---

* Unfortunately, that didn't stop the US military from conducting a test in 1957 in which it exposed several K-class blimps to nuclear attack (Operation Plumbbob) with predictable results.

GOODYEAR TIRE & RUBBER CO.

Of the six biggest tyre manufacturers in the United States, only Goodyear remains independent today. With 92,000 employees and $13 billion in annual sales, the company remains the largest tyre producer in the world. Goodyear got out of the airship-building business in 1987 when it sold its aerospace division to Loral. The company has had plenty of ups and downs since then, but has managed to outlast Firestone, Uniroyal, Goodrich, Armstrong and General Tire, all of which were sold to foreign competitors.

DR KARL ARNSTEIN

Arnstein had no trouble transferring his skills in stress analysis from airships to aeroplanes. When the Second World War broke out, he was in the fortunate position of being a naturalised American citizen, otherwise it's doubtful he'd have survived in Germany having been born a Jew. Still, Arnstein found himself in the unenviable position of building weapons to attack his former homeland, something fellow engineer, Werner von Braun, would also experience after the war ended. As America moved into the space age, Arnstein continued designing blimps for the Navy, which included the K, L, M and N-types.

Arnstein and Bertl remained happily married, raising a family in the Akron house they lived in for more than forty years.[7] When Arnstein retired from Goodyear's Aerospace division in 1957 he was Vice President in charge of engineering.

Just before retirement, Arnstein was honoured by the US Navy with its Distinguished Public Service Award for his contribution to its airship programme.[8] Always modest where his achievements were concerned, Arnstein noted, 'Naturally there were disappointments … One of the most glaring … was to find our original high hopes for … airships not fully obtainable.'[9] Arnstein continued to believe airships held a place in modern aviation, especially for sightseeing and luxury cruises. He died in 1974 at the ripe old age of 87.

ADMIRAL WILLIAM A. MOFFETT

Moffett had been dead for two years when the *Macon* crashed, but his contributions to naval aviation far outlived him. His use of aircraft carriers to integrate aeroplanes with the fleet not only transformed the US Navy into a modern fighting force but changed the face of naval warfare. Meanwhile, his wife Jeanette, who'd christened the *Macon*, never remarried, choosing to tend to her husband's legacy, instead. She died in 1958 at age 71 and is buried next to her husband in Arlington National Cemetery.

ADMIRAL ERNEST J. KING

After his stint as chief of the BUAER, Admiral King found himself shunted to the backwater of the Navy's Policy Board. The Second World War would revive his career. He was named Commander in Chief of the U.S. Fleet after Pearl Harbor, and Chief of Naval Operations in March 1942. Leaving active duty in 1945 as a five star Fleet Admiral, King died in 1956, aged 77.

COMMANDER GARLAND FULTON

Fulton, who'd been Admiral Moffett's right-hand man on LTA matters, continued working at the BUAER despite having no rigid airships to build. Instead, he focused on the Navy's blimp fleet.

Fulton took voluntary retirement from the Navy in 1940, ending his twenty-eight-year career, eighteen of which were spent on lighter-than-air flight. He kept in touch with his LTA colleagues after retiring, including Rosendahl (who became an admiral), George H. Mills (who became a commodore) and Jerome C. Hunsaker, who returned to MIT to teach aeronautical engineering. Surprisingly, Fulton also corresponded with Arnstein,[10] suggesting that whatever enmity existed between the two was eventually set aside.

Fulton died in 1974 aged 84 and is buried at Arlington National Cemetery. His personal papers are held at the National Air and Space Museum Archives in Virginia. He was never blamed for his role in the *Macon* crash.

COMMANDER ALGER H. DRESEL

The *Macon*'s former commanding officer was in charge of Moffett Field when the airship was lost. Disgusted by the politics of the LTA programme (which one Goodyear official likened to a 'clique' dominated by 'prima donnas'[11]), Dresel returned to the surface fleet. A heart condition invalided him out of the Navy in 1940. He died thirteen years later at age 64 and is buried at the Naval Academy Cemetery in Annapolis, Maryland, not far from his old boss, Admiral King.

COMMANDER CHARLES E. ROSENDAHL

Rosendahl was commander of NAS Lakehurst when the *Macon* crashed. He was still in command of the base when the *Hindenburg* burst into flames in 1937.

'Rosy's' career appeared to be on the wane until the Second World War provided ample opportunity to shine. When a Japanese torpedo blew the bow off the New Orleans-class cruiser he was commanding, Rosendahl's executive officer told him the ship would surely sink. 'Like hell!'[12] Rosendahl replied; a fitting response for the man who'd piloted the bow half of the *Shenandoah* to safety. Running the USS *Minneapolis* (CA-36) aground, Rosendahl and his crew eventually refloated the ship, sailing her to a safe port for repairs.

After distinguishing himself in battle, Rosendahl was promoted to rear admiral in 1943 and put in charge of Lakehurst's Naval Airship Training and Experimentation Command (NATEC). It was an ideal position for the LTA veteran. For the remainder of the war he oversaw approximately 200 pressure airships deployed on the Atlantic and Pacific coasts as well as in the Caribbean, South Atlantic and Mediterranean.[13]

Retiring from the Navy in 1946 at the rank of vice admiral, Rosendahl worked in the private sector for more than a decade before retiring in 1960 to Flag Point, his New Jersey estate. There, he entertained friends from his LTA days, including Fulton and Tex Settle.[14] Occasionally, a Navy blimp on its way to Lakehurst would tarry over Rosendahl's home – a tribute the irascible sky sailor surely enjoyed.

Rosendahl continued to be a vociferous (some might say annoying) advocate for airships well into his retirement. The author of three books and countless magazine articles, he tirelessly promoted lighter-than-air flight for the military and commercial markets. Shortly before he died in 1977, Rosendahl opined, 'It won't be many years before you have the return of the airship.'[15] As things turned out, he was overly optimistic.

After dying of natural causes at age 84, Rosendahl was posthumously inducted into the Hall of Honour at the National Museum of Naval Aviation in Pensacola, Florida. His personal papers can be found in the Vice Admiral Charles E. Rosendahl Lighter-than-Air Collection at the University of Texas' Eugene McDermott Library.

COMMANDER HERBERT V. WILEY

'Doc' Wiley remained on duty at NAS Sunnyvale for four months after the *Macon* crash, even though there were no rigid airships left for him to command. In June 1935, he was assigned to the heavy cruiser USS *Pensacola* (CA-24) as damage control officer. After commanding the world's largest, most expensive aircraft it must have seemed like a step down.

Wiley also remarried that year. Charlotte Mayfield Weeden was a socially prominent divorcée from Palo Alto, California. Nicknamed Blossom, she'd graduated from Stanford University before entering into a brief marriage with a local doctor. Wiley was famous enough that their union made newspapers as far afield as Baltimore.

In 1937, Wiley was put in command of the USS *Sirius* (AK-15), a creaky cargo ship built in 1919. He spent the next six months in the unglamorous task of towing a channel dredge from New York to Pearl Harbor.[16] Next, he was assigned to the United States Naval Academy as an instructor in the department of English, History and Government. None of the subjects were his strong suit. In February 1940, he returned to sea, serving as the executive officer of the USS *Mississippi* (BB-41), a Pacific Fleet battleship more to his liking.

The Second World War opened up a number of opportunities for Wiley. When Japan attacked Pearl Harbor, he was in the Pacific commanding Destroyer Squadron 29. Captaining the nearly obsolete USS *Black Hawk* (AD-9), he staged a daring attack that helped to slow Japan's invasion of Borneo. He also heavily damaged a Japanese convoy at the Battle of Makassar Strait during a night-time attack in January 1942.

Seven months later, Wiley was again posted to the US Naval Academy, this time as head of the Department of Electrical Engineering – a position for which he was better suited. Still, he must have found the administrative job frustrating with a war going on.

If there are any doubts as to whether Wiley was a giant, they were put to rest when he assumed command of the USS *West Virginia* (BB-48) in January 1944. The *Wee Vee*, as she was known, had been sunk during the attack on Pearl Harbor. She'd been refloated and retrofitted since then at a cost exceeding the Navy's entire LTA programme.[17] Wiley was 53 at the time but determined to make his mark. Participating in some of the fiercest naval battles of the Pacific war, Wiley and his crew supported the first landing of American troops in the Philippines in October 1944. That same month, the *Wee Vee* participated in the Battle of Surigao Strait, for which Wiley was awarded the Navy Cross. His citation reads:

For extraordinary heroism as … a brilliant and fearless leader, Captain
Wiley conducted a vigorous and unrelenting attack against the Japanese in
the face of intense opposition thereby rendering invaluable assistance in
sinking ten hostile combatant vessels including two of the enemy's most
powerful battleships.[18]

Wiley also commanded the *West Virginia* during the invasion of Iwo Jima,
winning him the Legion of Merit with Combat V, as well as participating
in the invasion of Okinawa. On the first day of the Okinawa landing, the
Wee Vee was hit by a kamikaze plane yet continued to fight. For his actions
during the Okinawa campaign, Wiley was awarded the Bronze Star Medal,
the citation reading:

Wiley skillfully maneuvered through dangerous navigational waters within
unusually close range of the island and with his vessel exposed to intense
fire and enemy shore guns, delivered prolonged and effective point blank,
counter battery fire against Japanese installations threatening our forces. A
brilliant and fearless leader, Wiley led his gallant ship in fighting off repeated
aerial attacks.[19]

What the citation doesn't mention is how Wiley 'sat on his perch' on the *West
Virginia*'s bridge during the battle, refusing to leave for more than eighteen
days.[20] According to his daughter, her father remained on the bridge not just
out of concern for his ship, but because he'd had a debilitating heart attack and
was afraid if he left the bridge he might not be able to return.[21]

Francis T. Kleber, a 20-year-old ensign aboard the *Wee Vee*, remembers Wiley
'was not the chatty type'; he was 'somewhat reserved'. But every time Kleber
made a verbal report to Wiley he felt as if 'I was standing next to God. He was
revered … by every man who served under him. I will not forget him.'[22]

Wiley did his best to shield his family from hearing about the depriva-
tions of war, which included frequent kamikaze attacks, severe food shortages
and heat so oppressive the walls of his cabin 'couldn't be touched'.[23] In
a September 1944 letter sent to Marie on her 14th birthday, Wiley makes no
mention of these hardships, but makes clear his love for his daughter:

This must be short just enough for you to know I am thinking of you on
your birthday. I wish I could have you aboard for dinner. I would have a swell
cake and have the orchestra play especially for you when it was brought in.
So, many many happy birthdays and much much love. Daddy.[24]

Wiley gave up command of the *West Virginia* in May 1945, returning to the United States for temporary duty with the Twelfth Naval District in San Francisco. It was around this time that Marie recalls going to the movies with her father and every man in the theatre standing up to salute him.

Wiley didn't remain stateside long. In February 1946 he was transferred to Guantanamo Bay, Cuba, to command its Naval Training Group, where he had another massive heart attack. Relieved of duty, he was transferred to the retired list in January 1947 after being advanced to the rank of rear admiral.

Wiley visited the Naval Department in Washington before retiring, where he enquired about the medals he'd been awarded. Reaching into his file, a secretary pulled out Wiley's Navy Cross, the second highest decoration for combat valour, and slid it across the desk to him. As Wiley was leaving, he ran into Admiral Chester W. Nimitz who asked, 'Why ... so sad, Doc?' When Wiley showed him the medal, Nimitz took it, saying to come back the next morning. During a hastily arranged ceremony, Nimitz personally pinned the medal on Wiley's chest.[25] It was the least he could do considering 'Doc's' thirty-one years of service.

After retiring from the Navy, Wiley was hired as a part-time assistant to the Dean of Engineering at the University of California, Berkeley. He and Blossom settled in San Francisco, where Wiley's heart condition was so severe he sometimes had trouble walking more than two blocks.[26] On top of that, his second marriage was an unhappy one. Blossom insisted on dragging her reticent husband to social events when he would have preferred to stay at home. Her increasing taste for alcohol, combined with Wiley's meagre retirement benefits, was a constant source of friction. The two finally separated in early 1954, when Wiley moved into a hotel.[27]

Wiley was on a business trip to Los Angeles in April that year when he died of a heart attack. Sixty-two years old, he was staying in Pasadena at the home of a long-time 'lady friend', raising a few eyebrows.[28] It might also explain why one newspaper reported him dying at home, while another said he collapsed at the Pasadena airport. Blossom was in the hospital at the time with a broken hip, possibly due to a fall caused by her drinking.

Wiley is buried in Golden Gate National Cemetery in San Mateo, California. He shares a headstone with his first wife, Marie. Their son, Gordon, is buried nearby, as is Blossom.

Until recently, Wiley has been an obscure naval figure. Rosendahl was so incensed by Wiley's meagre obituary in the *New York Times* he wrote a letter to the editor recounting his colleague's heroism. Fortunately, recent biographies by Wiley's grandson Ian Ross, and M. Ernest Marshall have helped revive interest in this complex man. Today, Wiley's copper wings can be found on the Famous Fliers' Wall at the Mission Inn in Riverside, California. Appearing alongside those of Charles Lindbergh and Amelia Earhart, he's in excellent company.

NAS SUNNYVALE

The Navy didn't have much use for NAS Sunnyvale after the *Macon* crashed. Seven months later, the airship base was swapped with the Army in exchange for some airfields, but the Second World War changed all that. The Army returned Moffett Field to the Navy in 1942, which based its K and L blimps there for coastal patrol.

Moffett Field continued as a military base for another forty-seven years, but the last Navy blimp was deflated at the base in 1947.[29] Shuttered as part of Congress's base closure act in 1994, Moffett Field languishes as a ghost town today, its streets largely deserted, including the two named after Dailey and Edquiba.

On any given day, tens of thousands of people drive by Hangar One, a skeleton now stripped of its asbestos-laden covering. Google has bought the structure, promising to refurbish it. Hard to miss from US Route 101, few people realise the hangar's original purpose, nor do they know who Admiral Moffett was.

NAS LAKEHURST

NAS Lakehurst was placed on restricted status after the *Macon* crash, its operating budget and personnel slashed to the bone. Although the base became the centre of Navy LTA operations during the First World War, it never again hosted another rigid airship after the *Hindenburg* disaster. When the war ended, the Navy's LTA programme continued at Lakehurst for another twenty years. The programme didn't end until its remaining LTA craft landed for the last time on 31 August 1962, twenty-seven years after the *Macon* crashed.[*,30]

Today the base is shared by the Army, Air Force and Navy, but like Moffett Field is a shadow of its former self. The enormous hangar once used to

---

[*] The US Navy occasionally experiments with LTA flight today but nowhere like it once did.

house the *Shenandoah*, *Los Angeles*, *Akron* and *Macon* still stands. Largely filled with memories, dust and pigeon droppings, it remains the largest structure for miles around.

BUAER

The Bureau of Aeronautics (BUAER) was eliminated in 1959 when the Navy merged it with the Bureau of Ordnance (BUORD) to form the Bureau of Naval Weapons (BUWEPS). Although the US Air Force has occasionally experimented with dropping and retrieving parasitic aircraft from mother ships, the Navy never again made hooking aeroplanes on to aircraft a regular part of its operations.

LUFTSCHIFBAU ZEPPELIN

The Second World War proved as much a boon to Luftschiffbau Zeppelin as it did for Goodyear. Although Arnstein's old firm had got out of the rigid airship business, it signed a contract with the Third Reich to produce rocket propellant tanks and fuselages for what would become the V-2 rocket.

Amazingly, the story comes full circle in 2011 when ZLT Zeppelin Luftschifftechnik GmbH, the modern offspring of Luftschiffbau Zeppelin, sold three semi-rigids to Goodyear, which assembled them at its Wingfoot Lake Airship Facility in Suffield, Ohio. Based on the German company's Zeppelin NT (New Technology) design, *Wingfoot One* was launched in 2014. Less than a third the length of the *Macon*, *Wingfoot One* is a 246ft-long semi-rigid containing 300,000 cu ft of helium. She and her sister airships, *Wingfoot Two* and *Three*, can be seen flying across the United States, providing television coverage for such events as the Daytona 500 and PGA Championship.

Neither Goodyear blimps nor Zeppelin NT airships have been problem free. A Zeppelin NT leased to DeBeers for diamond exploration was damaged beyond repair while moored to its mast by bad weather in 2007. Four years later, an American-built, Goodyear-branded blimp, *The Spirit of Safety*, caught fire over Germany, killing its pilot.

THE *MACON*'S LEGACY

Airships today have found their niche not in transporting wealthy passengers in luxury as Litchfield had imagined but as flying billboards. The business is distinctly unglamorous, but non-rigids continue to be built today by the American Blimp Corporation, the Worldwide Aeros Corporation, Lockheed Martin, Boeing and Northrop Grumman.

Every few years a start-up issues a press release announcing its design for a new, state-of-the-art airship. Various prototypes have been built but every project has experienced difficulty either with financing, flight tests or both. The problem remains the same for twenty-first-century airship designers as it was for Arnstein: they have more enthusiasm than paying customers. Litchfield would have sympathised.

It's a conundrum that rigid airships suffered far fewer fatal crashes than aeroplanes, yet neither the government, military nor private sector have much of a stomach for them. The truth is, far more people die in automobile accidents on Memorial Day weekend than ever died on an airship, but their reputation lies in tatters.[*]

So what strangled the American airship in its cradle? It wasn't the loss of the *Hindenburg*; the American airship was already dead by then. What killed the American airship is easy: after the *Macon* crash the market for them dried up. If that should change, large-scale airships will return. Until then, it's just wishful thinking.

Sceptics point out that had the McNary-Crosser bill passed in 1933 Litchfield's commercial airships would have only lasted a few years before being surpassed by the aeroplane. This is probably true, but Pan American's transpacific clipper service began in 1935 only lasted seven years. After that, a new generation of aircraft rendered it obsolete.

For perspective, all forms of transportation have a limited lifetime, but that's no reason to dismiss them. The golden age of passenger ships was relatively short but greatly admired. The horse may have lasted longest as transportation, but hardly anyone uses them as such anymore. One thing is certain. The point will come when aeroplanes and automobiles will seem every bit as antiquated as LTA flight. Who are we to say they had no value?

---

[*]   At the time of the *Macon* crash both the Associated Press and *Popular Science Monthly* estimated that 350 people died in airship crashes between 1913 and 1935. Later reports place the figure closer to 600. By comparison, 550 people die in vehicle accidents in the US every Memorial Day weekend, while approximately 4,000 people died in aeroplane crashes prior to the First World War.

The loss of the *Macon* marked the end of the American big rigid, yet she offers some important lessons. The passion Moffett, Litchfield, Arnstein and Wiley brought to a white elephant technology can serve as inspiration or a caution, but the question that most bears asking is whether it was worth the effort?

What few people realise is that most commercial ventures end in failure. Roughly 80 per cent of all new books, movies, music and videogames, not to mention more prosaic items such as new grocery products, never earn a profit. In other words, more commercial ventures fail than succeed. The odds are even worse for new inventions. As proof, approximately 90 per cent of all US patents never earn a dime.

Few new technologies work as planned, especially during their early days. The greater the paradigm shift, the steeper the learning curve. Yet no one knows for sure whether an invention will succeed until it's built. Sometimes, the only difference between success and failure is time, money and patience. That an invention takes longer to work out its bugs than planned only increases our impatience. Put another way, not every hole we dig is going to strike oil, but none will if we cease to drill.

It's often said we learn more from failure than success. Unfortunately, failure has a stigma. That's too bad. There's no shame in failing. If a man's reach should exceed his grasp then no one should be surprised at the outcome. But that doesn't mean we should stop striving. Where would we be if Magellan hadn't searched for a better trade route, or we'd never voyaged to the Moon? The world would be a lesser place. Moffett, Litchfield, Arnstein and Wiley may never have realised their dream, but they were better men for trying. So are we.

Sometimes, history is smug in its conclusions. What is often overlooked is the tremendous passion, courage and determination that goes into so many unsuccessful ventures. In many respects, failure is the purest expression of the human condition, but that's no reason to despair. There's beauty in failure if one only knows where to look.

For a brief time the rigid airship was an integral part of the American culture – proof that a better future lay just around the corner. The *Macon* operated for only twenty-three months, the *Akron* for twenty. Initially viewed as a disruptive technology, they succeeded in disrupting only themselves. The silver-skinned giants may never have fulfilled their promise, but they're still worth celebrating. After all, it's the drive to make things better that lies at the heart of human progress. Where would we be without it?

ACKNOWLEDGEMENTS

When I first undertook this project I heard the story that a well-regarded airship historian told a librarian that he'd 'skimmed all the cream' from the Goodyear archives, implying there'd be very little left for future airship historians to uncover. Needless to say this anecdote worried me. After fourteen years of research I am pleased to report he was mistaken; plenty of 'cream' is still left. For that I am grateful.

A book like this may be written alone but never without help. First and foremost, I am indebted to the airship historians who came before me, especially Richard K. Smith, whose book, *The Airships Akron & Macon*, I consider to be a well-balanced take on the subject. Smith and others may have been first to milk this cow, but we benefit from their efforts.

Thanks must also go to those who read and commented on earlier versions of my manuscript. Special praise goes to William Althoff; Juli Cortino; Thomas Crouch; C.P. Hall, II; Emil Petrinic; Alastair Reid; and Rick Zitarosa. I also want to thank the Mill Valley Library's Writers Drop-In Group for suffering through an early version, with a special nod to Kate Moore for her consistently superb insights and encouragement.

I also appreciate those who agreed to share their precious time and recollections with me, especially Marie Wiley Ross and Ian Ross. Mother and son provided invaluable insights into their father and grandfather, respectively. Chris Grech, the former Deputy Director of Marine Operations at the Monterey Bay Research Aquarium Institute (MBARI) was indispensable in recounting previous attempts to find the *Macon*, while Frederick 'Fritz' Trapnell shared important research about his father, the Sparrowhawk pilot, Lt Frederick M. 'Trap' Trapnell. I also appreciate Barry and Blaine Miller, the sons of Sparrowhawk Squadron Leader Harold B. Miller, for providing copies of their father's letters describing what it was like to serve in the *Macon*'s HTA unit. Ben Travis, who flew a Zeppelin NT semi-rigid for Airship Ventures, was also helpful in describing what it's like to pilot an airship, while Rachel Loya was kind enough to arrange the meeting. Sadly, Airship Ventures is no longer in business, but believe me when I say it was a thrill to watch its semi-rigid take off and land at Moffett Field just like the *Macon*.

I also want to thank my airship experts whose counsel proved invaluable. At the top of the list is Emil Petrinic. Emil not only illustrated the USS *Macon* diagrams in this book but spent countless hours discussing the ins and outs of airship history with me, including sharing his treasure trove of research. Put simply, Emil is my kind of rivet counter: honest, unselfish and incredibly thorough. Additionally, Alastair Reid and Eric Brothers provided useful insights that helped round out my understanding.

I'll also never forget the afternoon I spent with Rick Zitarosa, Vice President and Historian at the Navy Lakehurst Historical Society, high in the rafters of Hangar No. 1 at Lakehurst, New Jersey. As I listened to Rick recount his memories of LTAers like Commander Charles E. Rosendahl and Shaky Davis, I wondered whether I'd ever understand these people as well as Rick did. If I've fallen short, it's not Rick's fault. He not only helped school me in important aspects of airship history, he inspired me. Rick may not agree with all my interpretations, but we can all agree Rick is a priceless resource.

I am also grateful to James Gorman for helping spark this book. Jim started me on this journey by buying my pitch to write about the 2006 NOAA/ MBARI expedition to survey the *Macon* when he was Deputy Science Editor at the *New York Times*. I'm also appreciative to Carl van Wodtke, Editor in Chief at *Aviation History* magazine, for publishing my *Macon* cover story, which helped spur me to dig deeper into this amazing tale.

I normally do all of my own research, but in this case I required the assistance of Bonnie G. Rowan to help navigate the labyrinth stacks at the National Archives in Washington, DC. Bonnie, a true stoic, copied every page of the *Akron* and *Macon*'s logbooks, a mind-numbing task that she cheerfully undertook. Stephen L. Comfort was also a big help in uncovering Lt Cdr Wiley's personnel records (once feared missing) at the National Personnel Records Center in St Louis.

Archivists, librarians and historians largely (if undeservedly) go unsung yet were instrumental in helping me track down important documents. As a result, a special salute goes to Elizabeth C. Borja, CA, Reference Services Archivist, Smithsonian National Air and Space Musuem, Archives Division, Washington, DC; Mary Beth Brown, Manuscript Specialist, Western Historical Manuscript

Collection, University of Missouri-Columbia, Columbia, MO; Jennifer A. Bryan, Ph.D., Head of Special Collections & Archives/Archivist, Nimitz Library, US Naval Academy United States Naval Academy, Annapolis, MD; Sarah Clothier, Manager, AFI Catalog, American Film Institute, Los Angeles, CA; Sarah E. Dunne, MLIS, Archivist & Librarian, Owls Head Transportation Museum, Owls Head, ME; Vernon Early, Supervisor, Motion Picture, Sound and Video Research Room, National Archives and Records Administration, Washington, DC (now, sadly deceased) ; Cheryl R. Ganz, PhD, Chief Curator of Philately and Lead Curator of the William H. Gross Stamp Gallery, Smithsonian National Postal Museum and the new William H. Gross Stamp Gallery, Washington, DC; Olivia Garrison, Iowa State University Library, Reference Coordinator, Special Collections and University Archives, Ames, IA; Craig A. Holburt, Archives, University of Akron Libraries, Akron, OH; Peter L. Jakab, Chief Curator, Smithsonian National Air and Space Museum, Washington, DC; Allan Janus, Archives Division, Smithsonian National Air and Space Museum, Washington, DC; Janie Jorgensen, United States Naval Institute, Annapolis, MD; Jill D. Lane, Executive Director, Anderson-Abruzzo International Balloon Museum Foundation, Albuquerque, NM; Richard Leisenring, Jr., Curator, Glenn H. Curtiss Museum, Hammondsport, NY; Marilee Schmit Nason, Ph.D., Balloon Museum Curator of Collections, Albuquerque, NM; Carol O'Neil, Pt. Sur Historical State Mark, Monterey, CA; Kayla Siefker, Senior Media & Public Relations Manager, Gale, Farmington Hills, MI; Dean Smith, University of California, Berkeley, Bancroft Library, Berkeley, CA; Bill Stubkjaer, Curator, Moffett Field Historical Society, Mountain View, CA; Daniel Sullivan, Vice President, Moffett Field Historical Society, Mountain View, CA; Allen Testa, Reference Librarian, Marin County Free Library, San Rafael, CA; Tim Thomas, Museum Historian, Monterey Maritime & History Museum, Monterey, CA (an institution that is now sadly defunct); Bill Vas, Library and Archives, Western Museum of Flight, Torrance, CA; W.C. Watt of the University of California, Irvine, School of Social Sciences, Irvine, CA; and Tonya White, US Naval Academy Alumni Association, Communications Coordinator, Annapolis MD. The Marin County Free Library was also helpful in finding material especially the San Rafael and Novato branches, where no request was considered too obscure or difficult to oblige.

Tracking down photographs is always a tricky business. I owe a special thanks to S. Victor Fleischer, Head of Archival Services and Associate Professor of Bibliography at the University of Akron as well as John Ball, Library Associate Senior, Archival Services at the University of Akron, Akron, OH; Robert Hanshew, Naval History and Heritage Command, Washington, DC; Kate Igoe,

Rights Management Archivist at the National Air and Space Museum; Debbie Seracini, Archivist, San Diego Air & Space Museum, San Diego, CA; Susan von Thun, Science Communication and Content Manager at MBARI and Hendrick Stoops for the photos inside this book.

The 2006 NOAA/MBARI expedition was key to kindling my interest in the *Macon*. I have Rachel Saunders at the National Oceanic and Atmospheric Administration (NOAA) and Lisa Borok at MBARI to thank for arranging my attendance. I also want to thank NOAA's Bruce G. Terrell, Maritime Historian, Sanctuaries and Reserves Division; and Robert Schwemmer, Maritime Heritage Program, for sharing their knowledge about the *Macon*.

For their enthusiasm and scholarship, which helped keep the airship dream alive, I thank the Lighter-Than-Air Society, Akron, OH, www. blimpinfo.com; the Moffett Field Historical Society, Mountain View, CA, www.moffettfieldmuseum.org; the Naval Airship Association, Inc., United States, www.naval-airships.org; the Navy Lakehurst Historical Society, Lakehurst, NJ, www.nlhs.com; The Airship Association, United Kingdom, www.airship-association.org; and Dan Grossman's www.airships.net, a great place to start for anyone interested in the history of airships.

Richard G. Van Treuren's Atlantis Productions, with its airship-related books and DVDs, not only brought the past alive but filled in some important knowledge gaps. Additionally, I am grateful to F. Marc de Piolenc who gave me a well-deserved scolding for my snarky comments about atomic-powered airships. Marc's figurative smack aside the head fundamentally changed the way I view big rigids. Thanks for that, Marc. I appreciate it.

Finally, a shout out goes to Pete Brill; Peter E. Doane; Oli Mittermaier for his friendship (and excellent video production skills); Phyllis Matyi (who kept a roof over my head); Roy Mize, Eddie Ogden, Robert Prager and Dick Stettler for important contributions to my research; Amy Rigg, Commissioning Editor at The History Press, has my undying gratitude for acquiring this book, while I remain indebted to Jezz Palmer for her kindness and grace in shepherding it through the production process despite my many revisions. Any mistakes encountered here are mine, and mine alone.

SOURCES

BOOKS

Allen, Hugh, *The Story of the Airship*, Periscope Film, LLC, Los Angeles, CA, 2008–2010, reprint from the Goodyear Tire & Rubber Co., Seventh Edition, 1931.

Althoff, William F., *Sky Ships: A History of the Airship in the United States Navy*, Orion Books, New York, NY, 1990.

Archbold, Rick and Marschall, Ken, *Hindenburg: An Illustrated History*, Pacifica Press, Pacifica, CA, 1990.

Beaubois, Henry, *Airships Yesterday, Today and Tomorrow*, The Two Continents Publishing Group, New York, NY, 1976.

Botting, Douglas, Dr, *Eckener's Dream Machine*, Henry Holt and Company, New York, NY, 2001.

Cook, Jeffrey, *USS Akron and USS Macon: An Engineering History of Fin Design*, Atlantis Productions, Edgewater, FL, 2008.

Cross, Wilbur, *Disaster at the Pole: The Tragedy of the Airship Italia and the 1928 Nobile Expedition to the North Pole*, Lyons Press, Guilford, CT, 2000.

Crouch, Tom D., *Lighter Than Air: An Illustrated History of Balloons and Airships*, The John Hopkins University Press, Baltimore, MD, 2009.

Deighton, Len and Schwartzman, Arnold, *Airship Wreck*, Holt, Rinehart and Winston, New York, NY, 1978.

Dick, Harold G. and Robinson, Douglas H., *The Golden Age of Passenger Airships: Graf Zeppelin and Hindenburg*, Smithsonian Institution Press, Washington, DC, 1985.

Ege, Lennart, *Balloons and Airships*, Macmillan Publishing Co., Inc., New York, NY, 1974.

Ellsworth, Lincoln, *Search*, Brewer, Warren & Putnam, New York, NY, 1932.

Fraenkel, K.; Andrée, S.A. and Strindberg, S.A., *Andrée's Story: The Mystery and Adventure of the First Man Who Dreamed and Dared to Fly The Pole*, Blue Ribbon Books, Inc., New York, NY, 1930.

Fulton, Garland, Commander, (CC) US Navy, *Airship Progress and Airship Problems*, Wildside Press, Cabin John, MD, reprinted from *Journal of the American Society of Naval Engineers*, Vol. XLI, No. 1, February 1929.

Hoffman, Paul, *Wings of Madness: Alberto Santos-Dumont and the Invention of Flight*, Hachette Books, New York, NY, 2003.

Hoffman, Richard, Captain (ret.) US Navy, *Curtiss F9C Sparrowhawk Airship Fighters, Naval Fighters Number Seventy-Nine*, Steve Ginter, Simi Valley, CA, 2008.

Holmes, Richard, *Falling Upwards: How We Took to the Air*, Pantheon Books, New York, NY, 2013.

Hood, Joseph F., *When Monsters Roamed the Skies: The Saga of the Dirigible Airship*, Grosset & Dunlap, New York, NY, 1968.

Hook, Thom, *Flying Hookers for the Macon: The Last Great Rigid Airship Adventure*, Airsho Publishers, Baltimore, MD, 2001.

Kartman, Ben and Brown, Leonard (editors), *Disaster!*, Pellegrini & Cudahy, New York, NY, 1948.

Kirschner, Edwin J., *The Zeppelin in the Atomic Age: The Past, Present, and Future of the Rigid Lighter-Than-Air Aircraft*, University of Illinois Press, Urbana, IL, 1957.

Klein, Pitt, *Bombs Away! Zeppelins at War*, Lulu Publishing, Morrisville, NC, 2016.

Knabenshue, A. Roy, *Chauffeur of the Skies*, unpublished manuscript, National Air & Space Museum, A. Roy Knabenshue Collection, Washington, DC.

Krist, Gary, *City of Scoundrels: The Twelve Days of Disaster that Gave Birth to Modern Chicago*, Broadway Books, New York, NY, 2013.

Litchfield, Paul, *Industrial Voyage: My Life as an Industrial Lieutenant*, Doubleday & Co., Inc., Garden City, NY, 1954.

Litchfield, Paul W. and Allen, Hugh, *Why Has America No Rigid Airships?*, Corday & Gross, Co., Cleveland, OH, 1945.

Marshall, M. Ernest, *Rear Admiral Herbert V. Wiley: A Career in Airships and Battleships*, Naval Institute Press, Annapolis, MD, 2019.

Maxtone-Graham, John, *Safe Return Doubtful: The Heroic Age of Polar Exploration*, Charles Scribners & Sons, New York, NY, 1988.

McBride, William M., *Technological Change and the United States Navy 1865–1945*, The Johns Hopkins University Press, Baltimore, MD, 2000.

McPhee, John, *The Deltoid Pumpkin Seed*, Farrar, Straus and Giroux, New York, NY, 1992.

Partridge, Rowan, *ZRS*, Atlantis Productions, Edgewater, FL, 2000.

Pellegreno, Ann Holtgren, *Iowa Takes to the Air, Volume One, 1845–1910*, Aerodrome Press, Story City, Iowa, 1980.

Santos-Dumont, Alberto, *My Airships: The Story of My Life*, Grant Richards, London, 1904.

Regis, Ed, *Monsters: The Hindenburg Disaster and the Birth of Pathological Technology*, Basic Books, New York, NY, 2015.

Robinson, Douglas H., *Giants in the Sky: A History of the Rigid Airship*, University of Washington Press, Seattle, WA, 1973.

Robinson, Douglas H. and Keller, Charles L., *'Up Ship!': A History of the US Navy's Rigid Airship's 1919–35*, Annapolis, MD, Naval Institute Press, 1982.

Roland, Charles W., Captain, US Navy, *Handling Rigid Airships on the Ground*, Type-Ink, Berkeley, CA, 1979.

Rose, Alexander, *Empires of the Sky: Zeppelins, Airplanes, and Two Men's Epic Duel to Rule the World*, Random House, New York, NY, 2020.

Rosendahl, Charles E., Vice Admiral, US Navy (ret.), *SNAFU: The Strange Story of the American Airship*, Atlantis Productions, Edgewater, FL, 2004.

Rosendahl, Charles E., Lt Cdr, US Navy, *Up Ship!*, Dodd, Mead and Company, New York, NY, 1931.

Rosendahl, Charles E., Commander, US Navy, *What About the Airship? The Challenge to the United States*, Charles Scribner's Sons, New York, NY, 1938.

Ross, Ian, *Such is Life in the Navy: The Story of Rear Admiral Herbert V. Wiley*, self-published, 2014, 2016.

Seckman, JoAnne, *Captain Thomas S. Baldwin: Dean of the Aviators*, Spooky Valley Publishing, Mt Horeb, WI, 2003.

Shock, James R., *American Airship Bases & Facilities*, Atlantis Productions, Edgewater, FL, 1995.

Shock, James R., *US Navy Airships: A History by Individual Airship*, Atlantis Productions, Edgewater, FL, 2008.

Smith, Anthony, *Throw Out Two Hands*, George Allen and Unwin Ltd, London, UK, 1963.

Smith, Richard K., *The Airships Akron & Macon: Flying Aircraft Carriers of the United States Navy*, Naval Institute Press, Annapolis, MD, 1972.

Tobin, James, *To Conquer the Air: The Wright Brothers and the Great Race for Flight*, Free Press, New York, NY, 2003.

Toland, John, *The Great Dirigibles: Their Triumphs & Disasters*, Dover Publications, Inc., New York, NY, 1972.

Topping, Dale; Brothers, Eric (editor), *When Giants Roamed the Sky: Karl Arnstein and the Rise of Airships From Zeppelin to Goodyear*, University of Akron Press, Akron, OH, 2001.

Trimble, William F., *Admiral William A. Moffett: Architect of Naval Aviation*, Smithsonian Institution Press, Washington and London, 1994.

Tully, Anthony P., *Battle of Surigao Strait*, Indiana University Press, Bloomington, IN, 2009.

Ullmann, John F., *Mellone's Photo Encyclopedia of USS Akron and Macon Event Covers*, FDC Publishing Co., Stewartsville, NJ, 1996.

Ventry, Lord and Kolesnik, Eugene, M., *Jane's Pocket Book 7 Airship Development*, Macdonald and Jane's Publishers Ltd, London, UK, 1976.

Veronico, Nicholas A., *Moffett Field*, Arcadia Publishing, San Francisco, CA, 2006.

Vissering, Harry, *Zeppelin: The Story of a Great Achievement*, Hardpress Publishing, Miami, FL, 2016.

Waller, Douglas, *A Question of Loyalty: General Billy Mitchell and the Court-Martial that Gripped the Nation*, HarperCollins Publishers, New York, NY, 2004.

Wellman, Walter, *The Aerial Age: A Thousand Miles by Airship Over the Atlantic Ocean*, Forgotten Books, London, UK, 2015.

Wilkinson, Alec, *The Ice Balloon: S.A. Andrée and the Heroic Age of Arctic Exploration*, Knopf, New York, NY, 2012.

PERIODICALS

'Aeronautics: Dirigible Scene', *Time* magazine, 2 May 1932, Vol. XX, No. 18.

'*Akron*, World's Greatest Airship, Gets Outer Covering', *Popular Science Monthly*, May 1931, Vol. 118, No. 5, p. 52.

'America's Giant Airship Nearly Ready', *Flight*, 29 December 1932, p. 1228.

Arnstein, Karl, Dr, 'Developments in Lighter than Air Craft', *Society of Automotive Engineers Journal*, May 1929.

Arnstein, Karl, Dr, 'Some Design Aspect of the Rigid Airship', *Transactions*, The American Society of Engineers, June 1934.

'Big Changes Give Giants of the Air Far Wider Range', *Popular Science Monthly*, September 1930, p. 51.

Bolster, Calvin M., 'The Life and Death of USS *Macon*' in *Flying Hookers for the Macon*, Hook, Thom, Airsho Publishers, Baltimore, MD, 2001, Appendix B, p. 133, reprinted with the permission of the US Naval Academy Alumni Association.

'"Brain" of Giant Dirigible Is in Control Room', *Popular Mechanics*, August 1933, p. 207.

Burgess, C.P., 'New 6 Million Cubic-foot Airships for Our Navy', *Scientific American*, December 1926, p. 418.

Burton, Earl E., Ensign, US Navy, 'Down to the Sea in Blimps', *Flying*, October 1942.

Burton, Walter E., 'World's Biggest Airship to Fly in May', *Popular Science Monthly*, February 1931, Vol. 118, No. 2, pp. 24–25, 138.

Campbell, George, Lt, US Navy, 'They Won't Stay Down: The Dirigible Dilemma', *Collier's*, 28 May 1938, Vol. 101, No. 22, p. 12.

Copping, Jasper, 'America the Airship: The First Transatlantic Crossing', *The Daily Telegraph*, London, UK, 13 October 2010.

Crouch, Tom D., 'In the Museum: Dangerous Crossing', *Air & Space Magazine*, November 2010.

DeMary, R.C., 'USS *Macon*', *Universal Engineer*, March 1933.

'Dirigibles in Disrepute After *Macon*'s Loss', *The Literary Digest*, 23 February 1935, p. 8.

Draper, John, 'The Air Liners of the Future', *Popular Mechanics*, February 1930, p. 218.

Elliott, John M., 'Sparrowhawk Re-Marked', *American Aviation Historical Society Journal*, Summer 1972, Vol. 17, No 2.

'Flying Carrier for Warplanes', *Popular Mechanics*, May 1942, p. 14.

Fulton, Garland, Captain, US Navy (ret.), 'Recollections of the Early History of Naval Aviation', *Naval Engineers Journal*, October 1964, pp. 743–751.

'Giant "*Macon*" Berthed in Pacific Hangar', *Popular Mechanics*, October 1933, p. 71.

Glenshaw, Paul, 'Kings of the Air: Two Showmen, One dirigible, and the Flight that Changed Aviation', *Air & Space Magazine*, February 2013.

Goodspeed, M. Hill, 'Curtiss F9C Sparrowhawk', *Wings of Fame: The Journal of Classic Combat Aircraft*, Vol. 17, AIRtime Publishing, Inc., Westport, CT, under license from Aerospace Publishing Ltd, London, UK, 1999.

Gordon, Bob, 'Zeppelins Are Safe!', *Modern Mechanix*, August 1937.

Grech, Chris, Deputy Director Marine Operations, Monterey Bay Aquarium Research Institute (MBARI), 'Eighteen Years and Counting: Locating, Mapping, and Recovering the Remains of the USS *Macon*', *Noticias de Monterey: Into the Deep: Wreck and Rediscovery of America's Last Airship*, Monterey History and Art Association, Spring–Summer 2006, Vol. LV, No. 2–3.

'Guard Secrets of New Airship,' *Popular Science Monthly*, September 1932, Vol. 121, No. 3, p. 14.

'How the R-100 is Realising Britain's Dreams', *The Literary Digest*, 16 August 1930.

Jones, Bradley, Professor, University of Cincinnati, Department of Aeronautics, 'The *Macon* Christening', *US Air Services Magazine*, April 1933..

Kurtuz, Gary F., '"Navigating the Upper Strata" and the Quest for Dirigibility', *California History*, Vol. 58, No. 4, Winter 1979/1980, University of California Press in association with the California Historical Society, p. 339.

Martin John K., 'Americans Plan the World's Largest Airship', *Popular Science Monthly*, May 1926, Vol. 108, No. 5, pp. 34–35.

Metseger, Alfred B., Rear Admiral (ret.), US Navy, 'When *Macon* Went Down' in *Flying Hookers for the Macon*, Hook, Thom, Airsho Publishers, Baltimore, MD, 2001, Appendix C, p. 139.

Mikesh, Robert C., 'That Great Hook-Up in the Sky!', *Wings*, February 1975, Vol. 5, No. 1.

Miller, Harold B., Lt, US Navy, 'Navy Skyhooks', *Proceedings*, US Naval Institute, February 1935

Miller, Harold B., Rear Admiral (ret.), US Navy, 'Skyborne Aircraft Carriers: A Closed Chapter of Naval Aviation', *Shipmate*, March 1984.

Miller, Harold, 'The Violent Death of America's Last Dirigible', *True* magazine, Vol. 44, No. 315, August 1963.

Miller, H.B., Lt, US Navy, 'Last Flight Recalled' in *Flying Hookers for the Macon* *Flying Hookers for the Macon*, Hook, Thom, Airsho Publishers, Baltimore, MD, 2001, Appendix A, p. 129.

Moffett, William A., Rear Admiral, US Navy, 'Sky Leviathans of Tomorrow', *Popular Science Monthly*, October 1923, Vol. 103, No. 4.

'Navy's First Dirigible Meets Disaster', *Popular Mechanics*, June 1916, p. 819.

Novak, Matt, 'Don't Let Your Money Fly Away: A 1909 Warning to Airship Investors', *Smithsonian.com*, www.smithsonianmag.com/history/dont-let-your-money-fly-away-a-1909-warning-to-airship-investors-108767919/.

Polmar, Norman, 'Ships that Were Lighter Than Air', *Naval History Magazine*, US Naval Institute, May 2011, Vol. 25, No. 3, www.usni.org/magazines/naval-history-magazine/2011/may/ships-were-lighter-air.

'Return of Dirigible Predicted by Ralph Weyerbacher', *The Sunday Courier and Press*, Evansville, Indiana, 2 April 1950, p. 20A.

Rosendahl, C.E., Rear Admiral, US Navy, as told to Kyle Crichton, 'We Need Airships', *Colliers*, 10 June 1944, p. 14.

Stuart, Arthur A., 'Nine-Acre Nest for Dirigibles', *Popular Science Monthly*, September 1929, Vol. 115, No. 3, p. 20.

'Suns Rays to Drive Aerial Landing Field', *Modern Mechanix*, October 1934, p. 85.

Teale, Edwin, 'Does Latest Disaster Spell the Doom of the Dirigible?', *Popular Science Monthly*, May 1935, Vol. 126, No. 5, p. 26.

'The Future of the Air-Ship Revived: Interview with Anton Heinen', *The Literary Digest*, 7 April 1934, p. 50.

'The USS *Macon*: Construction of New American Airship Well Advanced', *Flight*, 20 May 1932, p. 444.

Thomas, Tim, 'The USS *Macon*: Also a Monterey Story', *Noticias de Monterey: Into the Deep: Wreck and Rediscovery of America's Last Airship*, Monterey History and Art Association, Spring-Summer 2006, Vol. LV, No. 2–3.

'Timber Traveler Erects Airship Dock', *Engineering News-Record*, 27 October 1932, Vol. 109, No. 17, p. 487.

'Transport: Last of the Last', *Time* magazine, 25 February 1935, Vol. XXV, No. 8, p. 39.

'U.S. Plans the Greatest Airship of All', *Popular Science Monthly*, March 1925, p. 40.

'Up Ship!', *Time* magazine, 10 August 1931, Vol. 18, Issue 6, p. 36.

Vaeth, J. Gordon, 'USS *Macon*: Lost and Found: Her Loss Marked the End of the Airship Era', *National Geographic* magazine, January 1992, Vol. 181, No. 1, Washington, DC, p. 114.

Vaeth, J. Gordon, 'The *Macon*: Last Queen of the Skies, Naval History Magazine', US Naval Institute, Annapolis, MD, Spring 1992, Vol. 6, No. 1.

'War Ideas, Flying Aircraft Carriers', *Popular Science*, February 1943, Vol. 142, No. 2, p. 122.

Watkins, John Elfreth, Jr, 'What May Happen in the Next Hundred Years', *Ladies Home Journal*, December 1900, Vol. XVIII, No. 1.

Wiley, H.V., Lt Cdr, US Navy, 'A Celestial Cruise', *Proceedings*, United States Naval Institute, April 1925, Vol. 51, No. 266, p. 604.

Wiley, H.V., Lt Cdr, US Navy, 'Value of Airships', *Proceedings*, US Naval Institute, May 1934.

Windsor, H.H., 'International Balloon Race of 1907', *Popular Mechanics*, January 1952, p. 170.

'Won in the Clouds', *Motion Picture News*, March–April 1914.

NEWSPAPERS

Akron Beacon Journal, Akron, OH; *Albany Evening News*, Albany, NY; Associated Press, New York, NY; *Brooklyn Daily Eagle*, Brooklyn, NY; *Chicago Daily Tribune*, Chicago, IL; *Christian Science Monitor*, Washington, DC; *Cleveland Plain Dealer*, Cleveland, OH; *El Paso Herald-Post*, El Paso, TX; *Kansas City Star*, Kansas City, MO; *Los Angeles Times*, Los Angeles, CA; *Milwaukee Journal*, Milwaukee, MN; *New York Evening Graphic*, New York, NY; *New York Times*, New York, New York; *Oakland Tribune*, Oakland, CA; *San Francisco Chronicle*, San Francisco, CA; *San Francisco Examiner*, San Francisco, CA; *San Rafael Independent*, San Rafael, CA; *Santa Ana Register*, Santa Ana, CA; *St. Louis Post-Dispatch*, St Louis, MO; *St. Petersburg Times*, St Petersburg, FL; *Taunton Daily Gazette*, Tauton, MA; *The Brooklyn Citizen*, Brooklyn, NY; *The Independent-Record*, Helena, MT; *The San Francisco Call*, San Francisco, CA; *The Washington Post*, Washington, DC.; *United Press*, New York, NY

Arnstein, Karl, Dr, 'Giant Airships Have Mission Over Oceans', *New York Times*, 4 December 1932, Section XX, p. 13.

Arnstein, Karl, Dr, 'How *Macon* Was Refined', *New York Times*, 30 April 1933, Section XX, p. 6.

Arnstein, Karl, Dr, 'Roomy Deck For Airship', *New York Times*, 23 December 1934, Section XX, p. 9.

Grant, Pat, 'Glendale and Airship Dreams', *Glendale News-Press*, Glendale, CA, 13 October 2010, www.latimes.com/socal/glendale-news-press/news/tn-gnp-grant-20101013-story.html.

Moffett, William A., Rear Admiral, 'Admiral Moffett Expresses His Faith in the Dirigible', *New York Times*, 12 October 1930.

Moffett, William A., Rear Admiral, 'Moffett Sees Air For Our Airships', *New York Times*, 21 October 1928.

Moffett, William A., Rear Admiral, 'Graf Zeppelin Opens a New Era in Air Travel', *New York Times*, 1 September 1929, Section S, p. 3.

US GOVERNMENT PUBLICATIONS

Contract for the Construction of Airship ZRS-5, Act of 24 June 1926.

Durand Committee Report, Special Committee on Airships, 'Technical Aspects of the Loss of the *Macon*', Report No. 3, 30 January 1937.

Hearings Before a Joint Committee to Investigate Dirigible Disasters, 73rd Congress of the United States, 22 May to 6 June 1933.

H.R. 9690, section 2, Lighter-than-Air, Providing for 2 Rigid Airships.

H.R. 9177, 73rd Congress, 2nd Session, House of Representatives, A Bill Authorizing the Reconstruction Finance Corporation to make a loan for the construction and operation of airships in overseas trade, and for other purposes, 17 April 1934.

Investigation of the Loss of the USS Akron, hearings before the United States House Committee on Naval Affairs, Subcommittee on Aeronautics, Seventy-Third Congress, 7 April 1933.

Sixteenth Census of the United States; 1940, Population Schedule, Department of Commerce – Bureau of the Census, Washington, DC.

US NAVY

Grossnick, Roy A. (editor), *Kite Balloons to Airships … the Navy's LTA Experience*, Naval History and Heritage Command, published by the Deputy Chief of Naval Operations (Air Warfare) and the Commander, Naval Air Systems Command, Washington, DC, www.history.navy.mil/research/histories/naval-aviation-history/navys-lighter-than-air-experience-monograph.html.

Logbook of the USS *Akron*, commanded by Frank C. McCord, Commander attached to Rigid Airship Training and Experimental Squadron.

Logbook of the USS *Macon*, commanded by A.H. Dresel, Commander, attached to Aircraft Division, Battle Force Squadron, United States Fleet.

Logbook of the USS *Macon*, commanded by Herbert V. Wiley, Lt Cdr, attached to Aircraft Division, Battle Force Squadron, United States Fleet.

Navy Court of Inquiry into the Loss of the *Akron*.

Navy Court of Inquiry into the Loss of the *Macon*.

The Lucky Bag, US Naval Academy, 1912, Vol. XIX.

The Lucky Bag, US Naval Academy, 1915, Vol. XXII.

Wiley, Herbert V., Commander, US Navy, *USS* Macon: *Doctrines and Policies for Operation and Upkeep*, US Navy, 6 May 1935.

AUTHOR INTERVIEWS

Chris Grech, 23 April 2013, Moss Landing, CA.
Ian Ross, 1 June 2013, Corte Madera, CA.
Fritz M. Trapnell, 13 January 2012, Los Altos, CA.
Marie Wiley Ross, 11 July 2008, Livermore, CA.

GOODYEAR CORPORATE MATERIAL

Building the World's Largest Airships, The Goodyear-Zeppelin Corporation, Akron,
      OH, 1929, p. 2.
Goodyear Blimp History, www.goodyearblimp.com.
Goodyear Corporate, corporate.goodyear.com/en-US.
Goodyear History, corporate.goodyear.com/en-US/about/history.html.
'The World's Largest Airship. USS *Macon*', The Goodyear News Service, *Airship
      Quarterly*, Fall 1934, p. 62.

LTA ASSOCIATION PUBLICATIONS

Airship: The Journal of the Airship Association, UK.
Brown, P. Rendall, *A Brief History of the Wingfoot Lake Airship Base* reprint, The LTA
      Society, September 1997.
Buoyant Flight, a publication of the Lighter-Than-Air Society, Akron, OH.
Mackey, Donald M., Lt Cdr, US Navy, 'What Really Happened to the *Macon*?',
      LTA Bulletin, c. 1965.
Mumma, Phil, '*Macon's* Men Rode Navy Flying Trapeze', *Moffett News*,
      16 October 1968, Vol. 51, No. 12, p. 4.
The Noon Balloon, official newsletter of the Naval Airship Association, Inc..
The Sparrowhawk, Moffett Field Historical Society newsletter, Sunnyvale, CA.

ORAL HISTORIES

Clarke, William, 'At the Helm of the USS *Macon* on February 12, 1935',
      interviewed by Robert Llewellyn on 8 September 1996, *Noticias de Monterey:
      Into the Deep: Wreck and Rediscovery of America's Last Airship*, Monterey History
      and Art Association, Spring–Summer 2006, Vol. LV, Nos 2–3, p. 17.
Clarke, William, interview conducted by Richard van Treuren, *Noon Balloon*,
      newsletter of the Naval Airship Association, Inc., Winter 2008.
Lust, John, interviewed by Michael J. Vinarcik, Oral History Project, United States
      Naval Airship Association, 17–30 March 1997, pp. 1–39.

SPEECHES

Arnstein, Karl, Dr, *Safety Problem of Airships*, Presented at Safety Conference in
      Cleveland, OH, 1934.
Burgess, C.P., *Some Airship Problems*, 25 July 1935.

Hunsaker, J.C., Vice President, Goodyear-Zeppelin Corp., *Airships for Commercial Purpose*, Presented at the International Automotive Engineering Congress of the Society of Automotive Engineers Palmer House, Chicago, IL, 28 August–4 September 1933.

Moffett, William A., Rear Admiral, Chief of the Bureau of Aeronautics, Speech on Recent Lighter-Than-Air Developments, *c.* 1928.

ONLINE SOURCES

Airships.net

Rao, Arun, and Scaruffi, Piero, *A History of Silicon Valley*, 2011, www.scaruffi.com/svhistory/sv/chap75.html.

MULTIMEDIA

1910 Los Angeles International Air Meet, www.youtube.com/watch?v=fKw8BKJ11xg.

Air Power: Battle in the Skies (PC videogame), Mindscape, Novato, CA, 1995.

Airship Handling (DVD), Atlantis Productions, Edgewater, FL.

Giants in the Sky: The Rise and Fall of Airships, New Museum, Los Gatos, CA, 2015.

Gordon Wiley Video Interview, conducted by the Maritime Museum of Monterey, Monterey, CA.

Here Comes the Navy (DVD), Warner Bros. Pictures, Inc., 1934.

Interview with Lt Cdr Herbert V. Wiley following the loss of the USS *Akron* (ZRS-4), www.airships.net/blog/worst-airship-disaster-history-uss-akron.

Into the Ether: Published Works on Ballooning & Atmospheric Studies, 1783–1910, San Francisco International Airport Aviation Museum and Library, June 2018–March 2019.

The Flying Carriers (DVD), Airship History Series, Atlantis Productions, Edgewater, FL, 2006.

USS *Akron*, British Pathé newsreel, USS *Akron* tail-smashing incident, www.youtube.com/watch?v=5sUFo57GqnE.

USS *Akron*, Part I, construction of, Goodyear Tire & Rubber Co., Inc., www.youtube.com/watch?v=1AxdJwWnkdQ.

USS *Akron*, Part II, christening and flight trials, Goodyear Tire & Rubber Co., Inc., www.youtube.com/watch?v=ZjPqK8dYD1A&t=422s.

USS *Akron*, miscellaneous footage including *Sparrowhawk* hook-ons, www.youtube.com/watch?v=DTGBFY82Gik.

USS *Akron*, San Diego incident resulting in death of two ground handlers, www.youtube.com/watch?v=pF5_OLJGPQY.

USS *Akron*, San Diego incident resulting in death of two ground handlers, British Movitone, www.youtube.com/watch?v=iJKF3RHKDtY.

USS *Akron*, Wiley newsreel interview following crash, 5 April 1933, www.youtube.com/watch?v=VRfoJKfCVco.

USS *Macon*, construction and trial flight, www.youtube.com/watch?v=_mNbC97MSVE.

USS *Macon Lost At Sea*, Universal Newsreel, www.youtube.com/
watch?v=rjzXfqB2Svc.

USS *Macon on Manoeuvres*, British Pathé newsreel, www.youtube.com/
watch?v=PH1mbzAIRJ8.

USS *Macon*, Part I, christening and trial flight, Goodyear Tire & Rubber Co., Inc.,
www.youtube.com/watch?v=4en-_yhxX-o.

USS *Macon*, Part II, christening and trial flight, Goodyear Tire & Rubber Co., Inc.,
www.youtube.com/watch?v=fOFZLLin19o.

MISCELLANEOUS

Drummond Hay, Grace, Lady, 'I Smoke a Lucky Instead of Eating Sweets',
American Tobacco Company, 1929, tobacco.stanford.edu/tobacco_web/
images/tobacco_ads/keeps_you_slim/sweet/large/sweet_12.jpg.

El-Zoghbi, Christine J., 'Airship Advocates: Innovation in the United States
Navy's Rigid Airship Program', A Dissertation submitted to the Faculty of
Columbian College of Arts and Sciences of the George Washington University
in partial satisfaction of the requirements for the degree of Doctor of
Philosophy, 31 January 2008.

Robinett, P.M., *Herbert V. Wiley, 16 May 1891–26 April 1954, Who Was
Born For High Adventure*, 1 August 1960, Western Historical Manuscript
Collection-Columbia, University of Missouri, Columbia, MO, Typescript
Collection (C995).

The Airdock: A Historic Landmark, Lockheed Martin, 2001.

NOTES

PREFACE

1 Smith, Richard K., *The Airships* Akron *& Macon: Flying Aircraft Carriers of the United States Navy*, Naval Institute Press, Annapolis, MD, 1972, p. 171.
2 Rosendahl, Charles E., Cdr, US Navy, *What About the Airship?: The Challenge to the United States*, Charles Scribner's Sons, New York, NY, 1938, p. 67.

1: ADMIRAL WILLIAM A. MOFFETT: A GIANT IN WINTER

1 'Aeronautics: Dirigible Scene', *Time* magazine, 2 May 1932, Vol. XX, No. 18.
2 Moffett, William A. Rear Admiral, 'Moffett Sees Air For Our Airships', *New York Times*, 21 October 1928.
3 Trimble, William F., *Admiral William A. Moffett: Architect of Naval Aviation*, Smithsonian Institution Press, Washington and London, 1994, p. 238.
4 Ibid., p. 5.
5 Ibid., p. 26.
6 Ibid., p. 16.
7 Ibid.
8 Ibid., p. 253.
9 Ibid., p. 260.
10 Ibid., p. 261.
11 Toland, John, *The Great Dirigibles: Their Triumphs & Disasters*, Dover Publications, Inc., New York, NY, 1972, p. 252.
12 Smith, *The Airships* Akron *& Macon*, pp. 63, 65.
13 Toland, *The Great Dirigibles*, p. 252.
14 Trimble, *Admiral William A. Moffett*, p. 2.

2: DEPARTURES

1   Trimble, *Admiral William A. Moffett*, p. 3.
2   Ibid.
3   *Building the World's Largest Airships*, The Goodyear–Zeppelin Corporation, Akron, OH, 1929, p. 2.
4   Trimble, *Admiral William A. Moffett*, p. 40.
5   Ibid., p. 4.
6   Ibid., p. 231.
7   Smith, *The Airships* Akron & Macon, p. 38.
8   Topping, Dale; Brothers, Eric (ed.), *When Giants Roamed the Sky: Karl Arnstein and the Rise of Airships From Zeppelin to Goodyear*, University of Akron Press, Akron, OH, 2001, p. 166.
9   'Mrs. Hoover Names Huge Airship *Akron*', *New York Times*, 9 August 1931, p. 1.
10 Smith, *The Airships* Akron & Macon, p. 39.
11 'Up Ship!', *Time* magazine, 10 August 1931, Vol. 18, Issue 6, p. 36.
12 Ibid.
13 Smith, *The Airships* Akron & Macon, Footnote 8, p. 211.
14 Trimble, *Admiral William A. Moffett*, p. 3.
15 Ibid., p. 264.
16 Ibid., p. 2.
17 Smith, *The Airships* Akron & Macon, p. 77.
18 Trimble, *Admiral William A. Moffett*, p. 2.
19 Wiley, Herbert V., Lt Cdr, US Navy, Statement before the House of Representatives, Subcommittee on Aeronautics of the Committee on Naval Affairs, *Investigation of the Loss of the USS* Akron, 7 April 1933, p. 4.
20 Trimble, *Admiral William A. Moffett*, p. 2.

3: A NIGHT TO REMEMBER

1   Rosendahl, Charles E., Lt Cdr, US Navy, *Up Ship!*, Dodd, Mead and Company, New York, NY, 1931, p. 270.
2   *Akron Beacon Journal*, 4 April 1933, p. 20.
3   Wiley, Statement before the House of Representatives, *Investigation of the Loss of the USS* Akron.
4   Smith, *The Airships* Akron & Macon, p. 66.
5   Vaeth, J. Gordon, 'USS *Macon*: Lost and Found: Her Loss Marked the End of the Airship Era', *National Geographic* magazine, January 1992, Vol. 181, No. 1, Washington, DC, p. 120.
6   Shock, James R., *US Navy Airships: A History by Individual Airship*, Atlantis Productions, Edgewater, FL, 2008, p. 64.
7   Hook, Thom, *Flying Hookers for the* Macon: *The Last Great Rigid Airship Adventure*, Airsho Publishers, Baltimore, MD, 2001, quoting Lt Harold B. Miller, p. 83.
8   Shock, *US Navy Airships*, p. 64.
9   Hook, *Flying Hookers for the* Macon, p. 40.

10 'Wiley Hails Heroism of Men As the *Akron* Plunged Into Sea', *New York Times*, 5 April 1933, p. 1; Rosendahl, Charles E., Vice Admiral, US Navy (ret.), *SNAFU: The Strange Story of the American Airship*, Atlantis Productions, Edgewater, FL, 2004, p. 29.

11 Lust, John, interviewed by Michael J. Vinarcik, Oral History Project, United States Naval Airship Association, 17–30 March 1997, p. 34.

12 Toland, *The Great Dirigibles*, p. 258.

13 Trimble, *Admiral William A. Moffett*, p. 264.

14 Wiley, Herbert V., Lt Cdr, Statement before the House of Representatives, *Investigation of the Loss of the USS* Akron.

15 *Akron Beacon Journal*, 4 April 1933, p. 10.

16 Deal, Richard, E., Boatswain's Mate, Second Class, US Navy, Statement before the House of Representatives, Subcommittee on Aeronautics of the Committee on Naval Affairs, *Investigation of the Loss of the USS* Akron, 7 April 1933, p. 7; 'Last Moments on *Akron* Told by Survivors', *Chicago Daily Tribune*, 8 April 1933, p. 1.

17 Deal, Statement before the House of Representatives, *Investigation of the Loss of the USS* Akron.

18 Toland, *The Great Dirigibles*, p. 254.

19 Deal, Statement before the House of Representatives, *Investigation of the Loss of the USS* Akron; 'Last Moments on *Akron* Told by Survivors', *Chicago Daily Tribune*.

20 Wiley, Statement before the House of Representatives, *Investigation of the Loss of the USS* Akron.

21 Trimble, *Admiral William A. Moffett*, p. 264.

22 Toland, *The Great Dirigibles*, p. 259.

23 Ibid.

24 Smith, *The Airships* Akron & Macon, p. 87.

25 Ibid., p. 65.

26 Ibid.

27 Hunsaker, J.C., Vice President, Goodyear-Zeppelin Corp., *Airships for Commercial Purpose*, Presented at the International Automotive Engineering Congress of the Society of Automotive Engineers Palmer House, Chicago, IL, 28 August–4 September 1933, p. 4.

28 Deal, Statement before the House of Representatives, *Investigation of the Loss of the USS* Akron.

29 Rosendahl, *What About the Airship?*, p. 125.

30 Toland, *The Great Dirigibles*, p. 258.

31 Ibid.

32 Ibid.

33 Smith, *The Airships* Akron & Macon, p. 78.

34 'Wiley Disapproved the *Akron*'s Course Eastward in Storm', *New York Times*, 11 April 1933, p. 1.

35 Rosendahl, *SNAFU*, p. 30.

36 Toland, *The Great Dirigibles*, p. 259.

37 Hood, Joseph F., *When Monsters Roamed the Skies: The Saga of the Dirigible Airship*, Grosset & Dunlap, New York, NY, 1968, p. 105.

38 Toland, *The Great Dirigibles*, p. 258.

39   Smith, *The Airships* Akron & Macon, p. 78.
40   Trimble, *Admiral William A. Moffett*, p. 265.
41   *Akron Beacon Journal*, 5 April 1933, p. 10.
42   'Wiley Hails Heroism of Men As the *Akron* Plunged Into Sea', *New York Times*.
43   Toland, *The Great Dirigibles*, p. 258.
44   Trimble, *Admiral William A. Moffett*, p. 265.
45   Ibid., p. 261.
46   Rosendahl, *What About the Airship?*, p. 116.
47   Smith, *The Airships* Akron & Macon, p. 79.
48   Ibid.
49   Rosendahl, *SNAFU*, p. 29.
50   Smith, *The Airships* Akron & Macon, p. 80, Rosendahl, *SNAFU*, p. 30.
51   Smith, p. 80.
52   'Wiley Hails Heroism of Men As the *Akron* Plunged Into Sea', *New York Times*.

4: FIGHT FOR SURVIVAL

1   Rosendahl, *SNAFU*, p. 32.
2   Erwin, Moody, E., Statement before the House of Representatives, Subcommittee on Aeronautics of the Committee on Naval Affairs, *Investigation of the Loss of the USS* Akron, 7 April 1933, p. 11.
3   Erwin, Statement before the House of Representatives, *Investigation of the Loss of the USS* Akron; Rosendahl, *SNAFU*, p. 32.
4   Owen, Russell, '*Akron* Broke in Sea', *New York Times*, 12 April 1933, p. 7.
5   Ibid.
6   Rosendahl, *SNAFU*, p. 32; *Chicago Daily Tribune*, 8 April 1933, pp. 1, 12.
7   Rosendahl, Ibid.
8   Toland, *The Great Dirigibles*, p. 265.
9   Ibid., p. 266.
10   Ibid., p. 262.
11   Rosendahl, *SNAFU*, p. 31.
12   Ibid.
13   *Chicago Daily Tribune*, 8 April 1933, p. 1.
14   *Chicago Daily Tribune*, 8 April 1933, p. 12; Toland, *The Great Dirigibles*, p. 266.
15   Erwin, Statement before the House of Representatives, *Investigation of the Loss of the USS* Akron.
16   Toland, *The Great Dirigibles*, p. 266.
17   Ibid., pp. 266–7.
18   *Akron Beacon Journal*, 5 April 1933, p. 10.
19   *New York Times*, 5 April 1933, p. 1.
20   Toland, *The Great Dirigibles*, p. 266.
21   Ibid., p. 267.
22   *New York Times*, 11 April 1933, p. 1.
23   'Hunt for Survivors', *New York Times*, 5 April 1933, p. 14; *Akron Beacon Journal*, 4 April 1933, p. 10.
24   Smith, *The Airships* Akron & Macon, p. 80.
25   Ibid.

26 Toland, *The Great Dirigibles*, pp. 266–7.
27 Ibid.
28 Ibid.
29 Ibid., p. 268.
30 Smith, *The Airships* Akron & Macon, p. 80.
31 *Akron Beacon Journal*, 4 April 1933, p. 10.
32 Ibid.
33 *San Francisco Chronicle*, 4 April 1933, p. 1.
34 Toland, *The Great Dirigibles*, pp. 269–70.
35 Ibid., p. 272.
36 *Akron Beacon Journal*, 4 April 1933, p. 10.
37 Toland, *The Great Dirigibles*, p. 271.
38 *Akron Beacon Journal*, 4 April 1933, p. 10.
39 Trimble, *Admiral William A. Moffett*, p. 267.
40 'Mrs. Moffett Refuses to Give Up Hope', *New York Times*, 5 April 1933, p. 14.
41 *Akron Beacon Journal*, 5 April 1933, p. 10.
42 Toland, *The Great Dirigibles*, p. 273.
43 Ibid.

5: SPOTLIGHT

1   'Designer of *Akron* Dazed by Disaster', *The Washington Post*, 5 April 1933, p. 2.
2   Ibid.
3   Ibid.
4   'Roosevelt Grieves at Loss to the Nation', *New York Times*, 5 April 1933, p. 1.
5   *New York Times*, 5 April 1933, p. 1.
6   *Akron Beacon Journal*, 4 April 1933, p. 23.
7   *New York Times*, 5 April 1933, p. 1.
8   Ibid.
9   Ibid.
10 Ibid.
11 Ibid.
12 Ibid.
13 Ibid.
14 *Akron Beacon Journal*, 5 April 1933, p. 1.
15 *Akron Beacon Journal*, 5 April 1933, Editorial, p. 4.
16 *Akron Beacon Journal*, 5 April 1933, p. 10.
17 Wiley newsreel interview, 5 April 1933, www.youtube.com/
    watch?v=VRfoJKfCVco.
18 'Navy Board Named for *Akron* Inquiry', *New York Times*, 6 April 1933, p. 1.
19 Ibid.
20 *Akron Beacon Journal*, 4 April 1933, p. 1.
21 Ibid.
22 Toland, *The Great Dirigibles*, p. 275.
23 *Akron Beacon Journal*, 4 April 1933, p. 1.
24 Smith, *The Airships* Akron & Macon, p. 77.

6: WILEY ON TRIAL

1   Ibid.
2   Trimble, *Admiral William A. Moffett*, p. 270.
3   'Wiley Disapproved the *Akron's* Course', *New York Times*, 11 April 1933, p.1.
4   Ibid.
5   Trimble, *Admiral William A. Moffett*, p. 269.
6   *Akron Beacon Journal*, 10 April 1933, p. 10.
7   *Akron Beacon Journal*, 11 April 1933, p. 15.
8   Ibid.
9   'Wiley Questions Inquiry Witness', *Akron Beacon Journal*, 12 April 1933, p. 11.
10 Ibid.
11 Ibid.
12 Ibid.
13 Toland, *The Great Dirigibles*, p. 275.
14 'Widow Takes News Bravely', *New York Times*, 11 April 1933, p. 10.
15 *New York Times*, 14 April 1933, p. 5.
16 '*Akron* Mishandled One Witness Hints', *New York Times*, 20 April 1933, p. 14.
17 'Dresel Tells Court Map Did Not Bar Fatal Flight', *New York Times*, 27 April 1933, p. 6.
18 Ibid.
19 'Aviation', *Akron Beacon Journal*, 20 April 1933, p. 6.
20 'Navy to Abandon Lakehurst Station', *The Washington Post*, 26 April 1933, p. 1.
21 *Akron Beacon Journal*, 27 April 1933, p. 1.
22 Topping, *When Giants Roamed the Sky*, pp. 183–4.
23 *Akron Beacon Journal*, 11 April 1933, p. 15.
24 Smith, *The Airships* Akron & Macon, p. 85.
25 Trimble, *Admiral William A. Moffett*, p. 273.
26 Smith, *The Airships* Akron & Macon, p. 87.
27 Robinson, Douglas H. and Keller, Charles, L., *Up Ship!*, Naval Institute Press, Annapolis, MD, 1982, pp. 185–6.
28 'Says Lakehurst Erred on Night of *Akron* Crash', *Akron Beacon Journal*, 1 June 1933, p. 21.
29 Smith, *The Airships* Akron & Macon, see Chapter 6, Footnote No. 12, p. 212.
30 Ibid., p. 77.

7: PAUL W. LITCHFIELD: A GIANT IN SPRING

1   Litchfield, Paul, *Industrial Voyage: My Life as an Industrial Lieutenant*, Doubleday & Co., Inc., Garden City, NY, 1954, p. 25.
2   Ibid., p. 26.
3   Ibid., p. 56.
4   Brown, P. Rendall, *A Brief History of the Wingfoot Lake Airship Base* reprint, The LTA Society, September 1997, p. 1.
5   Ibid.
6   Ibid.

7   Krist, Gary, *City of Scoundrels: The Twelve Days of Disaster that Gave Birth to Modern Chicago*, Broadway Books, New York, NY, 2013, p. 9. Note: Krist says the Wingfoot Air Express was filled with 10,000 cu ft of hydrogen but this is likely a typo.
8   Ibid., p. 6.
9   Ibid., p. 7.
10 Ibid., p. 4.
11 Ibid., p. 8.
12 *New York Times*, 22 July 1919, p. 5.
13 Krist, *City of Scoundrels*, p. 11.
14 Ibid., p. 13.
15 Benzkoferm, Stephan, '18 Years Before the *Hindenburg*, A Blimp Disaster Hit the Loop', *Chicago Daily Tribune*, 6 May 2012, www.chicagotribune.com/history/ct-per-flash-blimpdisasters-0506-20120506-story.html.
16 Krist, *City of Scoundrels*, p. 15.
17 Benzkoferm, '18 Years Before the *Hindenburg*'.
18 Ibid.
19 Herter, Debra, 'Chicago Disasters: The Wingfoot Express', *Disasters That Changed the World*, 21 April 2012, disastersthatchangedtheworld.blogspot.com/2012/04/chicago-disasters-wingfoot-express.html.
20 Benzkoferm, '18 Years Before the *Hindenburg*'.
21 Ibid.
22 Herter, 'Chicago Disasters: The Wingfoot Express'.
23 Allen, Hugh, *The Story of the Airship* reprint from The Goodyear Tire & Rubber Company, Akron, OH, 1931, Periscope Film LL, Edgewater, FL, 2008–10, p. 19.
24 Ibid., p. 19; Watson, Jim, 'Mysterious Island: Catalina by Blimp', *The Catalina Islander*, thecatalinaislander.com/mysterious-islandcatalina-by-blimp.

8: BLIMPS LEAD THE WAY

1   Litchfield, *Industrial Voyage*, p. 235.
2   Ibid., p. 52.
3   'Up Ship!', *Time* magazine.
4   Ibid.
5   Martin John K., 'Americans Plan the World's Largest Airship', *Popular Science Monthly*, May 1926, Vol. 108, No. 5, p. 35.
6   'Mayflower to Make Contact With Liner at Quarantine to Pick Up P.W. Litchfield', *New York Times*, 31 July 1930, p. 18.
7   'Up Ship!', *Time* magazine, p. 36.
8   Litchfield, *Industrial Voyage*, p. 235.
9   Ibid., p. 25.
10 Ibid., p. 36.

9: DAWN OF THE COMMERCIAL AIRSHIP

1 'Rufus Porter's Aeroport Airship-1853', *New England Aviation History*, 26 August 2016, www.newenglandaviationhistory.com/rufus-porters-aeroport-airship-1853.
2 Ibid.
3 Kurtuz, Gary F., '"Navigating the Upper Strata" and the Quest for Dirigibility', *California History*, Vol. 58, No. 4, Winter 1979/1980, University of California Press in association with the California Historical Society, p. 339.
4 'Would You If You Could', *Chicago Daily Tribune*, 26 June 1910, p. 15.
5 Novak, Matt, 'Don't Let Your Money Fly Away: A 1909 Warning to Airship Investors', *Smithsonian.com*, 31 May 2012.
6 Seckman, JoAnne, *Captain Thomas S. Baldwin: Dean of the Aviators*, Spooky Valley Publishing, Mt Horeb, WI, 2003, p. 40.
7 Kurtuz, '"Navigating the Upper Strata" and the Quest for Dirigibility', p. 344.
8 Seckman, *Captain Thomas S. Baldwin*, p. 40.
9 Ibid., p. 43.
10 *Oakland Tribune*, 8 August 1904, p. 12.
11 Seckman, *Captain Thomas S. Baldwin*, p. 37A.
12 Ibid., p. 79.
13 Ibid., p. 83.
14 Crouch, Tom D., *Lighter Than Air: An Illustrated History of Balloons and Airships*, The John Hopkins University Press, Baltimore, ML, 2009, p. 85.
15 Topping, *When Giants Roamed the Sky*, p. 32.
16 Knabenshue, *Chauffeur of the Skies*, unpublished manuscript, National Air & Space Museum, A. Roy Knabenshue Collection, Washington, DC, p. 4.
17 Ibid., p. 6.
18 Ibid., p. 10.
19 Ibid., p. 12.
20 1910 Los Angeles International Air Meet video, www.youtube.com/watch?v=fKw8BKJ11xg.
21 Knabenshue, *Chauffeur of the Skies*, pp. 185–6.
22 Ibid., p. 186.
23 Ibid., p. 187.
24 'Won in the Clouds', *Motion Picture News*, March–April 1914, p. 36.
25 *Popular Science*, January 1923, Vol. 102, No. 1, Cover.
26 Radecki, Alan, 'Slate's Strange Dirigible,' *Vintage Air*, 20 August 2013, vintageairphotos.blogspot.com/2013/08/slates-strange-dirigible.html.
27 Ibid.
28 Grant, Pat, 'Glendale and Airship Dreams', *Glendale News-Press*, 13 October 2010.
29 *Flight*, 7 February 1929, pp. 101–2.
30 Radecki, 'Slate's Strange Dirigible'.
31 Ibid.
32 Grant, 'Glendale and Airship Dreams'.
33 Radecki, 'Slate's Strange Dirigible'.
34 Grant, 'Glendale and Airship Dreams'.

35 'Leak to Delay Airship Flight for Thirty Days', *Los Angeles Times*, 20 December 1929, p. 21.
36 Ibid.
37 Radecki, 'Slate's Strange Dirigible'.
38 John, Finn J.D., 'Would inventor's steam-powered metal airship have worked?', *Off Beat Oregon*, 21 February 2016, offbeatoregon.com/1602c.pt2-slate-metal-airship-inventor-379.html.
39 Grant, 'Glendale and Airship Dreams'.
40 Seckman, *Captain Thomas S. Baldwin*, p. 47.

10: COMPETITION

1 *New York Times*, 12 February 1923, p. 12.
2 *New York Evening Graphic*, 9 November 1926, p. 1.
3 *Flight*, 22 May 1924, p. 285.
4 Arnstein, Karl, Dr, 'Giant Airships Have Mission Over Oceans', *New York Times*, 4 December 1932, Section XX, p. 13.

11: CUTTING A DEAL

1 Litchfield, *Industrial Voyage*, p. 40.
2 Goodyear Corporate History, corporate.goodyear.com/en-US/about/history.html.
3 Litchfield, *Industrial Voyage*, pp. 237–8.
4 Ibid., p. 238.
5 Ibid., p. 239.
6 Ibid., p. 236.
7 Ibid., pp. 248–9.

12: PITCHING COMMERCIAL AIRSHIPS

1 'Asserts Aerial Travel Soon to Be Big Success', *Akron Beacon Journal*, 15 October 1925, p. 31.
2 Montana, Helena, 'Would Have U.S. Own Powerful Air Lines', *The Independent-Record*, 31 October 1935, p. 4.
3 Martin, 'Americans Plan the World's Largest Airship', *Popular Science Monthly*, pp. 34–5.
4 Ibid.
5 Ibid.
6 Ibid.
7 Ibid.
8 Rosendahl, *What About the Airship?*, p. 343.
9 Moffett, William A., Rear Admiral, US Navy, Speech, on recent Lighter-Than-Air Developments, *c.* 1928, pp. 1–8.
10 'Greatest Dirigible Is Planned By Navy', *New York Times*, 16 December 1924, p. 20.
11 Litchfield, *Industrial Voyage*, p. 240.

13: THE DESIGN COMPETITION

1   Trimble, *Admiral William A. Moffett*, p. 231.
2   Moffett Memo, 21 December 1927, National Air & Space Museum Archives, Garland Fulton Collection, Series I, Box 5, Folder 5.
3   Trimble, *Admiral William A. Moffett*, p. 231.
4   Ibid., p. 236.
5   Smith, *The Airships* Akron & Macon, p. 18.
6   Grossnick, Roy A. (ed.), *Kite Balloons to Airships … the Navy's LTA Experience*, Naval History and Heritage Command, Published by the Deputy Chief of Naval Operations (Air Warfare) and the Commander, Naval Air Systems Command, Washington, DC.
7   Allen, *The Story of the Airship*, p. 31.
8   Litchfield, *Industrial Voyage*, p. 245.
9   'Dr Eckener to Push Ocean Airship Line', *New York Times*, 18 October 1928, p. 15.
10 Botting, Douglas, *Dr Eckener's Dream Machine*, Henry Holt and Company, New York, NY, 2001, Epigraph.
11 Drummond Hay, Grace, Lady, 'I Smoke a Lucky Instead of Eating Sweets', American Tobacco Company, 1929, tobacco.stanford.edu/tobacco_web/images/tobacco_ads/keeps_you_slim/sweet/large/sweet_12.jpg.

14: SUCCESS WITHIN REACH

1   1929 Aviation Statistics, en.wikipedia.org/wiki/1929_in_aviation.
2   Allen, *The Story of the Airship*, pp. 64–5.
3   Ibid., pp. 65–6.
4   'Hoover Favorable to Pacific Air Line', *New York Times*, 10 May 1929, p. 15.
5   Ibid., p. 15.
6   'Plans Two Airships to Dwarf Zeppelin', *New York Times*, 3 August 1929, p. 4.
7   Ibid., p. 4.
8   'Airship Lines Planner Here', *New York Times*, 11 August 1929, Section XX, p. 13.
9   *Popular Mechanics*, March 1935, Vol. 63, No. 3, p. 357; Arnstein, Karl, Dr, 'Roomy Deck For Airship', *New York Times*, 23 December 1934, Section XX, p. 9.
10 'Urge Federal Aid to Build Airships', *New York Times*, 29 January 1931, p. 16.
11 'Airship Mail Bill Called A Subsidy', *New York Times*, 20 May 1932, p. 41.
12 Ibid.
13 'Marin May Be Site of San Francisco-Tokyo Dirigible Line Base', *San Rafael Independent*, 30 June 1930, p. 1.
14 'Builders of Navy Airships Ready to Lay Down Still Larger Ocean Craft', *New York Times*, 18 September 1932, p. XX5.
15 'Backs Ocean Mail for Huge Dirigible', *New York Times*, 17 June 1932, p. 21.

15: FOR WANT OF A NAIL

1   *New York Times*, 18 September 1932, p. XX5.
2   'Press Merchant Airship Measure For Early Vote', *Akron Beacon Journal*, 2 March 1933, p. 15.

3   Hunsaker, *Airships for Commercial Purposes*, pp. 1–16.

4   Ibid.

5   Ibid.

6   Ibid., p. 54.

7   Arnstein, Karl, Dr, 'Giant Airships Have Mission Over Oceans', *New York Times*, 4 December 1932, Section XX, p. 13.

8   Rosendahl, *What About the Airship?*, p. 54.

9   Arnstein, 'Giant Airships Have Mission Over Oceans', *New York Times*.

10 Rosendahl, *What About the Airship?*, p. 134.

11 en.wikipedia.org/wiki/Motor_vehicle_fatality_rate_in_US_by_year.

12 Litchfield, *Industrial Voyage*, p. 235.

13 Ibid., p. 247.

14 Ibid.

15 *Akron Beacon Journal*, 2 March 1933, p. 15.

16: AIRSHIP FEVER

1   Rosendahl, *Up Ship!*, p. 45.

2   Waller, Douglas, *A Question of Loyalty: General Billy Mitchell and the Court-Martial that Gripped the Nation*, HarperCollins Publishers, New York, NY, 2004, p. 28.

3   Watkins, John Elfreth, Jr, 'What May Happen in the Next Hundred Years', *Ladies Home Journal*, December 1900, Vol. XVIII, No. 1, p. 8.

4   *The San Francisco Call*, 23 November 1896, p. 1.

5   www.unmuseum.org/airship.htm.

17: CONSEQUENCES

1   Smith, *The Airships* Akron & Macon, p. 82.

2   Memo from Bureau of Navigation to Judge Advocate General, Subject: Claim of Herbert V. Wiley, Lieutenant Commander, US Navy, for reimbursement of clothing lost in disaster to USS *Akron*, on 4 April 1933; 26 April 1933, National Personnel Records Center, St Louis, MO.

3   'Delaney Intimates Navy's Inquiry "Whitewashed Whole Thing"', *Akron Beacon Journal*, 1 June 1933, p. 21.

4   *Hearings Before A Joint Committee to Investigate Dirigible Disasters*, 73rd Congress of the United States, 22 May to 6 June 1933, p. 527; '*Akron* Crash Fails To Change Policy', *New York Times*, 1 June 1933, p. 13.

5   'Lindbergh Favors Building Airships', *New York Times*, 2 June 1933, p. 15.

6   Hunsaker, *Airships for Commercial Purposes*, p. 2.

7   'Delaney Intimates Navy's Inquiry "Whitewashed Whole Thing"', *Akron Beacon Journal*.

8   'Navy *Akron* Probe Assailed in Report', *New York Times*, 15 June 1933, p. 13.

9   'Recommends Two New Airships', *Akron Beacon Journal*, 10 June 1933, p. 1.

10 Smith, *The Airships* Akron & Macon, p. 91.

11 'New *Akron* Urged by Admiral King', *New York Times*, 13 July 1933, Section: Radio Automobiles, p. 26.
12 Hunsaker, *Airships for Commercial Purposes*, p. 8.
13 Letter from Claude A. Swanson, Secretary of the Navy to President Roosevelt, 21 July 1933, National Air & Space Museum Archives, Garland Fulton Collection.

18: BUILDING THE *MACON*

1   Toland, *The Great Dirigibles*, pp. 271–2.
2   *Cleveland Plain Dealer*, 4 April 1933, Cleveland, OH, p. 1.
3   *Brooklyn Daily Eagle*, 4 April 1933, Brooklyn, New York, NY, p. 1.
4   *The Brooklyn Citizen*, 4 April 1933, Brooklyn, New York, NY, p. 1.
5   *Akron Beacon Journal*, 4 April 1933, p. 13.
6   Ibid.
7   *Akron Beacon Journal*, 4 April 1933, p. 1.
8   'Roosevelt Grieves at Loss to the Nation', *New York Times*.
9   'Designer of *Akron* Dazed by Disaster', *The Washington Post*.
10 *Akron Beacon Journal*, 4 April 1933, pp. 1, 13.
11 Ibid.
12 Hook, *Flying Hookers for the* Macon, p. 19.
13 Allen, *The Story of the Airship*, p. 39; *Flight*, 20 May 1932, 'The USS *Macon* Construction of New American Airship Well Advanced', p. 444.
14 *Flight*, Ibid.
15 Allen, *The Story of the Airship*, pp. 39, 41.
16 Rosendahl, *SNAFU*, p. 21.
17 '*Macon*'s Ladders Made in Germany of Oregon Spruce', *Christian Science Monitor*, 14 December 1932, p. 3; Allen, *The Story of the Airship*, p. 43.
18 'Guard Secrets of New Airship', *Popular Science Monthly*, September 1932, Vol. 121, No. 3, p. 15.
19 Allen, *The Story of the Airship*, p. 39.
20 Burton, Walter E., 'World's Biggest Airship to Fly in May', *Popular Science Monthly*, February 1931, Vol. 118, No. 2, pp. 24–5, 138.
21 Ibid.
22 Allen, *The Story of the Airship*, p. 40.
23 *The Washington Post*, 5 July 1932, p. 5.
24 'Sky Mammoth Takes Shape', *The Washington Post*, 10 July 1932, p. A4.
25 Memo to Rear Admiral Moffett from Commander Fulton, 28 May 1930, National Air & Space Museum Archives, Fulton Collection, Folder 9.
26 Rosendahl, *What About the Airship?*, p. 393.
27 Memo from Rear Admiral Moffett, to Assistant Secretary Ingalls, Status of Expenditures, 8 June 1931, BUAER Records, National Archives Research Center, Washington, DC.
28 Memo from Rear Admiral Moffett, Chief of Bureau of Aeronautics, to Secretary of the Navy, Subject: Request change in ZRS-5 design, 25 April 1931, National Archives Research Center, Washington, DC.
29 Memo from Admiral W.V. Pratt, Chief of Naval Ops to Secretary of the Navy, 5 February 1932, National Archives Research Center, Washington, DC.

30 'Asks Navy to Set Price on the *Los Angeles*', *New York Times*, 2 February 1932, p. 7.

31 'Record Life Ending for Los Angeles', *The Washington Post*, 22 May 1932.

32 'Thrift Cuts Air Fleet', *New York Times*, 14 August 1932.

33 Arnstein, Karl, Dr, 'How *Macon* Was Refined', *New York Times*, 30 April 1933, Section XX, p. 6.

34 '*Macon* and *Akron* Cost $8,000,000', *New York Times*, 13 February 1935, p. 4.

35 *Macon* Group Change Order No. 1, 1 August 1932, University of Akron Libraries, Karl Arnstein Papers, Akron, OH.

36 Smith, *The Airships* Akron & Macon, p. 35.

37 BUAER records, National Archives Research Center, Washington, DC.

38 '"*Macon*" Name Chosen for Largest Airship', *The Washington Post*, 18 February 1932, p. 13.

39 Ibid.

40 DeMary, R.C., 'USS *Macon*: Uncle Sam's Latest Contribution to the Navy Ready to Take to the Air', *Universal Engineer*, March 1933.

19: CHRISTENING

1 'Scrip Talked Not Airships', *Akron Beacon Journal*, 13 March 1933, p. 15; Smith, *The Airships* Akron & Macon, p. 97.

2 Smith, Ibid., p. 97.

3 Jones, Bradley, Professor, University of Cincinnati, Department of Aeronautics, 'The *Macon* Christening', *US Air Services Magazine*, April 1933.

4 *Akron Beacon Journal*, 13 March 1933, p. 15.

5 Ibid.

6 'Big Airship *Macon* is Named at Akron', *New York Times*, 12 March 1933, Section F, p. 26.

7 'Mrs. Moffett to Name the *Macon*', *New York Times*, 5 February 1933, p. N5.

8 Smith, *The Airships* Akron & Macon, p. 97.

9 Ibid.

10 'Giant Dirigible to be Named Today', *New York Times*, 11 March 1933, Section: Sports, p. 21.

11 Jones, Bradley, Professor, University of Cincinnati, Department of Aeronautics, 'The *Macon* Christening', *US Air Services Magazine*, April 1933.

12 'The World's Largest Airship. USS *Macon*', The Goodyear News Service, *Airship Quarterly*, Fall 1934, p. 62.

13 Burton, Walter, E., 'World's Biggest Airship to Fly in May', *Popular Science Monthly*; DeMary, R.C., 'USS *Macon*', *Universal Engineer*.

14 Miller, Harold, 'The Violent Death of America's Last Dirigible', *True* magazine, Vol. 44, No. 315, August 1963, p. 28.

15 'The World's Largest Airship', *Airship Quarterly*, p. 59.

16 Arnstein, Karl, Dr, *New York Times*, 30 April 1933, Section XX, p. 6.

17 'The World's Largest Airship', *Airship Quarterly*, p. 58.

18 Rosendahl, *What About the Airship?*, p. 75.

19 'Guard Secrets of New Airship', *Popular Science Monthly*, September 1932, Vol. 121, No. 3, p. 15.

20 'The World's Largest Airship', The Goodyear News Service, p. 61.

21 Ibid.

22 Ibid.

23 Campbell, George, Lt US Navy, 'They Won't Stay Down: The Dirigible Dilemma', *Collier's*, 28 May 1938, Vol. 101, No. 22, p. 12.

24 Althoff, William F., *Sky Ships: A History of the Airship in the United States Navy*, Orion Books, New York, NY, 1990, p. 88.

25 Allen, *The Story of the Airship*, p. 43.

26 Ibid., p. 44.

27 Miller, 'The Violent Death of America's Last Dirigible', p. 30.

28 Allen, *The Story of the Airship*, p. 45.

29 *Macon* Group Change Order No. 1.

30 Memo from Commander Fulton to Admiral King, 9 September 1935, Actual memo attached 6 August 1935, BUAER Records, National Archives Research Center, Washington, DC.

31 Robinson and Keller, *Up Ship!*, p. 179.

32 *Akron Beacon Journal*, 13 March 1933, p. 15.

33 Shock, James R., *American Airship Bases & Facilities*; 'Giant Dirigible To Be Named Today', *New York Times*, p. 21; *Akron Beacon Journal*, 13 March 1933, p. 15.

34 'Big Airship *Macon* is Named at Akron', *New York Times*.

35 Jones, 'The *Macon* Christening', *US Air Services Magazine*.

36 *Akron Beacon Journal*, 13 March 1933, p. 15.

37 Trimble, *Admiral William A. Moffett*, p. 263.

20: TRIAL FLIGHTS

1 '*Macon* Soars Thru Sky on First Flight', *Taunton Daily Gazette*, Taunton, MA, 21 April 1933.

2 '*Macon* Up 12 hours in Maiden Flight', *New York Times*, 22 April 1933, p. 1.

3 Litchfield, *Industrial Voyage*, p. 246.

4 *USS* Macon *Trial Flight No. 3, Authorization Instructions For Personnel Participating in Trial Flights of the USS* Macon *(ZRS-5)*, p. 1.

5 '*Macon* Trial Flight Postponed 3 Days', *The Washington Post*, 9 April 1933.

6 Memo from Bureau of Navigation to Lt Cdr Herbert V. Wiley, US Navy, Subject: Travel Orders to Akron, Ohio. Trials of the USS *MACON*, 28 March 1933, Wiley Personnel file, Service Number: 9129, National Personnel Records Center, St Louis, MO.

7 'Reporters "Rush" '*Akron*' Survivor', *Akron Beacon Journal*, 24 April 1933, p. 10.

8 '*Macon* Superior to *Akron*, Wiley Says After Flight', *The Washington Post*, 24 April 1933, p. 3.

9 '*Macon* Up 13 Hours', *New York Times*, 24 April 1933, p. 29.

10 Ibid.

11 *Akron Beacon Journal*, 24 April 1933, p. 10.

12 *The Washington Post*, 24 April 1933, p. 3.

13 *Akron Beacon Journal*, 24 April 1933, p. 10.

14 *New York Times*, 22 April 1933, p. 1.

15 Memo from Commander Fulton to Admiral King, 9 September 1935.

16 Arnstein, *New York Times*, 30 April 1933, Section XX, p. 6.

17 Memo from Chief of Bureau of Aeronautics, Admiral E.J. King to Chief of Naval Operations, J.K. Taussig Acting, 23 May 1933, BUAER Records, National Archives Research Center, Washington, DC.

18 Keith, Phil, *Staying the Rising Sun: The True Story of USS Lexington, Her Valiant Crew, and Changing the Course of WWII*, Zenith Press, Minneapolis, MN, 2015, p. 209.

19 Naval History and Heritage Command, H-008-5: Admiral Ernest J. King— Chief of Naval Operations, 1942, www.history.navy.mil/about-us/leadership/director/directors-corner/h-grams/h-gram-008/h-008-5.html.

20 'Wiley Requested Sea Duty', *New York Times*, 17 June 1933, p. 1.

21 Althoff, *Sky Ships*, p. 107.

22 Ibid.

21: LAKEHURST

1 'New *Akron* Urged By Admiral King', *New York Times*.

2 Letter to Admiral Moffett from Congressman William H. Sutphin, 3rd Dist., NJ, Committee on Naval Affairs, 14 March 1933, BUAER Records, National Archives Research Center, Washington, DC.

3 Memo from Commanding Officer A.H. Dresel to Chief of Naval Operations, Subject: USS *Macon* – Schedule of employment, 1 July to 1 October 1933, 6 July 1933, BUAER Records, National Archives Research Center, Washington, DC.

4 Ibid.

5 Althoff, *Sky Ships*, p. 107.

6 Dresel Memo, 6 July 1933, Subject: USS *Macon* – Schedule of employment, BUAER Records, National Archives Research Center, Washington, DC.

7 Smith, *The Airships* Akron & Macon, p. 119.

8 Topping, *When Giants Roamed the Sky*, p. 165.

9 Hunsaker, J.C., Notes, University of Akron Libraries, Karl Arnstein Papers.

10 Letter from Arnstein to Inspector of Naval Aircraft, 13 June 1933, University of Akron Libraries, Karl Arnstein Papers.

11 Memo from Commander Garland Fulton to Admiral King, 28 June 1933, BUAER Records, National Archives Research Center, Washington, DC.

12 Ibid.

13 *Macon's Report on Acceptance Trials held April 10–June 14 at Akron and August 30–31 at Lakehurst*, BUAER Records, National Archives Research Center, Washington, DC.

22: DR KARL ARNSTEIN: A GIANT DISPLACED

1 'Karl Arnstein, Airship Designer Chief Engineer of *Akron* and *Macon* Projects is Dead', *New York Times*, 13 December 1974, p. 48.

2 Litchfield, *Industrial Voyage*, p. 239.

3 Biography of Karl Arnstein, University of Akron Libraries, Karl Arnstein Papers, rave.ohiolink.edu/archives/ead/OhAkUAS0012.

4 Topping, *When Giants Roamed the Sky*, p. 237.

5   Ibid., p. 85.
6   Litchfield, *Industrial Voyage*, p. 239.
7   Topping, *When Giants Roamed the Sky*, p. 54.
8   Ibid., p. 8.
9   Litchfield, *Industrial Voyage*, p. 239.
10   Robinson and Keller, *Up Ship!*, pp. 124–5.
11   Topping, *When Giants Roamed the Sky*, p. 91.
12   Ibid., p. 92.
13   Ibid., p. 102.
14   Ibid., p. 104.
15   Ibid., p. 103.
16   Ibid., p. 108.
17   Ibid., p. ix.
18   Litchfield, *Industrial Voyage*, p. 75.
18   Topping, *When Giants Roamed the Sky*, p. 101.
20   Litchfield, *Industrial Voyage*, p. 240.
21   Topping, *When Giants Roamed the Sky*, p. 75.
22   Smith, *The Airships* Akron & Macon, p. 40.

23: DOUBTS

1   *New York Times*, 27 April 1933, p. 6.
2   Cook, Jeffrey, *USS* Akron *and USS* Macon: *An Engineering History of Fin Design*, Atlantis Productions, Edgewater, FL, 2008, p. 6.
3   Topping, *When Giants Roamed the Sky*, p. 152.
4   Cook, *USS* Akron *and USS* Macon, p. 21.
5   DeMary, 'USS *Macon*', *Universal Engineer*.
6   'The World's Largest Airship', The Goodyear News Service, p. 59.
7   Topping, *When Giants Roamed the Sky*, p. 155.
8   Bolster, Calvin A., Lt, US Navy, Testimony at Navy Court of Inquiry into the Loss of the *Macon*, p. 111, University of Akron Libraries, Karl Arnstein Papers.
9   Arnstein, Karl, Dr, 'Factors of Safety in Airship and Other Engineering Structures', Karl Arnstein Papers, University of Akron Libraries, Akron, OH.
10   Topping, *When Giants Roamed the Sky*, p. 156.
11   Cook, *USS* Akron *and USS* Macon, p. 28.
12   Ibid., p. 29.
13   Ibid.
14   Ibid.; Topping, *When Giants Roamed the Sky*, p. 176.
15   Topping, *When Giants Roamed the Sky*, p. 176.
16   Cook, *USS* Akron *and USS* Macon, p. 26.
17   Topping, *When Giants Roamed the Sky*, p. 177.
18   Cook, *USS* Akron *and USS* Macon, p. 29.
19   Topping, *When Giants Roamed the Sky*, p. 202.
20   Trimble, *Admiral William A. Moffett*, p. 273.
21   Topping, *When Giants Roamed the Sky*, p. 177.
22   Cook, *USS* Akron *and USS* Macon, p. 33.
23   Topping, *When Giants Roamed the Sky*, pp. 183–4.

24 Ibid.
25 *Investigation of the Loss of the USS* Akron; House of Representatives; Subcommittee on Aeronautics of the Committee on Naval Affairs, 7 April 1933, p. 1.
26 *Building the World's Largest Airships*, Goodyear-Zeppelin Corporation, Moffett Field Museum, Mountain View, CA, p. 3.
27 Letter marked PERSONAL from Arnstein to Commander Garland Fulton, Bureau of Aeronautics, Washington, DC, 8 July 1933, BUAER Records, National Archives Research Center, Washington, DC.
28 Ibid.
29 Letter from G. Fulton to Dr Arnstein, 10 July 1933, BUAER Records, National Archives Research Center, Washington, DC.

24: FULTON

1 Topping, *When Giants Roamed the Sky*, p. 196.
2 Cook, *USS* Akron *and USS* Macon, p. 21.
3 Fulton, Garland, Commander (CC), US Navy, 'Airship Progress and Airship Problems', February 1929, *Journal of the American Society of Naval Engineers*, Vol XLI, No. 1, pp. 32–3.
4 Ibid.
5 Fulton, Garland, Captain, US Navy (ret.), 'Recollections of the Early History of Naval Aviation', *Naval Engineers Journal*, October 1964, pp. 743–51.
6 Letter from Arnstein to Fulton, 22 July 1932, BUAER Records, National Archives Research Center, Washington, DC.
7 Fulton Memorandum, 6 August 1935, p. 4.
8 Memorandum from K. Bauch, Subject: *Macon* Fin Reinforcement, 12 November 1935, University of Akron Libraries, Karl Arnstein Papers.
9 Fulton Memorandum, 6 August 1935, p. 6.
10 Ibid., p. 5.
11 *The Lucky Bag*, US Naval Academy, 1912, Vol. XIX, p. 74.
12 Topping, *When Giants Roamed the Sky*, p. 114; Robinson and Keller, *Up Ship!*, pp. 125, 127.
13 Robinson and Keller, *Up Ship!*, pp. 124, 127.
14 National Air & Space Museum Archives, The Garland Fulton Collection, sova. si.edu/record/NASM.XXXX.0101?s=0&n=10&t=C&q=garland+fulton&i=0.
15 Robinson and Keller, *Up Ship!*, p. 124.
16 Quarterly Hull Inspection Report, 30 September 1933, USS *Macon*, BUAER Records, National Archives Research Center, Washington, DC.

25: SUNNYVALE

1 Miller, Harold B., Rear Admiral, US Navy (ret.), 'Skyborne Aircraft Carriers: A Closed Chapter of Naval Aviation', *Shipmate*, March 1984, p. 16.
2 Robinson and Keller, *Up Ship!*, p. 186.
3 Hook, *Flying Hookers for the* Macon, p. 27.

4   *San Francisco Examiner*, 16 October 1933, p. 5.
5   Ibid.
6   *New York Times*, 12 April 1933, p. 7.
7   *San Francisco Examiner*, 16 October 1933, p. 5.
8   Hook, *Flying Hookers for the* Macon, p. 28.
9   *San Francisco Examiner*, 16 October 1933, p. 5.
10 Ibid.
11 Ibid.
12 Ibid.
13 Moffett Field 60th Anniversary 1933–1993 Commemorative Brochure, p. 4.
14 Ibid.
15 Ibid., p. 1.
16 Ibid., p. 4.
17 Western Union Telegram from R.W. Peterson, Chairman of Santa Clara County Consolidated Chambers of Commerce, to Admiral Moffett, 2 December 1930, Moffett Field Museum.
18 Moffett Field 60th Anniversary 1933–1993 Commemorative Brochure, p. 5.
19 *New York Times*, 18 May 1933, p. 8.
20 Veronico, Nicholas A., *Moffett Field*, Arcadia Publishing, San Francisco, CA, 2006, p. 10.
21 Memo from Chief of Naval Operations to Commander in Chief, US Fleet, Subject: US *Macon*-operations with view to determining her military value, 26 October 1933, BUAER Records, National Archives Research Center, Washington, DC.

26: UP TO THE TASK?

1   Letters, *Time* magazine, 3 April 1933, Vol. XXI, No. 14.
2   Rosendahl, *Up Ship!*, p. 97.
3   Smith, *The Airships* Akron & Macon, p. 90.
4   Ibid., p. 63.
5   Ibid.
6   Ibid.
7   Ibid.
8   Toland, *The Great Dirigibles*, p. 279.
9   Smith, *The Airships* Akron & Macon, Footnote No. 11, p. 214; *New York Times*, 27 April 1933, p. 6.
10 Ibid., p. 3.
11 Grossnick, Roy A. (ed.), *Kite Balloons to Airships*, p. 30.
12 Althoff, *Sky Ships*, p. 94.
13 Grossnick, Roy A. (ed.), *Kite Balloons to Airships*, pp. 31–2.
14 Letter from E.J. King to Commander A.H. Dresel, Subject: USS *Macon*, 11 January 1934, National Air & Space Museum Archives, The Garland Fulton Collection, Folder 8.
15 Smith, *The Airships* Akron & Macon, pp. 103, 105.
16 Ibid., p. 105.
17 Ibid., p. 69.

18 Grossnick, Roy A. (ed.), *Kite Balloons to Airships*, p. 32.
19 Smith, *The Airships* Akron & Macon, pp. 69, 70, 112.
20 Letter from E.J. King to Commander A.H. Dresel, Subject: USS *Macon*, 11 January 1934.
21 Letter from E.J. King, To Rear Admiral John Halligan, Commander Aircraft, Battle Forces, USS *Saratoga*, Navy Yard, Bremerton, Washington, 11 January 1934, BUAER Records, National Archives Research Center, Washington, DC.
22 Ibid.
23 Smith, *The Airships* Akron & Macon, p. 113.
24 Ibid.; Robinson and Keller, *Up Ship!*, p. 187.
25 Rosendahl, *SNAFU*, p. 36; Miller, 'Skyborne Aircraft Carriers', *Shipmate*, pp. 15–17.
26 Memo from Commanding Officer to Chief Bureau of Aeronautics, Subject: *USS Macon-Structural Failure*, 7 April 1934, BUAER Records, National Archives Research Center, Washington, DC.

27: FLYING AIRCRAFT CARRIERS

1 Hoffman, Richard, Capt. (ret.) US Navy, 'Curtiss F9C Sparrowhawk: Airship Fighters', *Naval Fighters*, No. 79, 2008, p. 25.
2 Ibid., pp. 25–6.
3 Goodspeed, M. Hill, 'Curtiss F9C Sparrowhawk', *Wings of Fame: The Journal of Classic Combat Aircraft*, Vol. 17, AIRtime Publishing, Inc., Westport, CT, under licence from Aerospace Publishing Ltd, London, UK, 1999, p. 102.
4 Smith, *The Airships* Akron & Macon, p. 27; Hoffman, 'Curtiss F9C Sparrowhawk', *Naval Fighters*, p. 15.
5 Smith, *The Airships* Akron & Macon, p. 74; Hoffman, 'Curtiss F9C Sparrowhawk', *Naval Fighters*, p. 21.
6 Hoffman, 'Curtiss F9C Sparrowhawk', *Naval Fighters*, p. 21.
7 Smith, *The Airships* Akron & Macon, pp. 135, 137.
8 Lust, John, interviewed by Michael J. Vinarcik, p. 11.
9 Goodspeed, 'Curtiss F9C Sparrowhawk', *Wings of Fame*, p. 102; Hook, *Flying Hookers for the* Macon, p. 81.
10 Mikesh, Robert C., 'That Great Hook-Up in the Sky!', *Wings*, February 1975, Vol. 5, No. 1, p. 20.
11 Mumma, Phil, '*Macon's* Men Rode Navy Flying Trapeze', *Moffett News*, 16 October 1968, Vol. 51, No. 12, p. 4.
12 Goodspeed, 'Curtiss F9C Sparrowhawk', *Wings of Fame*, p. 102.
13 Hoffman, 'Curtiss F9C Sparrowhawk', *Naval Fighters*, p. 27.
14 Ibid., p. 25; Mikesh, 'That Great Hook-Up in the Sky!', *Wings*, p. 24.
15 *HTA Report Operations*, USS *Akron*, 1931–1932, BUAER Records, National Archives Research Center, Washington, DC.
16 Letter to Lt J.R. Dudley, US Navy, 24 September 1934, Attachment: *Operation of HTA from LTA*, p. 3, courtesy of Blaine Miller.
17 Smith, *The Airships* Akron & Macon, pp. 29–30.
18 Ibid., p. 139; Hoffman, 'Curtiss F9C Sparrowhawk', *Naval Fighters*, p. 33.
19 Trimble, *Admiral William A. Moffett*, pp. 238–9.

20 Smith, *The Airships* Akron & Macon, p. 69.
21 Ibid.
22 Hoffman, 'Curtiss F9C Sparrowhawk', *Naval Fighters*, p. 22.
23 Smith, *The Airships* Akron & Macon, p. 19.
24 Hoffman, 'Curtiss F9C Sparrowhawk', *Naval Fighters*, p. 2; Miller, Harold B., Lt, US Navy, 'Navy Skyhooks', *Proceedings*, US Naval Institute, February 1935, p. 235; Smith, *The Airships* Akron & Macon, p. 19.
25 Hoffman, 'Curtiss F9C Sparrowhawk', *Naval Fighters*, p. 2; Smith, *The Airships* Akron & Macon, pp. 19–20; Miller, 'Navy Skyhooks', *Proceedings*, pp. 236–7.
26 Hoffman, 'Curtiss F9C Sparrowhawk', *Naval Fighters*, p. 2; Smith, *The Airships* Akron & Macon, pp. 19, 21; Miller, 'Navy Skyhooks', *Proceedings*, p. 236.
27 Hoffman, 'Curtiss F9C Sparrowhawk', *Naval Fighters*, p. 2.
28 Miller, 'Navy Skyhooks', *Proceedings*, p. 238.
29 Hoffman, 'Curtiss F9C Sparrowhawk', *Naval Fighters*, p. 4; Smith, *The Airships* Akron & Macon, pp. 21, 23.
30 Smith, *The Airships* Akron & Macon, pp. 21, 23.
31 Miller, 'Navy Skyhooks', *Proceedings*, p. 239.
32 Hoffman, 'Curtiss F9C Sparrowhawk', *Naval Fighters*, p. 19.

28: PERIL IN THE SKY

1   Smith, *The Airships* Akron & Macon, p. 115.
2   Fulton Memorandum, 6 August 1935, p. 4.
3   Ibid., p. 47.
4   Ibid., pp. 47–8.
5   Ibid., p. 48.
6   Memo from A.H. Dresel to Commander Aircraft, Battle Force, 5 December 1933, BUAER Records, National Archives Research Center, Washington, DC.
7   Robinson and Keller, *Up Ship!*, p. 188; Smith, *The Airships* Akron & Macon, p. 115.
8   Robinson and Keller, *Up Ship!*, p. 188.
9   Memo from Commanding Officer of USS *Macon* to Chief of the Bureau of Aeronautics, Subject: USS *Macon* Flight to Opa-locka, Florida and Return, 11 June 1934, BUAER Records, National Archives Research Center, Washington, DC.
10 Smith, *The Airships* Akron & Macon, p. 101.
11 Memo from Commanding Officer to Chief of the Bureau of Aeronautics, Subject: USS *Macon* Flight to Opa-locka, Florida and Return-Material report on, p. 1, BUAER Records, National Archives Research Center, Washington, DC.
12 Mackey, *What Really Happened to the* Macon?, p. 4, quoting Dr A.D. Topping's review of Richard K. Smith's book, *The Airships* Akron & Macon, in the *Wingfoot LTA Bulletin*.
13 Smith, *The Airships* Akron & Macon, p. 117.
14 Ibid.
15 Ibid.
16 Robinson and Keller, *Up Ship!*, p. 188.

17 Daniels, A.L., Lt, US Navy, Testimony at Navy Court of Inquiry into the Loss of the *Macon*, p. 94, University of Akron Libraries, Karl Arnstein Papers.

18 Smith, *The Airships* Akron & Macon, p. 117.

19 Memo from Commanding Officer to Chief of the Bureau of Aeronautics, Subject: USS. MACON-Damage to Structure in Flight to Opa-locka, Florida-Report of, p. 1, BUAER Records, National Archives Research Center, Washington, DC.

20 Klemperer, W., *Damages suffered by USS* Macon *in flight to Florida*, 15 May 1934, University of Akron Libraries, Karl Arnstein Papers.

21 Ibid.; Memo from Commanding Officer to Chief of the Bureau of Aeronautics, Subject: USS MACON-Flight to Opa-locka, Florida, and return-Material report on, p. 9; Althoff, *Sky Ships*, p. 119.

22 Althoff, *Sky Ships*, p. 119.

23 Klemperer, W., *Damages suffered by USS* Macon *in flight to Florida*.

24 Smith, *The Airships* Akron & Macon, p. 117.

25 Memo from Commanding Officer to Chief of the Bureau of Aeronautics, Subject: USS. MACON-Damage to Structure in Flight to Opa-locka, Florida-Report of, pp. 1–2.

26 '*Macon's* Loss Laid to a Break at Fins', *New York Times*, 16 February 1935, p. 2.

27 Mackey, Donald M., Lt Cdr, *What Really Happened to the* Macon?, p. 12, ABAC Acq#1604; Memo from Commanding Officer to Chief of the Bureau of Aeronautics, Subject: USS. MACON-Damage to Structure in Flight to Opa-locka, Florida-Report of, p. 2.

28 Toland, *The Great Dirigibles*, p. 277.

29 Ibid.

30 Smith, *The Airships* Akron & Macon, p. 117.

31 Toland, *The Great Dirigibles*, p. 277.

32 *The Washington Post*, 13 February 1935.

33 Smith, *The Airships* Akron & Macon, Footnote No. 14, p. 214.

34 Bolster, Testimony at Navy Court of Inquiry into the Loss of the *Macon*, p. 44; 'Construction Officer Asserts Airship Was Nearly Lost', *New York Times*, 16 February 1935, p. 1.

35 Robinson and Keller, *Up Ship!*, Chapter 12, Footnote No. 13, p. 229.

29: FLEET PROBLEM XV

1 Toland, *The Great Dirigibles*, p. 278.

2 Smith, *The Airships* Akron & Macon, p. 119.

3 Topping, *When Giants Roamed the Sky*, p. 156.

4 Memo from Commanding Officer to Chief of the Bureau of Aeronautics, Subject: USS MACON-Flight to Opa-locka, Florida, and return-Material report on, p. 3.

5 Ibid., pp. 1–10; Hoffman, 'Curtiss F9C Sparrowhawk', *Naval Fighters*, p. 30; Robinson and Keller, *Up Ship!*, p. 188.

6 Fulton Memorandum, 6 August 1935, p. 7.

7 Bolster, Calvin M., Rear Admiral, US Navy (ret.), 'The Life and Death of USS *Macon*', in *Flying Hookers for the* Macon, Airsho Publishers, Baltimore, MD, p. 134.

8   Report From Commanding Officer of USS *Macon* To Chief of the Bureau of Aeronautics, Subject: USS *Macon* Flight to Opa-locka, Florida and Return, p. 3.

9   Ibid., p. 4.

10 Ibid., p. 3.

11 Ibid., pp. 4–5.

12 Ibid., p. 5.

13 Smith, *The Airships* Akron & Macon, p. 119.

14 Ibid., p. 5.

15 Hook, *Flying Hookers for the Macon*, p. 28.

16 Report From Commanding Officer of USS *Macon* To Chief of the Bureau of Aeronautics, Subject: USS *Macon* Flight to Opa-locka, Florida and Return, p. 3; Bolster, 'The Life and Death of USS *Macon*', p. 134.

17 Western Union Telegram from Kurt Bauch to Karl Arnstein, 29 April 1934. University of Akron Libraries, Karl Arnstein Papers.

18 Smith, *The Airships* Akron & Macon, p. 119.

19 To Dr Karl Arnstein from Rear Admiral E.J. King, Chief of the Bureau of Aeronautics, 22 May 1934, University of Akron Libraries, Karl Arnstein Papers.

20 Memo from Commanding Officer to Chief of the Bureau of Aeronautics, Subject: USS MACON-Flight to Opa-locka, Florida, and return-Material report on, p. 6.

21 Smith, *The Airships* Akron & Macon, p. 119.

22 Ibid., p. 121.

23 Grossnick, Roy A. (ed.), *Kite Balloons to Airships*, p. 33.

24 '*Macon* "Destroyed" by "Enemy" Planes', *New York Times*, 9 May 1934, Section: Books-Arts, p. 23.

25 Memo from Commanding Officer to Chief of the Bureau of Aeronautics, Subject: USS MACON-Flight to Opa-locka, Florida, and return-Material report on, p. 6.

26 'Swanson denies he said USS *Macon* Prove Worthless in Caribbean Sea Fleet Maneuvers', *Akron Beacon Journal*, 10 May 1934, p. 1.

27 Smith, *The Airships* Akron & Macon, pp. 122–3.

28 'Standley Praises Fleet Efficiency He Doubts *Macon's* Value Says Airship Has Shown Her Vulnerability', *New York Times*, 13 May 1934, pp. 1–2.

29 Ibid.

30 Ibid.

31 Ibid.

32 Cable from Dresel to King, 9 May 1934, BUAER Records, National Archives Research Center, Washington, DC.

33 Smith, *The Airships* Akron & Macon, p. 123.

34 Memo from Commanding Officer to Chief of the Bureau of Aeronautics, Subject: USS MACON-Flight to Opa-locka, Florida, and return-Material report on, p. 8.

35 Toland, *The Great Dirigibles*, p. 279.

36 Letter from Arnstein to Fulton, 30 April 1934, University of Akron Libraries, Karl Arnstein Papers, p. 1.

37 Ibid.

38 Ibid.

39 Ibid.

40 Ibid., p. 2.
41 Memo from Commanding Officer to Chief of the Bureau of Aeronautics, Subject: USS *Macon*-Damage to Structure in flight to Opa-locka, Florida-Report of, p. 4.
42 Klemperer, W., *Damages suffered by USS* Macon *in flight to Florida.*
43 Fulton Memorandum, 6 August 1935, p. 9.
44 Rosendahl, *SNAFU*, p. 23.
45 Minutes covering conference of Dr Arnstein's visit with Commander Fulton, J.C. Peeples, Secretary. Bureau of Aeronautics in Washington, DC, 17 July 1934, BUAER Records, National Archives Research Center, Washington, DC.
46 Memo from G.V. Whittle, Lt Cdr, Inspector of Naval Aircraft, to Goodyear Zeppelin, 2 August 1934, University of Akron Libraries, Karl Arnstein Papers.
47 Memo from Commanding Officer to Commander in Chief, US Fleet, *c.* May 1934, p. 4, BUAER Records, National Archives Research Center, Washington, DC.
48 Ibid.
49 Ibid., p. 5.
50 Ibid.
51 McBride, William M., *Technological Change and the United States Navy 1865–1945*, The Johns Hopkins University Press, Baltimore, MD, 2000, p. 188.
52 Smith, *The Airships* Akron & Macon, p. 125.
53 Ibid., p. 127.
54 Fisher Research Labs, Company History, www.fisherlab.com/about.htm.

30: A GIANT IN WAITING

1   'Wiley Requested Sea Duty', *New York Times.*
2   Ibid.
3   Author interview with Ian Wiley, 1 June 2013, Corte Madera, CA.
4   Author interview with Marie Wiley Ross, 11 July 2008, Livermore, CA.
5   Ross, Ian, *Such is Life in the Navy: The Story of Rear Admiral Herbert V. Wiley*, self-published, 2014, 2016, p. 3.
6   Memo from The Chief of the Bureau of Aeronautics to The Chief of the Bureau of Navigation, Re: Orders, 27 March 1931, Wiley Personnel File, National Personnel Records Center, St Louis, MO.
7   Author interview with Marie Wiley Ross.
8   Video interview with Gordon Wiley, conducted by Monterey Maritime History Museum; Thomas, Tim, 'The USS *Macon*: Also a Monterey Story', p. 5, *Noticias de Monterey: Into the Deep: Wreck and Rediscovery of America's Last Airship*, Monterey History and Art Association, Spring–Summer 2006, Vol. LV, Nos 2–3.
9   Author interview with Marie Wiley Ross.
10 Topping, *When Giants Roamed the Sky*, p. 194.
11 Ibid.; Vaeth, J. Gordon, 'The *Macon*: Last Queen of the Skies', *Naval History* magazine, Spring 1992, Vol. 6, No. 1, p. 55.

31: THE *HOUSTON* INCIDENT

1 Smith, *The Airships* Akron & Macon, p. 128.
2 Rosendahl, *SNAFU*, p. 33.
3 Vaeth, 'The *Macon*: Last Queen of the Skies', *Naval History* magazine, p. 55.
4 Smith, *The Airships* Akron & Macon, p. 128.
5 Toland, *The Great Dirigibles*, p. 279.
6 Lust, John, interviewed by Michael J. Vinarcik, p. 19.
7 Smith, *The Airships* Akron & Macon, p. 128.
8 Ibid.
9 Memo from Commanding Officer to Commander Aircraft, Battle Force, Subject: USS *Macon*-Operations, July 1934, p. 1, BUAER Records, National Archives Research Center, Washington, DC; Althoff, *Sky Ships*, p.116; Smith, *The Airships* Akron & Macon, p. 126.
10 Letter from Harold Miller, to Ward Harrigan, 2 March 1935, p. 6, courtesy of Blaine Miller.
11 Smith, *The Airships* Akron & Macon, p. 128.
12 Video interview with Gordon Wiley, conducted by Monterey Maritime History Museum.
13 Memo from Commanding Officer to Commander Aircraft, Battle Force, Subject: USS MACON-Operations, p. 2.
14 Ibid.
15 Ibid; Robinson and Keller, *Up Ship!*, p. 189.
16 Memo from Commanding Officer to Commander Aircraft, Battle Force, Subject: USS MACON-Operations, p. 2.
17 Ibid.
18 Ibid., p. 3.
19 Ibid.
20 Ibid., p. 2.
21 Memo from Commanding Officer to Chief of Naval Operations, Subject: Operations of USS *Macon*, 18–21 July 1934; Contact with USS *Houston*, p. 2, BUAER Records, National Archives Research Center, Washington, DC.
22 Letter from H.B. Miller, Pan Am, Director of Public Relations, to Mr. William A. Riley, Jr, 22 January 1958, p. 3, courtesy of Blaine Miller.
23 Miller, 'Skyborne Aircraft Carriers', *Shipmate*, p. 17.
24 Smith, *The Airships* Akron & Macon, p. 129.
25 Vaeth, 'USS *Macon*: Lost and Found', *National Geographic* magazine, p. 127.
26 United Press, *Santa Ana Register*, Santa Ana, CA, 20 July 1934.
27 Smith, *The Airships* Akron & Macon, p. 131.
28 Hook, *Flying Hookers for the* Macon, p. 83.
29 Miller, 'Skyborne Aircraft Carriers', *Shipmate*, pp. 15–17.
30 Ibid.; Smith, *The Airships* Akron & Macon, pp. 129, 131.
31 United Press, *Santa Ana Register*, Santa Ana, CA, 20 July 1934.
32 Memo from Commanding Officer to Chief of Naval Operations, Subject: Operations of USS *Macon*, 18–21 July 1934; Contact with USS *Houston*, p. 2.
33 Ibid.
34 Smith, *The Airships* Akron & Macon, p. 128; Vaeth, 'The *Macon*: Last Queen of the Skies', *Naval History* magazine, p. 55.

35 Ullmann, John F., *Mellone's Photo Encyclopedia of USS* Akron *and* Macon *Event Covers*, FDC Publishing Co., Stewartsville, NJ, 1996, p. 147.

36 Ibid.

37 Memo from Commanding Officer to Chief of Naval Operations, Subject: Operations of USS *Macon*, 18–21 July 1934; Contact with USS *Houston*, p. 1.

38 Ibid.

39 Smith, *The Airships* Akron *&* Macon, p. 131.

40 Ibid.

41 Cable from USS *Macon* to Admiral King, 19 July 1934, BUAER Records, National Archives Research Center, Washington, DC.

42 Cable from COMBATFOR to Admiral King, Chief of Bureau of Aeronautics, 20 July 1934, BUAER Records, National Archives Research Center, Washington, DC.

43 Memo from Commanding Officer to Chief of Naval Operations, Subject: Operations of USS *Macon*, 18–21 July 1934; Contact with USS *Houston*, p. 1.

44 Schick, Jack H., 'Herbert Victor Wiley: American Hero Extraordinaire', *SearchWarp.com*, 5 May 2012.

45 Video interview with Gordon Wiley, conducted by Monterey Maritime History Museum.

46 Vaeth, 'USS *Macon*: Lost and Found', *National Geographic* magazine, p. 118.

47 Rosendahl, *SNAFU*, p. 37.

32: LT CDR WILEY: A GIANT REVEALED

1   Robinett, P.M., *Herbert V. Wiley 16 May 1891–26 April 1954 Who Was Born For High Adventure*, 1 August 1960, Western Historical Manuscript Collection-Columbine, Ellis Library, University of Missouri, Columbia, MO, Typescript Collection (C995), p. 1; Marshall, M. Ernest, *Rear Admiral Herbert V. Wiley: A Career in Airships and Battleships*, Naval Institute Press, Annapolis, MD, 2019, p. 6; Ross, *Such is Life in the Navy*, p. 3.

2   Robinett, *Herbert V. Wiley*, p. 1.

3   Marshall, *Rear Admiral Herbert V. Wiley*, p. 6.

4   Ross, *Such is Life in the Navy*, p. 7.

5   Robinett, *Herbert V. Wiley*, p. 1.

6   Ibid.

7   Ibid.

8   'Dirigible Commander Liked Mechanical Toys as a Boy', *St Louis Post-Dispatch*, 24 October 1928.

9   Ibid.

10 Robinett, *Herbert V. Wiley*, p. 1.

11 'Dirigible Commander Liked Mechanical Toys as a Boy', *St Louis Post-Dispatch*.

12 Ross, *Such is Life in the Navy*, p. 10.

13 'Dirigible Commander Liked Mechanical Toys as a Boy', *St Louis Post-Dispatch*; Ross, *Such is Life in the Navy*, p. 10.

14 Ibid., p. 11.

15 Ibid., p. 13.

16 Marshall, *Rear Admiral Herbert V. Wiley*, p. 8; Ross, *Such is Life in the Navy*, p. 13.

17 Author interview with Marie Wiley Ross.
18 Wiley, Herbert Victor, Health and Physical Records, Nimitz Library, United States Naval Academy, Annapolis, MD.
19 Demerit Record of Midshipman, Herbert Victor Wiley, Nimitz Library, United States Naval Academy, Annapolis, MD.
20 'Dirigible Commander Liked Mechanical Toys as a Boy', *St Louis Post-Dispatch*.
21 Marshall, *Rear Admiral Herbert V. Wiley*, p. 8; Ross, *Such is Life in the Navy*, p. 11.
22 Author interview with Marie Wiley Ross.
23 *The Lucky Bag*, US Naval Academy, 1915, Vol. XXII, p. 199.
24 Memo from President, Permanent Medical Examining Board to Superintendent, Subject: Physical examination of Midshipman Herbert Victor Wiley, First Class, Nimitz Library, United States Naval Academy, Annapolis, MD.
25 Ross, *Such is Life in the Navy*, p. 23.
26 Memo from Navy Department, Bureau of Navigation, Washington, DC, to Naval Academy, Subject: Wiley, Herbert Victor, 5 April 1915, Nimitz Library, United States Naval Academy, Annapolis, MD.
27 Memo from Special Medical Examining Board to Superintendent, Subject: Wiley, Herbert V., Midshipman First Class, Re rejection of, 27 May 1915, Nimitz Library, United States Naval Academy, Annapolis, MD.
28 Marshall, *Rear Admiral Herbert V. Wiley*, p. 11.
29 Ibid., pp. 21–2.
30 Ibid., p. 25.
31 Ibid., pp. 25–6.
32 Ibid., p. 26.
33 Rosendahl, *Up Ship!*, p. 3.
34 Ibid., p. 5.
35 Robinson and Keller, U*p Ship!*, p. 68.
36 Ibid.
37 Report of Examining Board, US Naval Air Station, Lakehurst, NJ, 12 September 1924, Wiley Personnel file, National Personnel Records Center, St Louis, MO.
38 Memo from Lieutenant Commander Herbert V. Wiley to The Chief of the Bureau of Navigation; Subject: Leave and Change of Duty—Request for, 12 August 1926, Wiley Personnel file, National Personnel Records Center, St Louis, MO.
39 Ibid.
40 Memo from The Commanding Officer to The Chief of the Bureau of Navigation, Subject: Lieutenant Commander Wiley requests leave and change of duty; 13 September 1926; 1st Endorsement, USS. Los Angeles, Naval Air Station, Lakehurst, NJ, 22 September 1926, Wiley Personnel file, National Personnel Records Center, St Louis, MO.
41 'Dirigible Commander Liked Mechanical Toys as a Boy', *St Louis Post-Dispatch*.
42 'Over the Old Home Town', *Kansas City Star*, 9 October 1928.
43 Smith, *The Airships* Akron & Macon, p. 40.
44 Author interview with Ian Wiley.
45 Author interview with Marie Wiley Ross.
46 Ibid.

47 Toland, *The Great Dirigibles*, p. 279.
48 Smith, *The Airships* Akron & Macon, p. 127.
49 Wiley, H.V., Lt Cdr, US Navy, 'Value of Airships', *Proceedings*, US Naval Institute, May 1934, p. 665.

33: A GIANT EXCELS

1   Memo from Commanding Officer to Chief of Naval Operations, Subject: Operations of USS *Macon*, 18–21 July 1934; Contact with USS *Houston*, p. 3.
2   Ibid.
3   Letter From Wiley to King, 28 August 1934, p. 1.
4   Smith, *The Airships* Akron & Macon, p. 131.
5   Letter from H.V. Wiley to Admiral King, 28 August 1934, p. 1.
6   Ibid.
7   Ibid.
8   Ibid.
9   Video interview with Gordon Wiley, conducted by Monterey Maritime History Museum.
10 Memo from Commanding Officer to Commander Aircraft, Battle Force; Subject: USS MACON-Operation Report-week ending 28 October 1934, p. 1, BUAER Records, National Archives Research Center, Washington, DC.
11 USS *Macon* Operational Flight Log, Moffett Field Museum, Sunnyvale, CA.
12 Robinson and Keller, *Up Ship!*, p. 190.
13 Memo from Commanding Officer to Commander Aircraft, Battle Force, Subject: USS MACON-Operations-Week 6–12 August 1934, p. 2, BUAER Records, National Archives Research Center, Washington, DC; Letter from H.B. Miller to Lt J.R. Dudley, 34 September 1934, attachment: Operation of H.T.A. from L.T.A., pp. 3–4, courtesy of Blaine Miller; Letter From H.B. Miller, to Mr. William A. Riley, Jr, 22 January 1958, p. 4, courtesy of Blaine Miller.
14 Hoffman, 'Curtiss F9C Sparrowhawk', p. 32; Smith, *The Airships* Akron & Macon, p. 131.
15 Althoff, *Sky Ships*, p. 118.
16 Bolster, 'The Life and Death of USS *Macon*', p. 135; Smith, *The Airships* Akron & Macon, p. 55; 'Efficiency of *Macon* Gains in Long Cruises', *New York Times*, 30 December 1934, p. 2; Smith, *The Airships* Akron & Macon, pp. 133–5.
17 Memo from Commanding Officer to Commander Aircraft, Battle Force, Subject: USS MACON-Operation Report-week ending 2 September 1934, pp. 1–2, BUAER Records, National Archives Research Center, Washington, DC.
18 Smith, *The Airships* Akron & Macon, pp. 133–5.
19 Letter from H.B. Miller to Mr. William A. Riley, Jr, 22 January 1958, p. 4, courtesy of Blaine Miller.
20 Althoff, *Sky Ships*, p. 117.
21 Memo from Commanding Officer to Commander Aircraft, Battle Force, Subject: USS MACON-Operations, July 1934, p. 2.
22 Memo from Commanding Officer to Commander Aircraft, Battle Force, Subject: USS MACON-Operations, July 1934, p. 3; Memo from Commanding Officer to Commander Aircraft, Battle Force, Subject:

USS MACON-Operation Report-Week ending 2 September 1934, p. 2, BUAER Records, National Archives Research Center, Washington, DC.

23 Memo from Commanding Officer to Commander Aircraft, Battle Force, Subject: USS MACON-Operations, July 1934, p. 4.

24 Letter from Wiley to Fulton, 3 August 1934, BUAER Records, National Archives Research Center, Washington, DC.

25 Memo from Commanding Officer to Commander Aircraft, Battle Force, Subject: USS MACON-Operations-Week of 6–12 August 1934, p. 1.

26 Memo from Commanding Officer to Commander Aircraft, Battle Force, Subject: USS MACON-Operation Report-Week ending 19 August 1934, p. 1; Memo from Commanding Officer to Commander Aircraft, Battle Force, Subject: USS MACON-Operation Report-Week ending 16 September 1934, p. 1, BUAER Records, National Archives Research Center, Washington, DC.

27 Memo from Commanding Officer to Commander Aircraft, Battle Force, Subject: USS MACON-Operation Report-Week ending 28 October 1934, pp. 3–4.

28 Toland, *The Great Dirigibles*, p. 279.

29 'Wiley Did Not Rush Repairing of *Macon*', *New York Times*, 20 February 1935, Section: Sports, p. 28.

30 Letter from Inspector General of Naval Aircraft to Goodyear-Zeppelin Corp., 27 August 1934, University of Akron Libraries, Karl Arnstein Papers, Akron, OH.

31 Cook, *USS* Akron *& USS* Macon, p. 34; Rosendahl, *SNAFU*, pp. 23–4; Robinson and Keller, *Up Ship!*, p. 191; Topping, *When Giants Roamed the Sky*, pp. 195–6, Smith, *The Airships* Akron *&* Macon, pp. 147, 149.

32 Rosendahl, *SNAFU*, pp. 23–4.

33 Topping, *When Giants Roamed the Sky*, p. 196.

34 Ibid.

35 Litchfield, Paul W., and Allen, Hugh, *Why Has America No Rigid Airships?*, Corday & Gross, Co., Cleveland, OH, 1945, pp. 31–2; Cook, *USS* Akron *and USS* Macon, Footnote No. 101, p. 88.

36 Smith, *The Airships* Akron *&* Macon, p. 140; Robinson and Keller, *Up Ship!*, p. 190.

37 Toland, *The Great Dirigibles*, p. 280.

38 Letter from Lt H.B. Miller to Lt Ward Harrigan, 2 March 1935, p. 1, courtesy of Blaine Miller.

39 Hoffman, 'Curtiss F9C Sparrowhawk', *Naval Fighters*, p. 36.

40 Ibid., p. 34.

41 *New York Times*, 30 December 1934, p. 2.

42 Memo from Commanding Officer to Commander Aircraft, Battle Force, Subject: USS MACON-Operation Report-Week ending 13 January 1935, p. 1.

43 Letter from Lt H.B. Miller to Lt Ward Halligan, 2 March 1935, p. 2; Smith, *The Airships* Akron *&* Macon, pp. 67, 69, 112, 133.

44 Memo from The Chief of Bureau of Aeronautics to Commanding Officer, USS. MACON, Subject: USS MACON-Schedule, 11 January 1935, BUAER Records, National Archives Research Center, Washington, DC.

45 '*Macon* Aftermath – Is the US Airship Program Down for the Count', *The Washington Post*, 17 February 1935.

46 Smith, *The Airships* Akron *&* Macon, p. 147.

47 Memo from Chief of Naval Operations (acting J.S. Taussig) to Commander-in-Chief, US Fleet, 4 December 1934, BUAER Records, National Archives Research Center, Washington, DC.

48 Memo from Commander in Chief, US Fleet, (J.M. Reeves) to Chief of Bureau of Aeronautics, 24 December 1934, BUAER Records, National Archives Research Center, Washington, DC.

49 Letter from Lt H.B. Miller to Lt Ward Harrigan, 2 March 1935, p. 2, courtesy of Blaine Miller; 'Coxswain Proves He Can Take It', *New York Times*, 16 February 1935, p. 2

50 Letter from Lt H.B. Miller to Lt Ward Harrigan, 2 March 1935, p. 2, courtesy of Blaine Miller.

51 Wiley, 'Value of Airships', *Proceedings*, p. 671.

52 'Coxswain Proves He Can Take It', *New York Times*, p. 2; Robinson and Keller, *Up Ship!*, p. 190.

53 Letter from Lt H.B. Miller to Lt Ward Harrigan, 2 March 1935, p. 2, courtesy of Blaine Miller; Smith, *The Airships* Akron & Macon, p. 149.

54 Marshall, *Rear Admiral Herbert V. Wiley*, p. 191.

34: A GIANT IN DANGER

1 Goodspeed, 'Curtiss F9C Sparrowhawk', *Wings of Fame*, p. 101.

2 Campbell, George W., Lt US Navy, 'Five O'Clock, Off California' in *Disaster!*, Kartman, Ben and Brown, Leonard (eds), Pellegrini & Cudahy, New York, NY, 1948, p. 240.

3 Ibid.

4 Ibid.

5 Ibid., p. 241.

6 Lust, John, interviewed by Michael J. Vinarcik, p. 13.

7 'Fleet Ships Head North', *Los Angeles Times*, 12 February 1935, Section II, p. A5.

8 Toland, *The Great Dirigibles*, p. 281.

9 Smith, *The Airships* Akron & Macon, p. 151; Althoff, *Sky Ships*, p. 120.

10 Letter from Lt H.B. Miller to Lt Ward Harrigan, 2 March 1935, p. 2, courtesy of Blaine Miller

11 Toland, *The Great Dirigibles*, p. 281.

12 Mackey, Donald M., Lt Cdr, US Navy, 'What Really Happened to the *Macon*?', *LTA Bulletin*, c. 1965, p. 6.

13 Miller, H.B., Lt, US Navy, 'Last Flight Recalled', in *Flying Hookers for the Macon*, Airsho Publishers, Baltimore, MD, p. 129.

14 *Macon* Logbook, 1200 to 1600 hours, 12 February 1935, p. 591, BUAER Records, National Archives Research Center, Washington, DC.

15 Ibid.

16 Letter from Lt H.B. Miller to Lt Ward Harrigan, 2 March 1935, p. 3, courtesy of Blaine Miller.

17 *Macon* Logbook, 1200 to 1600 hours, 12 February 1935, p. 591.

18 Rosendahl, *What About the Airship?*, p. 125.

19 Rosendahl, *SNAFU*, Footnote No. 7, p. 219.

20 Toland, *The Great Dirigibles*, p. 282.

21 Ibid., p. 283.

22 Letter from Harold Miller to Ward Harrigan, 2 March 1935, p. 3, courtesy of Blaine Miller.
23 Campbell, 'Five O'Clock, Off California,' p. 243.
24 'Fleet Ships Head North', *Los Angeles Times*, p. 5.
25 Campbell, 'Five O'Clock, Off California', p. 243.
26 Letter from Lt H.B. Miller to Lt Ward Harrigan, 2 March 1935, p. 3, courtesy of Blaine Miller.
27 Letter marked Personal and Confidential from C.M. Bolster to Commander Fulton, 26 March 1935, BUAER Records, National Archives Research Center, Washington, DC.
28 Letter from Lt H.B. Miller to Lt Ward Harrigan, 2 March 1935, p. 3, courtesy of Blaine Miller.
29 Miller, 'The Violent Death of America's Last Dirigible', *True* magazine, p. 60.
30 *Macon* Logbook, 1600 to 1800 hours, 12 February 1935, p. 592.
31 Letter marked Personal and Confidential from C.M. Bolster to Commander Fulton, 26 March 1935.
32 Peck, Scott E., Lt Cdr, Navigator, Testimony at the Navy Court of Inquiry into the Loss of the *Macon*, p. 99, University of Akron Libraries, Karl Arnstein Papers.
33 Toland, *The Great Dirigibles*, p. 283.
34 Ibid.
35 Ibid.
36 Mackey, 'What Really Happened to the *Macon*?', *LTA Bulletin*, p. 7, ABAC Acq#1604.
37 Toland, *The Great Dirigibles*, p. 284.
38 Smith, *The Airships* Akron & Macon, p. 151.
39 *Macon* Logbook, 1600 to 1800 hours, 12 February 1935, p. 592.
40 Ibid.
41 Smith, *The Airships* Akron & Macon, p. 153.
42 Toland, *The Great Dirigibles*, pp. 283–4.
43 Ibid., p. 285.
44 Letter marked Personal and Confidential from C.M. Bolster to Commander Fulton, 26 March 1935.
45 Smith, *The Airships* Akron & Macon, p. 153.
46 Mackey, 'What Really Happened to the *Macon*?', *LTA Bulletin*, p. 5, ABAC Acq#1604.
47 Davis, Robert J., Chief Boatswain's Mate, US Navy, Testimony at Navy Court of Inquiry into the Loss of the *Macon*, University of Akron Libraries, Karl Arnstein Papers; Letter marked Personal and Confidential from C.M. Bolster to Commander Fulton, 26 March 1935; Smith, *The Airships* Akron & Macon, p. 153.
48 Conover, William M., Aviation Metal Smith, First Class, US Navy, Testimony at Navy Court of Inquiry into the Loss of the *Macon*, University of Akron Libraries, Karl Arnstein Papers.
49 Ibid.
50 Letter marked Personal and Confidential from C.M. Bolster to Commander Fulton, 26 March 1935.
51 *Macon* Logbook, 1600 to 1800 hours, 12 February 1935, p. 592.

52 Peck, Testimony at Navy Court of Inquiry into the Loss of the *Macon*, p. 99.
53 Conover, Testimony at Navy Court of Inquiry into the Loss of the *Macon*.
54 Miller, 'The Violent Death of America's Last Dirigible', *True* magazine, p. 60.
55 Peck, Testimony at Court of Inquiry into the Loss of the *Macon*, p. 99.
56 Ibid.
57 Campbell, George W., Lt (jg), US Navy, Testimony at Navy Court of Inquiry into the Loss of the *Macon*, University of Akron Libraries, Karl Arnstein Papers.
58 'Wiley's Story of *Macon* Crackup', *San Francisco Chronicle*, 15 February 1935, p. 7.
59 Clarke, William, 'At the Helm of the USS *Macon* on February 12, 1935', interviewed by Robert Llewellyn on 8 September 1996, *Noticias de Monterey: Into the Deep: Wreck and Rediscovery of America's Last Airship*, Monterey History and Art Association, Spring–Summer 2006, Vol. LV, Nos 2–3, p. 17.
60 Clarke, William H., Coxswain, US Navy, Testimony at Navy Court of Inquiry into the Loss of the *Macon*, p. 77, University of Akron Libraries, Karl Arnstein Papers.
61 Conover, Testimony at Navy Court of Inquiry into the Loss of the *Macon*.
62 Ibid.
63 Clarke, Testimony at Navy Court of Inquiry into the Loss of the *Macon*, p. 77.
64 Letter marked Personal and Confidential from C.M. Bolster to Commander Fulton, 26 March 1935; Galatian, Andrew B., Aviation Chief Machinist's Mate, US Navy, Testimony at Navy Court of Inquiry into the Loss of the *Macon*, University of Akron Libraries, Karl Arnstein Papers.
65 Fraas, Matthew G., Jr, Aviation machinist Mate, Second Class, Testimony at Navy Court of Inquiry into the Loss of the *Macon*, p. 111, University of Akron Libraries, Karl Arnstein Papers.
66 Ibid.; Peck, Testimony at Navy Court of Inquiry into the Loss of the *Macon*, p. 99; Letter marked Personal and Confidential from C.M. Bolster to Commander Fulton, 26 March 1935.
67 Reppy, John D., Lt (jg), US Navy, Testimony at Navy Court of Inquiry into the Loss of the *Macon*, p. 35, University of Akron Libraries, Karl Arnstein Papers.
68 Toland, *The Great Dirigibles*, p. 286.
69 Herndon, William H., Jr, Ship's Cook, First Class, US Navy, Statement to Navy Court of Inquiry into the Loss of the *Macon*, University of Akron Libraries, Karl Arnstein Papers.
70 Class, Theodore. Ship's Cook, Second Class, Statement to Navy Court of Inquiry into the Loss of the *Macon*, University of Akron Libraries, Karl Arnstein Papers.
71 Davis, Robert J., Testimony at Navy Court of Inquiry into the Loss of the *Macon*.
72 Smith, *The Airships* Akron & Macon, p. 154.
73 Ibid., p. 153.
74 Ibid.
75 'Transport: Last of the Last', *Time* magazine, 25 February 1935, Vol. XXV, No. 8, p. 39.
76 Miller, Harry Russell, Assistant Lighthouse Keeper, Point Sur, Testimony at Navy Court of Inquiry into the *Macon* crash, p. 67, University of Akron Libraries, Karl Arnstein Papers.
77 Toland, *The Great Dirigibles*, p. 289.

78 Connolly, Joseph R., Coxswain, US Navy, Testimony at Navy Court of Inquiry
    into the Loss of the *Macon*, p. 129, University of Akron Libraries, Karl Arnstein
    Papers; Schellberg, Leonard E., Boatswain's Mate, First Class, US Navy,
    Testimony at Navy Court of Inquiry into the Loss of the *Macon*, University of
    Akron Libraries, Karl Arnstein Papers.
79 Smith, *The Airships* Akron & Macon, p. 153.
80 Ibid.
81 Toland, *The Great Dirigibles*, p. 286.
82 Kenworthy, Jesse L., Lt Cdr, US Navy, Testimony at Navy Court of Inquiry into
    the Loss of the *Macon*, p. 16, University of Akron Libraries, Karl Arnstein Papers.
83 Wiley, Testimony at the Navy Court of Inquiry into the Loss of the *Macon*,
    p. 2, University of Akron Libraries, Karl Arnstein Papers.
84 'Macon's Men Land, Saved From Death', *New York Times*, 14 February 1935, p. 1.
85 Campbell, Testimony at Navy Court of Inquiry into the Loss of the *Macon*.
86 Woodson, Walter B., Captain, USS *Houston*, US Navy, Testimony at Navy
    Court of Inquiry into the Loss of the *Macon*, p. 93, University of Akron
    Libraries, Karl Arnstein Papers.
87 'Witnesses Tell of Crumpling Fins "Went to Pieces Like Paper Sack", *Los
    Angeles Times*, 17 February 1935, p. 7.
88 Reppy, Testimony at Navy Court of Inquiry into the Loss of the *Macon*, p. 35.
89 Bolster, 'The Life and Death of USS *Macon*', p. 136.
90 Lust, John, interviewed by Michael J. Vinarcik, pp. 20–1.
91 Letter from Lt Roland G. Mayer to Commander Fulton, Re: *Macon* loss,
    10 April 1935, BUAER Records, National Archives Research Center,
    Washington, DC.
92 Glowacki, Arthur F., Seaman, First Class, US Navy, Testimony at Navy Court
    of Inquiry into the Loss of the *Macon*, University of Akron Libraries, Karl
    Arnstein Papers.
93 Toland, *The Great Dirigibles*, p. 290.
94 Henderson, Thomas, Lighthouse Keeper, Point Sur, Testimony at Navy Court
    of Inquiry into the Loss of the *Macon*, University of Akron Libraries, Karl
    Arnstein Papers.
95 Toland, *The Great Dirigibles*, p. 295.
96 Cochrane, Edwin F., Lt Cdr, US Navy, Testimony at Navy Court of Inquiry
    into the Loss of the *Macon*, University of Akron Libraries, Karl Arnstein Papers.
97 'Coxswain Proves He Can Take It', *New York Times*, p. 2.
98 Wiley, Testimony at Navy Inquiry into the Loss of the *Macon*, p. 2.
99 Ibid.; 'Wiley's Own Story of *Macon* Plunge', *New York Times*, 14 February 1935, p. 2.
100 Campbell, Testimony at Navy Court of Inquiry into the Loss of the *Macon*, p. 108.

35: A GIANT IS LOST

1 Associated Press, *Albany Evening News*, 13 February 1935, p. 1.
2 Kenworthy, Testimony at Navy Court of Inquiry into the Loss of the *Macon*, p. 16.
3 Toland, *The Great Dirigibles*, pp. 293, 295.
4 Adams, Charles E., Aviation Machinist's Mate, Second Class, US Navy,
   Testimony at Navy Court of Inquiry into the Loss of the *Macon*, University of
   Akron Libraries, Karl Arnstein Papers.

5   Kenworthy, Testimony at Navy Court of Inquiry into the Loss of the *Macon*, p. 16.

6   Campbell, Testimony at Navy Court of Inquiry into the Loss of the *Macon*, p. 108.

7   Ibid.; 'Wiley's Own Story of *Macon* Plunge', *New York Times*, p. 2.

8   Miller, 'The Violent Death of America's Last Dirigible', *True* magazine, p. 62.

9   Hook, *Flying Hookers for the* Macon, p. 95.

10 '*Macon*'s Stern "Crumbled"', *New York Times*, 13 February 1935, p. 1.

11 Wiley, Testimony at Navy Court of Inquiry into the Loss of the *Macon*, p. 2; 'Wiley's Own Story of *Macon* Plunge', *New York Times*, p. 2.

12 Toland, *The Great Dirigibles*, p. 295.

13 Campbell, Testimony at Navy Court of Inquiry into the Loss of the *Macon*, p. 108.

14 Peck, Testimony at Court of Inquiry into the Loss of the *Macon*, p. 99.

15 Campbell, Testimony at Navy Court of Inquiry into the Loss of the *Macon*, p. 108.

16 Kenworthy, Testimony at Navy Court of Inquiry into the Loss of the *Macon*, p. 16.

17 Mackey, 'What Really Happened to the *Macon*?', *LTA Bulletin*, p. 15.

18 Ibid.; Hammond, Worther M., Coxswain, US Navy, Testimony at Navy Court of Inquiry into the Loss of the *Macon*, University of Akron Libraries, Karl Arnstein Papers; 'Coxswain Proves He Can Take It', *New York Times*, p. 2.

19 Miller, 'The Violent Death of America's Last Dirigible', *True* magazine, p. 62.

20 Kenworthy, Testimony at Navy Court of Inquiry into the Loss of the *Macon*, p. 16. Note: Other sources say it was 1739 hours.

21 Mackey, Donald M., Flight Control Officer, Testimony at the Navy Court of Inquiry into the Loss of the *Macon*, University of Akron Libraries, Karl Arnstein Papers; 'Wiley's Own Story of *Macon* Plunge', *New York Times*, p. 2.

22 Miller, H.B., Lt, US Navy, 'Last Flight Recalled', pp. 129–30.

23 Miller, 'The Violent Death of America's Last Dirigible', *True* magazine, p. 136.

24 Clarke, William, 'At the Helm of the USS *Macon* on February 12, 1935', interviewed by Robert Llewellyn, p. 19.

25 Miller, 'The Violent Death of America's Last Dirigible', *True* magazine, p. 136.

26 Hammond, Testimony at Navy Court of Inquiry into the Loss of the *Macon*.

27 'Coxswain Proves He Can Take It', *New York Times*, p. 2.

28 Ibid.

29 Mackey, 'What Really Happened to the *Macon*?', *LTA Bulletin*, p. 15.

30 Ibid.; Toland, *The Great Dirigibles*, p. 299.

31 Toland, *The Great Dirigibles*, p. 295.

32 Ibid.

33 Miller, 'The Violent Death of America's Last Dirigible', *True* magazine, p. 31.

34 Toland, *The Great Dirigibles*, p. 291.

35 Campbell, 'Five O'Clock, Off California', p. 249.

36 Wiley, Testimony at Navy Court of Inquiry into the Loss of the *Macon*, p. 2.

37 Miller, 'The Violent Death of America's Last Dirigible', *True* magazine, p. 62; Clarke, William, 'At the Helm of the USS *Macon* on February 12, 1935', interviewed by Robert Llewellyn, p. 19; 'Wiley's Own Story of *Macon* Plunge', *New York Times*, p. 2.

38 '*Macon* Survivors Reach Shore with Tales of Heroism', *United Press*, 13 February 1933.

39 Kenworthy, Testimony at Navy Court of Inquiry into the Loss of the *Macon*, p. 16.

40 Mackey, Testimony at the Navy Court of Inquiry into the Loss of the *Macon*; Kenworthy, Testimony at Navy Court of Inquiry into the Loss of the *Macon*,

p. 16; Bolster, 'The Life and Death of USS *Macon*', p. 137; 'Wiley's Own Story of *Macon* Plunge', *New York Times*, p. 2.

41   Campbell, Testimony at Navy Court of Inquiry into the Loss of the *Macon*, p. 108; Campbell, 'Five O'Clock, Off California', pp. 248–9; 'Transport: Last of the Last', *Time* magazine, p. 39; Adams, Testimony at Navy Inquiry into the Loss of the *Macon*.

42   'Wiley's Own Story of *Macon* Plunge', *New York Times*, p. 2.

43   Wiley, Testimony at Navy Court of Inquiry into the Loss of the *Macon*, p. 2; Adams, Testimony at Navy Court of Inquiry into the Loss of the *Macon*.

44   'Witnesses Tell of Crumpling Fins', *Los Angeles Times*, p. 2.

45   Miller, 'Last Flight Recalled', p. 131.

46   Wiley, Testimony at Navy Court of Inquiry into the Loss of the *Macon*, p. 2.

47   Hook, *Flying Hookers for the* Macon, p. 68.

48   Glowacki, Testimony at Navy Court of Inquiry into the Loss of the *Macon*.

49   Miller, 'Last Flight Recalled', p. 131.

50   Clarke, Testimony at Navy Court of Inquiry into the Loss of the *Macon*, p. 77.

51   '*Macon* Survivors Reach Shore with Tales of Heroism', *United Press*.

52   Rosendahl, *SNAFU*, Footnote No. 6, p. 219.

53   Clarke, Testimony at Navy Court of Inquiry into the Loss of the *Macon*, p. 77.

54   Ibid.; Hooper, Sydney, Aviation Machinist's Mate, US Navy, Testimony at Navy Court of Inquiry into the Loss of the *Macon*, University of Akron Libraries, Karl Arnstein Papers; Toland, *The Great Dirigibles*, pp. 301, 304.

55   '*Macon's* Men Land, Saved From Death', *New York Times*, p. 1.

56   Lehtonen, L.E., Aviation Machinist's Mate, Third Class, US Navy, Testimony at Navy Court of Inquiry into the Loss of the *Macon*, University of Akron Libraries, Karl Arnstein Papers; 'Navy Gives Praise to *Macon* Heroes', *New York Times*, 29 August 1935, p. 23.

57   Hooper, Testimony at Navy Court of Inquiry into the Loss of the *Macon*.

58   Toland, *The Great Dirigibles*, p. 298.

59   Cariaso, Maximo, Mess Attendant, First Class, US Navy, Testimony at Navy Court of Inquiry into the Loss of the *Macon*, University of Akron Libraries, Karl Arnstein Papers; Toland, *The Great Dirigibles*, p. 301.

60   Miller, 'Last Flight Recalled', p. 131.

61   Toland, *The Great Dirigibles*, p. 303.

62   Ibid., pp. 302–3, 306.

63   '*Macon's* Men Land, Saved From Death', *New York Times*, p. 1.

64   Adams, Testimony at Navy Court of Inquiry into the Loss of the *Macon*.

65   '*Macon's* Men Land, Saved From Death', *New York Times*, p. 1.

66   Bolster, 'The Life and Death of USS *Macon*', p. 137.

67   '*Macon's* Men Land, Saved From Death', *New York Times*, p. 1.

68   Morris, Edward R., Aviation Machinist's Mate, First Class, US Navy, Testimony at Navy Court of Inquiry into the Loss of the *Macon*, University of Akron Libraries, Karl Arnstein Papers.

69   Bolster, 'The Life and Death of USS *Macon*', p. 137; Toland, *The Great Dirigibles*, p. 300.

70   Lehtonen, Testimony at Navy Court of Inquiry into the Loss of the *Macon*.

71   Hook, *Flying Hookers for the* Macon, p. 87.

72   Miller, 'Last Flight Recalled', p. 131.

73 Clarke, William, 'At the Helm of the USS *Macon* on February 12, 1935', interviewed by Robert Llewellyn, p. 21.

74 Lehtonen, Testimony at Navy Court of Inquiry into the Loss of the *Macon*.

75 Ibid.; Adams, Testimony at Navy Court of Inquiry into the Loss of the *Macon*; Kenworthy, Testimony at Court of Navy Inquiry into the Loss of the *Macon*, p. 16.

36: A GIANT IS RESCUED

1   *New York Times*, 13 February 1935, p. 2.

2   'Dirigibles in Disrepute After *Macon*'s Loss', *The Literary Digest*, 23 February 1935, p. 8.

3   '*Macon*'s Men Land', *New York Times*, p. 1.

4   Toland, *The Great Dirigibles*, p. 307.

5   Bolster, 'The Life and Death of USS *Macon*', p. 137.

6   Hammond, Testimony at Navy Court of Inquiry into the Loss of the *Macon*.

7   Letter from Lt H.B. Miller to Lt Ward Harrigan, 2 March 1935, p. 4, courtesy of Blaine Miller; Miller, 'Last Flight Recalled', p. 131.

8   Toland, *The Great Dirigibles*, p. 305.

9   Clarke Interview.

10 Toland, *The Great Dirigibles*, p. 305.

11 Ibid., p. 306.

12 Ibid., p. 307.

13 Wiley, Testimony at the Navy Court of Inquiry into the Loss of the *Macon*, p. 7.

14 Miller, 'Last Flight Recalled', p. 132.

15 Metseger, Alfred B., Rear Admiral (ret.), US Navy, 'When *Macon* Went Down', in *Flying Hookers for the* Macon, Airsho Publishers, Baltimore, MD, p. 139.

16 '*Macon*'s Men Land', *New York Times*, p. 1.

17 Metseger, 'When *Macon* Went Down', p. 140.

18 '*Macon*'s Men Land', *New York Times*, p. 1.

19 Metseger, 'When *Macon* Went Down', p. 140.

20 Ibid., p. 142.

21 'Transport: Last of the Last', *Time* magazine.

22 Toland, *The Great Dirigibles*, pp. 307–8.

23 Campbell, 'Five O'Clock, Off California', p. 250.

24 Ibid.

25 Metseger, 'When *Macon* Went Down', p. 140; Toland, *The Great Dirigibles*, p. 308.

26 Metseger, 'When *Macon* Went Down', p. 140.

27 Ibid., pp. 140–1.

28 '*Macon*'s Men Land', *New York Times*, p. 1.

29 Kenworthy, Testimony at Navy Court of Inquiry into the Loss of the *Macon*, p. 16; Adams, Testimony at Navy Court of Inquiry into the Loss of the *Macon*; '*Macon*'s Men Land', *New York Times*, p. 1; Miller, 'Last Flight Recalled', p. 131; Metseger, 'When *Macon* Went Down', p. 141; Bolster, 'The Life and Death of USS *Macon*', p. 137.

30 '*Macon*'s Men Land', *New York Times*, p. 1.

31 Bolster, *The Life and Death of USS* Macon, Hook, *Flying Hookers for the* Macon, Appendix B, p. 137; Kenworthy, Testimony at Navy Court of Inquiry into the

Loss of the *Macon*, p. 16; '*Macon*'s Men Land', *New York Times*, p. 1; Toland, *The Great Dirigibles*, p. 307.

32   Adams, Testimony at Navy Court of Inquiry into the Loss of the *Macon*.

33   Miller, 'Last Flight Recalled', pp. 131–2.

34   Metseger, 'When *Macon* Went Down', p. 141.

35   Miller, 'Last Flight Recalled', p. 132.

36   Metseger, 'When *Macon* Went Down', p. 141.

37   Letter from Lt H.B. Miller to Lt Ward Harrigan, 2 March 1935, p. 4, courtesy of Blaine Miller.

38   Metseger, 'When *Macon* Went Down', p. 141.

39   Ibid.

40   'Navy to Call Investigation Action', *San Francisco Chronicle*, 13 February 1935, p. 1; 'Airship Building Will Come to a Halt', *New York Times*, 14 February 1935, p. 3.

41   *Los Angeles Times*, 13 February 1935, p. 1.

42   *St Petersburg Times*, 13 February 1935, p. 1.

43   *San Francisco Chronicle Extra*, 13 February 1935, p. 1.

44   Associated Press, *Albany Evening News*, 13 February 1935, p. 1.

45   *New York Daily Mirror*, 13 February 1935, p. 1.

46   'Officers and Crew of *Macon*', *New York Times*, 13 February 1935, p. 2.

47   'Reeves Orders Inquiry Court in *Macon* Crash', *The Washington Post*, 14 February 1935, p. 3.

48   '*Macon*'s Men Land', *New York Times*, p. 1.

49   'Last of the Last', *Time* magazine, p. 39; 'President to Bar Dirigible Funds', *The Washington Post*, 14 February 1935, p. 1.

50   Metseger, 'When *Macon* Went Down', p. 142.

51   '*Macon* Survivors Reach Shore with Tales of Heroism', *United Press*.

52   *San Francisco Chronicle*, 14 February 1935.

53   'Wiley's Own Story of *Macon* Plunge', *New York Times*.

54   'Reeves Orders Inquiry Court in *Macon* Crash', *The Washington Post*, p. 3.

55   Metseger, 'When *Macon* Went Down', p. 141.

56   *San Francisco Examiner*, 14 February 1935, p. 1.

57   'Reeves Orders Inquiry Court in *Macon* Crash', *The Washington Post*.

58   'Awaits Word From Lost Son', *Los Angeles Times*, 14 February 1935, p. 2.

59   'Lost Radio Man's Birthday Today', *The Washington Post*, 16 February 1935, p. 3.

60   'El Paso Man, Mechanic on *Macon*', *El Paso Herald-Post*, 13 February 1935, p. 14.

61   'Airship Building Will Come to a Halt', *New York Times*, p. 3.

37: A GIANT ON TRIAL

1   'Builders Offer Aid', *New York Times*, 13 February 1935, p. 2.

2   'Dirigibles' Use in Navy Doomed Vinson Asserts', *The Washington Post*, 13 February 1935, p. 3.

3   Ibid.

4   Smith, *The Airships Akron & Macon*, p. 157.

5   'President to Bar Dirigible Funds', *The Washington Post*.

6   'Airship Building Will Come to a Halt', *New York Times*.

7   'President to Bar Dirigible Funds', *The Washington Post*.
8   'Commander of *Akron* Hits Craft Critics', *San Francisco Chronicle*,
    16 February 1935.
9   'Replace the *Macon*', *The Washington Post*, 16 February 1935, p. 3.
10 Letter From Carl Fritsche to President Roosevelt, 14 February 1935.
11 'Japan Regrets *Macon* Loss', *New York Times*, 14 February 1935, p. 3.
12 Letter from Dr Hugo Eckener to President Roosevelt, April 1934.
13 'Dirigibles' Use in Navy Doomed', *The Washington Post*, p. 3.
14 Ibid.
15 'The *Macon* Dies', *New York Times*, 17 February 1935, p. E1.
16 'Mitchell Flays Navy, Defends Our Dirigibles', *The Washington Post*,
    15 February 1935, p. 4.
17 'Airship Use Defended', *New York Times*, 24 February 1935, p. X19.
18 'Builders Offer Aid', *New York Times*.
19 'Wiley's Own Story of *Macon* Plunge', *New York Times*.
20 Wiley, Testimony at the Navy Court of Inquiry into the Loss of the *Macon*, p. 8.
21 'Wiley's Story of *Macon* Crackup', *San Francisco Chronicle*, p. 7.
22 Ibid.; 'Wiley Says *Macon* Showed No Strain', *New York Times*, 15 February 1935, p. 3.
23 Ibid.
24 Wiley, Testimony at the Navy Court of Inquiry into the Loss of the *Macon*,
    pp. 57–8.
25 Ibid., pp. 58, 63.
26 Ibid.
27 Ibid.
28 Ibid.
29 Ibid.
30 Ibid.
31 Miller, Testimony at the Navy Court of Inquiry into the Loss of the *Macon*, p. 67.
32 Bolster, Testimony at the Navy Court of Inquiry into the Loss of the *Macon*, p. 44.
33 Ibid., p. 82.
34 '*Macon's* Loss Laid To A Break At Fins', *New York Times*, p. 1.
35 '*Macon* Quiz Goes Deeper', *Los Angeles Times*, 18 February 1935, p. 9.
36 'Airship Failure Due to Unknown Stress', *New York Times*, 17 February 1935, p. E7.
37 Topping, *When Giants Roamed the Sky*, p. 201.
38 '*Macon* Service is Held', *New York Times*, 18 February 1935, p. 15.
39 'Wiley Did Not Rush Repairing the *Macon*', *New York Times*, Section:
    Sports, p. 28.
40 Wiley, Testimony at the Navy Court of Inquiry into the Loss of the *Macon*, p. 115.
41 Toland, *The Great Dirigibles*, p. 279.
42 '"God and Wiley Saved Our Lives"', *San Francisco Chronicle*, 20 February 1935.
43 Findings of the Navy Court of Inquiry into the Loss of the *Macon*,
    20 May 1935, University of Akron Libraries, Karl Arnstein Papers.
44 Memorandum from Assistant Chief of Bureau (McCrary) to The Chief of
    Bureau (King), Subject: Endorsement on Court of Inquiry on Loss of the
    USS *Macon*, 11 April 1935, BUAER Records, National Archives Research Center,
    Washington, DC.
45 Memo from The Chief of Bureau of Aeronautics to The Chief of Naval
    Operations, Re: Court of Inquiry to Inquire into the Loss of the USS *Macon*,

10 May 1935, p. 2, BUAER Records, National Archives Research Center, Washington, DC.

46   Findings of the Navy Court of Inquiry into the Loss of the *Macon*, 20 May 1935.

47   Mackey, 'What Really Happened to the *Macon*?', *LTA Bulletin*, p. 2.

48   'Sunnyvale Men Move to Lakehurst Shortly', *The Washington Post*, 31 March 1935, p. SS11.

49   'Navy Gives Praise to *Macon* Heroes', *New York Times*, p. 23.

50   'Radio Operator Honored', *New York Times*, 31 May 1935, p. 29.

51   'Sunnyvale Men Move to Lakehurst Shortly', *The Washington Post*.

52   Topping, *When Giants Roamed the Sky*, p. 202.

53   Ibid.; Letter from Karl Arnstein to P.W. Litchfield, 3 July 1935, University of Akron Libraries, Karl Arnstein Papers.

54   Ibid., p. 1.

55   Ibid., pp. 3–4.

38: ASSIGNING BLAME

1   Handwritten memo from Admiral King, Chief of Bureau of Aeronautics, Undated, BUAER Records, National Archives Research Center, Washington, DC.

2   Memo For Admiral King (from G. Fulton), 10 August 1935, p. 1, National Air & Space Museum Archives, Garland Fulton Collection, Washington, DC.

3   Memo from Arnstein to P.W. Litchfield, Subject: History of Suggested Reinforcement on Frame 17.5 of USS *Macon*, 9 September 1935, University of Akron Libraries, Karl Arnstein Papers.

4   Handwritten letter from Karl Arnstein to P.W. Litchfield, 3 July 1935, University of Akron Libraries, Karl Arnstein Papers.

5   Letter from G. Fulton to Dr Arnstein, 9 September 1935, pp. 1–2, University of Akron Libraries, Karl Arnstein Papers.

6   Ibid., p. 1.

7   Letter from Arnstein to Commander Fulton, 6 November 1935, p. 1, University of Akron Libraries, Karl Arnstein Papers.

8   Topping, *When Giants Roamed the Sky*, pp. 198–9.

9   Fulton Memorandum to King, 9 September 1935, Memo attachment, 6 August 1935.

10   Letter from G. Fulton to Dr Arnstein, 10 July 1933, BUAER Records, National Archives Research Center, Washington, DC.

11   Fulton Memorandum, 6 August 1935, p. 5.

12   Campbell, Testimony at Navy Court of Inquiry into the Loss of the *Macon*, p. 108.

13   Letter marked Personal and Confidential from C.M. Bolster to Commander Fulton, 26 March 1935.

14   Letter from Lieutenant Commander Roland G. Mayer to Commander Garland Fulton, 10 April 1935.

15   Ibid.

16   Mackey, 'What Really Happened to the *Macon*?', *LTA Bulletin*, quoting Danis Testimony at the Navy Court of Inquiry into the Loss of the *Macon*, p. 10.

17 Ibid.
18 Ibid., p. 11, quoting Peck Testimony at the Navy Court of Inquiry into the Loss of the *Macon*.
19 Mackey, 'What Really Happened to the *Macon*?', *LTA Bulletin*, p. 8.
20 Ibid., p. 5.
21 Ibid., p. 9.
22 Letter marked Personal and Confidential from C.M. Bolster to Commander Fulton, 26 March 1935.
23 Letter from Roland G. Mayer to Fulton, 10 April 1935.
24 Ibid.
25 Mackey, 'What Really Happened to the *Macon*?', *LTA Bulletin*, p. 13.
26 Bolster, Testimony at the Navy Court of Inquiry into the Loss of the *Macon*, pp. 104–5.
27 Letter from Lt H. B. Miller to Lt Ward Harrigan, 2 March 1935, p. 4, courtesy of Blaine Miller.
28 Rosendahl, *SNAFU*, p. 27.
29 Wiley, Testimony at the Navy Court of Inquiry into the Loss of the *Macon*, p. 2.
30 Letter marked Personal and Confidential from C.M. Bolster to Commander Fulton, 26 March 1935.
31 Rosendahl, *SNAFU*, p. 34.
32 Topping, *When Giants Roamed the Sky*, p. 196.
33 Cook, *USS* Akron *and USS* Macon, pp. 34–5.
34 Letter From Roland G. Mayer to Fulton, 10 April 1935.
35 Litchfield and Allen, *Why Has America No Rigid Airships?*, pp. 31–2.
36 Burgess, C.P., *Some Notes on Airship Problems*, 25 July 1935.
37 Hook, *Flying Hookers for the* Macon, p. 65.
38 Letter From Roland G. Mayer to Fulton, 10 April 1935.
39 Ibid.
40 Lust, John, interviewed by Michael J. Vinarcik, pp. 20–1.
41 Topping, *When Giants Roamed the Sky*, p. 198.

39: AFTERMATH

1   Topping, *When Giants Roamed the Sky*, pp. 204, 206.
2   Wiley, Herbert V., Commander, US Navy, *USS* Macon: *Doctrines and Policies for Operation and Upkeep*, US Navy, 6 May 1935.
3   'Dirigibles Inquiry Ordered by Swanson', *New York Times*, 21 February 1935, p. 6.
4   Cook, *USS* Akron *and USS* Macon, p. 38.
5   'Blames the Navy for Macon Crash', *New York Times*, 27 July 1935, Section: Sports/Books, p. 13.
6   'Macon's Crash Navy's Fault?', *Akron Beacon Journal*, 26 July 1935, p. 16.
7   'Blames the Navy for *Macon* Crash', *New York Times*, p. 13.
8   Ibid.
9   Ibid.
10 Letter from Secretary of the Navy Swanson to Dr Durand, 2 August 1935, National Air & Space Archives, Fulton Collection, Washington, DC.

11 'Swanson Acts on De Forest's Criticism of Navy', *New York Times*, 1 August 1935, p. 2.

12 Rosendahl, *SNAFU*, p. 170, quoting the Durand Committee Report.

13 Durand Committee Report, Special Committee on Airships, 'Technical Aspects of the Loss of the *Macon*', Report No. 3, 30 January 1937, p. 11.

14 Ibid., p.13.

15 'Big Airship Endorsed', *New York Times*, 2 February 1936, p. XX5.

16 McBride, *Technological Change and the United States Navy 1865–1945*, p. 189.

17 Shock, *US Navy Airships*, p. 74.

18 Ibid.

19 McBride, *Technological Change and the United States Navy 1865–1945*, p. 190.

20 Smith, *The Airships* Akron & Macon, p. 167.

21 McBride, *Technological Change and the United States Navy 1865–1945*, p. 189.

22 Letter from D.J. Callaghan, Captain, US Navy, Naval Aide to the President, to Paul W. Litchfield, Goodyear Tire & Rubber Co., 21 June 1939, University of Akron Libraries, Karl Arnstein Papers.

23 McBride, *Technological Change and the United States Navy 1865–1945*, p. 190.

24 Smith, *The Airships* Akron & Macon, p. 170.

25 Polmar, Norman, 'Ships that Were Lighter Than Air', *Naval History Magazine*, US Naval Institute, May 2011, Vol. 25, No. 3, www.usni.org/magazines/naval-history-magazine/2011/may/ships-were-lighter-air.

26 Smith, *The Airships* Akron & Macon, p. 170.

27 Topping, *When Giants Roamed the Sky*, p. 206.

40: A GIANT IS FOUND

1 Vaeth, 'USS *Macon*: Lost and Found', *National Geographic* magazine, p. 117.

2 Ibid.

3 Grech, Chris, Deputy Director Marine Operations, Monterey Bay Aquarium Research Institute (MBARI), 'Eighteen Years and Counting: Locating, Mapping, and Recovering the Remains of the USS *Macon*', *Noticias de Monterey: Into the Deep: Wreck and Rediscovery of Americas Last Airship*, Monterey History and Art Association, Spring–Summer 2006, Vol. LV, Nos 2–3, p. 26.

4 Author interview with Chris Grech, 23 April 2013, Moss Landing, CA.

5 Ibid.

6 Ibid.

7 Ibid.

8 Ibid.

9 Ross, *Such is Life in the Navy*, p. i.

10 Grech, 'Eighteen Years and Counting', *Into the Deep*, pp. 29–30; Vaeth, 'USS *Macon*: Lost and Found', p. 29.

11 Author interview with Chris Grech.

12 Ibid.

13 Vaeth, 'USS *Macon*: Lost and Found', *National Geographic* magazine, p. 117.

14 NASA, Historic Preservation Office, Moffett Field History, *The Discovery of the USS* Macon.

15 Grech, 'Eighteen Years and Counting', *Into the Deep*, p. 30.

16 Author interview with Chris Grech.
17 Ibid.
18 Ibid.
19 Ibid.
20 NASA, Historic Preservation Office, *The Discovery of the USS* Macon.
21 Grech, 'Eighteen Years and Counting', *Into the Deep*, p. 33.
22 Ibid., p. 38.

EPILOGUE

1   Rosendahl, *SNAFU*, p. 10.
2   Litchfield, *Industrial Voyage*, p. 249.
3   Rosendahl, *SNAFU*, Footnote No. 4, p. 218.
4   'Flying Carrier for Warplanes', *Popular Mechanics*, Vol. 77, No. 5, May 1942, pp. 14–15.
5   Rosendahl, *SNAFU*, p. 17.
6   Shock, *US Navy Airships*, p. 75.
7   Topping, *When Giants Roamed the Sky*, p. 237.
8   Ibid., p. 236.
9   Ibid., p. 237.
10 Commander Garland Fulton biography, National Air & Space Museum Archives, Garland Fulton Collection.
11 Letter from J.C. Hunsaker to Commander Fulton, National Air & Space Museum Archives, Garland Fulton Collection.
12 'Vice Adm. Charles Rosendahl Dies', *New York Times*, 15 May 1977, p. 36.
13 Robinson and Keller, *Up Ship!*, p. 195.
14 Rosendahl, *SNAFU*, p. 6, Foreword by Hepburn Walker Jr.
15 'Vice Adm. Charles Rosendahl Dies', *New York Times*.
16 Marshall, *Rear Admiral Herbert V. Wiley*, p. 216.
17 Rosendahl, *What about the Airship?*, p. 370.
18 USS *West Virginia* Veterans' Organization, www.usswestvirginia.org/veterans/personalpage.php?id=3433.
19 Ibid.
20 Notes from Commander Herbert V. Wiley's personal diary, collection of Marie Wiley Ross.
21 Author interview with Marie Wiley Ross.
22 Email from Francis T. Kleber CDR, US Navy (ret.), 27 May 2005.
23 Notes from Commander Herbert V. Wiley's personal diary.
24 Personal letter from Commander Herbert V. Wiley to his daughter, Marie Wiley, collection of Marie Wiley Ross.
25 Ross, *Such is Life in the Navy*, pp. 267–8.
26 Notes from Commander Herbert V. Wiley's personal diary.
27 Ross, *Such is Life in the Navy*, p. 278.
28 Ibid.
29 Veronico, *Moffett Field*, p. 52.
30 Rosendahl, *SNAFU*, p. 6, Foreword by Hepburn Walker Jr; Smith, *The Airships* Akron & Macon, Footnote No. 8, p. 218.

INDEX

Note: *italicised* page references indicate illustrations, and the suffix 'n' indicates a footnote.

Adams, Charles E. 303, 307
Adams, Charles F., III 150
Adams, Roger J. 76
Adams Aerial Transportation
    Company 76
advertising 80–2, 92, 108, 115, 133–5,
    160, 347, 359, 369
An Aerial Honeymoon (farce) 132
Aerial Navigation Company 84
aerodynamics 147, 161, 167, 178, 184–5,
    187–8, 195, 268, 337–41, 346
aeroplanes *see* passenger aeroplanes
The Air Ship (musical) 132
Aircraft Development Corporation
    112, 123
'airship' as term 18, 92
The Airship Destroyer (film) 133
Akron, Ohio 32, 74–5, 81–2, 107, 131,
    139–40, 148, 181–2, 322, 345,
    360–1
USS *Akron* (ZRS-4) 16, 17–18, 21–70,
    99, 133, 135–6, 158, 161, 176,
    192, 198, 370
    christening 32–5, 154–5
    construction 32, 82n, 117, 148,
        160–1, 165, 168, 185–8, 192
    construction cost 32, 192, 349
    crash 36–53, 60, 62–3, 127–8,
        138–41, 145–6, *220*, 293

crash investigations, Congressional
    138–40
crash investigations, House Naval
    Affairs Committee 59–60, 189
crash investigations, Navy Court of
    Inquiry 55, 60–9, 138–9, 165,
    169, 184, 189–90, 206, *221*, 332
frame 17.5 178, 187–8, 192
lifesaving equipment 50, 67
weight 35, 155, 186, 188
wreckage located 67
Akron Beacon Journal 57–8, 66, 68,
    108, 145
Alcock, John 14n, 129
Allen, Hugh 108, 120, 148–9, 167, 181,
    184, 190, 199, 359
Aluminum Company of America 117
Alvin 354
America-Hawaiian Lines 118
American Blimp Corporation 369
Amundsen, Roald 130
Andrée, S.A. 129–30
Annapolis 31, 65, 195–6, 259, 265–7
Arnstein, Bertha Jehle (Bertl)
    180–1, 361
Arnstein, Dr Karl 16, 107, 113, 138,
    149, 151, 163, 166, 168, 177–83,
    184–5, *218–19*, *221*, 242, 245,
    325, 332–3, 339, 344–5, 360–1

Akron, building the 33, 63, 66, 160–1, 177–8, 183, 185–8
Akron, crash of the 54, 66, 68, 146, 183, 189
frame 17.5 on the *Macon* 178, 187–8, 190–2, 195, 248–9, 253, 277, 332–4, 340
Fulton, disputes with 175, 188–95, 242, 248, 278, 330, 333–4, 341, 362
Litchfield, relationship with 178, 183, 253, 278, 330–1
Macon, building the 146–7, 150, 160–2, 174–6, 178, 183–4, 188, 190–1, 195, 248–9, 277–8, 340, 346
Macon, crash of the 325, 328, 330–1, 340–1, 343, 346, 349
Navy Courts of Inquiry 66, 68, 177, 184
private life 178–82, 361
Atlantik (S.L. 101) 97
automobiles 74–5, 91, 106, 125–6, 133, 369

Balbo, Italo 174
Baldwin, Thomas S. 80n, 85–7, 89, 92
Balestreri, Vincent 353, 356–7
ballast 39, 45, 140, 157–8, 238, 247, 275, 340
  dumped during flights 45, 56, 198–9, 200, 239, 241, 245, 284, 292–5, 297, 299, 339–40, 342
ballooning 75, 82, 84–5, 87–9, 129–31, 233, 268
Bauch, Kurt 181, 187, 195, 243, 245
Beetleware 159
Belgium 97, 100
Berry, Fred T. 27, 37n
bicycles 74–5
big rigid airships 17–19, 80–1, 102–3, 106–7, 109, 197
USS *Black Hawk* (AD-9) 364
blimps 17–18, 32, 33, 53, 64, 75–9, 80–4, 102–3, 107, 111, 125, 177, 199, 233, 358, 368
  J-3 53
  K-class 358n, 360n, 361, 367
  L-class 177, 359, 361, 367
  M-class 177, 361
  N-class 177, 360, 361
  Pony 79
Bodensee (LZ-120) 100
Boeing 369
Boettner, Jack 76–8
Bolster, Calvin M. *228*, 242, 277, 284, 286, 288–90, 293–4, 300, 311, 314, 324–7, 330, 334–8
Brandes, Theodore C. 292
Brazil 13, 35, 115, 123–5, 135
Brown, Arthur 14n, 129
Brown-Boveri Electric Corporation 112
Buckley, William A. *228*, 299, 330
Bureau of Aeronautics (BUAER) 23, 68–9, 106, 140, 150–1, 155, 159, 170, 182, 187, 193, 195–6, 233, 248–9, 276–9, 328, 332, 347, 368
  see also Fulton, Garland 'Froggy'; King, Ernest J.; Moffett, William A.
Burgess, C.P. 193, 277, 341, 345
Butler, Henry V. 67, 278
Byrd, Richard 14n, 130

California Arrow 87, 89
Callaghan, D.J. 347–8
Camp Kearny incident 24
Campbell, George W. 145, *228*, 286–8, 293, 299, 303, 314, 316, 330, 334–5, 338–9
Canada 114, 121, 133
Canepa, David 353–4
Carbon and Carbide Chemicals Corporation 117–18
Cariaso, Maximo 301–2, 306
cars 74–5, 91, 106, 125–6, 133, 369
Catalina Service 79
Cecil, Henry B. 37n
Cesar, M. 111
Chanute, Octave 98
USS *Cincinnati* (CL-6) 70, 100, 251–3, 269, 278–9
circumnavigation of the globe 14, 117, 130–1, 200, 244
City of Glendale 92–4
City of Long Beach 111

Clarke, William H. 286, 289, 300, 302, 304–5, 308, 311, 314, 334
Clipper planes 348
Cochrane, Edwin F. 63–4, 286, 310, 330
Cold War 359
USS *Colorado* (ACR-7) 267
Columbia 81
Comet 344
Commander Aircraft, Battle Forces (COMBATFOR) 209, 263, 274, 277
USS *Concord* (CL-10) 313
Connecticut Aircraft Company 75n, 87
Connolly, Joseph R. 292
Conover, Wilmer M. 285–90, 334–5
Cook, Arthur B. 347
Cook, Frederick 14n, 130
Cook, Jeffrey 185
Coolidge, Calvin 116, 130, 155
Copeland, Robert W. 48–51
Coulter, Howard N. *228*
Courtney, Charles E. 313
Cracker Jack boxes 133
Crosser, Robert 119
Curtiss, Glenn 74, 244
Curtiss Aeroplane and Motor Company 230
Curtiss F9C-2 fighters *see* Sparrowhawks (Curtiss F9C-2 fighters)

Dailey, Ernest E. 284, 293, 298–9, 304–5, 315, 317, 326, 330, 367
Dalldorf, Karl 50, 51
Danis, Anthony L. *228*, 335–6
Davenport, Earl H. 76–8
Davis, Robert J. 'Shaky' 241–2, 247, 287–9, 291, 298, 311, 315, 324, 327, 330, 337
Day, George C. 166, 168, 171, 175
de Havilland aeroplanes 234
Deal, Richard E. ('Lucky Deal') 41–3, 48–53, 55, 58–9, 63, 68, 190, *221*
Dean, Carl 48
DeBeers 368
Defender 81
DELAG (Deutsche Luftschifffahrts-Aktiengesellschaft) 79n, 87, 96, 99

Delaney, John J. 68
Denby, Edwin 103
USS *Denver* (CL-16) 267
Depression 25, 34, 36, 66, 83, 94, 102, 116, 120–1, 140–1, 150, 172, 201, 276, 344, 347–9
Deutschland I (LZ-7) 87–8
Deutschland II (LZ-8) 87
Dirigible (film) 133
'dirigibles', term 18
Distant Early Warning (DEW) system 359–60
Dixmude 126
DN-1 87n, 103n
Dollar Lines 118
Dresel, Alger H. 169, 248–51, 257, 337, 362–3
    Akron, captain of 66, 204–5
    Akron crash, comments on the 66, 146
    and the *Los Angeles* 206n, 232, 236
    Macon, captain of 66, 166–8, 171, 173–4, 176, 197–200, 203–12, 235–47, 249
    weather, attitude to 66, 198, 206, 210, 237, 247
Drummond-Hay, Lady Grace Marguerite Hay 115–16
DuPont 160
Duralumin 67, 93, 117, 135, 146, 155, 158–9, 179–80, 292, 307, 337, 341, 350, 355
Durand, Dr William F. 344–5
Durand Committee 344–6
Dürr, Ludwig 177, 180

Earhart, Amelia 33, 81, 115, 244, 279, 367
Eckener, Dr Hugo 103–4, 107, 115–16, 118, 196, 321, 325
Edquiba, Florentino 301–2, 306, 315, 326, 367
elevator wheels
    Akron 39, 43, 45
    Macon 285, 287–90
Ellsworth, Lincoln 130
Empire State Building 15, 135
engines 17–18, 31, 85–7, 156

Akron 30, 39, 42, 46–7, 161–2
City of Glendale 93
Macon 157, 160, 162, 246
Wingfoot Air Express 76–7
Erwin, Moody E. 47–9, 51, 53, 55,
    58–9, 63, 65, 69, 190, *221*, 339
Ewa, Oahu 281, 359

F4U Corsairs 359
Federal Aviation Commission (FAC)
    280, 321
Finter, Clyde V. 234
Firestone 75, 361
First World War 64, 75, 87, 98–101,
    104n, 133, 179–80, 233, 275, 367
Fisher, Dr Gerhard 250, 258
fleet exercises 174, 206–12, 235, 245–8,
    250, 277–9, 282–5, 348
Ford, Edsel 112
Ford, Henry 112, 115, 117
Forest, A.V. de 345
Fraas, Matthew G. Jr 290, 292
France 25n, 81n, 97–8, 100, 111, 126,
    131, 133, 135
Fritsche, Carl 320, 345
Fulton, Garland 'Froggy' 68–9, 149,
    168, 180, 189, 192–6, *219*, *225*,
    235, 242–3, 249, 253, 327, 345,
    362–3
    Arnstein, disputes with 175,
        188–95, 242, 248, 278, 330,
        333–4, 341, 362
    and frame 17.5 188, 190–2, 195,
        248–9, 334, 341
    and *Macon*'s crash 328, 331–4,
        337–43
    on *Akron*'s fins 185, 187–8
    on *Macon*'s fins 195, 333–4
    on *Macon*'s weight 174–5, 188,
        190–1

Galatian, Andrew B. 290, 292
Garner, Ken 350
General Electric 160
General Motors Research Corporation
    117–18
Germany 81n, 133–5, 148, 156–7,
    180–1, 233, 330–1

airship industry 14–15, 32, 35, 59,
    79n, 87–91, 96–7, 99–100, 102–5,
    111n, 114–18, 121, 135, 188–9
    First World War 16, 99–101, 180, 275
    Second World War 358
    see also Luftschiffbau Zeppelin
Giffard, Henri 84
Glowacki, Arthur F. 294, 304
Goodrich 75, 103n, 361
Goodrich, Benjamin Franklin 74
Goodyear Aircraft Corporation 359
Goodyear Tire & Rubber Company
    15–16, 32, 33, 36, 81–2, 87, 102,
    109, 361
    Litchfield grows business 33, 73,
        83, 94
    tyre business 74–5, 80, 82, 102, 109,
        137, 361
Goodyear-Zeppelin Corporation 16, 32,
    54, 65, 104–8, 119, 137, 140, 154,
    166, 178, 278, 328, 332–3, 359
    Akron, building the 149, 185, 187–9,
        193, 332
    Air Dock 32, 34, 81n, 117, 146, 148,
        158, 161, 163, 166, 171
    end of 344, 349
    establishment of 103–4, 180–1
    Macon, building the 146–51, 155,
        167–9, 174–6, 182–3, 243, 245n,
        249, 332
    US Navy design competitions 32,
        111–13
Gorton, Adolphus W. 'Jake' 234, 258
Graf Zeppelin (LZ-127) 14, 35, 114–17,
    119, 121, 123–5, 130–1, 133, 135,
    170, 185, 198, 200, 244, 268, 321
Graf Zeppelin II (LZ-130) 15
Grech, Chris 351–7
Greyson M.P. Murphy Company 118
GZ-1 107–8

Haga Haig, Rollo Amyatt de 234
Halligan, John 210
Hamburg-America Line 118
Hammond, Worther M. 295, 299, 311
Hansa (LZ-13) 87
Hardesty, Fred S. 138
Harmon, Stormy 353

Harrigan, Ward 'Crash Helmet' 205,
    212, 234–5, 337
Harter, Dow W. 139
Hawaii 111, 120, 207, 210, 259, 274,
    279–81, 358–9
Hearst, William Randolph 200, 315
Heavier-Than-Air (HTA) flight 13, 98,
    138–9, 174, 348
    see also Sparrowhawks (Curtiss
    F9C-2 fighters)
Heinen, Anton 64–5, 69
helium 17, 39, 41, 81, 150, 156, 160,
    166, 236, 243, 291, 349n
    capacity 81n, 106, 107, 113, 152,
    156, 359, 368
    during crash of the Macon 288,
    291–7, 302, 305–7, 339
    venting 41, 45, 157–8, 198, 241,
    294–7, 302, 339
Helma, Paul 330
Here Comes the Navy (film) 202
Herndon, William H. Jr 306
High Treason (film) 133
Hindenburg (LZ-129) 14–15, 17, 88,
    115–16, 349, 369
Hodgdon, John 111
Hooper, Sydney 305–6, 311
Hoover, Herbert 118, 152
Hoover, Lou 32–5, 155, 223, 225
USS Hornet (CV-8) 359
House Military Affairs Committee 320
House Naval Affairs Committee 24,
    59–60, 141, 152, 198, 319–20
House Naval Appropriations
    Subcommittee 109
House Patents Committee 320
USS Houston (CA-30) 259–63, 278–9,
    288, 293
Hovgaard, Dr William 345
Howell, Clark 321
Huff, Gerald L. 228
Hughes, Howard 150
Hunsaker, Jerome C. 65, 118, 120, 124,
    125n, 138, 140, 166, 174, 178,
    193, 195, 219, 238, 345, 362
hydrogen 17, 75–7, 79, 81, 86, 89, 93–4,
    116, 156, 349n

Imperial Airship scheme (UK) 114
International Zeppelin Transport
    Company 36, 41, 117, 124
Italy 14, 25n, 80, 97–100, 130,
    135, 174
Iwo Jima 365

Japan 23–5, 97–8, 100, 114, 120–1, 133,
    135, 154–5, 281, 321, 347, 349,
    358–9, 363
Jewett, Frank B. 345
Johnson, Hiram 139–40
Jones, Bradley 345

Kármán, Dr Theodore von 343, 345
Kenworthy, Jesse L. Jr 52–3, 286, 297,
    299, 303, 310–18, 323, 330, 334
Kettering, Charles F. 345
King, Ernest J. 141, 173, 189, 196, 247,
    344–5, 347, 362
    Akron replacement, argues for 140,
    172, 347
    becomes BUAER chief 140, 170, 251
    and Dresel 171, 209–10, 247–8,
    250–1, 253
    and the Macon 169–71, 175, 207,
    209–10, 245–8, 250, 253, 276–7,
    280, 328, 332
    and Wiley 253, 257, 263, 269, 273–4,
    279–80
King, Moses 131–2
King, William H. 59, 138–40, 319, 328
King Committee 138–40, 172, 280
Kitty Hawk 86
Kivette, Fred 'Nappy' 260–1, 314
Kleber, Francis T. 365
Klemperer, Dr Wolfgang 248
Knabenshue, Ausgustus Roy ('Roy')
    79n, 88–91, 94–5
Knox, Frank 348
Koepenick, Steve 350–1

NAS Lakehurst, New Jersey 27, 36, 53,
    112, 131, 140, 145, 172–6, 234–5,
    244, 252, 267, 270, 321, 329,
    349, 367–8
    decommission threats 66, 139, 173
    and the Graf Zeppelin 114, 321

Macon's base after *Akron* crash 169–71, 173

Navy Courts of Inquiry at 60–1, 63, 169, *221*

role in Navy's airship programme 29, 200, 363, 367

M/V *Laney Chouest* 354

The Last Zeppelin (film) 130

Leahy, William D. 347

Lehman Brothers 118

Lehtonen, Leonard E. 308

Leonard, Jack F. 299–301

USS *Lexington* 281

Lighter-Than-Air (LTA) flight 14, 45, 89, 107, 155, 177, 345, 348–9, 363

  Cold War 359–60

  early days 18, 25, 75, 84–95, 131–6, 138–9

  Goodyear, importance to 33, 75, 80, 82, 103–4, 137, 360

  Naval LTA programme 25, 33, 43, 59–60, 69, 75, 80–1, 104, 139–40, 149, 156, 171–3, 247, 251, 267–9, 319, 328–9, 348–9, 362, 367

  opposition to Naval LTA program 25, 27, 66, 69, 138–41, 172–3, 247, 319, 349

  Second World War 358–9

Lilienthal, Otto 98

Lindbergh, Charles 138–9, 367

Litchfield, Paul W. 16, 32–3, 58, 73–83, 96–7, 137, 149–50, 163–4, 166, *217*, *219*, *223*, 321, 344, 360

  Akron crash 146

  Arnstein, relationship with 178, 183, 253, 278, 330–1

  'client is always right' mentality 175, 183, 192, 253

  Luftschiffbau Zeppelin, deal with 102–5, 180

  Macon crash 309, 319, 341, 346

  Second World War 358–9

Litchfield's passenger airships dream 16, 32–3, 35, 75, 79, 81–3, 94–5, 101, 106–9, 113–14, 116, 118–22, 126–8, 131, 137–8, 176, 281, 344, 359

end of 348

and the *Macon* crash 309, 319, 346

Moffett supports 109, 113, 154, 155

Lockheed 201, 369

Loral 361

USS *Los Angeles* (ZR-3) 133–4, 136, 139, 150–1, 155, 171, 176, 196, 204, 206, 236, 280, 286, 344, 347–8

  aeroplanes on 232, 234

  construction of 100n, 146, 152, 160, 177, 180

  as passenger airship 100, 109, 150

  track record 24, 58, 127

  Wiley on 43, 252, 257–8, 268–9

Los Angeles Steamship Company 118

Luftschiffbau Zeppelin 15, 18, 32, 64, 100, 103–4, 115, 118, 138, 177, 179–81, 188–9, 196, 321, 368

  see also Graf Zeppelin (LZ-127)

SS *Lurline* 274

Lust, John 342

LZ-7 (*Deutschland I*) 87–8

LZ-8 (*Deutschland II*) 87

LZ-10 (*Schwaben*) 87

LZ-11 (*Viktoria Luise*) 87

LZ-13 (*Hansa*) 87

LZ-17 (*Sachsen*) 87

LZ-120 (*Bodensee*) 100

LZ-126 100n, 121

LZ-127 *see Graf Zeppelin* (LZ-127)

LZ-129 (*Hindenburg*) 14–15, 17, 88, 115–16, 349, 369

LZ-130 (*Graf Zeppelin II*) 15

LZ-131 15

Mack Trucks, Inc. 36

Mackey, Donald M. 235, 246, 285, 329, 336

Macon, Georgia 152, 155, 163, 198

USS *Macon* (ZRS-5) 16–18, 24, 32, 60, 66, 70, 141, 143–253, *213–15*, *223–4*, *226*, *228*, 255–357

  christening 154, 163–4, *223*

  construction 146–53, 155–62, 174–6, 192–4, *222*, 341

  construction cost 150–1, 175–6, 349

  crash 285–309

crash investigations, Congressional
316, 320
crash investigations, House Naval
Affairs Committee 320
crash investigations, Navy Court
of Inquiry 316–18, 320, 322–5,
327–9, 332, 337, 338, 341–3, 345
finds Roosevelt in the Pacific
259–63, 270–4
in fleet exercises 174, 206–12, 235,
245–8, 250, 277–9, 282–5, 348
frame 17.5 180, 188, 190–1, 195,
241–3, 245, 248–9, 253, 277–8,
281–2, 300, 324–7, 332, 334,
337–9
lifesaving equipment 242, 298, 341
rescue 310–18
Sparrowhawk hangar 211, *216*, *226*,
230–2, 234
Texas, incident over 240–2, 248–9,
277, 287, 323–4, 326–7, 338
trial flights 165–71, 175–6, 195
weight 146–7, 151, 155–9, 161,
165, 174–5, 190–1, 197, 238–9,
245, 298
wreckage located *228*, 350–7
Madam Satan (film) 133
mail delivery 118–21, 124, 261–3, 348
Makassar Strait, Battle of 364
Malak, Julius E. 295, 301–2, 311
Marshall, M. Ernest 366–7
Martin Company 200
Masury, Alfred F. 36, 37n, 40, 43–4, 49,
52, 65, 118
Matson Navigational Company 118
Mayer, Roland and Nan 270, 335–7,
340, 342
Mayflower (blimp) 82
Mayflower (ship) 73
McCord, Frank C. 27–9, 36–8, 40,
42–5, 49, 52, 56, 61–2, 65, 68–9
McLeod, Rep. 320
McNary, Charles L. 119, 127
McNary-Crosser bill 119–24, 127,
164, 369
Merchant Airship Act 119
Metsger, Alfred 311
Midway Island 281

Miller, Harold B. 'Min' *228*, 232, 258,
260–1, 275, 284–7, 289, 300,
306–8, 311, 313, 337
Miller, Harry (assistant lighthouse
keeper) 291–2, 295
Mills, George *228*, 307, 314, 330, 362
USS *Milwaukee* (CL-5) 313
USS *Minneapolis* (CA-36) 363
USS *Mississippi* (BB-41) 364
Mitchell, Billy 321
Moffett, Jeannette 26, 52, 65, 155,
163–4, 211, 362
Moffett, William A. 16, 23–37, 43, 52,
54, 65, 80, 99, 103–4, 108–10,
112–13, 115, 148–9, 172, 208,
217, 232, 361–2
Akron crash 38, 40–2, 45, 49, 52, 59,
61–2, 68, 69
insists on all-weather flights 27–8,
30–1, 36, 38, 42, 68, 189, 194
and the *Macon* 149–50, 154–5,
163–4, 167, 211
Moffett Field 201–2, 310, 342, 362, 367
see also NAS Sunnyvale, California
USS *Montana* (ACR-13) 267
Monterey Bay Aquarium Research
Institute (MBARI) 351, 354–6
Montgolfier brothers 131
Montgomery, John J. 233
Morris, Edward R. 308
Morro Castle 125
Morrow, Colonel Joseph C. 76
Mountain View, California 131, 201

N.1 (Italian airship) 97–8
N2Y-1 trainer plane 36, 197, *225*, 230n,
276, 356n
Nagumo, Admiral 358–9
SS *Naitamba* 274
National Advisory Committee for
Aeronautics (NACA) 187–8
National Chicle Company 69
National City Company 118
National Ocean and Atmospheric
Administration (NOAA) 355–6
Navy Courts of Inquiry

for the *Akron* 55, 60–5, 66–9, 138–9, 165, 169, 177, 184, 189–90, 206, *221*, 332
   for the *Macon* 316–29, 332, 337–8, 341–3, 345
USS *New Orleans* (CA-32) 259
New York Times 32, 62, 97, 107n, 118–19, 123, 138, 151, 169–70, 177, 246–7, 279, 321–2, 325, 344, 346, 366
Nimitz, Chester W. 366
Nobile, Umberto 97–8, 130
non-rigid airships 17, 76, 80n, 81, 346, 360
   see also blimps
Norge 14, 130
North Pole 14, 129–30, 132
Northrop Grumman 369
Norton, Milton 76–8
Norway 130
nuclear energy 360

ocean liners *see* passenger ships
Okinawa 365
Opa-locka, Florida 236, 242–5, 247

Pacific 16, 73, 245, 263, 279, 281, 348
   Macon finds Roosevelt in 259–63, 270–4
   Pacific war 358, 363–5
   transpacific crossings 15, 33, 41, 117–19, 281, 369
Pacific (S.L. 103) 97
Pacific Zeppelin Transport Corporation 118, 281
Packard 134
Packard, David 351–2, 354–5
Pan Am 118, 123, 348, 369
Panama 109, 127, 132, 206, 236, 245
Panamerica (S.L. 102) 97
Parseval 134–5
Pasadena 89–91
passenger aeroplanes 13, 88, 91, 98–9, 115, 117–18, 123, 125–6, 128, 174, 348
passenger ships 14–15, 58, 60, 107–8, 118, 120, 123–5, 126n
   see also Titanic

USS *Patoka* 236
Pearl Harbor 281, 358, 364
Peary, Robert 14n, 130
Peck, Scott E. 286–7, 289, 298–9, 316, 330, 336
USS *Pennsylvania* (BB-38) 312–13, 315
USS *Pensacola* (CA-24) 364
Philippines 348, 364
Phoebus 50–1, 53, 59
Pilgrim 81–2
Point Lobos 351–2
Popular Science 92, 107, 111, 369n
Porter, Rufus 84
Pratt, William V. 59, 66
promotional flights 136, 173–4, 276–7
Puerto Rico 123

R33 101, 234
R34 14, 101, 121, 129
R36 101
R38 (*ZR-2*) 8n, 24, 101–2, 126, 177, 185, 192, 267
R100 117, 121
R101 114, 117, 121, 126
radar 349, 359–60
radio 38, 42, 44, 50, 57, 133, 160, 205, 208, 235, 237, 275, 279, 293, 298–9, 304
radio direction finders 205, 211, 250, 258, 297–8
range
   of airships 13, 30, 88, 98–9, 107, 150, 156, 162, 205, 271
   of Sparrowhawks 230, 235, 250, 258, 284
Rasmussen, Robert 351
Reeves, Joseph M. 'Bull' 260–3, 273–4, 278, 280–1, 284–5, 315, 317
Reliance 81
Reppy, John D. 290, 293, 298, 305, 330
The Republic Steel Corporation 160
Resolute 81
Revere Brass 160
Richardson, Harry W. 276
USS *Richmond* (CL-9) *228*, 311–15
ring design 48, 147, 160–1, 186, 188, 294, 340
Roma 80, 126

Roosevelt, Eleanor 52, 155, 259
Roosevelt, Franklin D. 26, 54, 59, 140,
    146, 163, 170, 247, 274, 314, 320
    and airships 59, 141, 280, 319, 347–8
    Macon finds in the Pacific 259–63,
    270–4
Roosevelt, Henry L. 259, 317
Rose, Alexander 98
Rosendahl, Charles E. 55, 125n, 149,
    185, 204–5, 211, 237, 242, 267–9,
    320, 339, 345, 347, 349, 358,
    362–3, 366
Ross, Ian 366–7
Rounds, Clinton S. 307
Rowe, Herbert R. 307, 311
Russia/Soviet Union 25, 97–8, 114,
    133, 135, 359–60
Rutan, Lucius 48–9

Sachsen (LZ-17) 87
safety of airships 15, 58, 88, 115, 124–6,
    140–1, 186–8, 317
St. Louis Fair 89
USS *San Diego* (ACR-6) 267
San Francisco Express 92
Sands, Richard 351, 353–4
Santa Barbara 284–5
Santos-Dumont, Alberto 13, 85–6,
    94, 233
USS *Saratoga* (CV-3) 278
SC-1 80n, 87
Scanlon, Pat 354
Schellberg, Leonard E. 'Gene' 290, 297,
    300–1
Schütte, Dr Johann 97
Schütte-Lanz 59, 97, 135, 138
Schwaben (LZ-10) 87–8
Scientific American 84
Sea Cliff 354–5
Sears-Roebuck & Company 109
Second World War 348–9, 358–9,
    361–8
Seiberling, Frank and Charles 74,
    81, 102
Sellers, David F. 197, 238, 250
semi-rigid airships 17, 80, 97, 107,
    130, 368

Settle, Thomas George W. ('Tex')
    168, 363
USS *Shenandoah* (ZR-1) 44, 64, 130,
    133, 136, 174, 176–7, 198–200,
    206, 236–7, 257–8, 268, 335n
    construction 65, 80–1, 102, 134
    crash 24, 41, 59, 64–5, 126, 185
Sherwin-Williams 160
Simpler, Leroy C. *228*
USS *Sirius* (AK-15) 364
The Skyhawk (film) 133
Slate, Thomas B. 92–4
Slate Aircraft Corporation 92
Smith, Richard K. 13, 336
Solar, Charles S. 'Chick' 342
South America 13–15, 35, 118, 123–5,
    135, 321
Soviet Union/Russia 25, 97–8, 114,
    133, 135, 359–60
Spain 98, 135
Sparrowhawks (Curtiss F9C-2 fighters)
    173–4, 229–35, 244, 337
    on the *Akron* 36, 208, 231–2, 234–5
    on the *Macon* 162, 173–4, 176, 197,
    208–9, *213*, *216*, *226–8*, 229–33,
    235, 238, 246, 250, 258, 260–1,
    270–1, 274–5, 277–9, 284–5,
    296–8, 355–6
speed 15, 98, 123, 135, 230, 336, 348
    Akron 30, 39
    Graf Zeppelin 14, 130–1
    Macon 161, 169, 175–6, 195, 229, 242
Sperry, Lawrence B. 233
Sperry Aircraft 233–4
The Spirit of Safety 368
spy basket (sub-cloud observation car)
    30, 275, 278, 284
Standard Oil Company of
    California 118
Standley, William V. 175–6, 197, 202–3,
    207, 209, 246–7, 263, 317, 319
Stanley, Charles 84–5
Stanley Aerial Navigation
    Company 84–5
Steele, Joseph E. 288, 291, 324
stress analysis 177–80, 184–5, 187,
    249, 340
submarines 39, 267, 358

NAS Sunnyvale, California 169–70, 174, 197–203, 236, 247, 253, 270, 276–8, 281, 316, 329, 345, 367
see also Moffett Field
Suriago Strait, Battle of 364–5
Sutphin, William H. 172
Swanson, Claude A. 26, 58–9, 62, 65, 140–1, 170, 172, 246, 317, 319, 329–30, 344–5

USS *Tennessee* (BB-43) 251–2, 269, 317, 322
Texaco 134
Texas 198–9, 237, 268
    Macon incident over 240–2, 248–9, 277, 287, 323–4, 326–7, 338
Thomas A. Edison, Inc. 160
Thurman, Emmett C. 290
Titanic 14–15, 59–60, 67, 121n, 138
Todd, James F. 317
Toland, John 205, 270–1
trains 14, 58, 60, 91–2, 97n, 107, 117–18, 125, 135, 344
transatlantic crossings 14, 76, 82, 96, 101, 107–9, 114–17, 124–5, 127–8, 138, 174, 268, 321
Transcontinental Air Transport 117
transpacific crossings 15, 33, 41, 117–19, 281, 369
Trapnell, Frederick M. 'Trap' 38, 230n
USCGC *Tucker* (CG-23) 53

U-boats 358
United Aircraft and Transport Corporation 117–18
United Dry Docks, Inc. 118
United Kingdom (UK) 14, 24, 45, 81n, 96–7, 99–100, 101, 114, 117, 121, 126, 133, 135, 154–5, 233–4
Up (film) 18
Upson, Ralph 112, 123
US Army 80, 87, 99, 103, 130, 154–5, 233–4, 367
US Navy 15–16, 23–4, 31, 75, 80, 87, 93, 99, 100, 102–4, 108–9, 130, 139, 150–1, 164, 251, 267, 348, 367
    design competitions 32, 110–14

opposition to LTA program 25, 27, 66, 69, 138–41, 172–3, 247, 319, 349
    see also Bureau of Aeronautics (BUAER); Lighter-Than-Air (LTA) flight: Naval LTA programme

V-2 rockets 368
Van Swearingen, Earl K. *228*
Ventana 351–2, 355
Verne, Jules 131
Versailles, Treaty of 100, 180, 206
Vickers 96–7, 121
Viktoria Luise (LZ-11) 87
Vinson, Carl 59–60, 141, 152, 198, 319
von Braun, Werner 181, 361

Wacker, Harry 76–8
Walker, Bill 350
Walsh, Thomas J. 127
weather 13, 99, 229
    forecasting 36, 69, 189
    Moffett insists big rigids fly in poor 27–8, 30–1, 36, 38, 42, 68, 189, 194
    Zeppelins and 188–9
Weaver, Carl 76, 78
Weeden, Charlotte Mayfield ('Blossom') 364, 366
Weeks, John W. 103
weight of airships 17, 39, 106, 147, 156, 174–5, 192
    Akron 35, 155, 186, 188
    Macon 146–7, 151, 155–9, 161, 165, 174–5, 190–1, 197, 238–9, 245, 298
Wellman, Walter 129n
Wells, H.G. 131
USS *West Virginia* (BB-48) (*'Wee Vee'*) 364–6
Western Air Express 118
Western Flyer 356
Westinghouse 160
Whipple, Laura T. 200–1
White City (previously, *Pasadena*) 91
White City Amusement Park 76
Wilbur, Curtis D. 113, *219*
Wiley, David *218*, 252, 270

Wiley, Gordon *218*, 252, 270, 274, 351, 353, 366
Wiley, Herbert V. ('Doc') 16, 27–8, 115, 168–9, 204–5, *218, 221, 227*, 264–72, 326, 344, 364–7
  Akron crash 40–6, 49, 50–1, 53, 55–9, 62, 269
  Akron crash investigations 61–4, 67–9, 138, 168–9, 189–90, 338–9
  Arnstein queries *Akron* crash with 66, 189–91
  character 55, 257–8, 264, 266, 270–1, 273, 282, 365
  on the USS *Los Angeles* 43, 252, 258, 268–9
  Macon, captain of 253, 257–63, 269–309
  Macon crash 285–90, 292–300, 302–4, 307, 311, 315–17, 329–30, 338–43
  Macon crash investigations 317–18, 322–4, 326–9, 338–9, 345
  personal life *218*, 252–3, 264–7, 270, 282
  sea duties 69–70, 170, 251–3, 267–9
  Second World War 364–6
Wiley, Joel ('J.A') (Wiley's father) 264–5, 282
Wiley, Marie (Wiley's daughter) *218*, 252, 270, 282, 350, 352–3, 365–6
Wiley, Marie Frances (née Scroggie) 252, 267, 366
Willard, Charles F. 89–90
Winchester Repeating Arms Company 160
Wingfoot Air Express 76–9, 125n
Wingfoot Lake Airship Base 75, 167, 368

Wingfoot One, Two and *Three* 368
Won in the Clouds (film) 90–1
Worldwide Aeros Corporation 369
Wright, Wilbur and Orville 13n, 74, 86, 87, 98

Zeppelin, Count Ferdinand von 18, 87, 94, 99, 103, 179, 322
Zeppelin NT airships 368
Zeppelin Stories 133
Zeppelins 32, 87–8, 98–9, 100n, 103–5, 111n, 114, 124, 133, 156, 177, 179–80, 189, 275
  definition 18
  First World War 16, 87, 99, 205, 233, 359
  see also DELAG (Deutsche Luftschifffahrts-Aktiengesellschaft); Luftschiffbau Zeppelin
Zepperplane 111
Zimmerman, Walter 242
ZLT Zeppelin Luftschifftechnik GmbH 368
ZMC-2 ('Tin Bubble') 93, 112, 320
ZPG-3W 360
ZR-1 *see Shenandoah* (ZR-1)
ZR-2 (*R38*) 8n, 24, 101–2, 126, 177, 185, 192, 267
ZR-3 *see Los Angeles* (ZR-3)
ZRCV 347–8
ZRN 347–8, 359
ZRS-4 *see Akron* (ZRS-4)
ZRS-5 *see Macon* (ZRS-5)
ZRS-6 208
ZRS-7 208

ABOUT THE AUTHOR

John J. Geoghegan specialises in reporting on unusual inventions that fail in the marketplace despite their innovative nature. He helped popularise the phrase white elephant technology (WETech), and his articles on this and related subjects have appeared in the *New York Times*, *The Wall Street Journal*, *WIRED*, *BusinessWeek*, *Smithsonian Air & Space* magazine and numerous other publications. Additionally, Mr Geoghegan is the author of *Operation Storm*, which tells the true but little-known story of a squadron of underwater aircraft carriers purpose-built by Japan during the Second World War to launch an aerial attack against New York City and Washington, DC, as a follow-up to Pearl Harbor. The *Wall Street Journal* called *Operation Storm* 'a fascinating, meticulously researched and deft account'. He is also author of a memoir, *Hear Today, Gone Tomorrow*, about how a precipitous hearing loss rendered him deaf virtually overnight. Bookauthority.com ranked *Hear Today* number one among the '38 best hearing loss books of all time'. Mr Geoghegan currently serves as the Director of the SILOE Research Institute's Archival Division in Marin County, California. You can learn more about his reporting on WETech inventions at www.johnjgeoghegan.com.

You may also enjoy ...

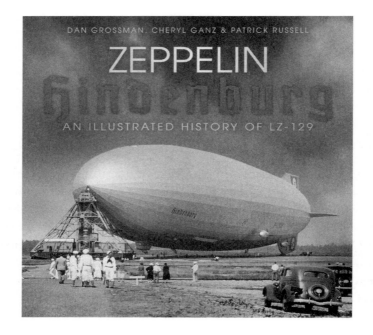

DAN GROSSMAN, CHERYL GANZ & PATRICK RUSSELL

ZEPPELIN

AN ILLUSTRATED HISTORY OF LZ-129

9780 7509 8991 6

'It burst into flames! ... It's burning, bursting into flames and it's – and it's falling on the mooring mast and ... this is terrible. This is one of the worst catastrophes in the world.'

In *Zeppelin Hindenburg*, three experts collaborate to create the definitive history of a cutting-edge invention – and to explain the the shocking disaster that signalled the end of airship travel.

You may also enjoy ...

978 0 7509 9746 1

'A worthy tribute to Britain's woman aviation pioneers.'
Sharon Nicholson FRAeS

Full of adventure and anecdotes, *Magnificent Women and Flying Machines* tells the tales of the female pioneers who achieved real firsts in various forms of aviation: in ballooning, parachuting, airships, gliding and fixed-wing flight – right up to a trip to the International Space Station!

You may also enjoy …

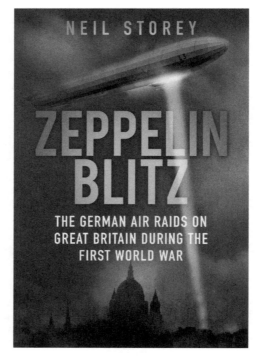

NEIL STOREY

ZEPPELIN BLITZ

THE GERMAN AIR RAIDS ON GREAT BRITAIN DURING THE FIRST WORLD WAR

978 0 7524 5625 3

In the early years of the First World War, German Zeppelins undertook a series of attacks on the British mainland in an attempt to subdue Britain. *Zeppelin Blitz* is the first full account of these assaults – raid-by-raid, year-by-year – and the terror they left in their wake.